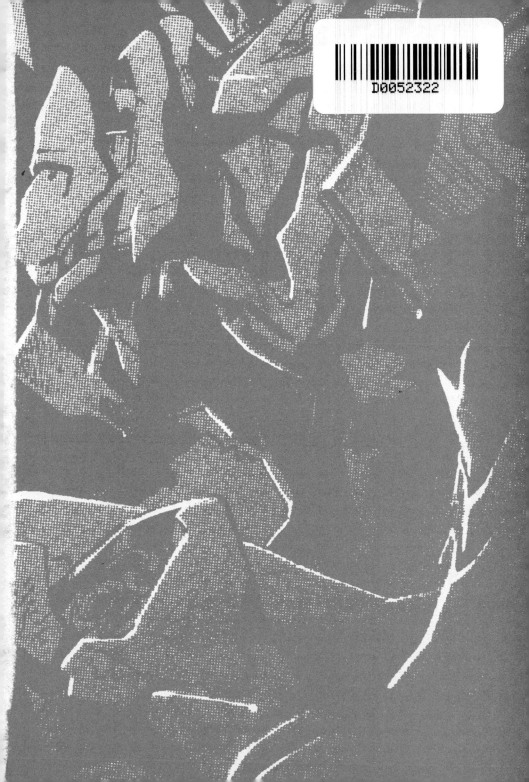

NEON GENESIS EVANGELION

Volume 3

Story & Art by
Yoshiyuki Sadamoto
Created by
GAINAX

GOD'S IN HIS HEAVEN. ALL'S RIGHT WITH THE WORLD.

Neon Genesis EVANGELION
Vol.3

CONTENTS

This volume contains NEON GENESIS EVANGELION Book Three #1 through #6 in their entirety.

Story & Art by Yoshiyuki Sadamoto
Created by GAINAX

English Adaptation by Fred Burke

Translation/Lillian Olsen
Touch-Up Art & Lettering/Wayne Truman
Cover Design/Hidemi Sahara
Editor/Carl Gustav Horn
Assistant Editor/Annette Roman

Director of Sales & Marketing/Oliver Chin
Senior Editor/Trish Ledoux
Managing Editor/Hyoe Narita
Editor-in-Chief/Satoru Fujii
Publisher/Seiji Horibuchi

Printed in Canada

Published by Viz Communications, Inc.
P.O. Box 77010
San Francisco, CA 94107

10 9 8 7 6 5 4 3 2 1
First printing, July 1999

Vizit us at our World Wide Web site at www.viz.com and our Internet magazine, j-pop.com, at www.j-pop.com!

<u>NEON GENESIS EVANGELION GRAPHIC NOVELS TO DATE</u>
NEON GENESIS EVANGELION VOL. 1
NEON GENESIS EVANGELION VOL. 2
NEON GENESIS EVANGELION VOL. 3

Stage 1: WHITE SCARS

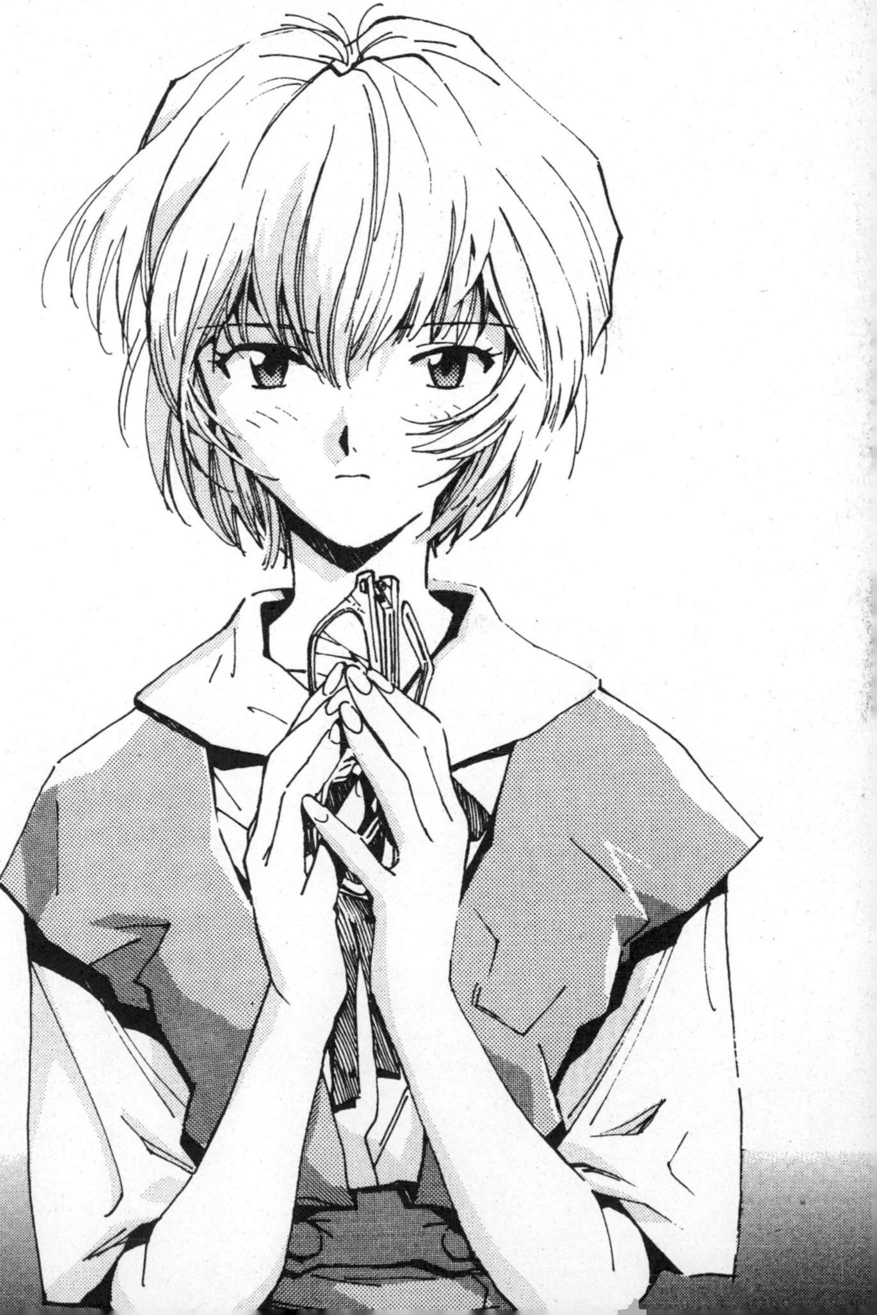

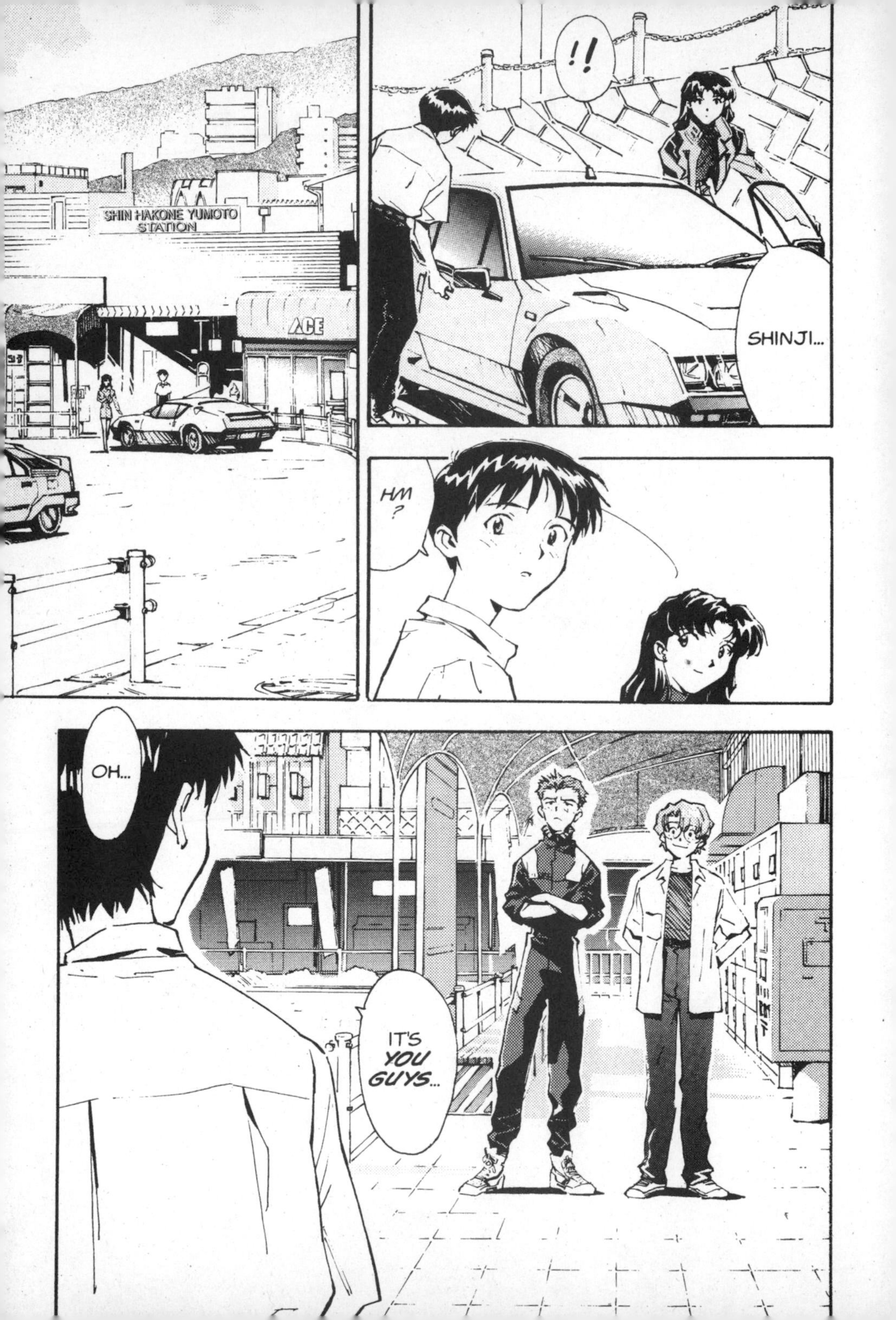
SHIN HAKONE YUMOTO STATION
ACE
!!
SHINJI...
HM?
OH...
IT'S YOU GUYS...

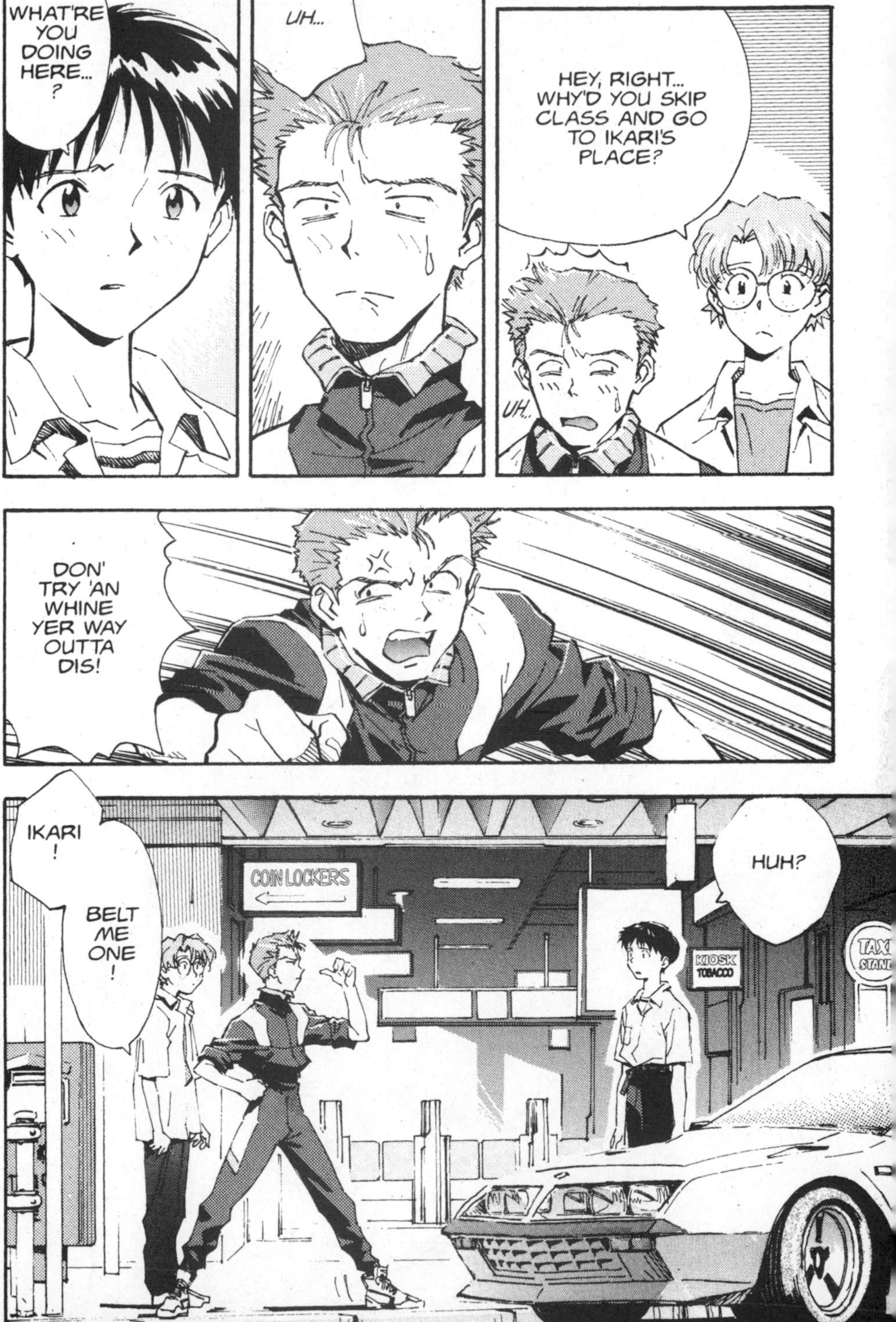
WHAT'RE YOU DOING HERE... ?
UH...
HEY, RIGHT... WHY'D YOU SKIP CLASS AND GO TO IKARI'S PLACE?
UH..
DON' TRY 'AN WHINE YER WAY OUTTA DIS!
IKARI !
BELT ME ONE !
COIN LOCKERS
HUH?
KIOSK TOBACCO
TAXI STAND

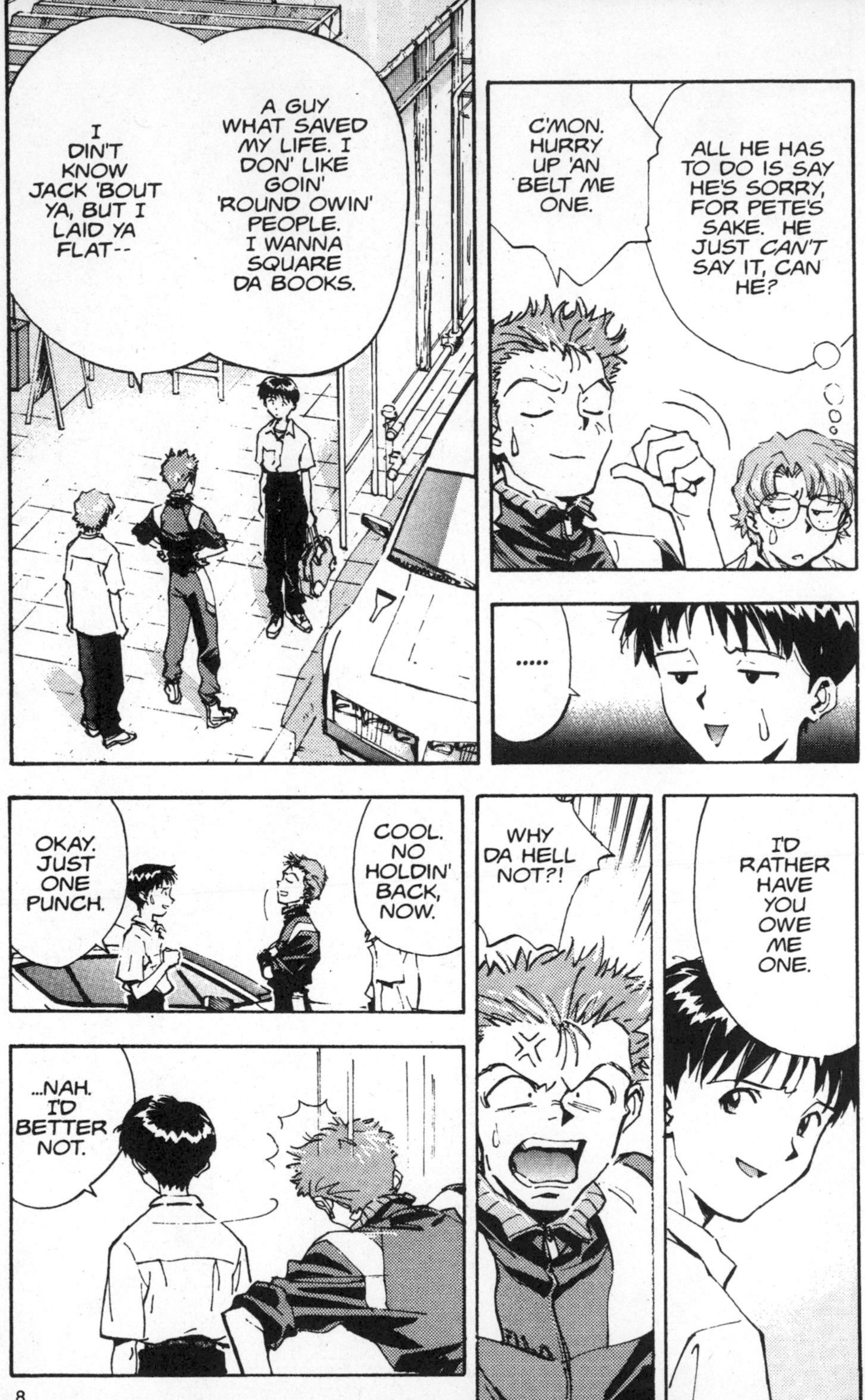
I DIN'T KNOW JACK 'BOUT YA, BUT I LAID YA FLAT--
A GUY WHAT SAVED MY LIFE. I DON' LIKE GOIN' 'ROUND OWIN' PEOPLE. I WANNA SQUARE DA BOOKS.
C'MON. HURRY UP 'AN BELT ME ONE.
ALL HE HAS TO DO IS SAY HE'S SORRY, FOR PETE'S SAKE. HE JUST *CAN'T* SAY IT, CAN HE?
......
OKAY. JUST ONE PUNCH.
COOL. NO HOLDIN' BACK, NOW.
...NAH. I'D BETTER NOT.
WHY DA HELL NOT?!
I'D RATHER HAVE YOU OWE ME ONE.

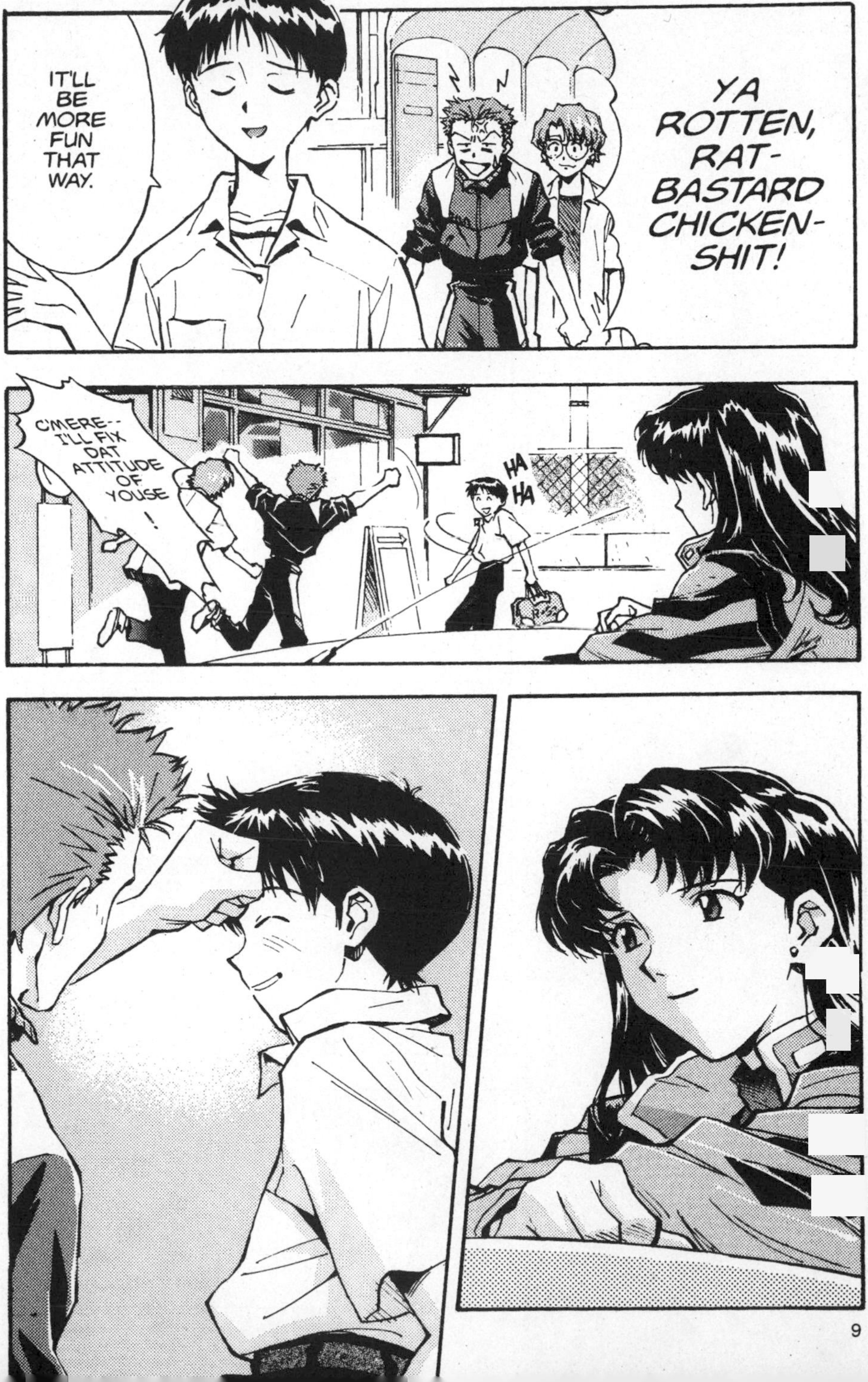
IT'LL BE MORE FUN THAT WAY.
YA ROTTEN, RAT-BASTARD CHICKEN-SHIT!
C'MERE-- I'LL FIX DAT ATTITUDE OF YOUSE!
HA HA

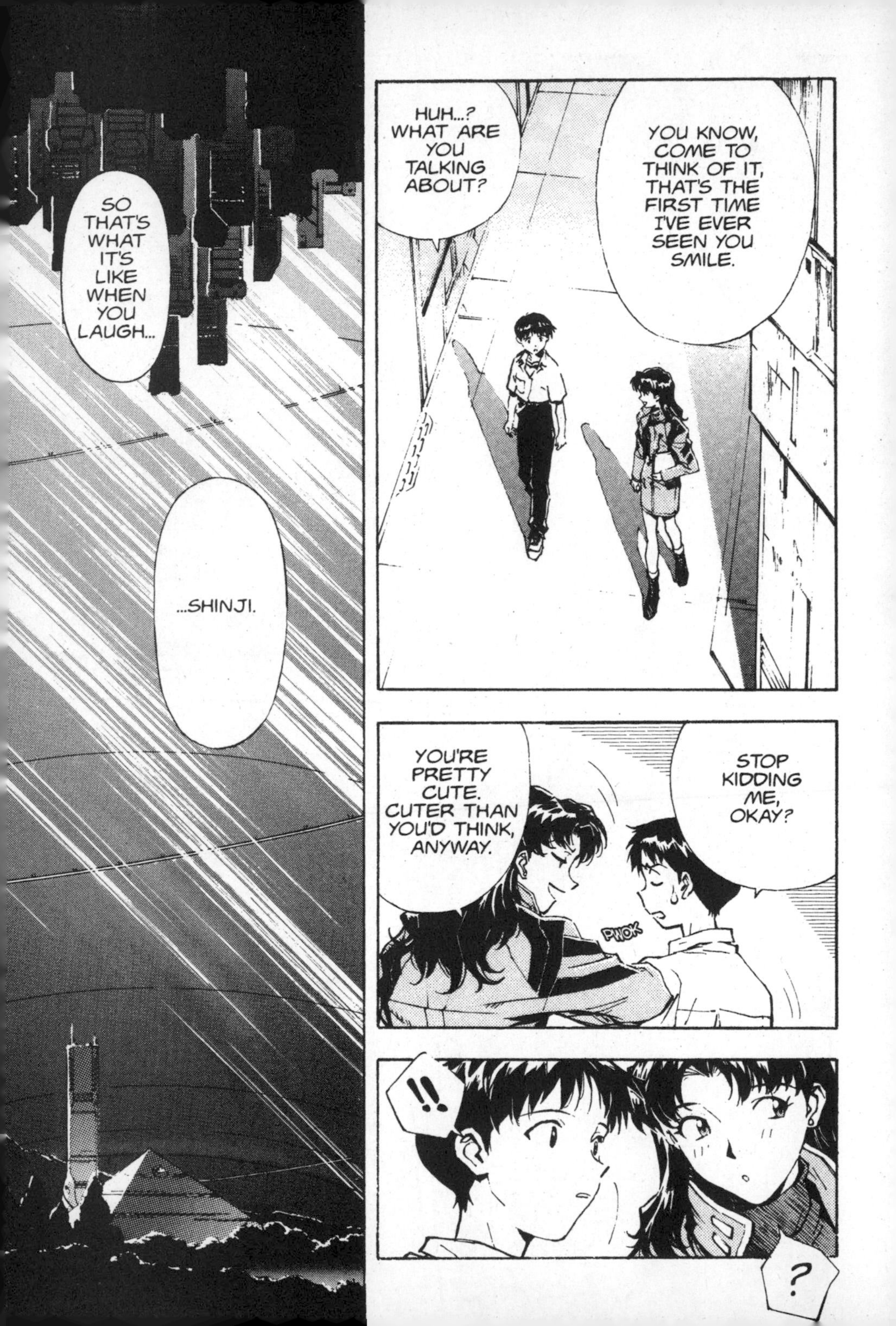
SO THAT'S WHAT IT'S LIKE WHEN YOU LAUGH...
...SHINJI.
HUH...? WHAT ARE YOU TALKING ABOUT?
YOU KNOW, COME TO THINK OF IT, THAT'S THE FIRST TIME I'VE EVER SEEN YOU SMILE.
YOU'RE PRETTY CUTE. CUTER THAN YOU'D THINK, ANYWAY.
STOP KIDDING ME, OKAY?
PWOK
!!
?

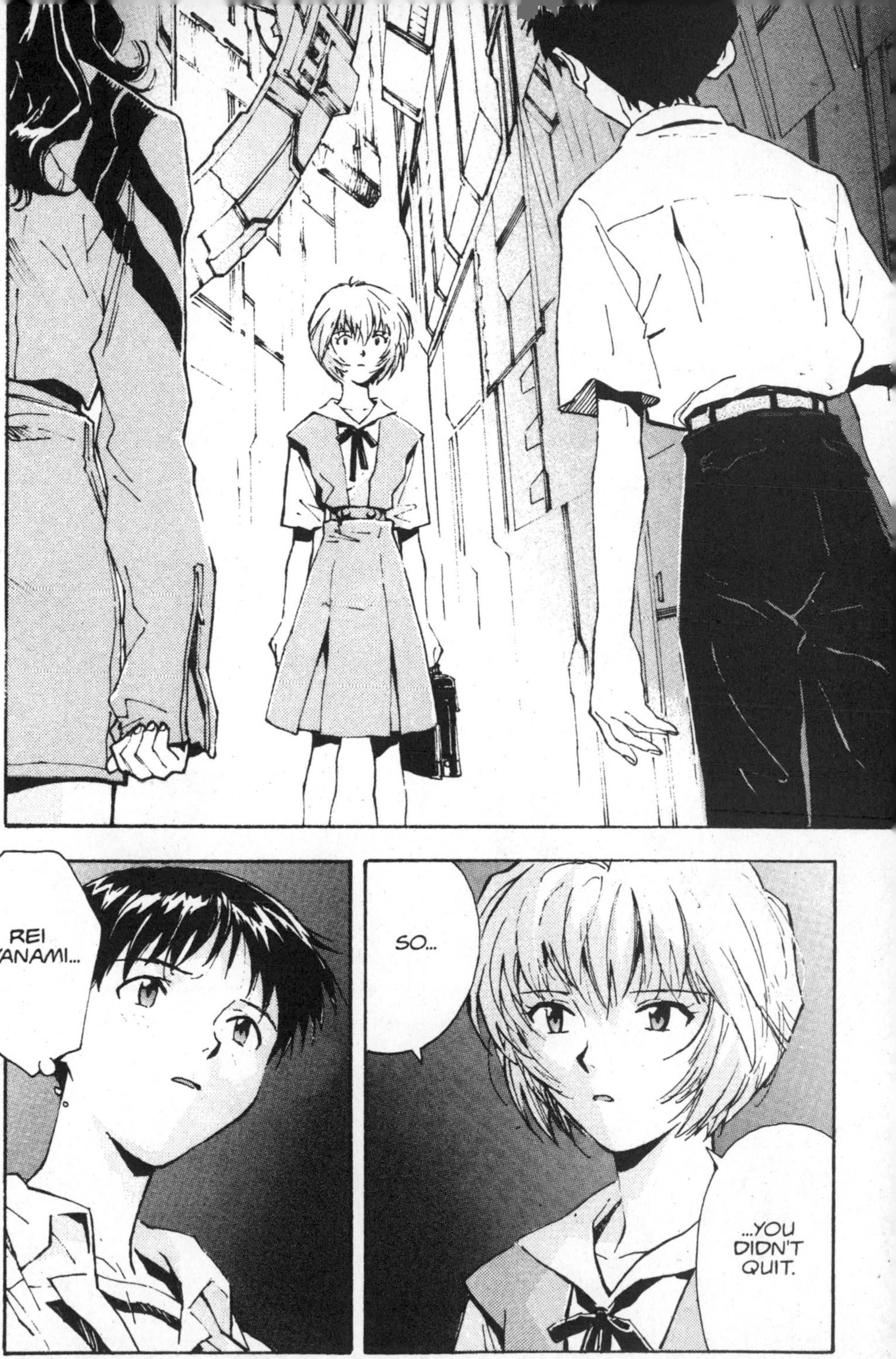
REI AYANAMI...
SO...
...YOU DIDN'T QUIT.

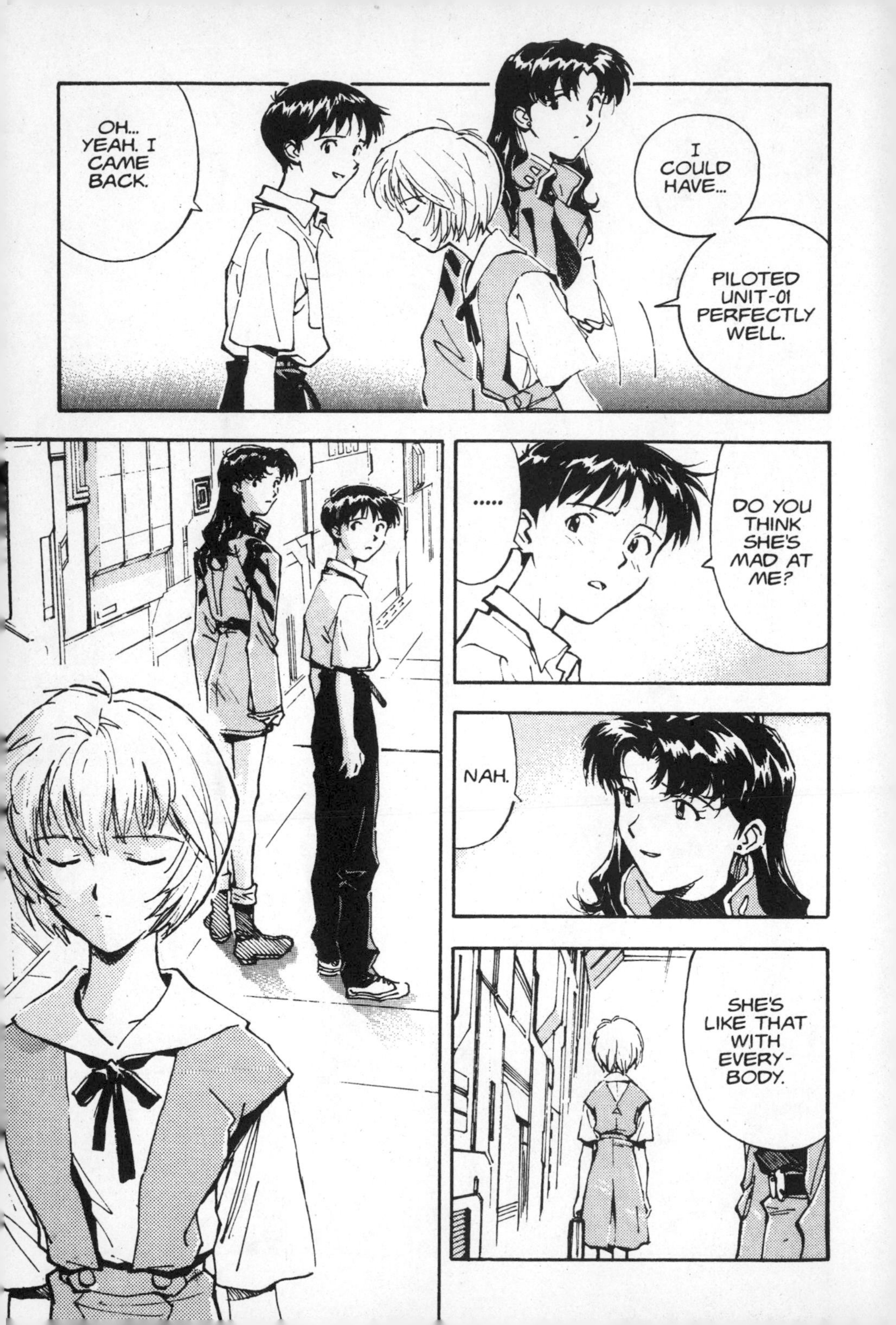
OH... YEAH. I CAME BACK.
I COULD HAVE...
PILOTED UNIT-01 PERFECTLY WELL.
......
DO YOU THINK SHE'S MAD AT ME?
NAH.
SHE'S LIKE THAT WITH EVERY-BODY.

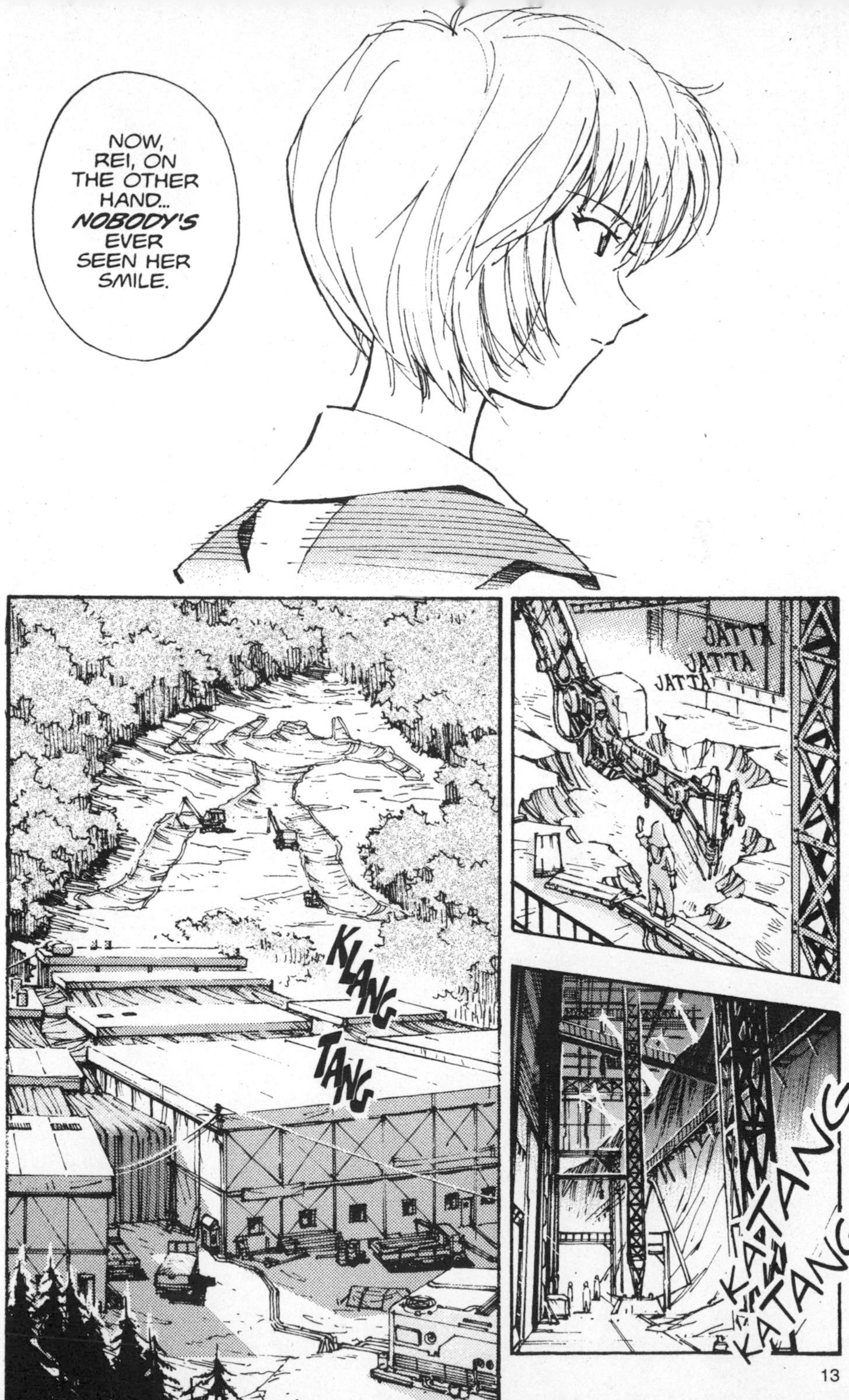
NOW, REI, ON THE OTHER HAND... *NOBODY'S* EVER SEEN HER SMILE.
KLANG
TANG
JATTA
JATTA
JATTA
KATANG
KATANG

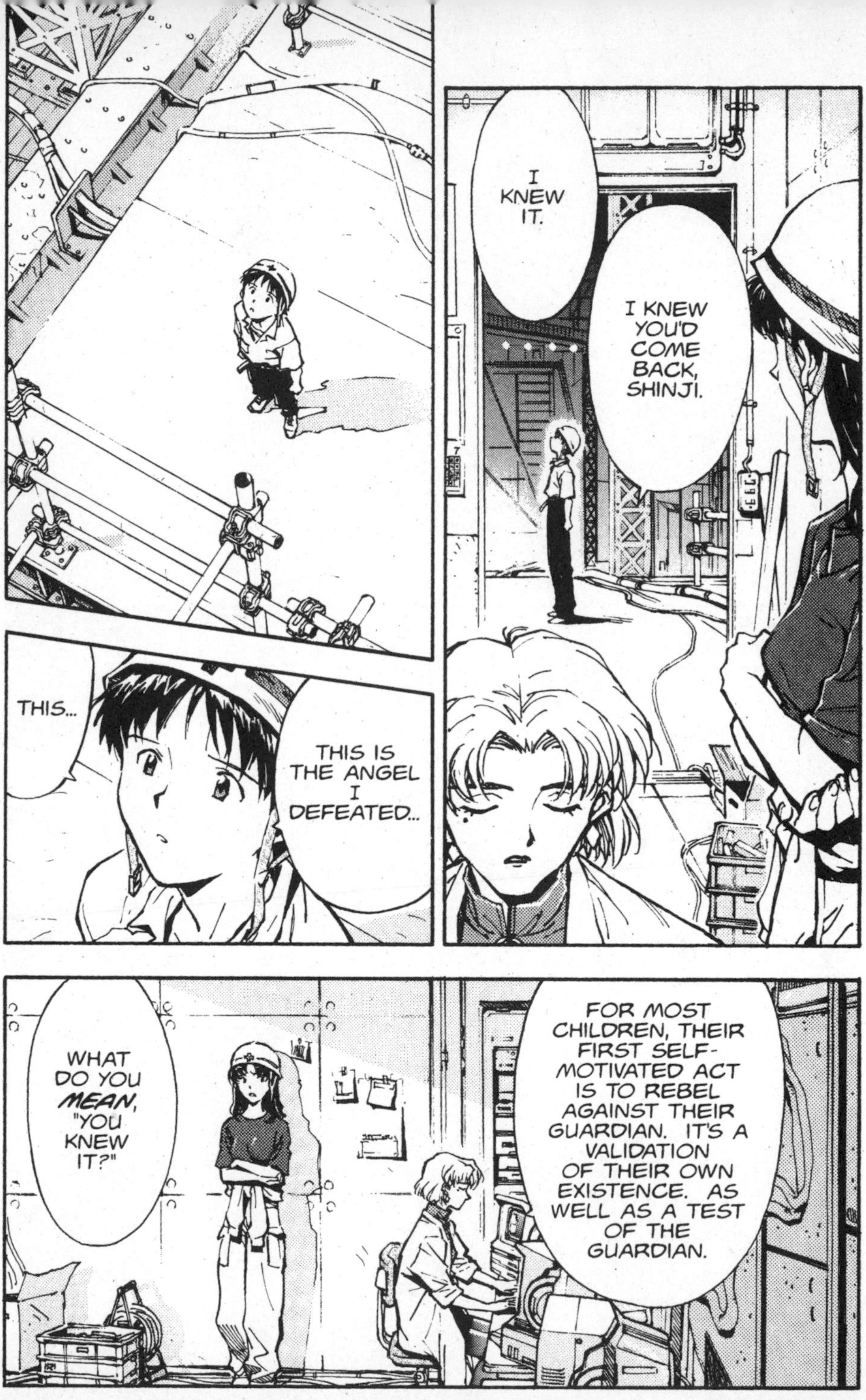
I KNEW IT.
I KNEW YOU'D COME BACK, SHINJI.
THIS...
THIS IS THE ANGEL I DEFEATED...
WHAT DO YOU *MEAN*, "YOU KNEW IT?"
FOR MOST CHILDREN, THEIR FIRST SELF-MOTIVATED ACT IS TO REBEL AGAINST THEIR GUARDIAN. IT'S A VALIDATION OF THEIR OWN EXISTENCE. AS WELL AS A TEST OF THE GUARDIAN.

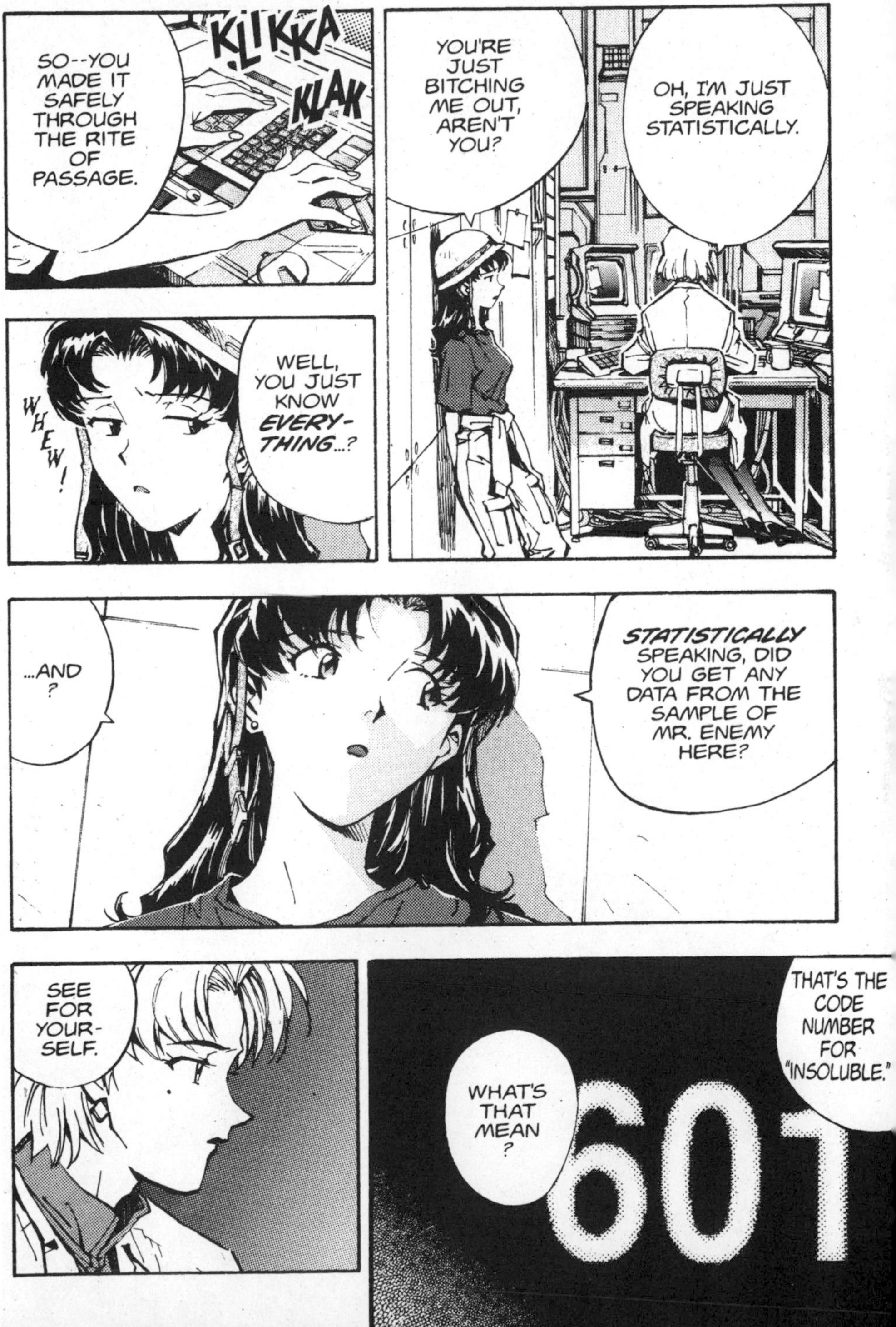
KLIKKA
KLAK
SO--YOU MADE IT SAFELY THROUGH THE RITE OF PASSAGE.
YOU'RE JUST BITCHING ME OUT, AREN'T YOU?
OH, I'M JUST SPEAKING STATISTICALLY.
WHEW!
WELL, YOU JUST KNOW *EVERY-THING...?*
...AND ?
STATISTICALLY SPEAKING, DID YOU GET ANY DATA FROM THE SAMPLE OF MR. ENEMY HERE?
SEE FOR YOUR-SELF.
WHAT'S THAT MEAN ?
THAT'S THE CODE NUMBER FOR "INSOLUBLE."
601

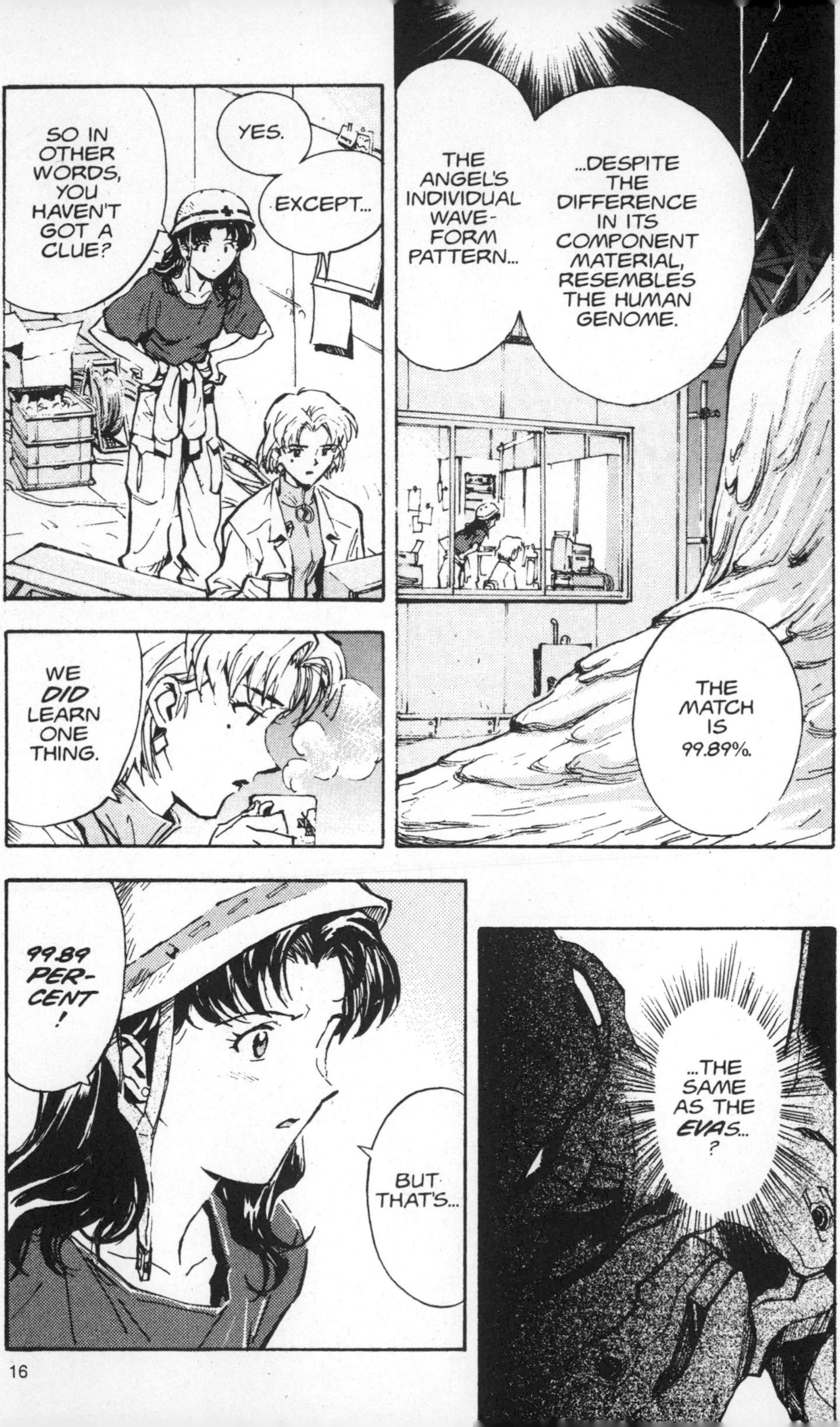
SO IN OTHER WORDS, YOU HAVEN'T GOT A CLUE?
YES.
EXCEPT...
WE *DID* LEARN ONE THING.
THE ANGEL'S INDIVIDUAL WAVE-FORM PATTERN...
...DESPITE THE DIFFERENCE IN ITS COMPONENT MATERIAL, RESEMBLES THE HUMAN GENOME.
THE MATCH IS 99.89%.
99.89 PERCENT!
BUT THAT'S...
...THE SAME AS THE *EVAS*...?

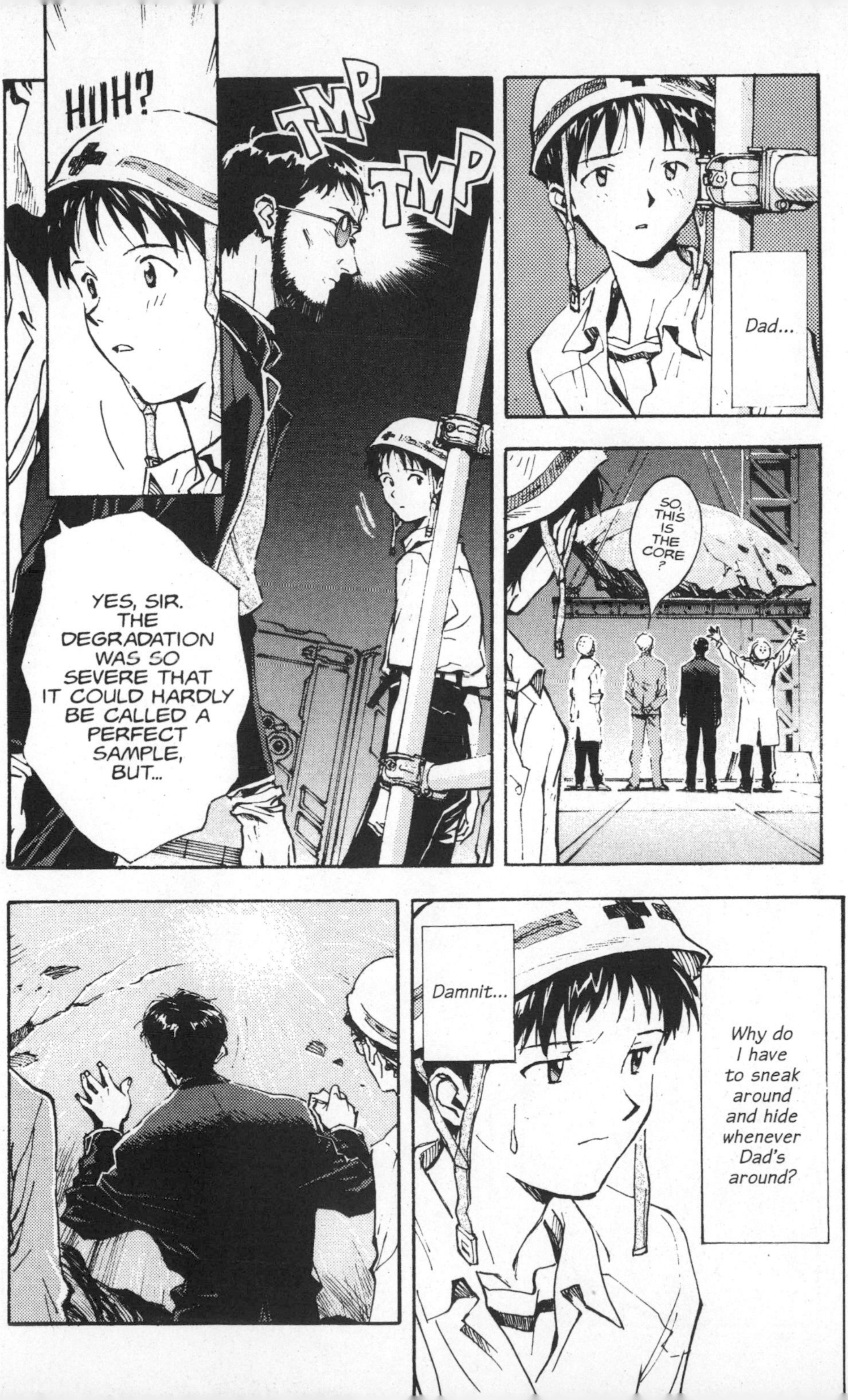
HUH?
TMP
TMP
YES, SIR. THE DEGRADATION WAS SO SEVERE THAT IT COULD HARDLY BE CALLED A PERFECT SAMPLE, BUT...
Dad...
SO, THIS IS THE CORE?
Damnit...
Why do I have to sneak around and hide whenever Dad's around?

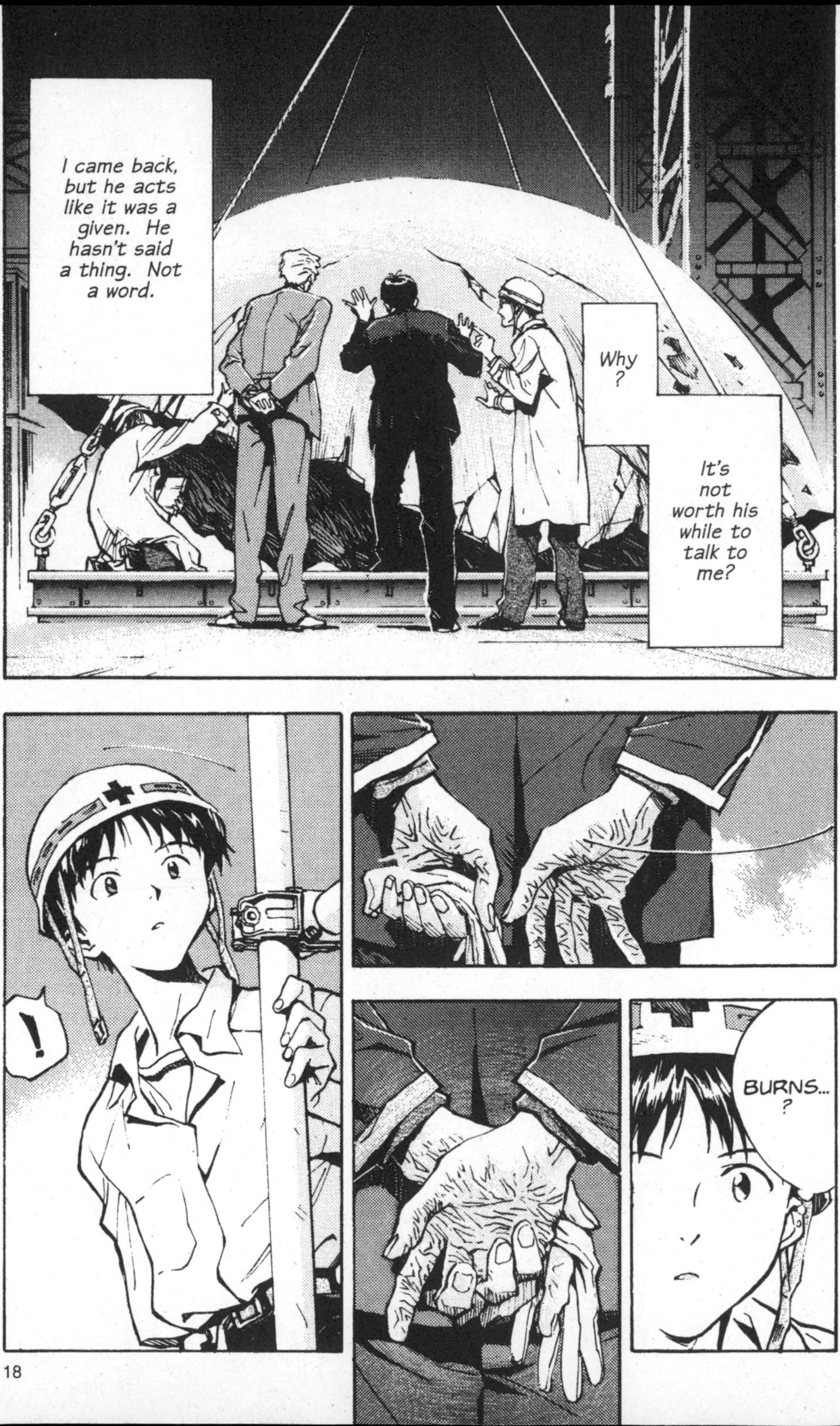

I came back, but he acts like it was a given. He hasn't said a thing. Not a word.
Why?
It's not worth his while to talk to me?
!
BURNS...?

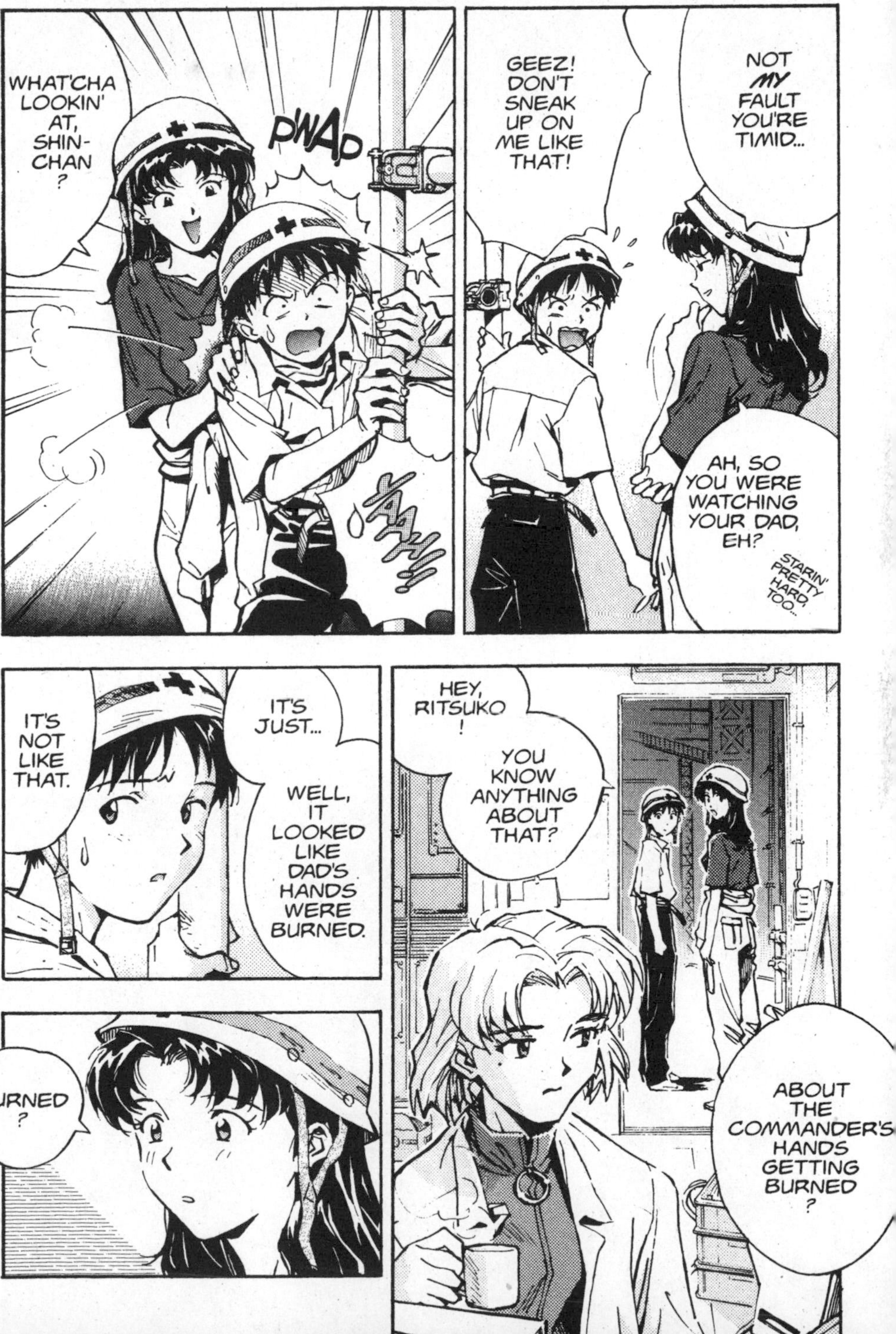
WHAT'CHA LOOKIN' AT, SHIN-CHAN ?
PWAP
YAAH!!
GEEZ! DON'T SNEAK UP ON ME LIKE THAT!
NOT MY FAULT YOU'RE TIMID...
AH, SO YOU WERE WATCHING YOUR DAD, EH?
STARIN' PRETTY HARD, TOO...
IT'S NOT LIKE THAT.
IT'S JUST...
WELL, IT LOOKED LIKE DAD'S HANDS WERE BURNED.
BURNED ?
HEY, RITSUKO !
YOU KNOW ANYTHING ABOUT THAT?
ABOUT THE COMMANDER'S HANDS GETTING BURNED ?

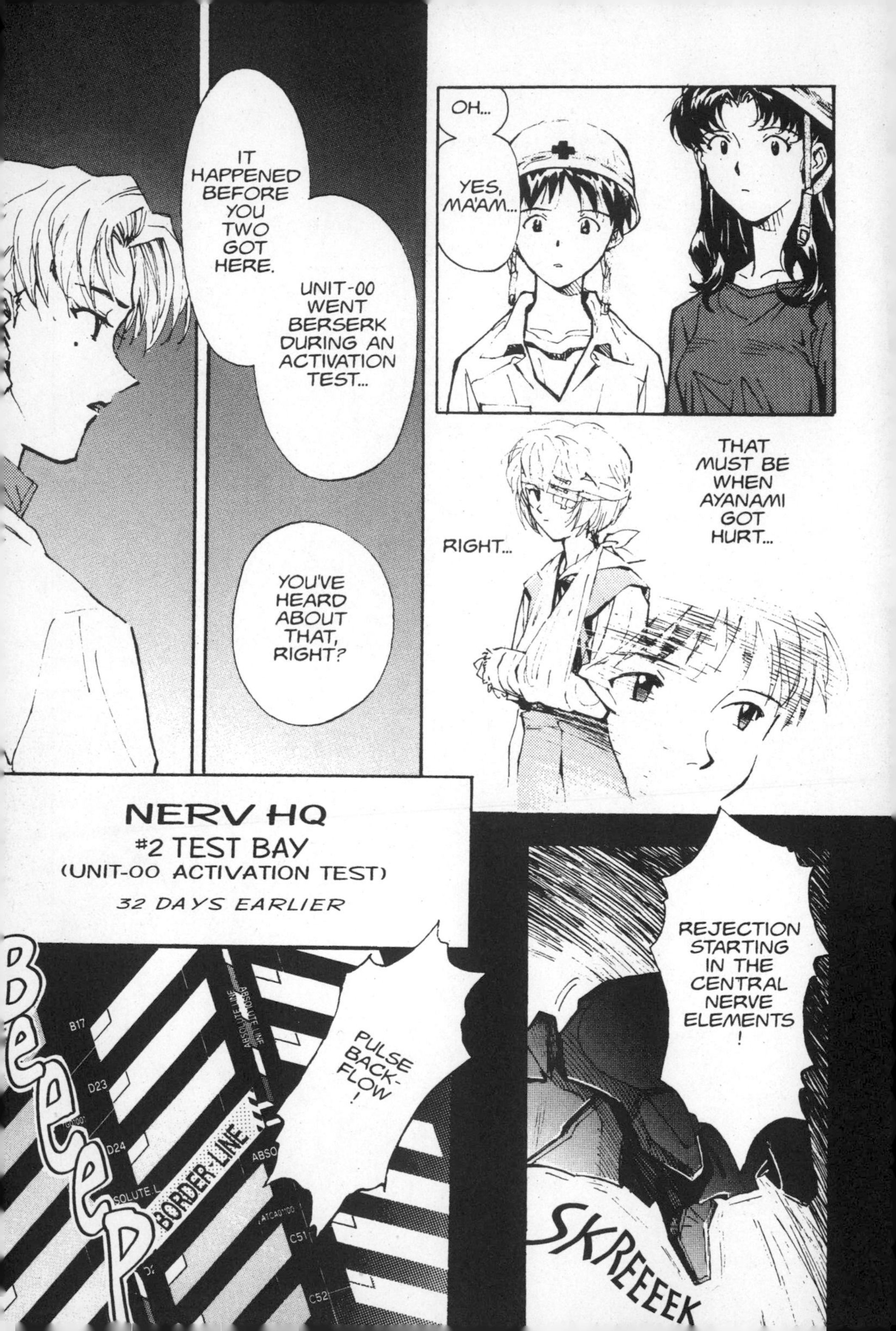
IT HAPPENED BEFORE YOU TWO GOT HERE.
UNIT-00 WENT BERSERK DURING AN ACTIVATION TEST...
YOU'VE HEARD ABOUT THAT, RIGHT?
OH...
YES, MA'AM...
RIGHT...
THAT MUST BE WHEN AYANAMI GOT HURT...
NERV HQ
#2 TEST BAY
(UNIT-00 ACTIVATION TEST)
32 DAYS EARLIER
BEEEEP
ABSOLUTE LINE
BORDER-LINE
PULSE BACK-FLOW!
REJECTION STARTING IN THE CENTRAL NERVE ELEMENTS!
SKREEEEK

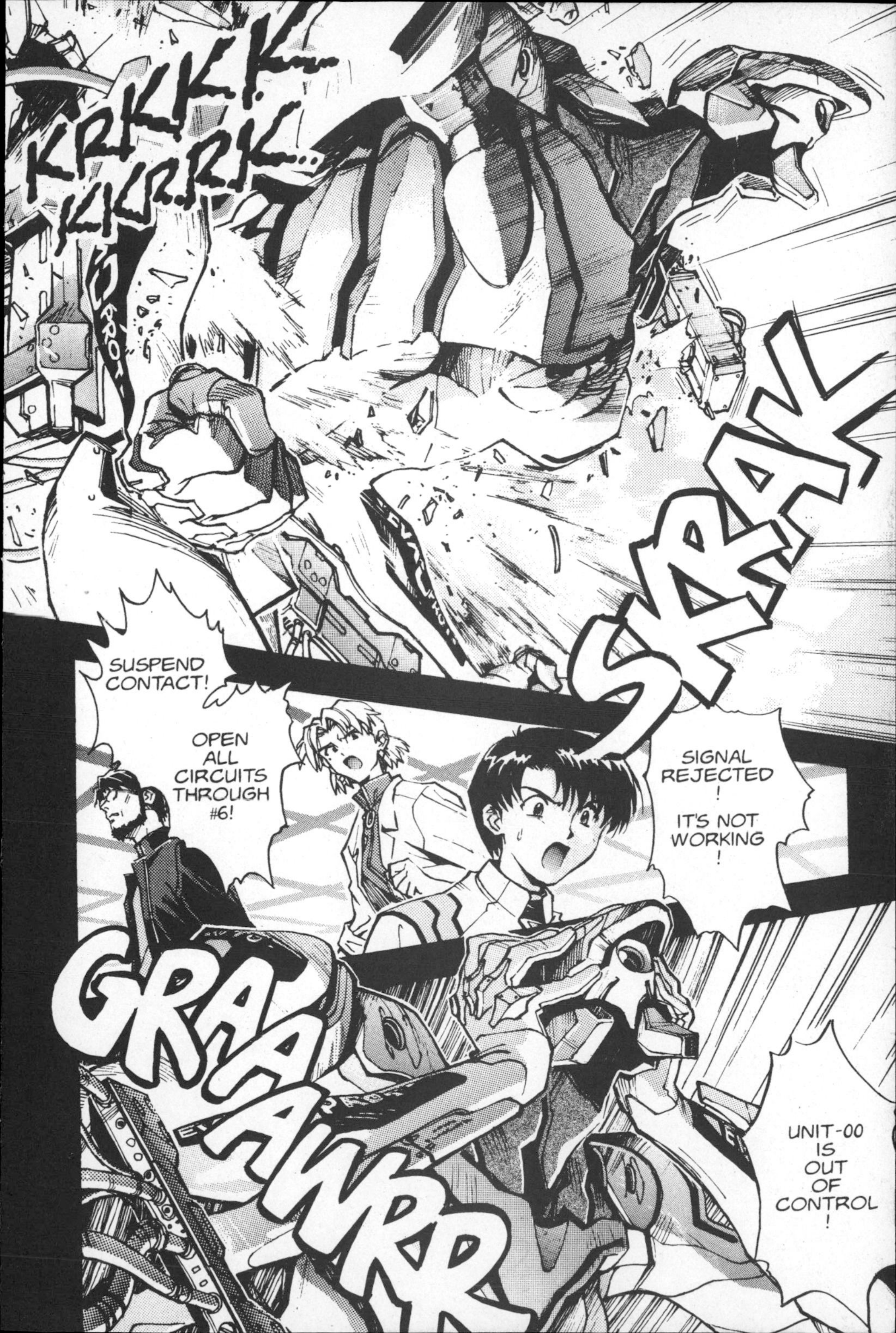
KRKK.K...
KKR.R.K...
SPRAK
SUSPEND CONTACT!
OPEN ALL CIRCUITS THROUGH #6!
SIGNAL REJECTED! IT'S NOT WORKING!
GRAAAWRR
UNIT-00 IS OUT OF CONTROL!

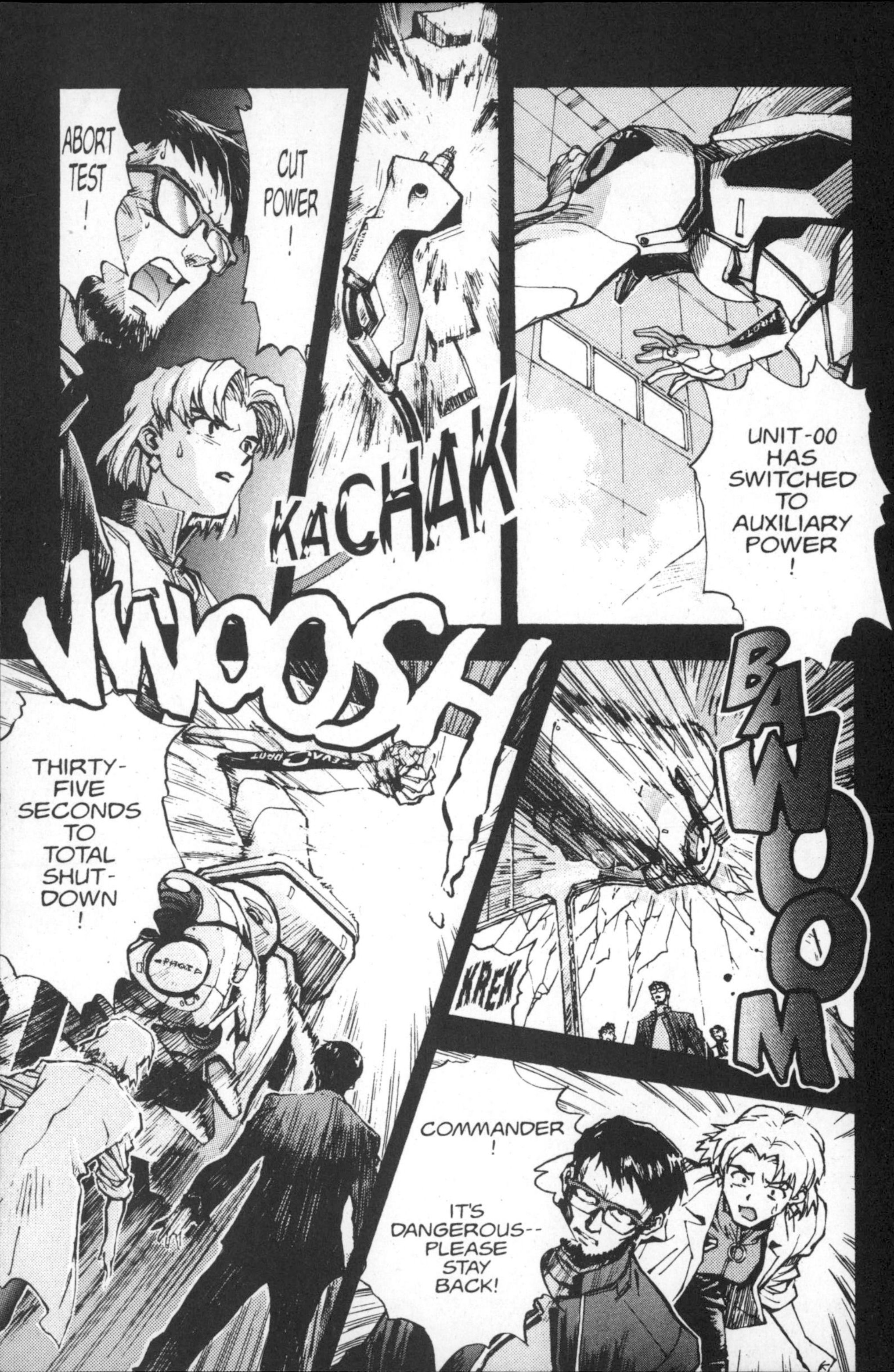

ABORT TEST !
CUT POWER !
KACHAK
UNIT-00 HAS SWITCHED TO AUXILIARY POWER !
VWOOSH
THIRTY-FIVE SECONDS TO TOTAL SHUT-DOWN !
BAWOOM
KREK
COMMANDER !
IT'S DANGEROUS-- PLEASE STAY BACK!

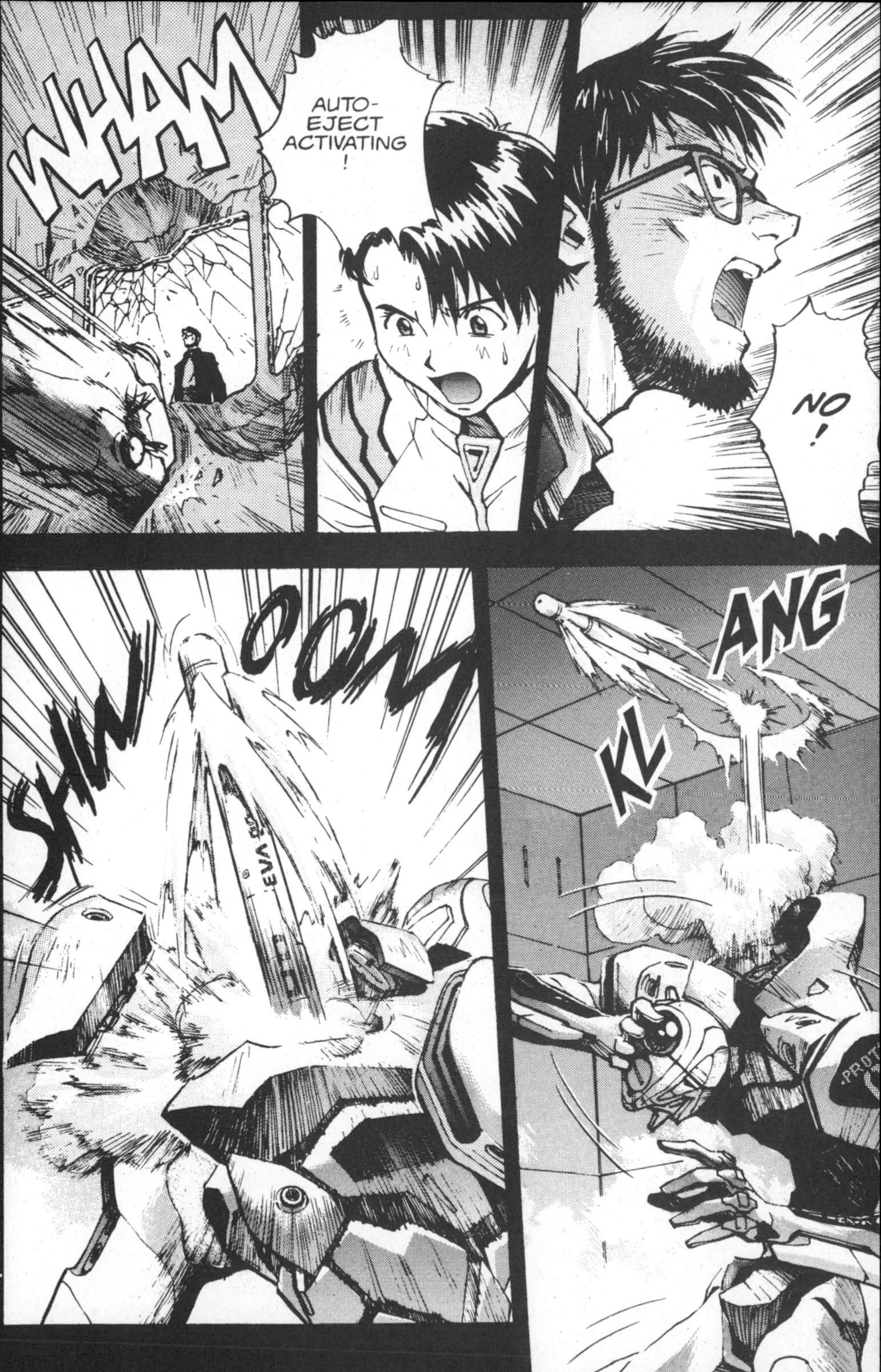
WHAM
AUTO-EJECT ACTIVATING!
NO!
SHWOOM
EVA
KLANG

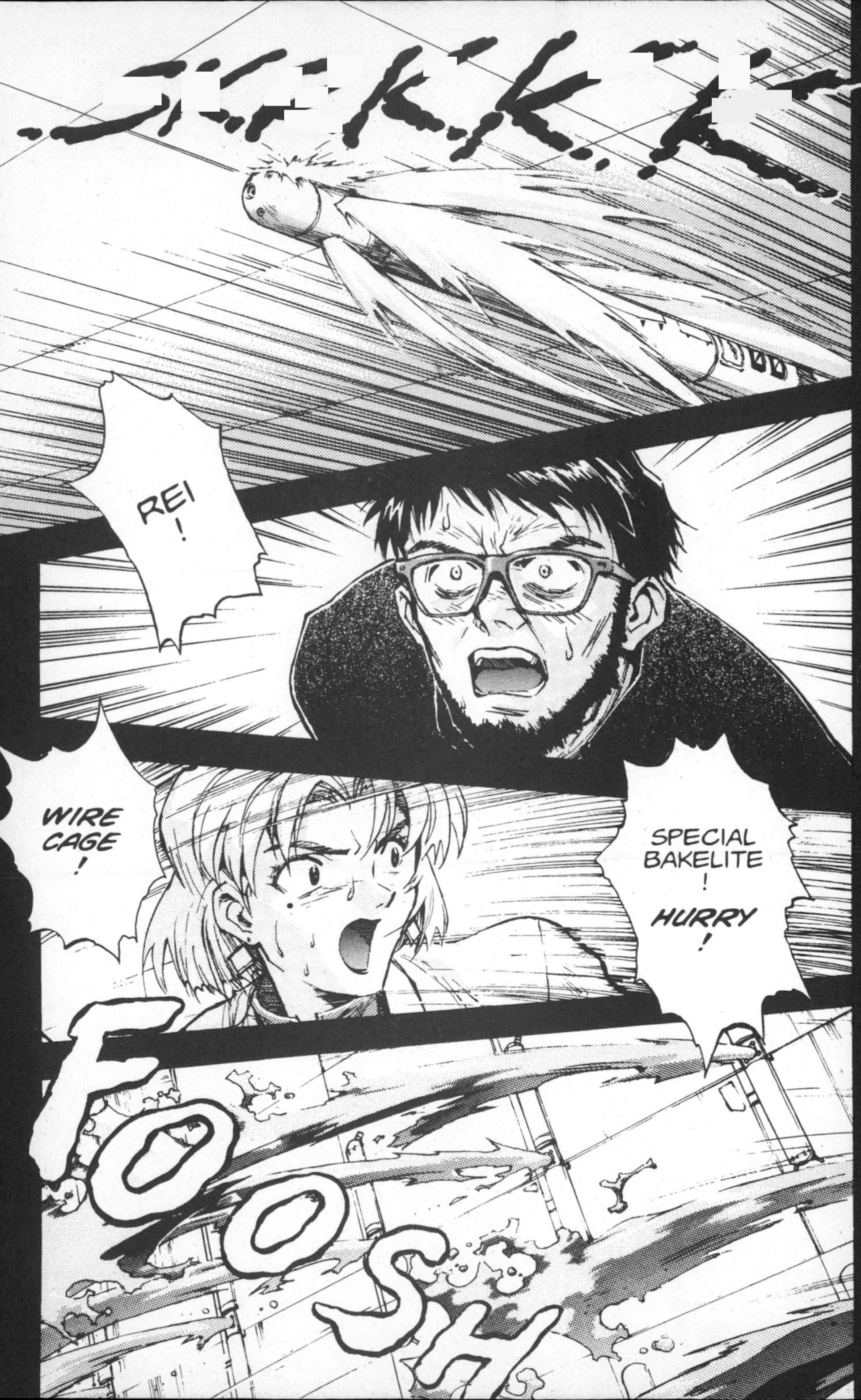
REI!
WIRE CAGE!
SPECIAL BAKELITE! HURRY!
FOOSH

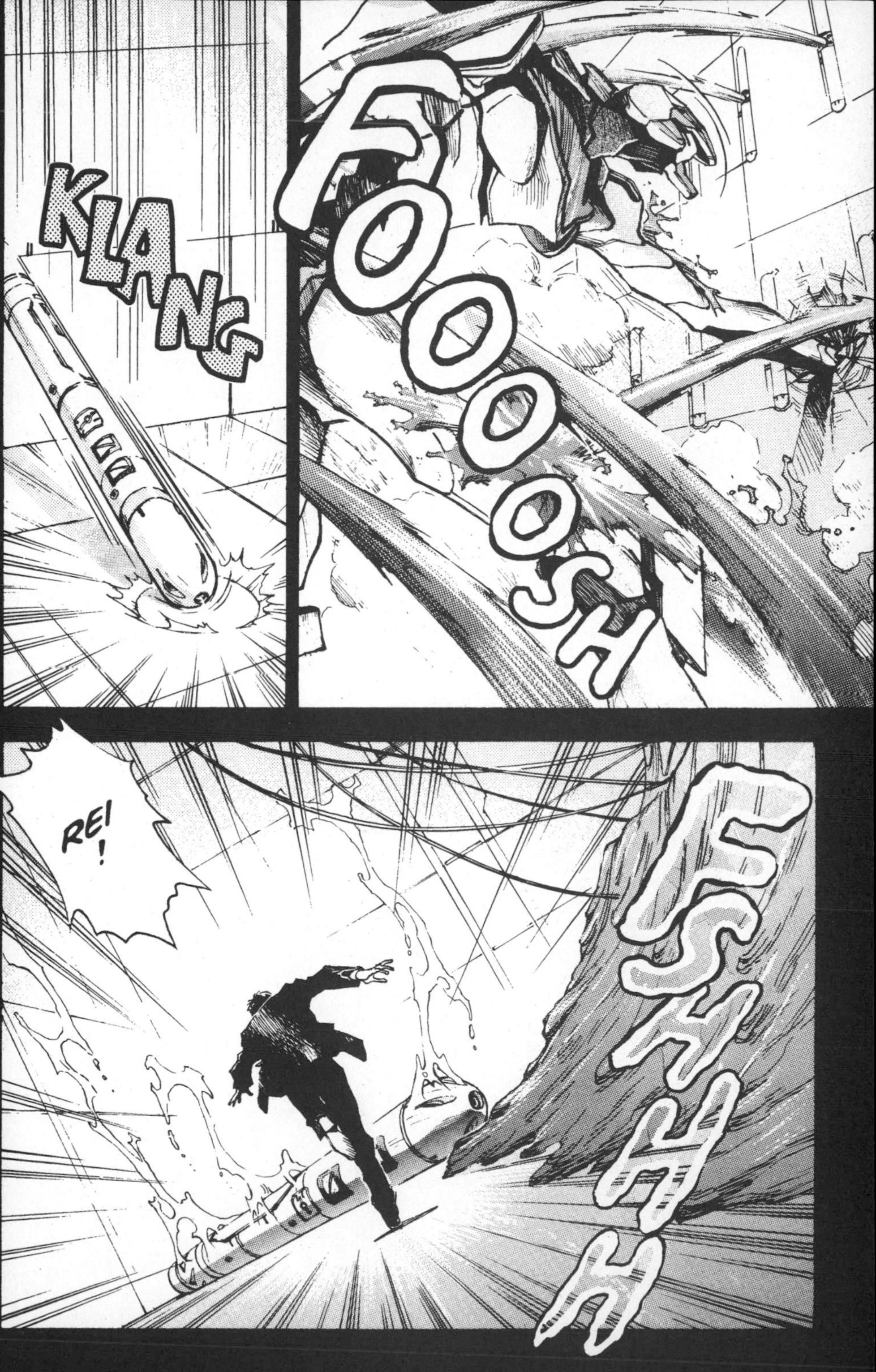
KLANG
FOOOOOSH
REI!
FSHHH

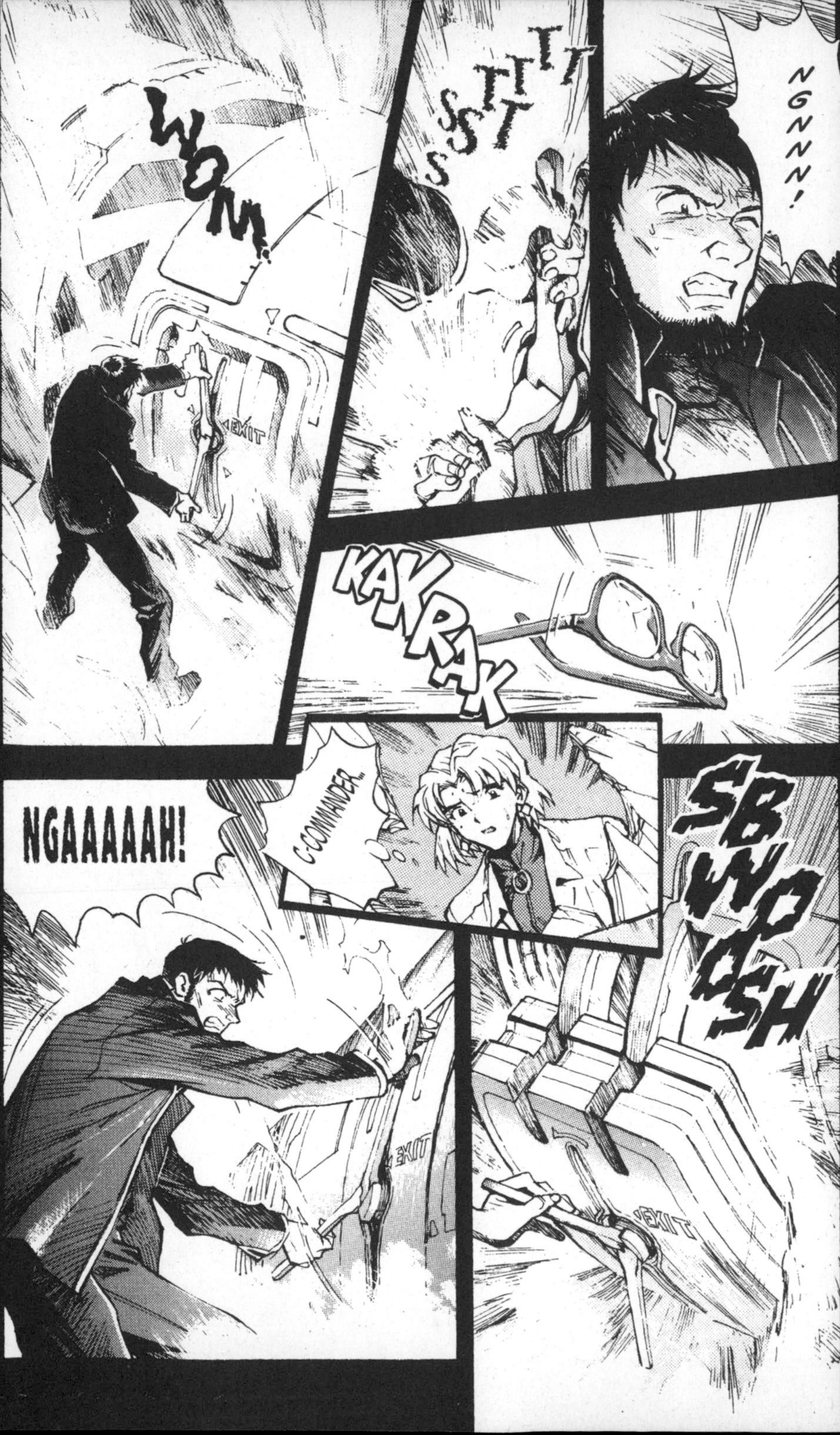
WOM
SSSTTTT
NGNNNN!
KAKRAK
NGAAAAAH!
C-COMMANDER...
SBWOOSH
EXIT
EXIT
EXIT

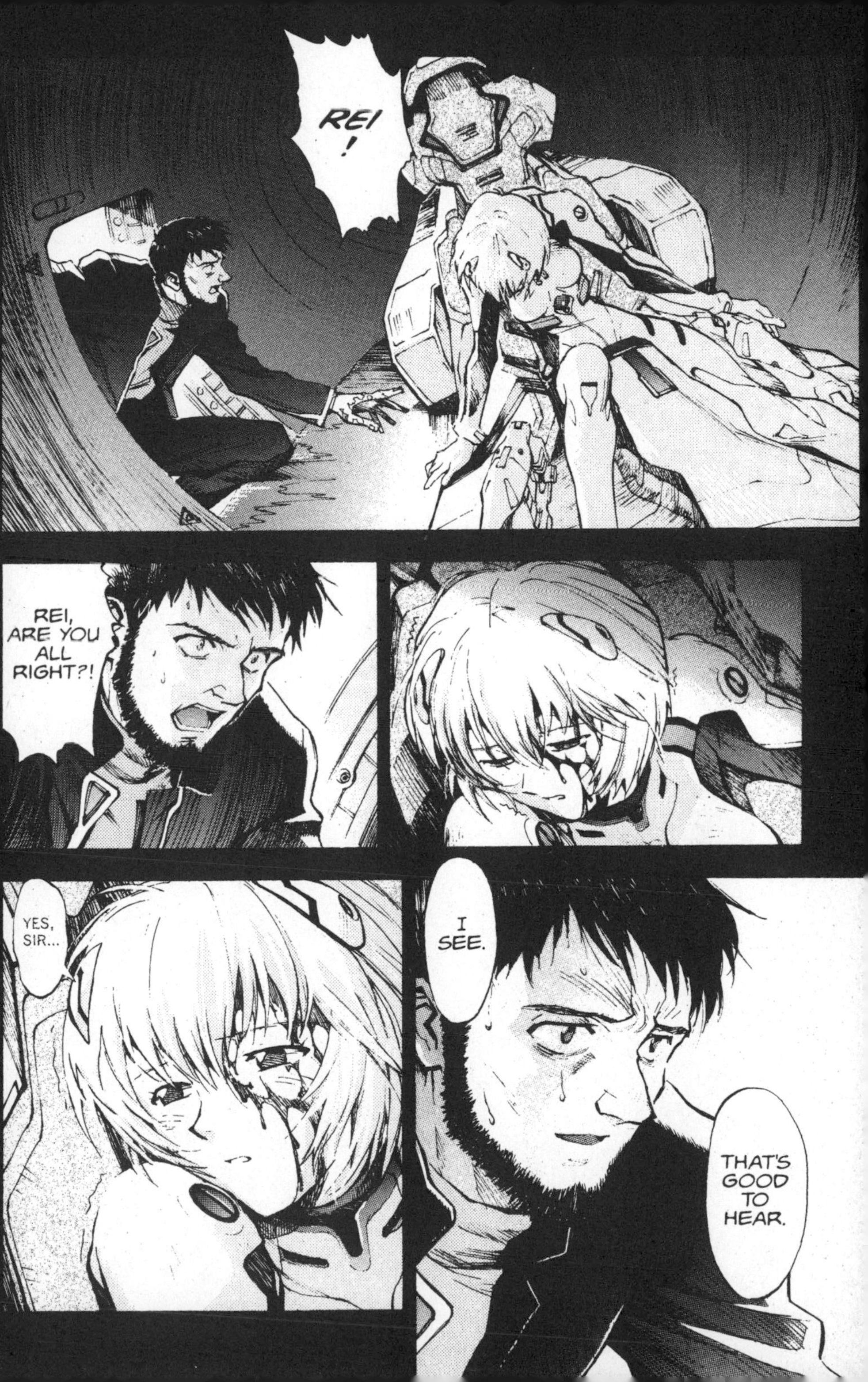
REI!
REI, ARE YOU ALL RIGHT?!
YES, SIR...
I SEE.
THAT'S GOOD TO HEAR.

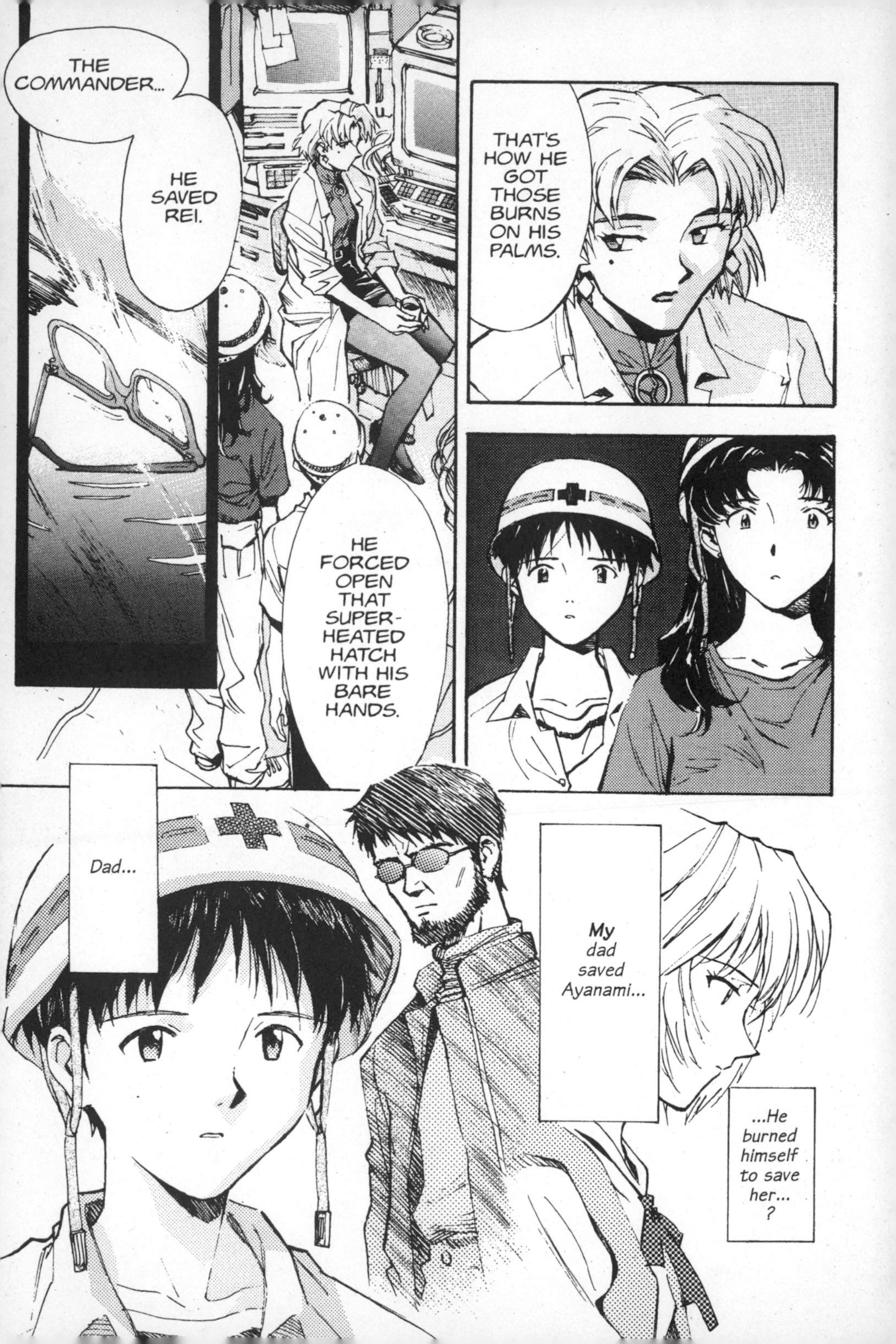
THE COMMANDER...
HE SAVED REI.
HE FORCED OPEN THAT SUPER-HEATED HATCH WITH HIS BARE HANDS.
THAT'S HOW HE GOT THOSE BURNS ON HIS PALMS.
Dad...
My dad saved Ayanami...
...He burned himself to save her... ?

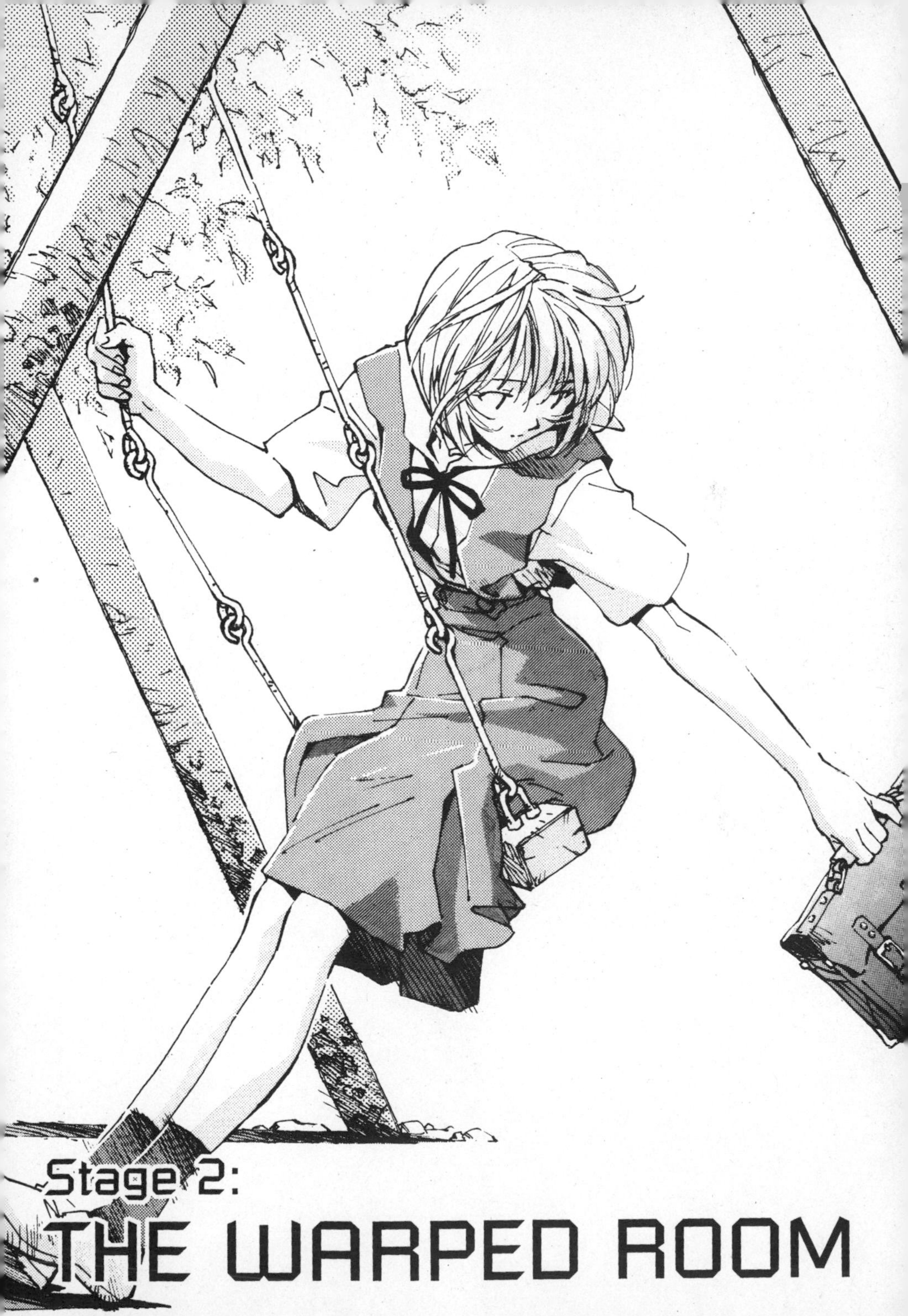

Stage 2: THE WARPED ROOM

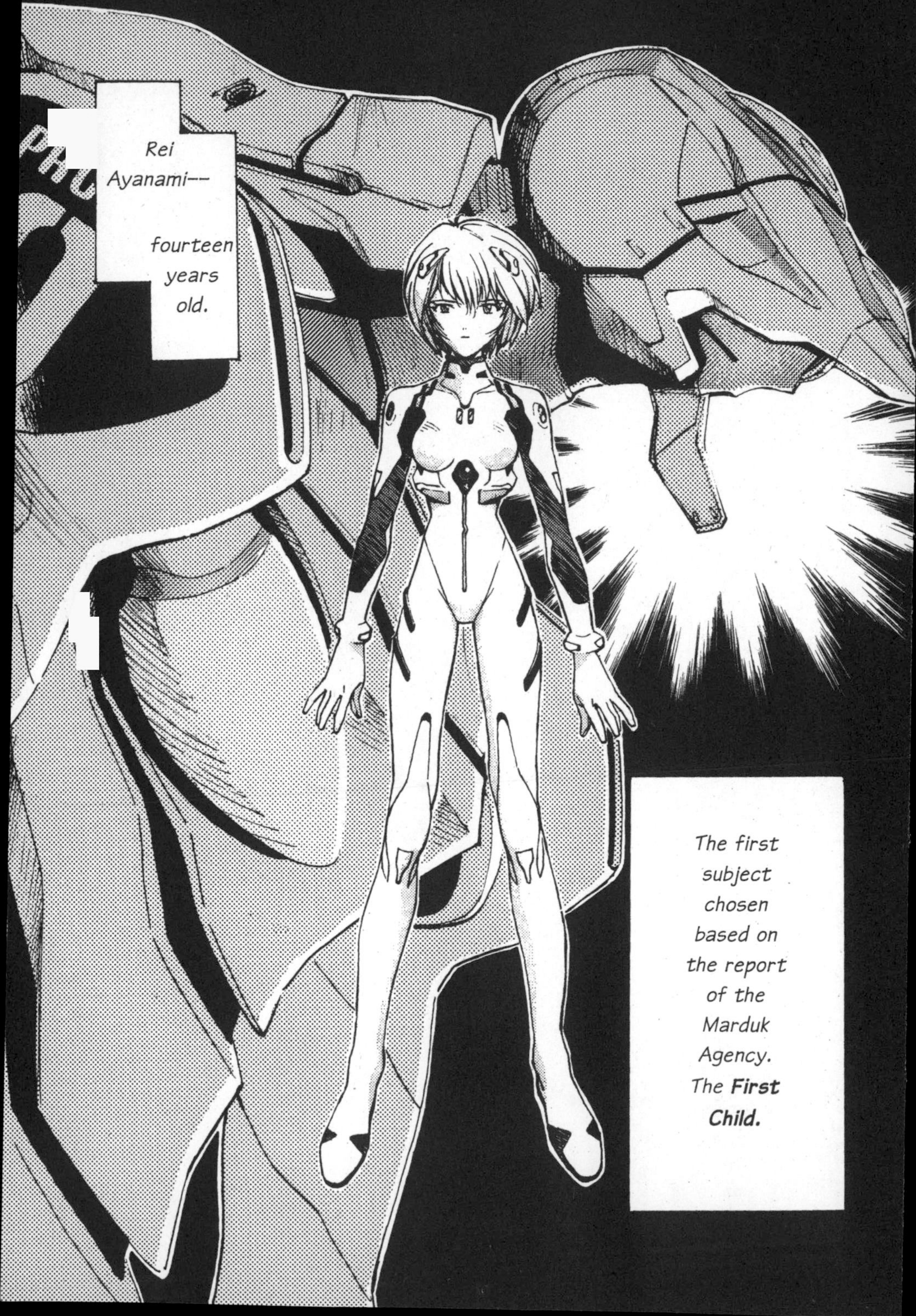
Rei Ayanami--
fourteen years old.
The first subject chosen based on the report of the Marduk Agency. The First Child.

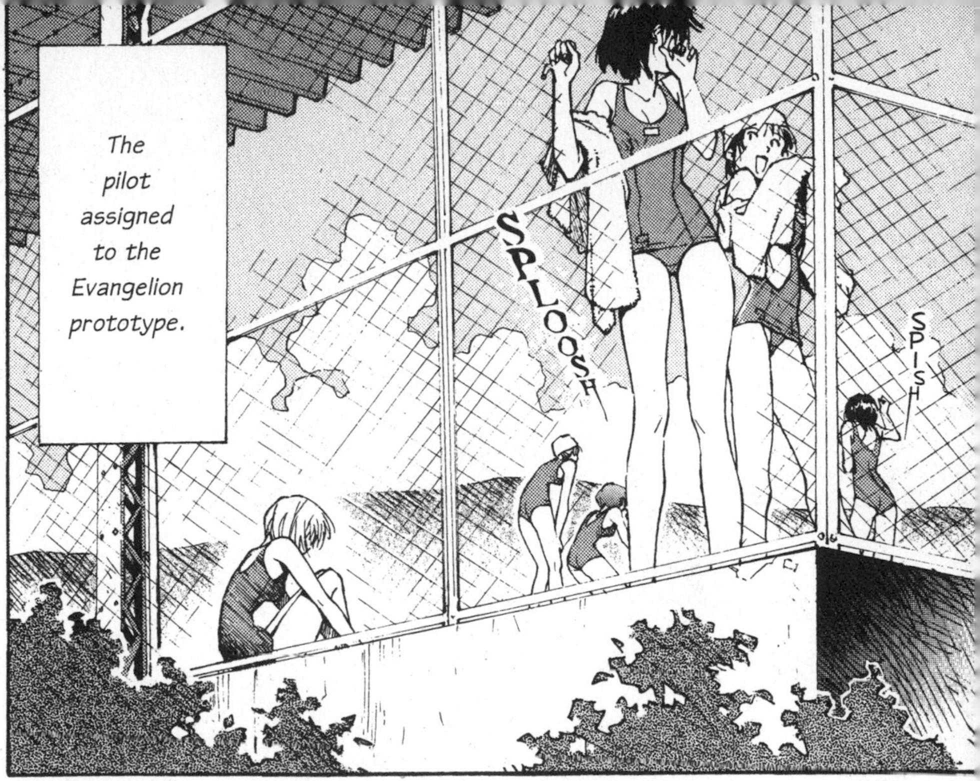
The pilot assigned to the Evangelion prototype.
SPLOOSH
SPISH

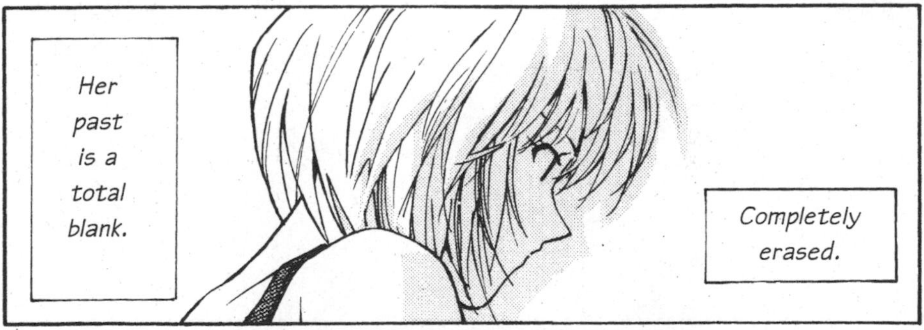
Her past is a total blank.
Completely erased.

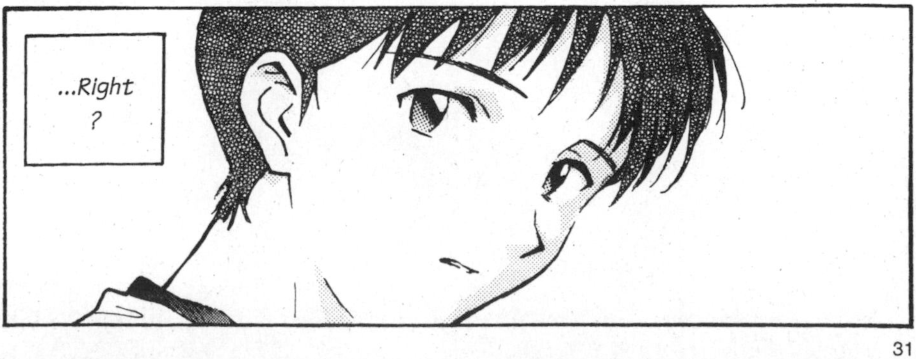
...Right?

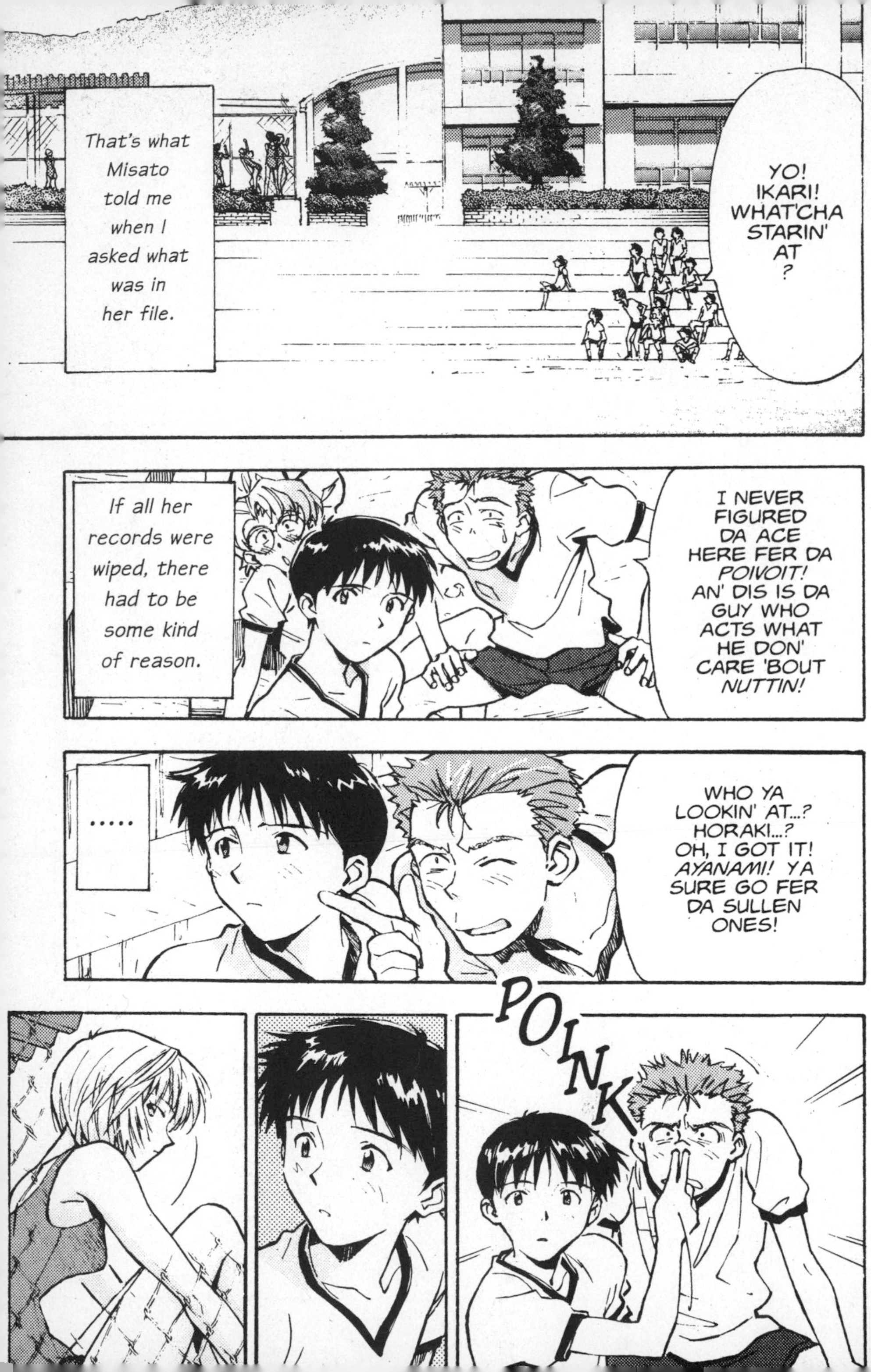
That's what Misato told me when I asked what was in her file.
YO! IKARI! WHAT'CHA STARIN' AT ?
If all her records were wiped, there had to be some kind of reason.
I NEVER FIGURED DA ACE HERE FER DA POIVOIT! AN' DIS IS DA GUY WHO ACTS WHAT HE DON' CARE 'BOUT NUTTIN!
.....
WHO YA LOOKIN' AT...? HORAKI...? OH, I GOT IT! AYANAMI! YA SURE GO FER DA SULLEN ONES!
POINK

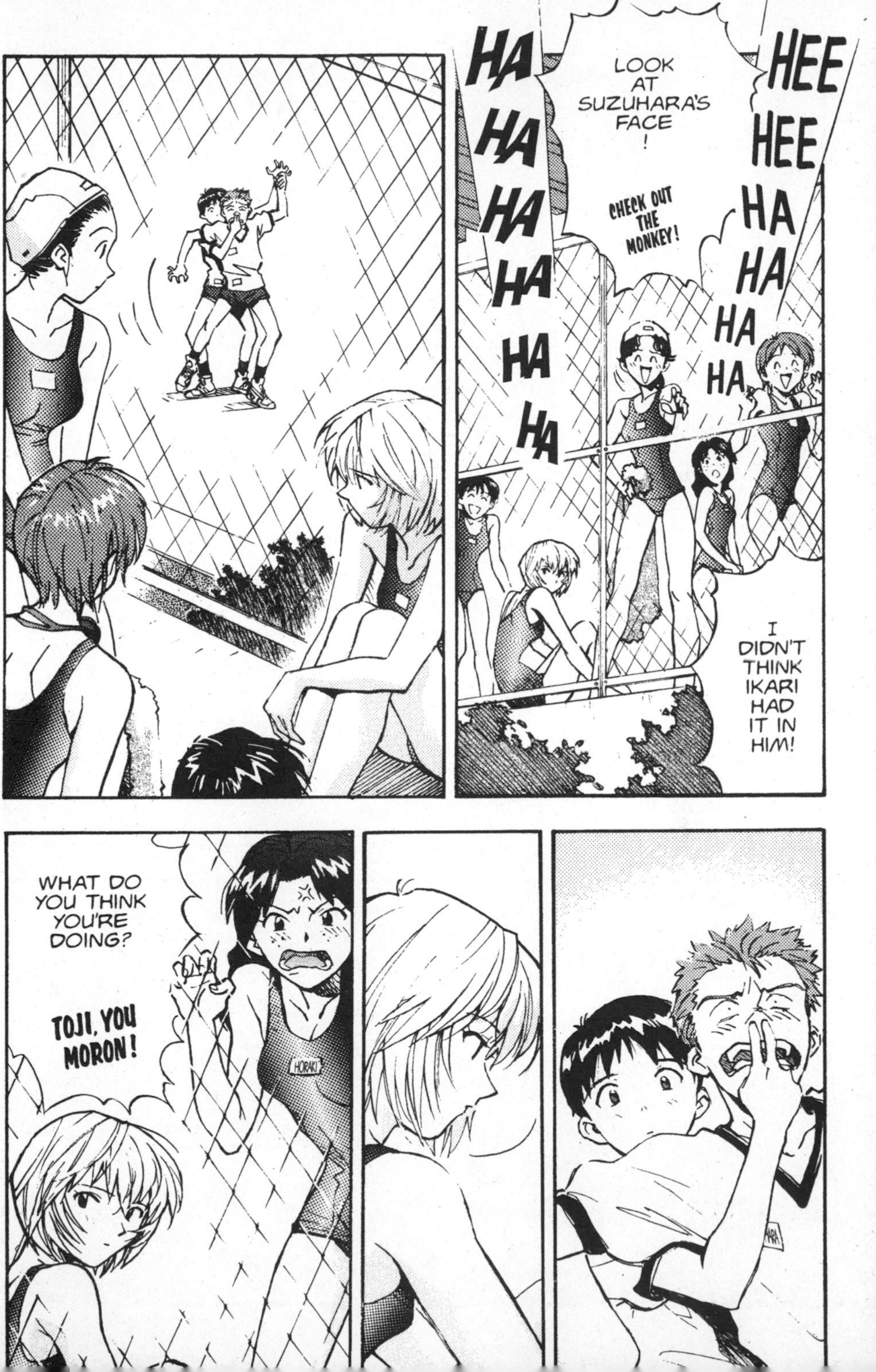
HA HA HA HA HA HA HA
LOOK AT SUZUHARA'S FACE!
CHECK OUT THE MONKEY!
HEE HEE HA HA HA HA
I DIDN'T THINK IKARI HAD IT IN HIM!
WHAT DO YOU THINK YOU'RE DOING?
TOJI, YOU MORON!
HORAKI

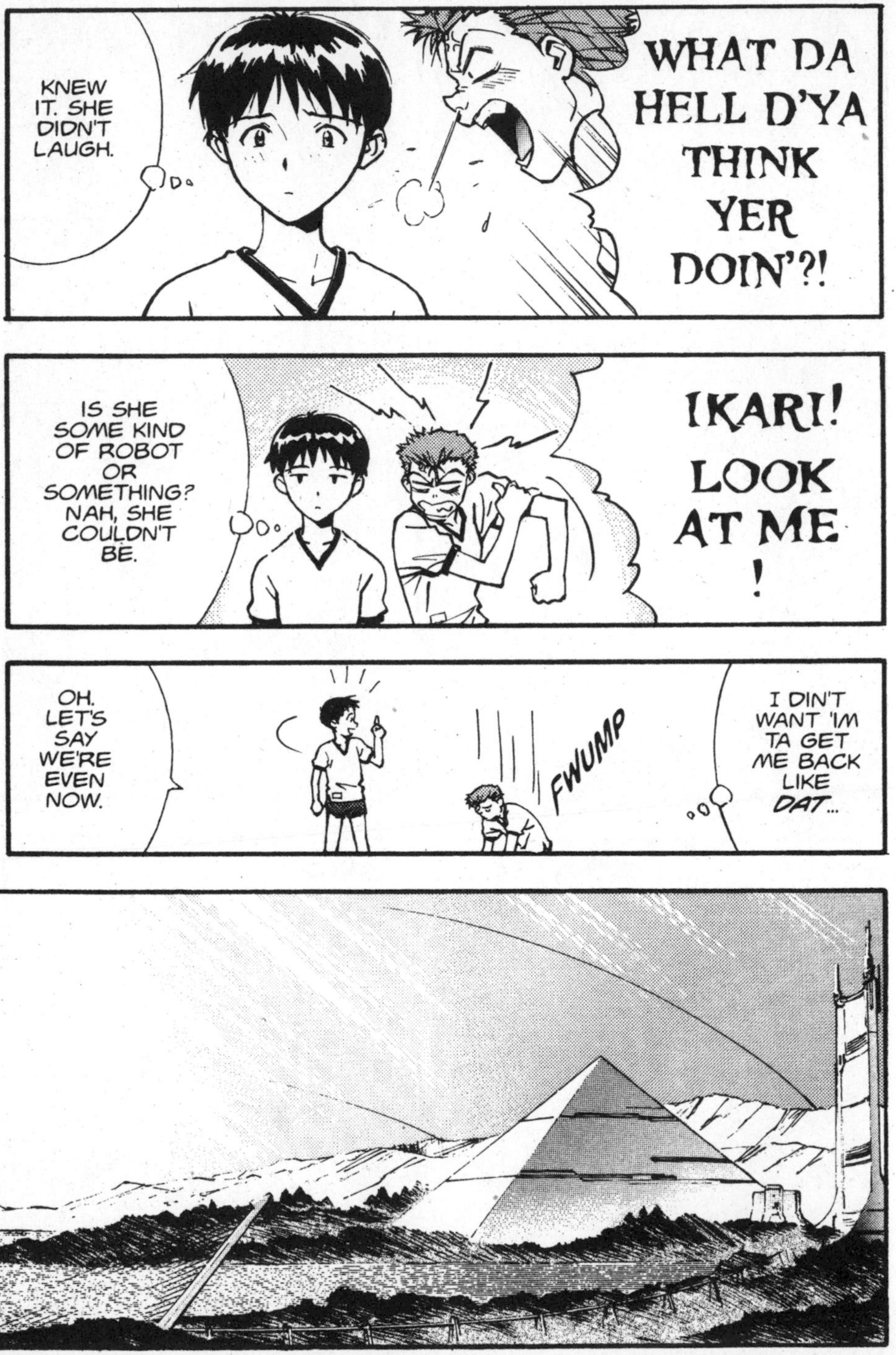
KNEW IT. SHE DIDN'T LAUGH.
WHAT DA HELL D'YA THINK YER DOIN'?!
IS SHE SOME KIND OF ROBOT OR SOMETHING? NAH, SHE COULDN'T BE.
IKARI! LOOK AT ME!
OH. LET'S SAY WE'RE EVEN NOW.
FWUMP
I DIN'T WANT 'IM TA GET ME BACK LIKE DAT...

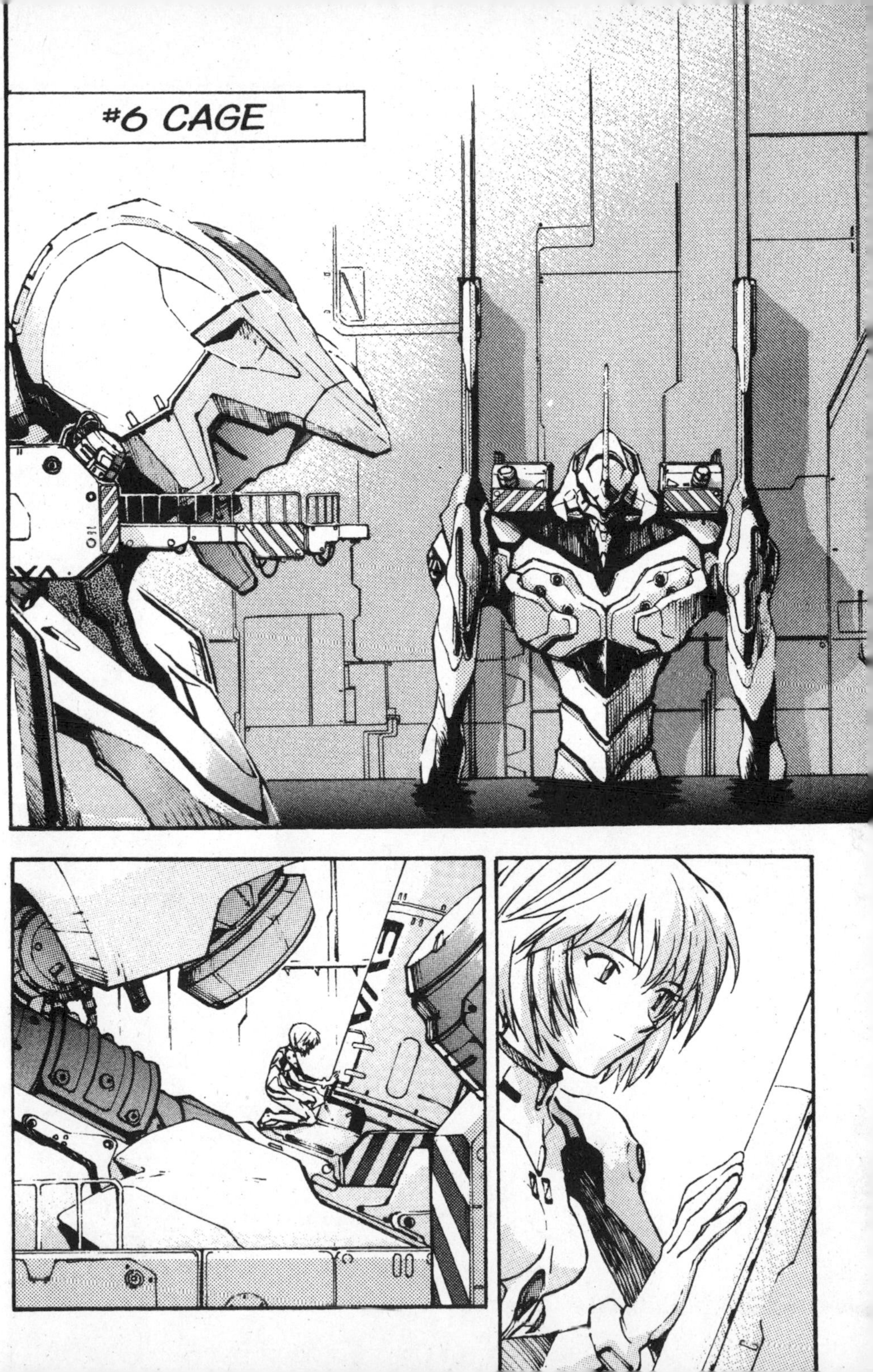
#6 CAGE

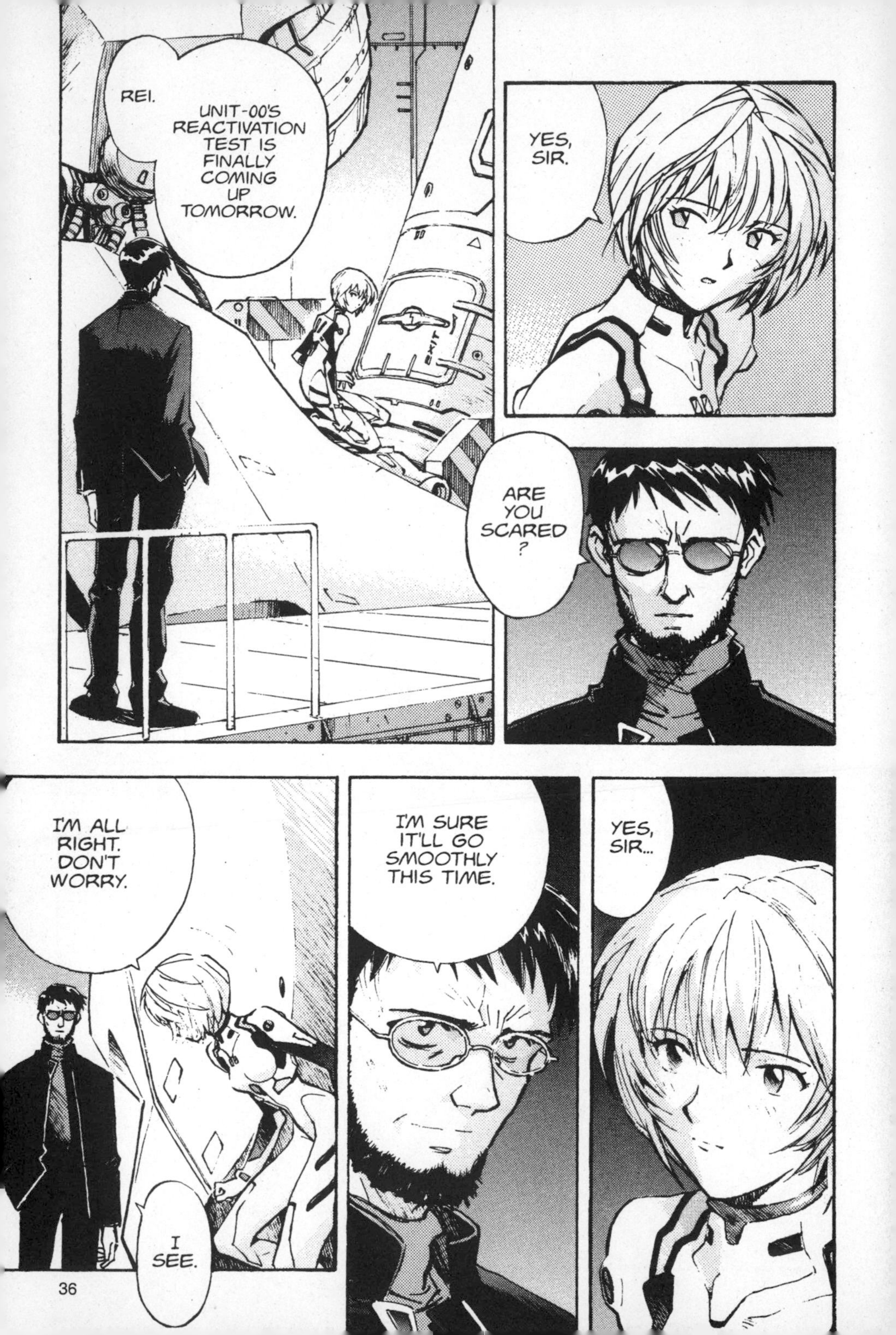
REI.
UNIT-00'S REACTIVATION TEST IS FINALLY COMING UP TOMORROW.
YES, SIR.
ARE YOU SCARED?
I'M ALL RIGHT. DON'T WORRY.
I SEE.
I'M SURE IT'LL GO SMOOTHLY THIS TIME.
YES, SIR...

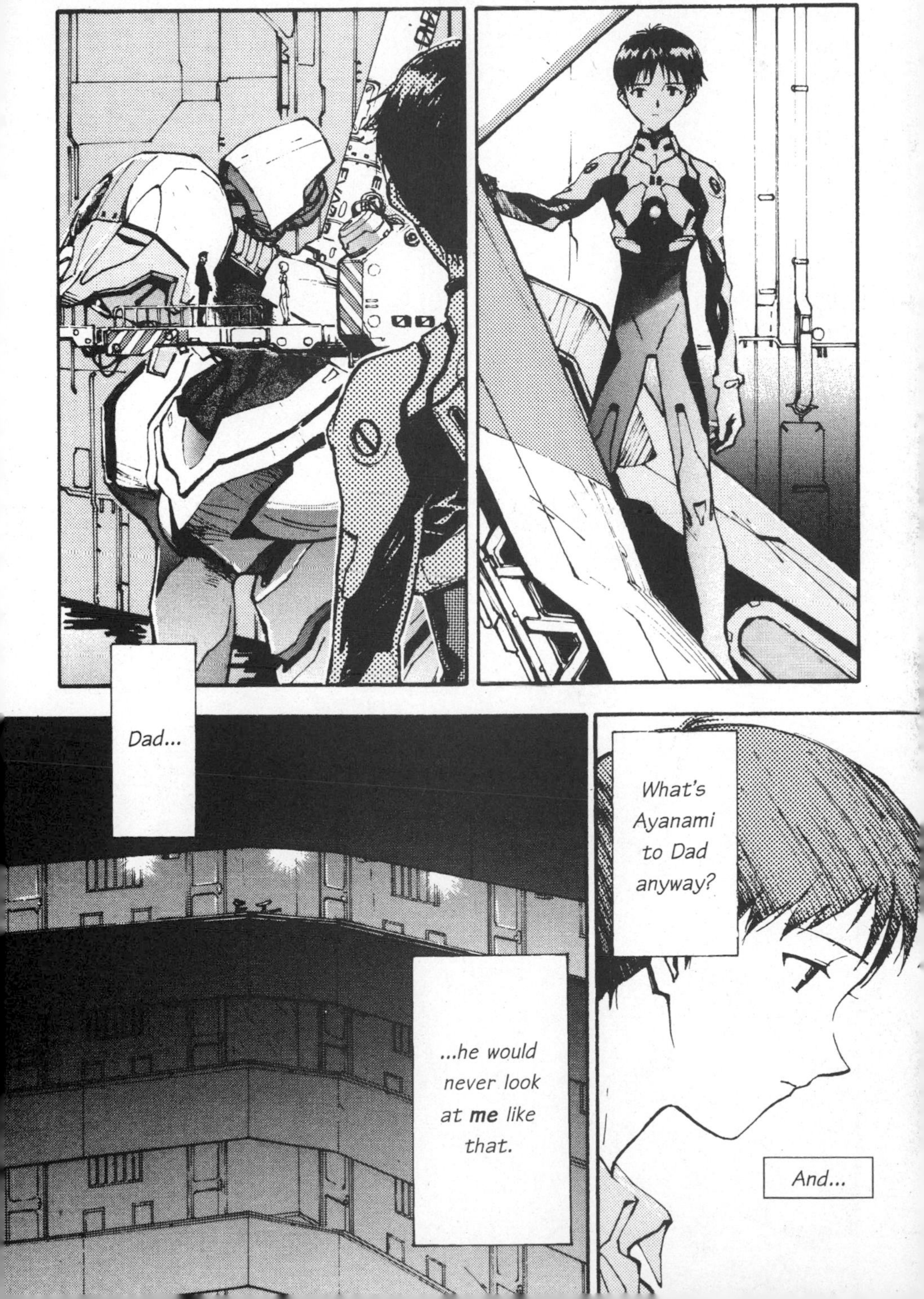
Dad...
...he would never look at **me** like that.
What's Ayanami to Dad anyway?
And...

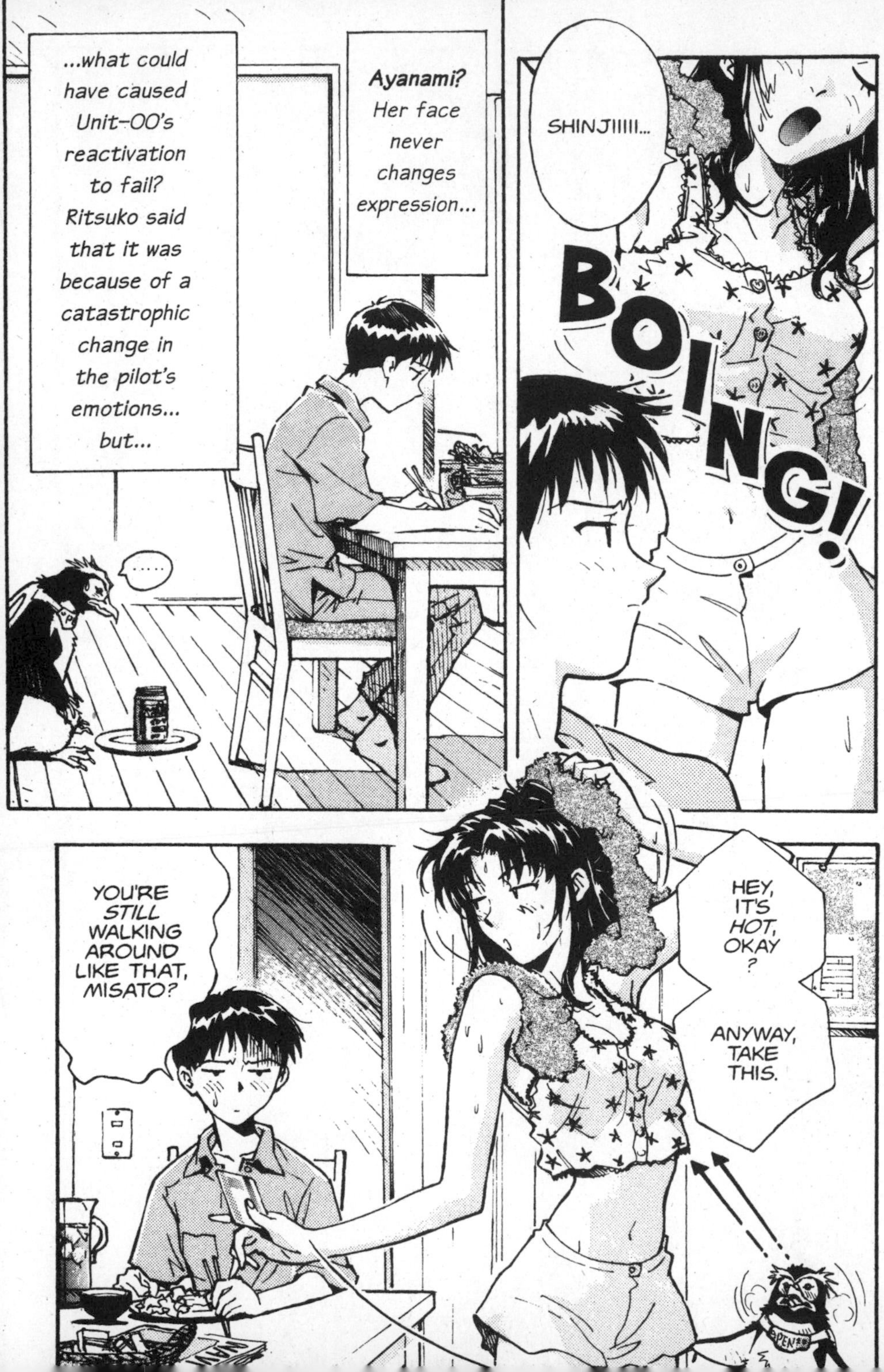
...what could have caused Unit-00's reactivation to fail? Ritsuko said that it was because of a catastrophic change in the pilot's emotions... but...
Ayanami? Her face never changes expression...
......
SHINJIIIII...
BOING!
YOU'RE STILL WALKING AROUND LIKE THAT, MISATO?
HEY, IT'S HOT, OKAY?
ANYWAY, TAKE THIS.

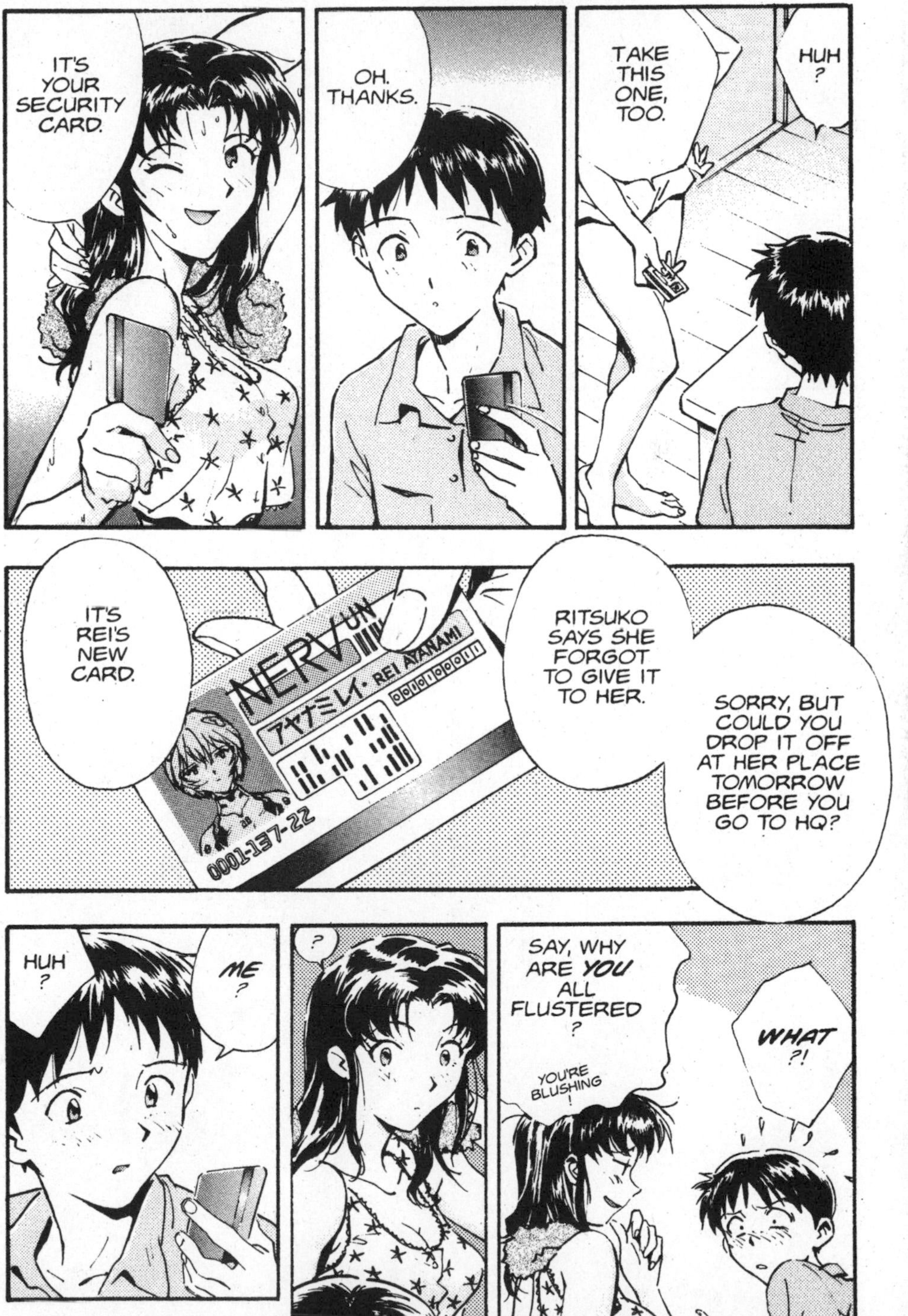
IT'S YOUR SECURITY CARD.
OH. THANKS.
TAKE THIS ONE, TOO.
HUH?
IT'S REI'S NEW CARD.
NERV UN
アヤナミレイ・REI AYANAMI
0001-137-22
RITSUKO SAYS SHE FORGOT TO GIVE IT TO HER.
SORRY, BUT COULD YOU DROP IT OFF AT HER PLACE TOMORROW BEFORE YOU GO TO HQ?
HUH?
ME?
?
SAY, WHY ARE ***YOU*** ALL FLUSTERED?
YOU'RE BLUSHING!
WHAT?!

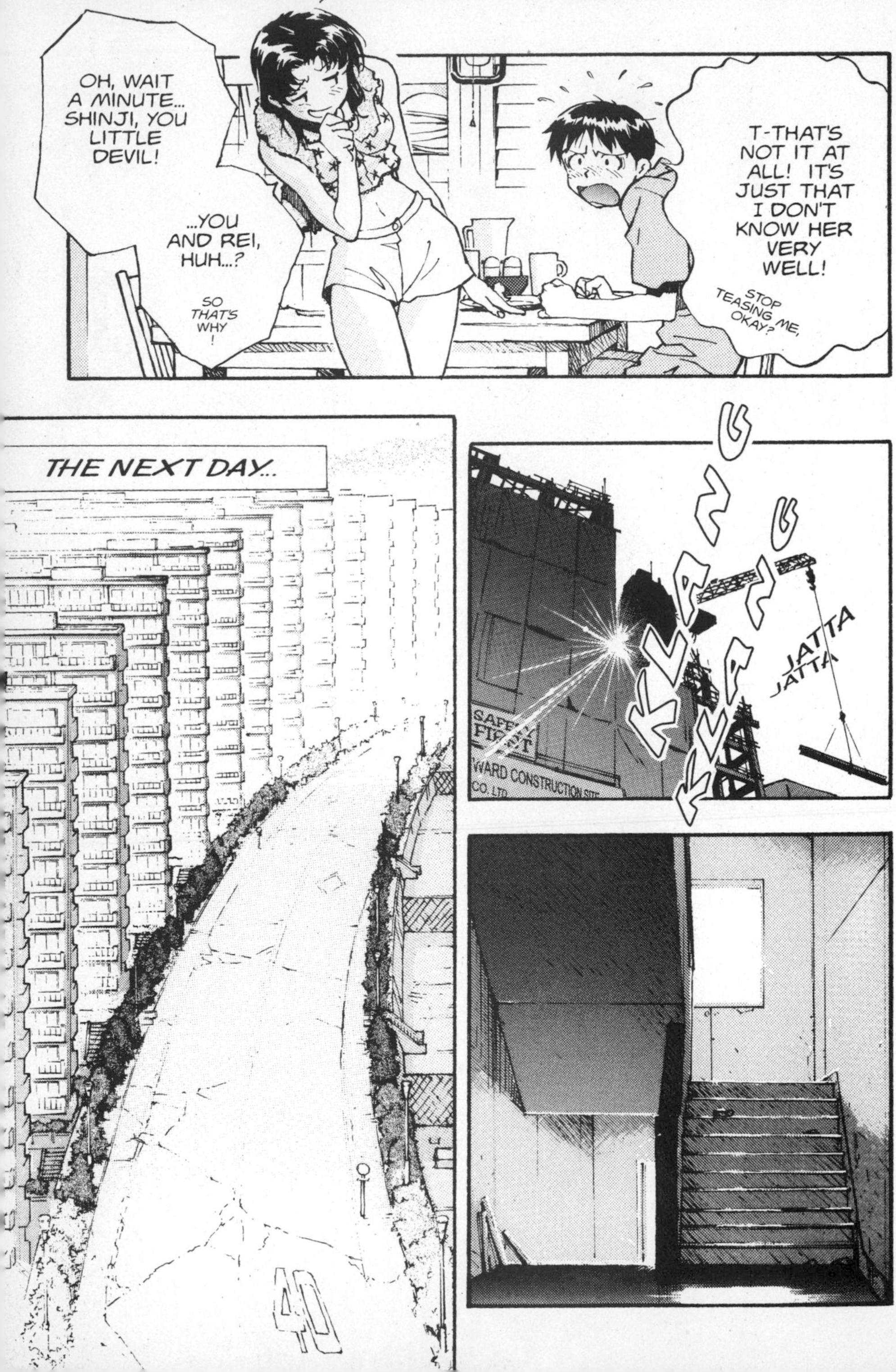
OH, WAIT A MINUTE... SHINJI, YOU LITTLE DEVIL!
...YOU AND REI, HUH...?
SO THAT'S WHY!
T-THAT'S NOT IT AT ALL! IT'S JUST THAT I DON'T KNOW HER VERY WELL!
STOP TEASING ME, OKAY?
THE NEXT DAY...
KLANG
KLANG
JATTA JATTA
SAFETY FIRST
WARD CONSTRUCTION SITE
CO. LTD.

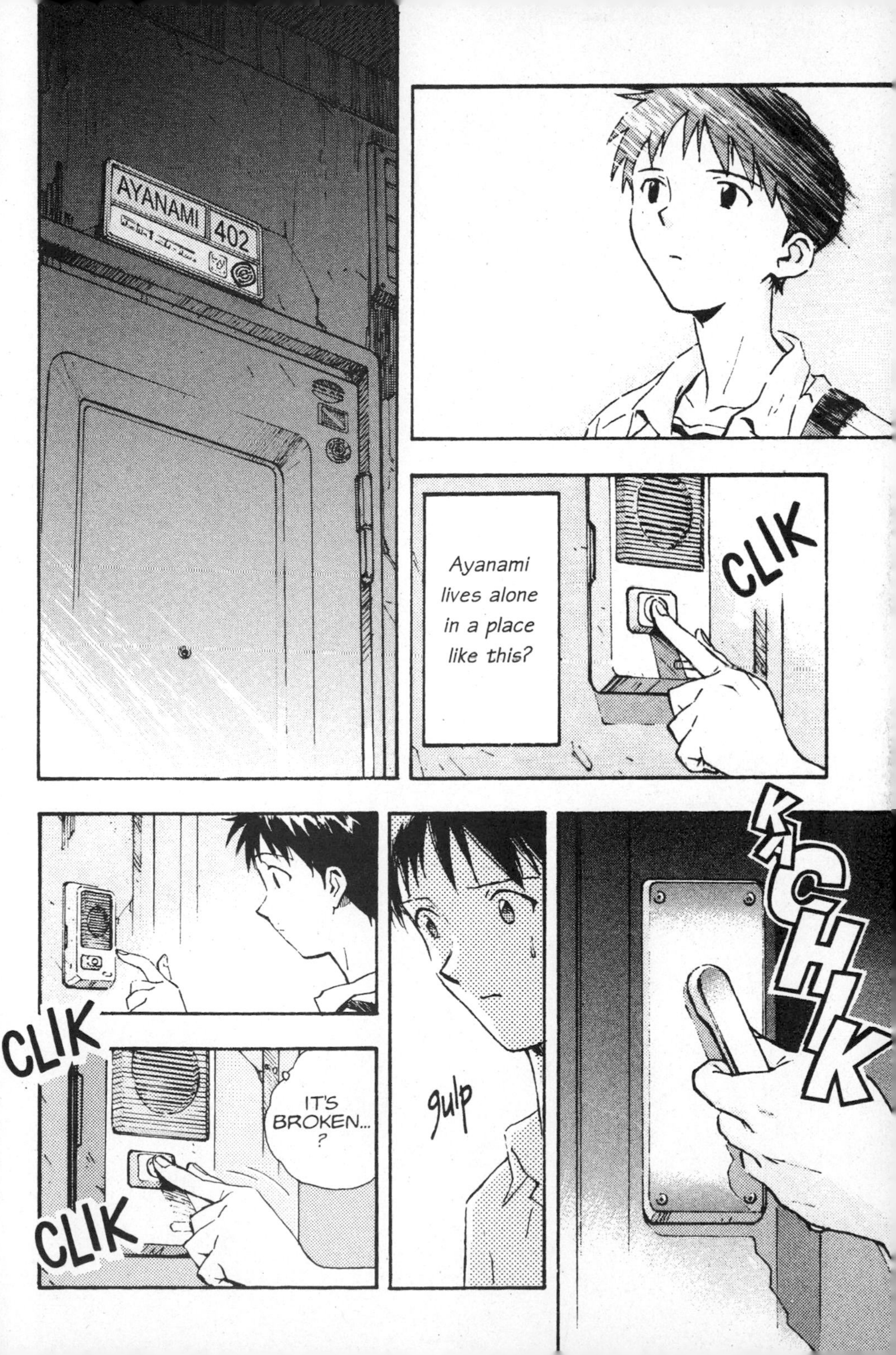
AYANAMI 402
Ayanami lives alone in a place like this?
CLIK
CLIK
IT'S BROKEN... ?
CLIK
gulp
KACHIK

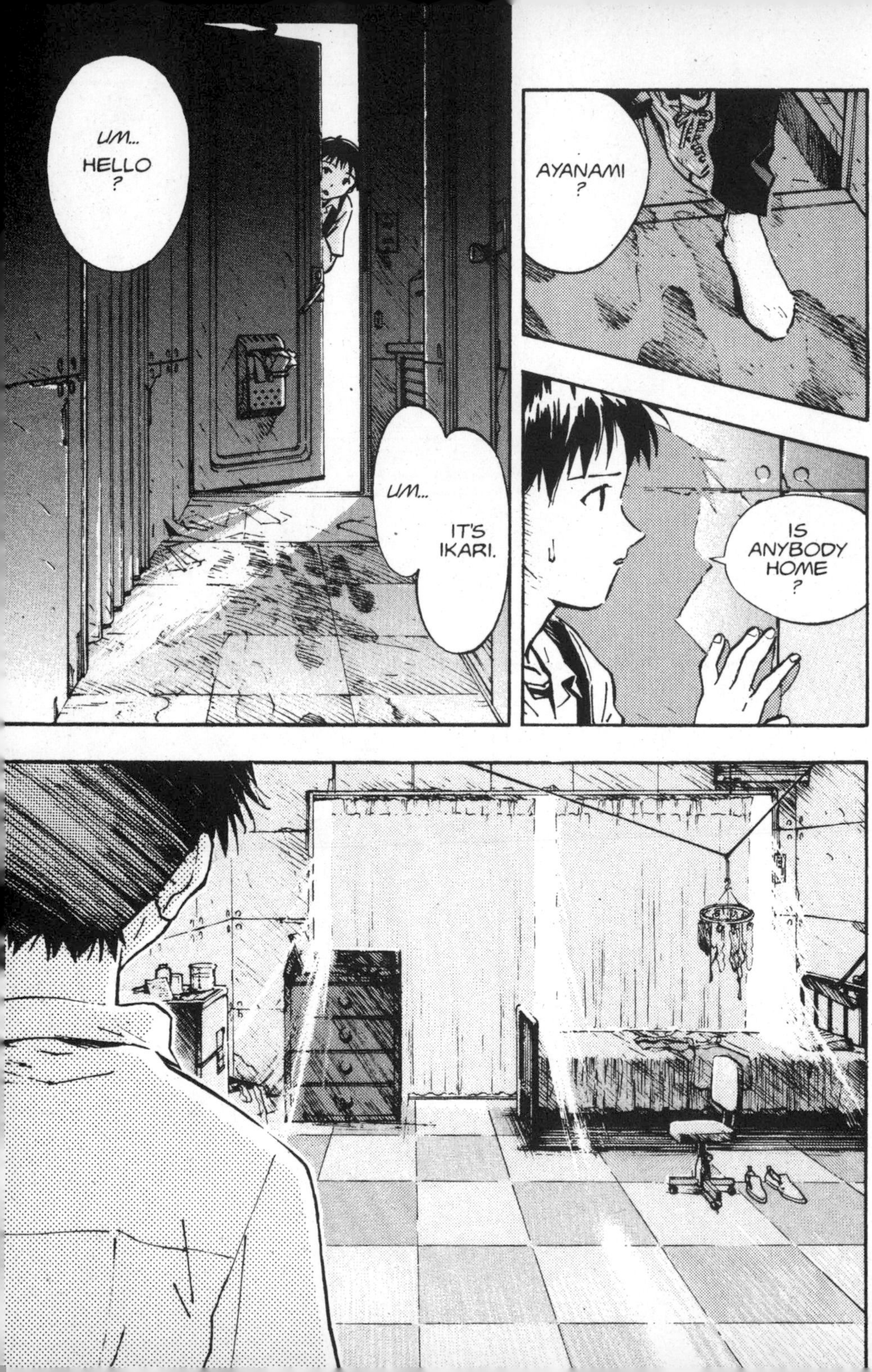
UM... HELLO ?
UM... IT'S IKARI.
AYANAMI ?
IS ANYBODY HOME ?

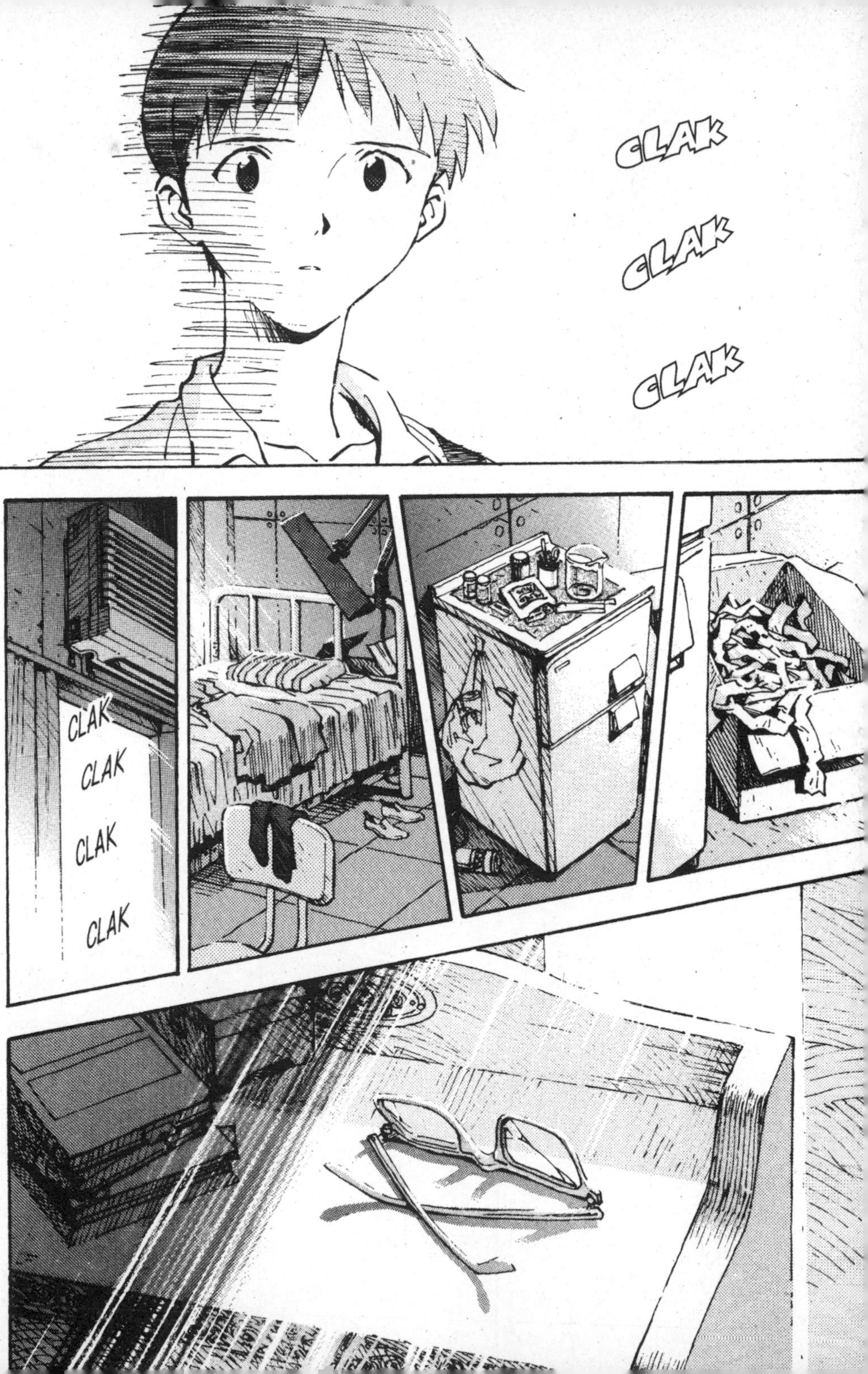
CLAK
CLAK
CLAK
CLAK
CLAK
CLAK
CLAK

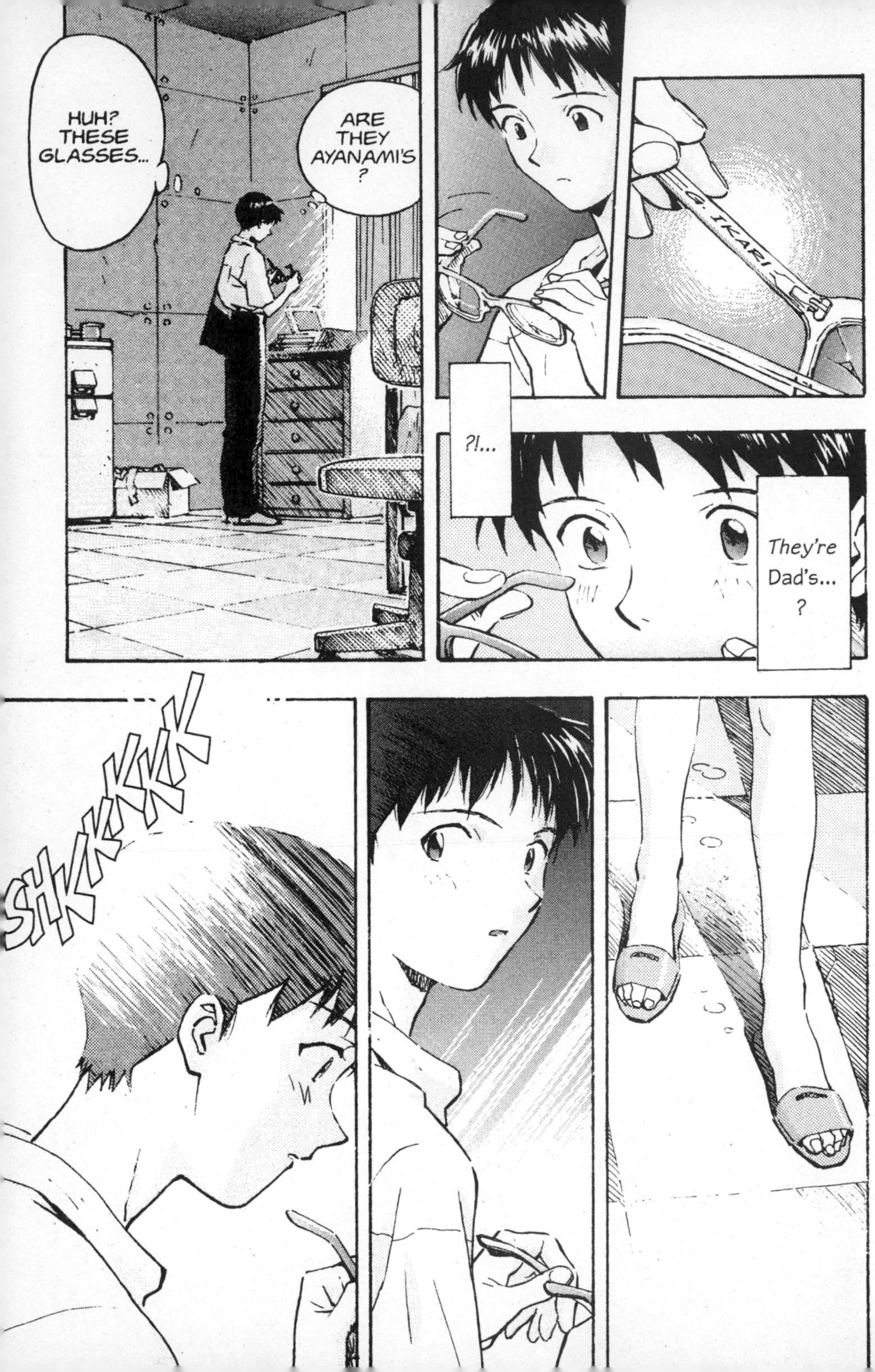
HUH? THESE GLASSES...
ARE THEY AYANAMI'S?
G. IKARI
?!...
They're Dad's...?
SHKKKKK

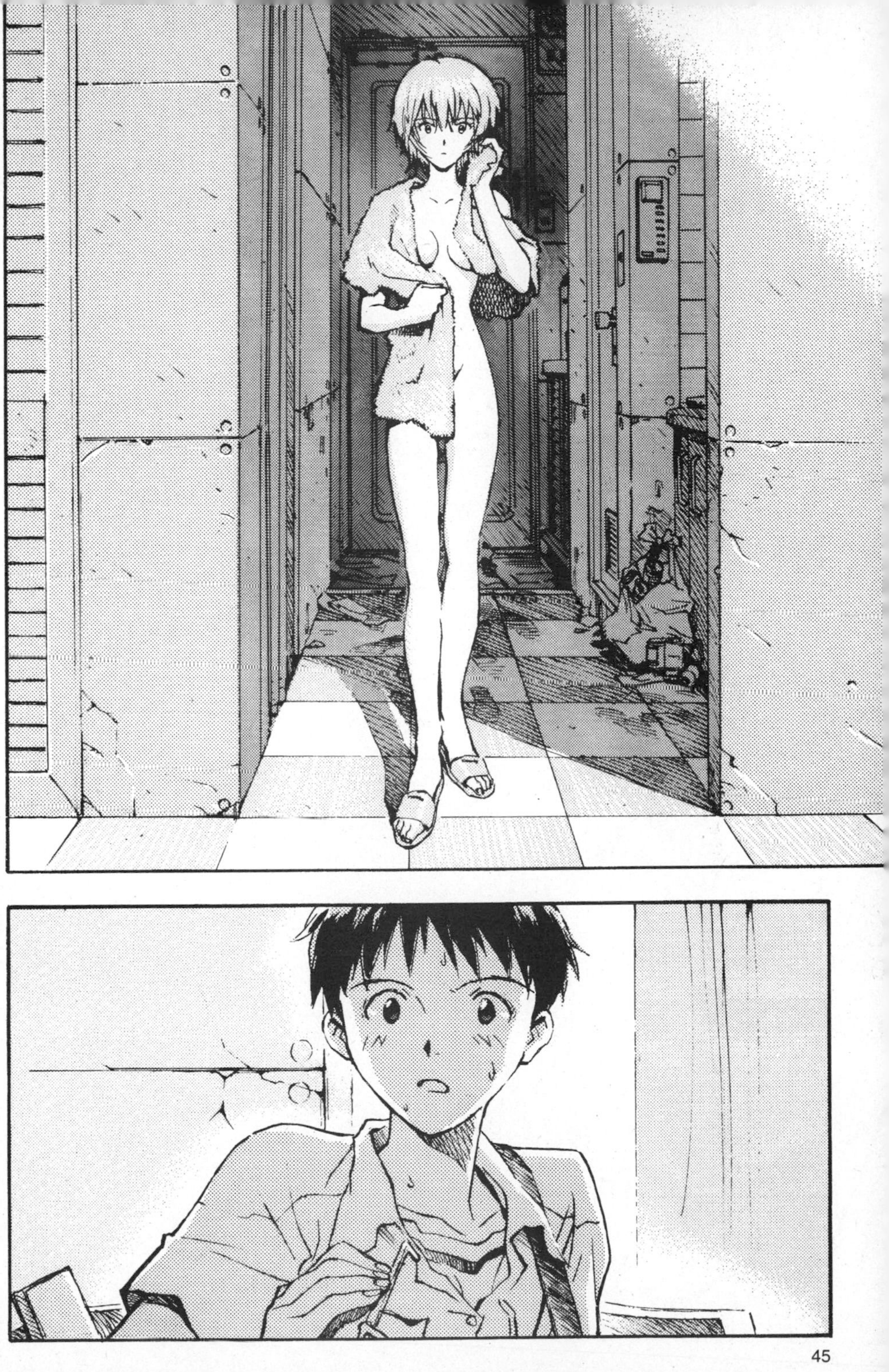

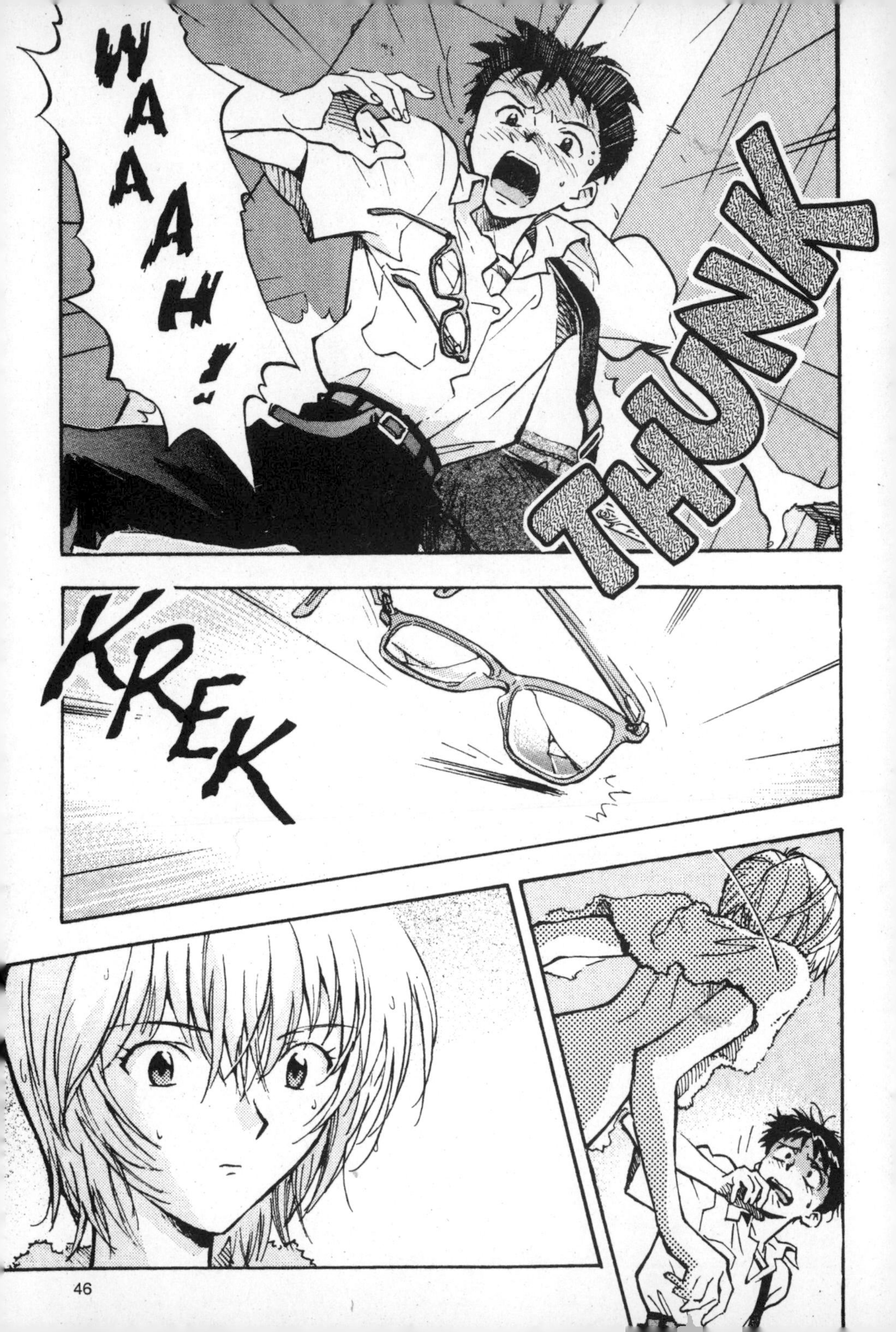
WAAAH!!
THUNK
KREK

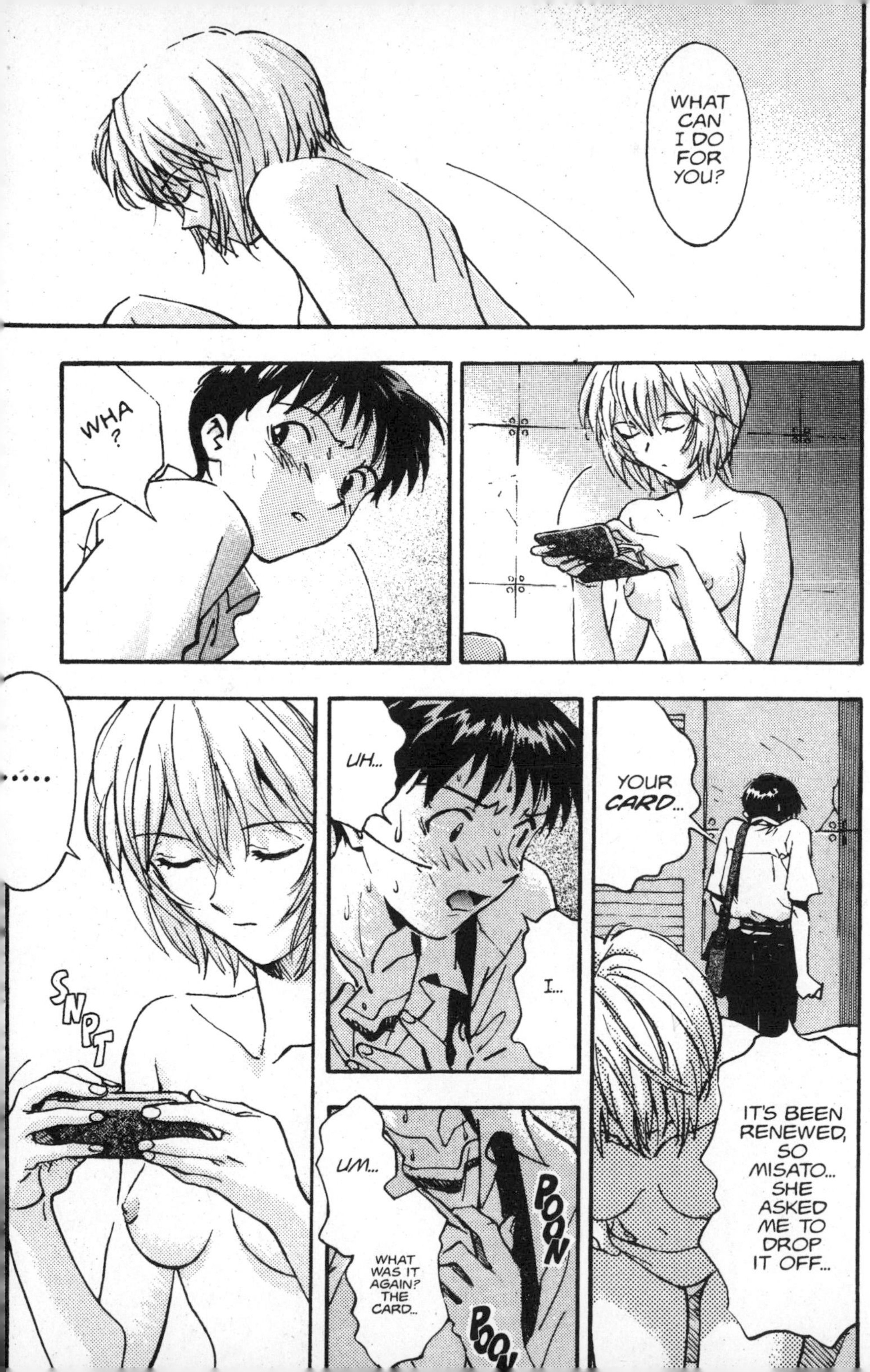
WHAT CAN I DO FOR YOU?
WHA ?
.....
SNPT
UH...
I...
UM...
WHAT WAS IT AGAIN? THE CARD...
POON
POO
YOUR CARD...
IT'S BEEN RENEWED, SO MISATO... SHE ASKED ME TO DROP IT OFF...

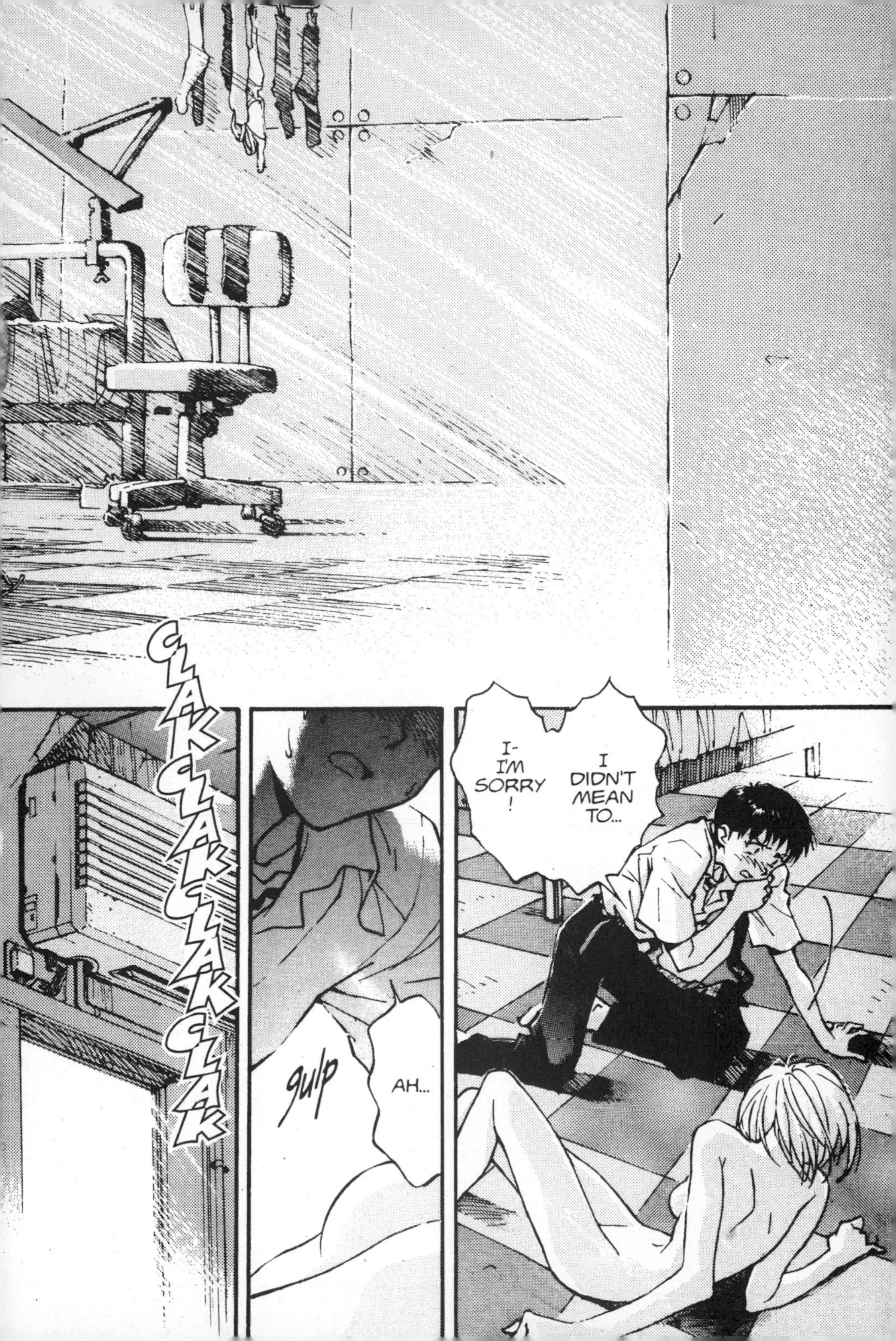
CLAK CLAK CLAK CLAK
gulp
AH...
I- I'M SORRY!
I DIDN'T MEAN TO...

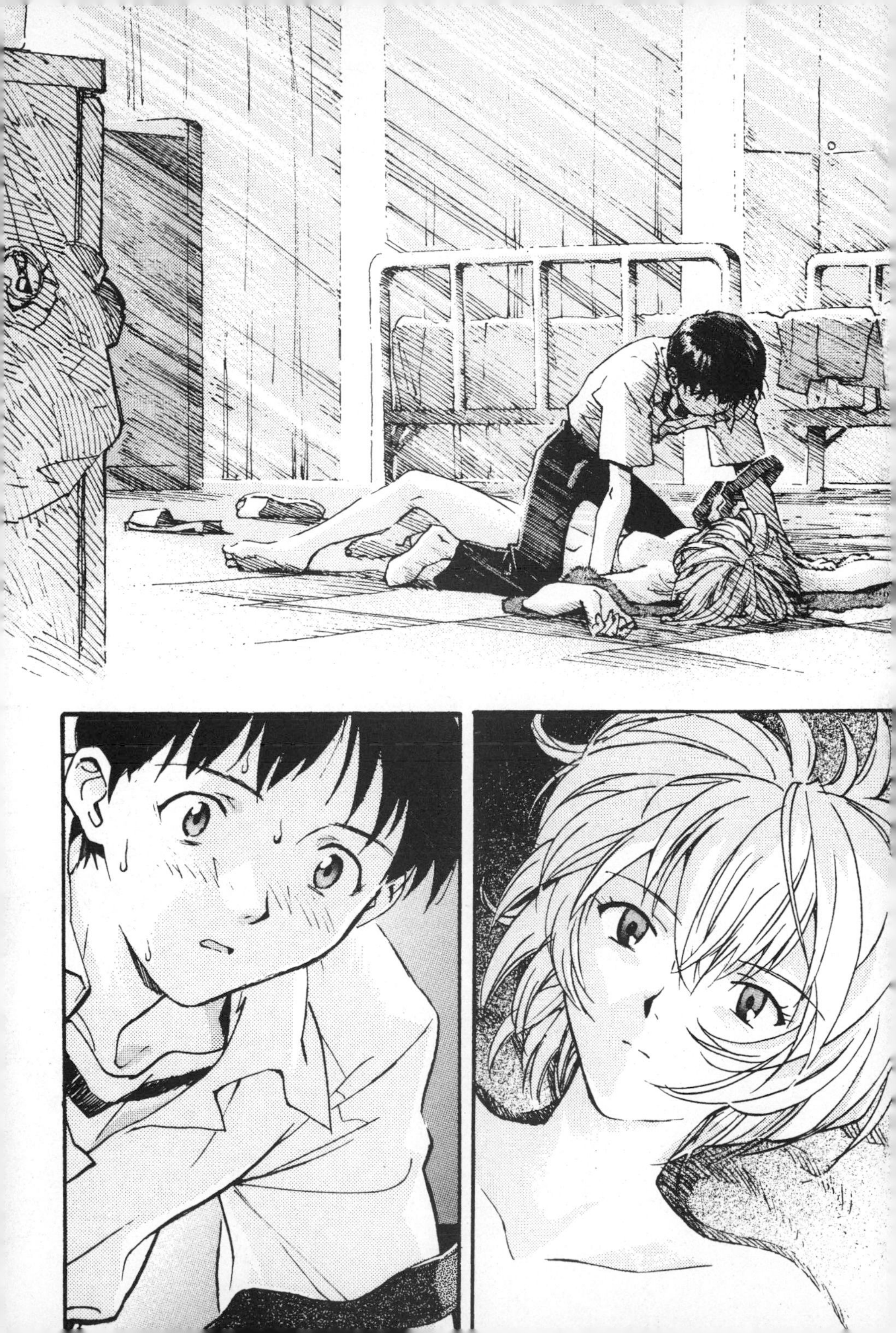

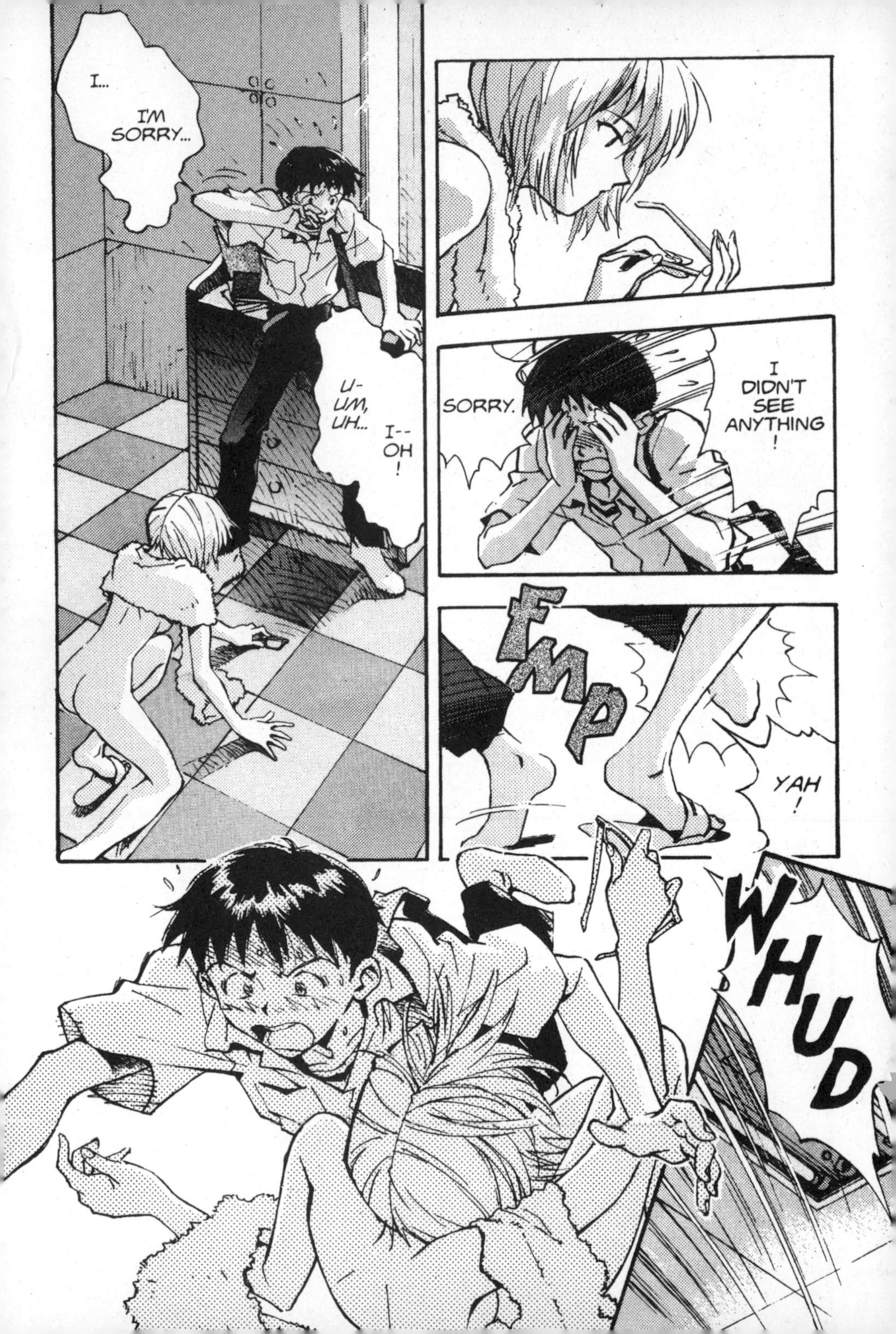
I...
I'M SORRY...
U-UM, UH...
I-- OH!
SORRY.
I DIDN'T SEE ANYTHING!
FMP
YAH!
WHUD

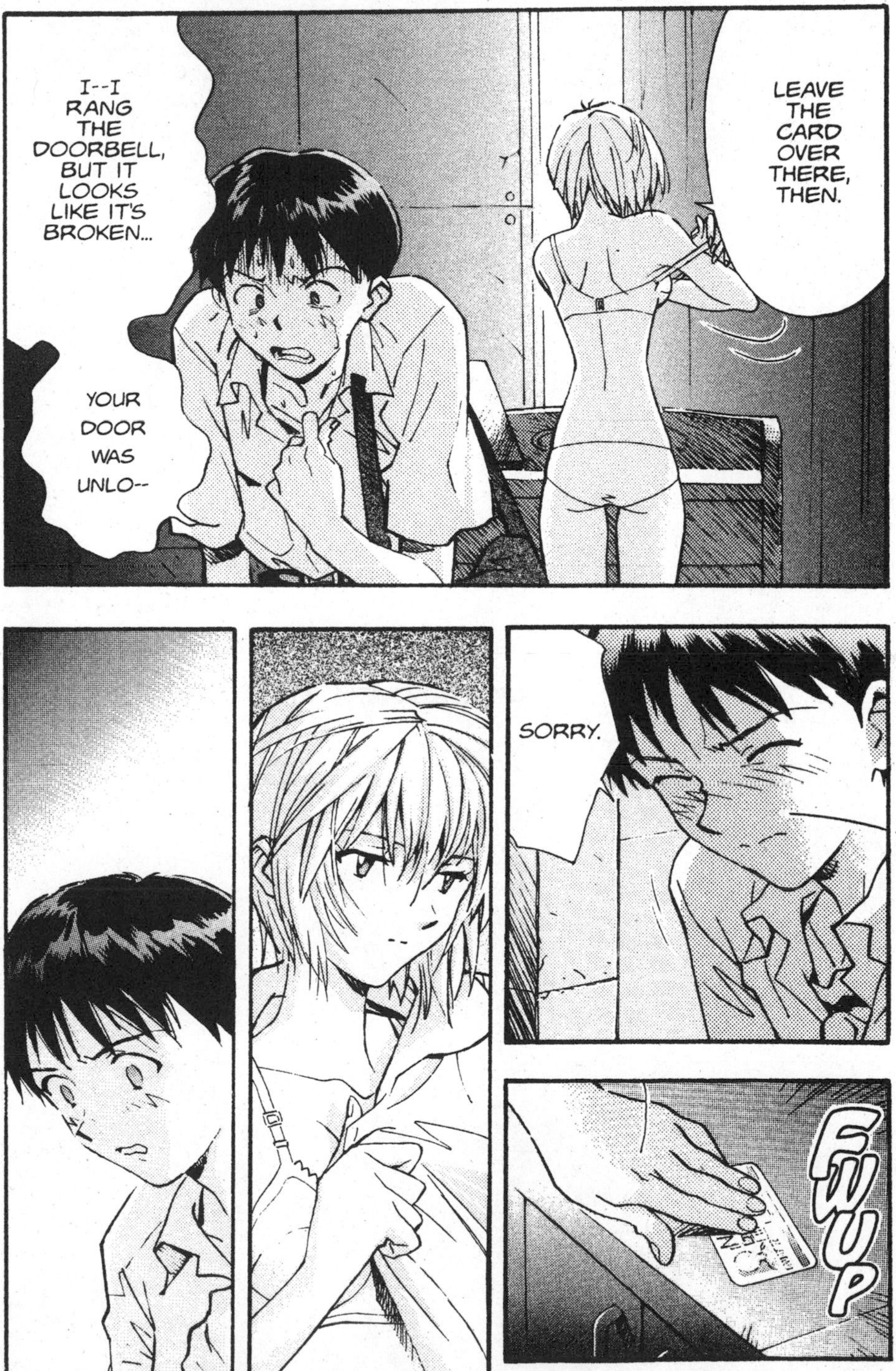
I--I RANG THE DOORBELL, BUT IT LOOKS LIKE IT'S BROKEN...
YOUR DOOR WAS UNLO--
LEAVE THE CARD OVER THERE, THEN.
SORRY.
FWUP

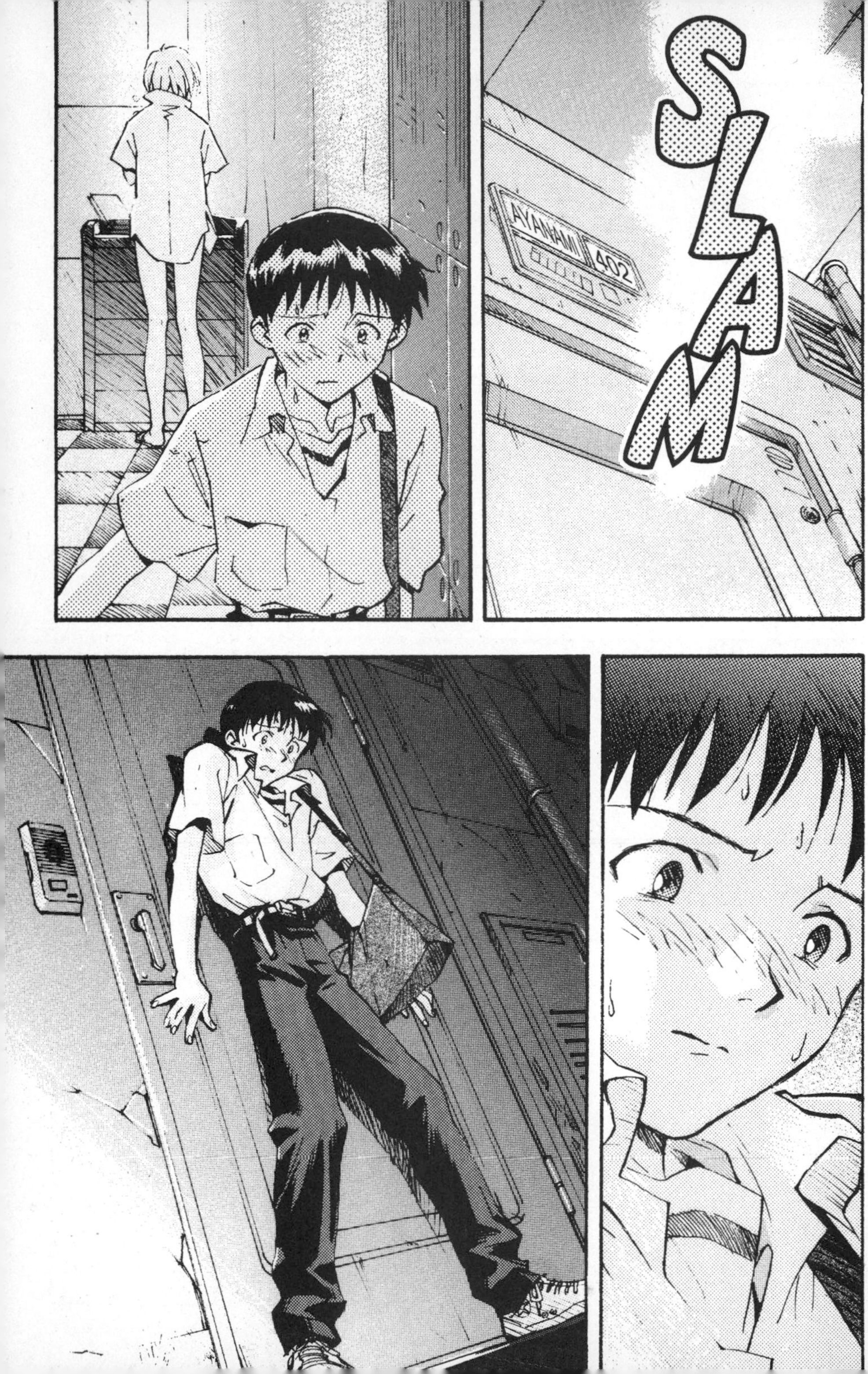
SLAM
AYANAMI 402

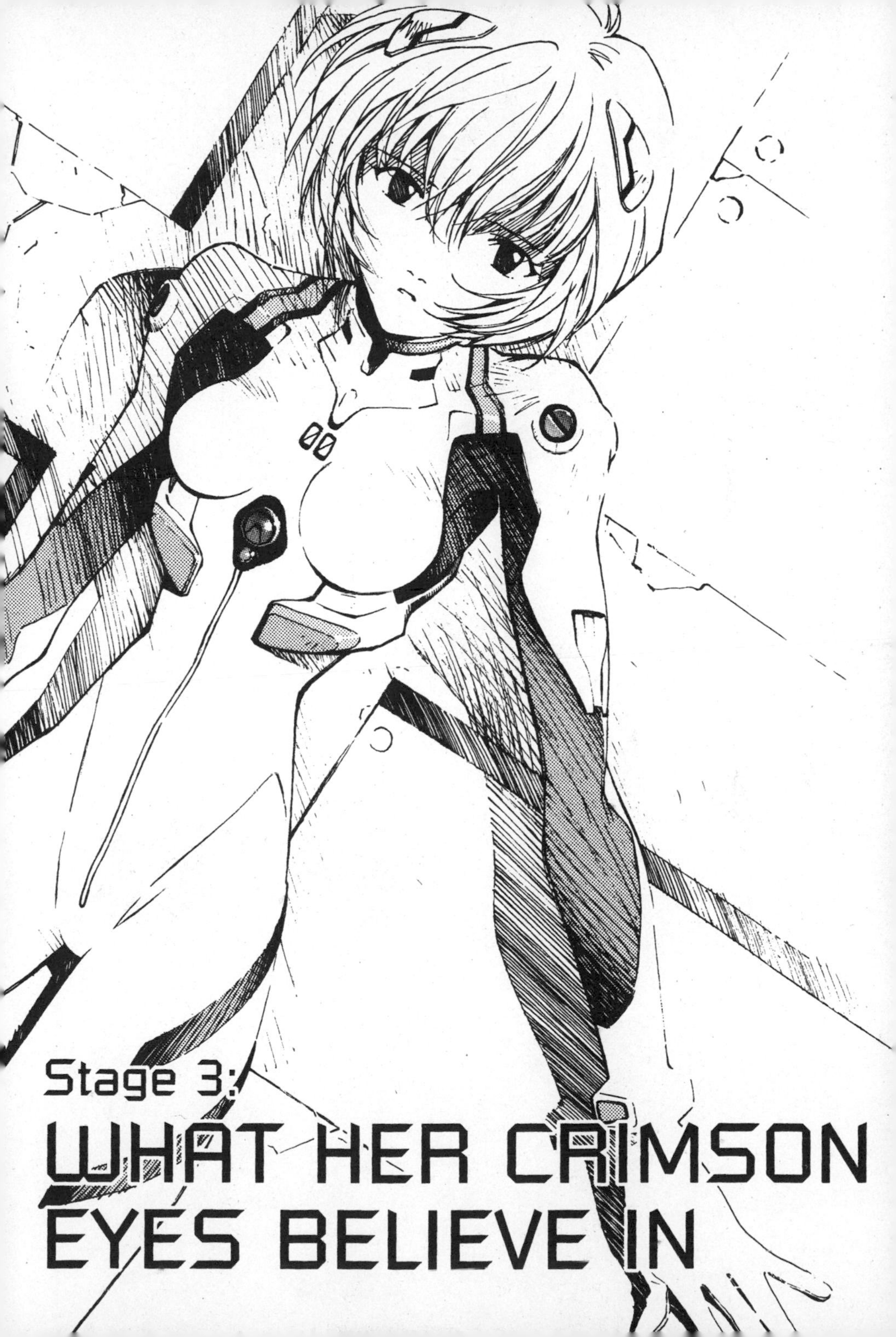

Stage 3: WHAT HER CRIMSON EYES BELIEVE IN

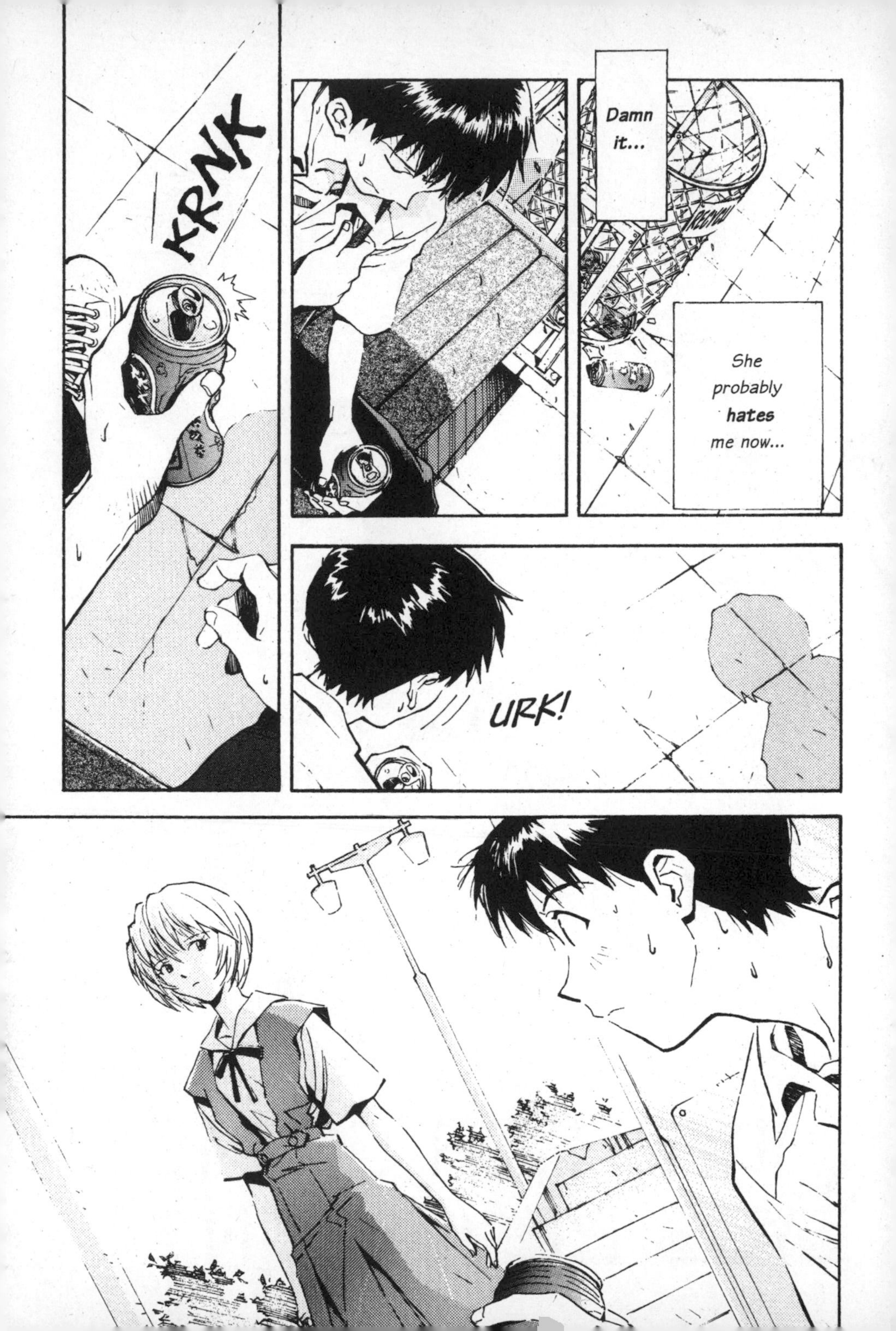
KRNK
Damn it...
She probably **hates** me now...
URK!

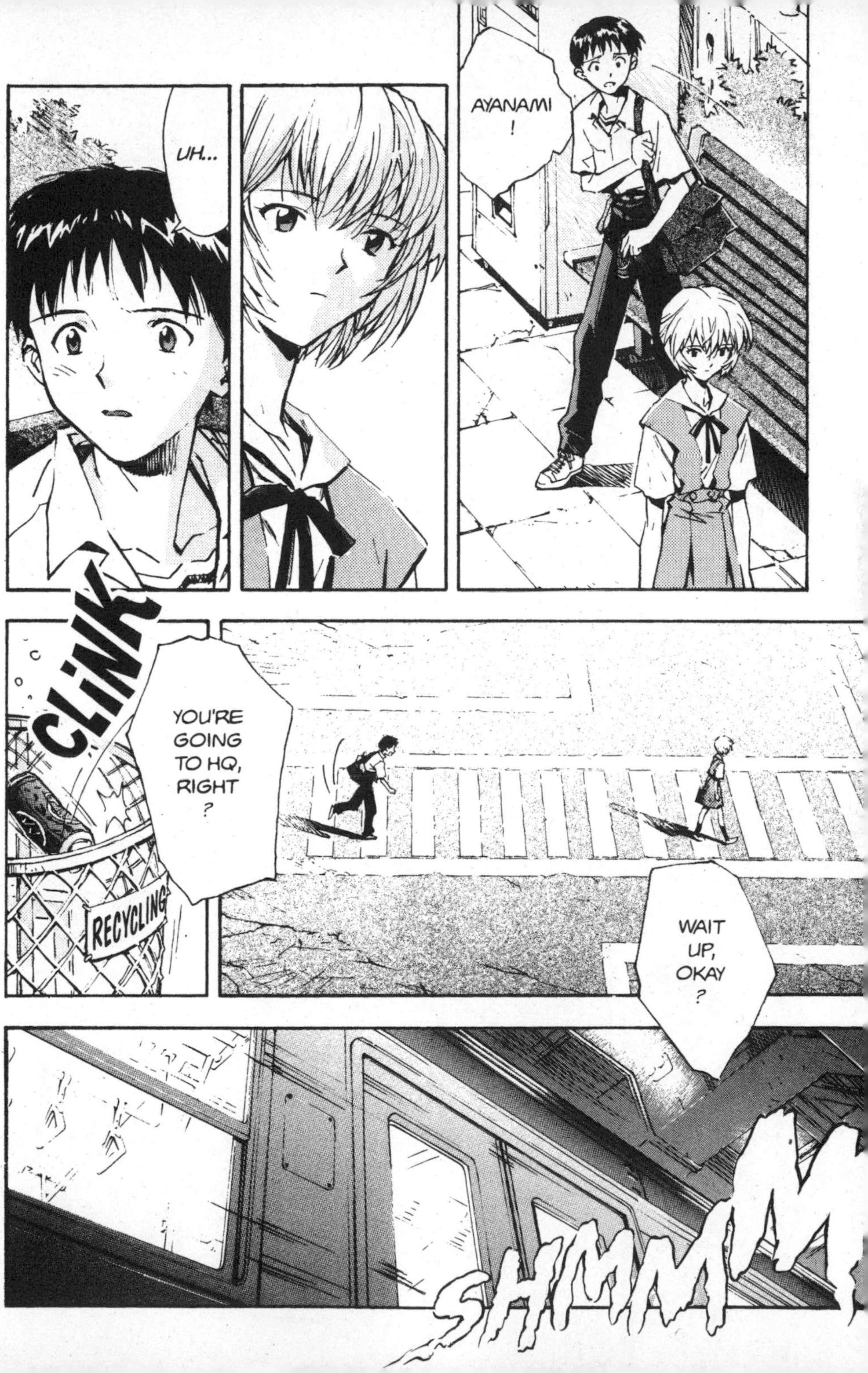
AYANAMI !
UH...
CLINK
YOU'RE GOING TO HQ, RIGHT ?
WAIT UP, OKAY ?
SHMMM

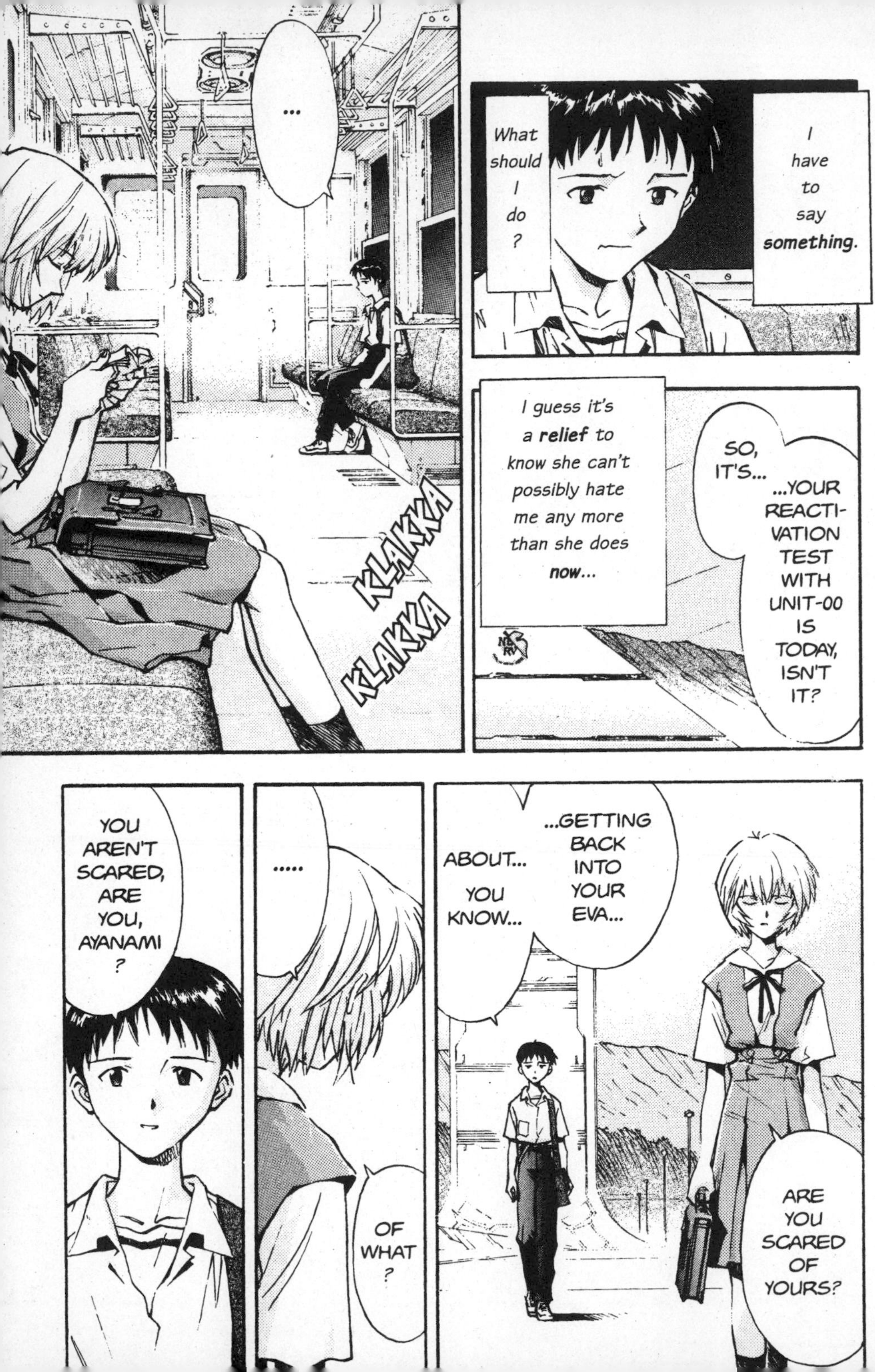
...
KLAKKA KLAKKA
What should I do?
I have to say **something**.
I guess it's a **relief** to know she can't possibly hate me any more than she does **now**...
SO, IT'S...
...YOUR REACTI-VATION TEST WITH UNIT-00 IS TODAY, ISN'T IT?
YOU AREN'T SCARED, ARE YOU, AYANAMI?
.....
OF WHAT?
ABOUT...
YOU KNOW...
...GETTING BACK INTO YOUR EVA...
ARE YOU SCARED OF YOURS?

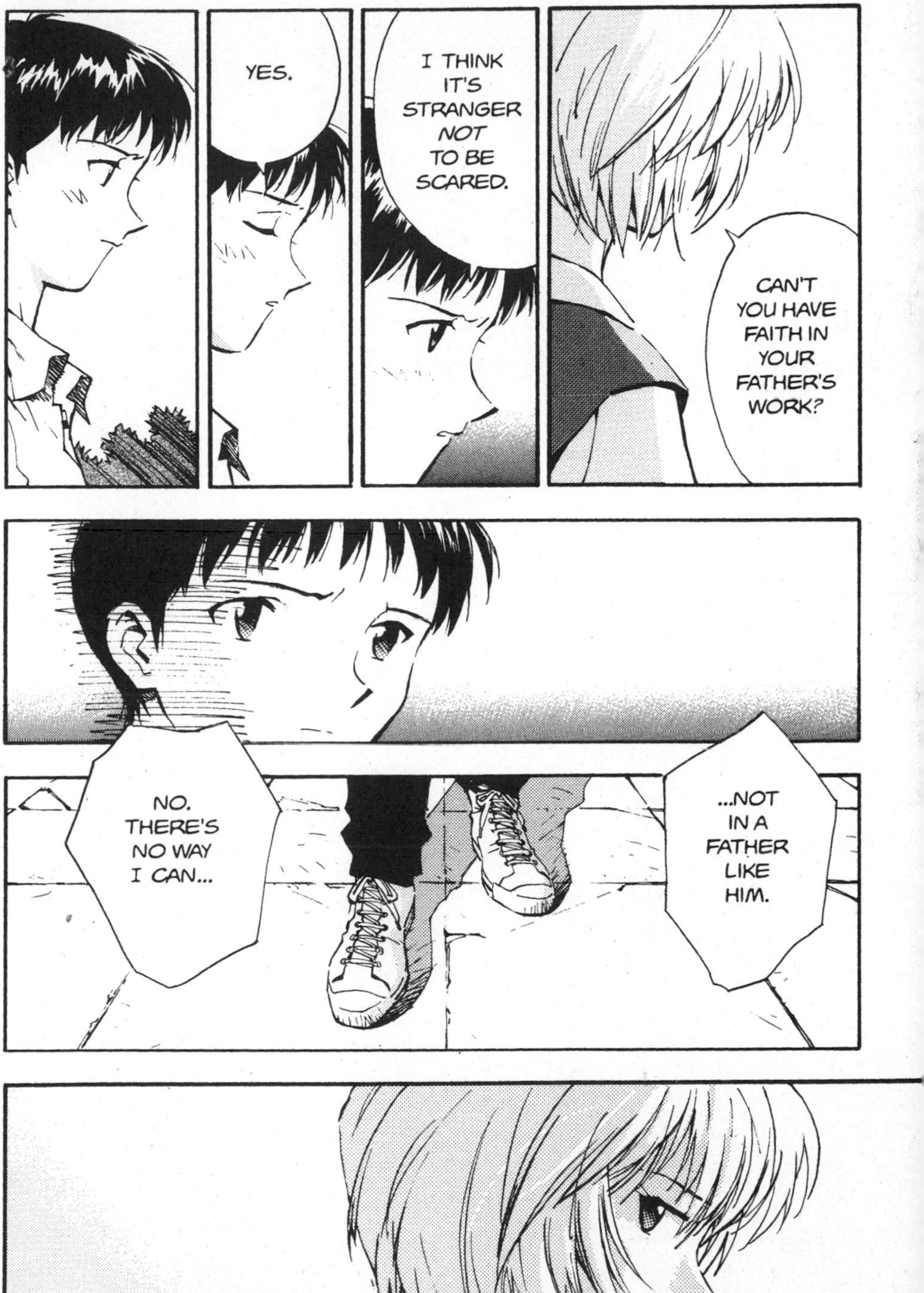
YES.
I THINK IT'S STRANGER NOT TO BE SCARED.
CAN'T YOU HAVE FAITH IN YOUR FATHER'S WORK?
NO. THERE'S NO WAY I CAN...
...NOT IN A FATHER LIKE HIM.

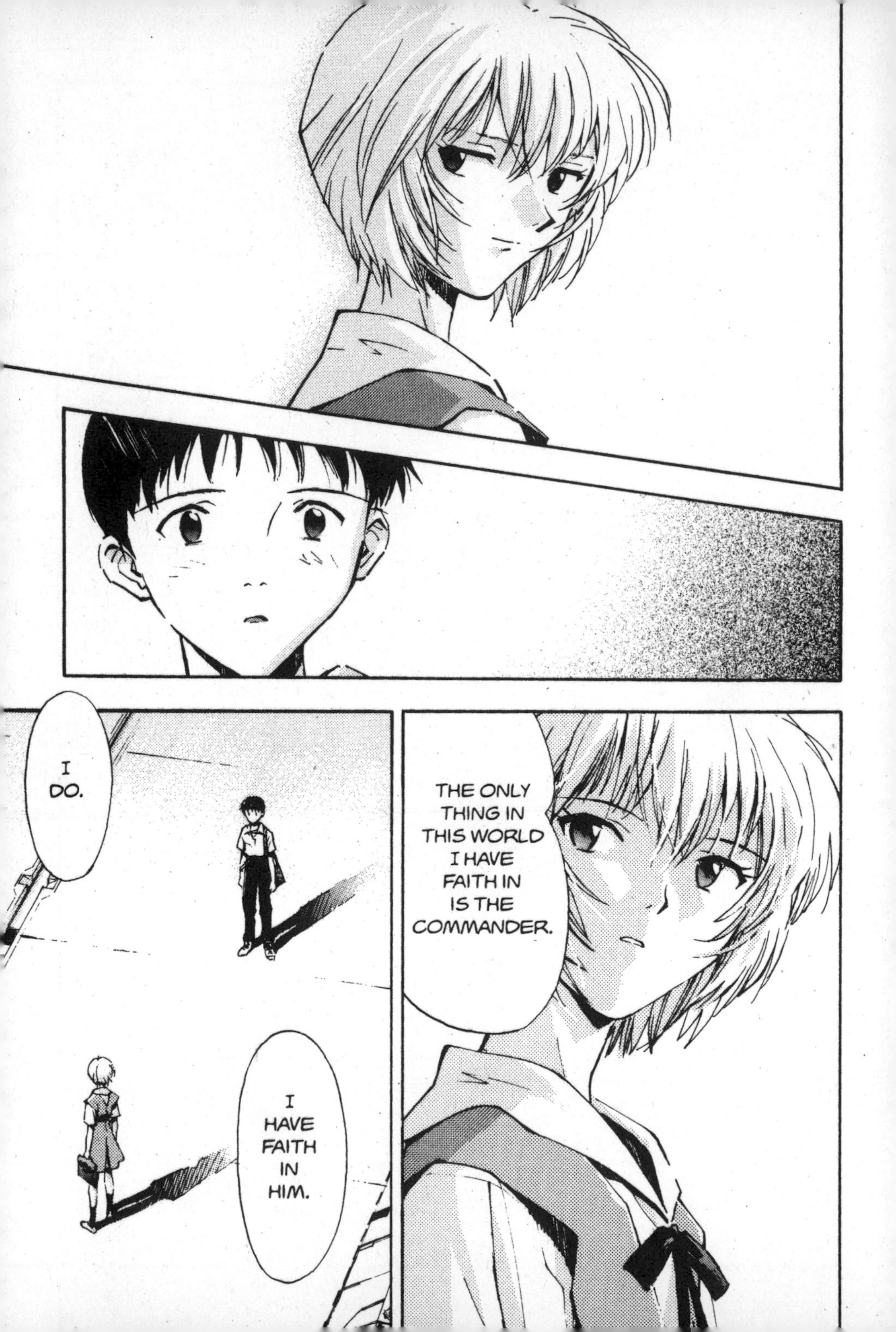
I DO.
I HAVE FAITH IN HIM.
THE ONLY THING IN THIS WORLD I HAVE FAITH IN IS THE COMMANDER.

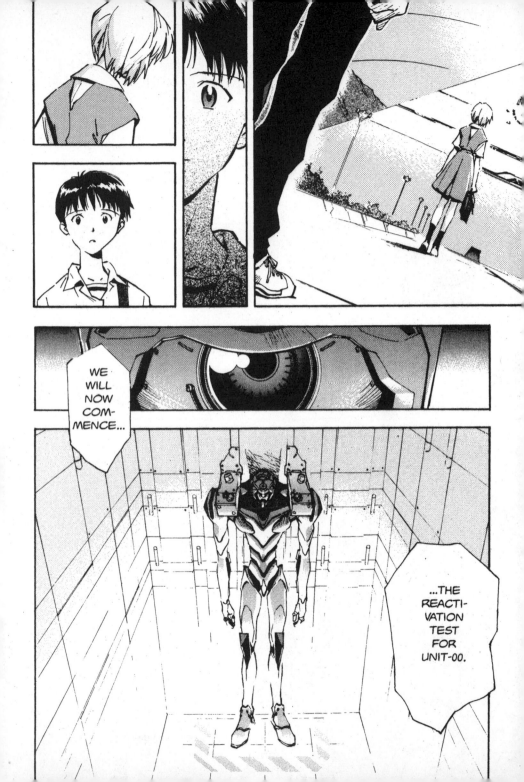

WE WILL NOW COMMENCE...

...THE REACTIVATION TEST FOR UNIT-00.

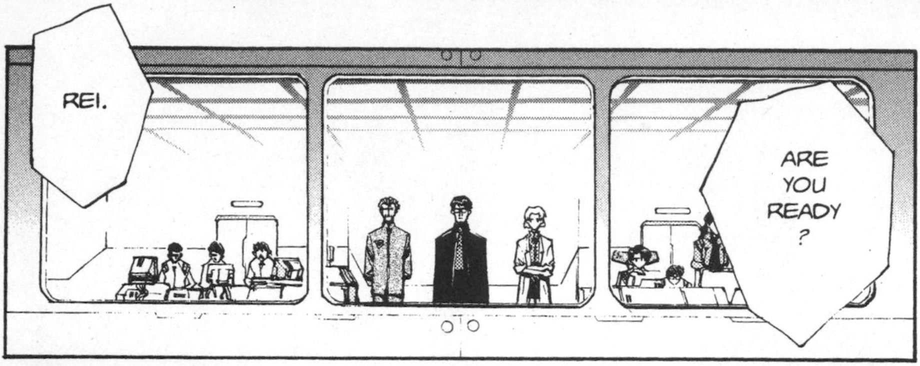
REI.
ARE YOU READY?
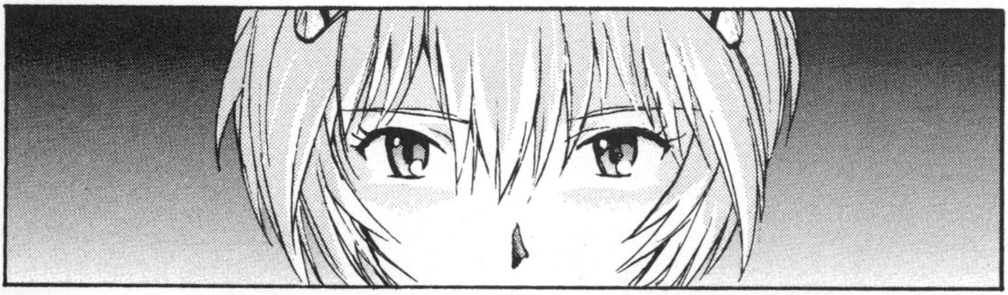
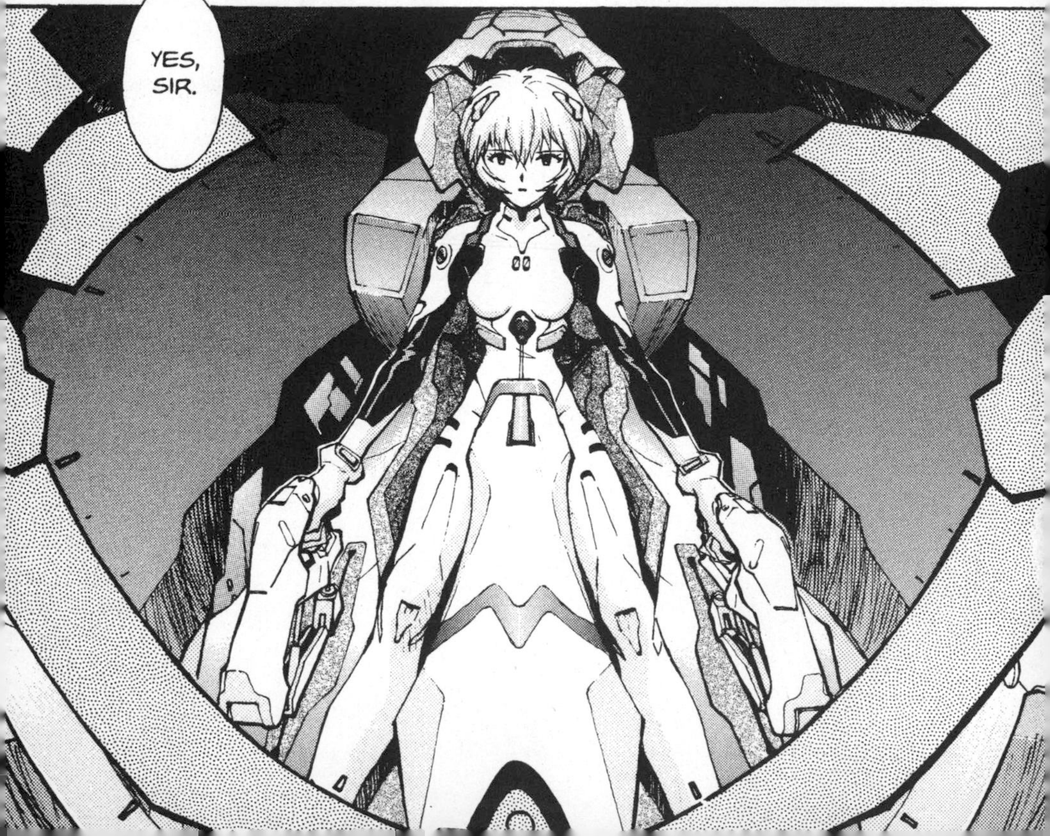
YES, SIR.

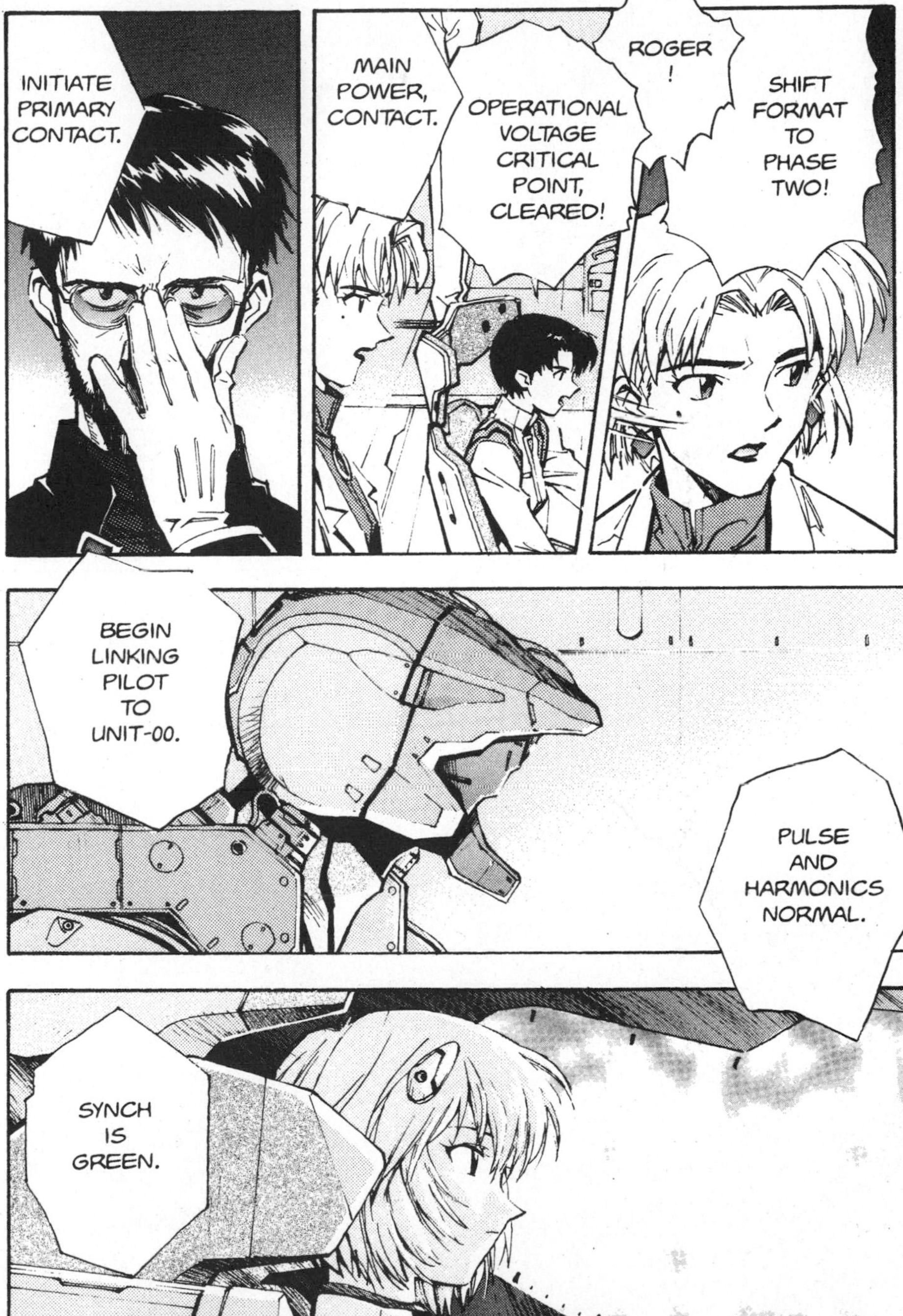
INITIATE PRIMARY CONTACT.
MAIN POWER, CONTACT.
OPERATIONAL VOLTAGE CRITICAL POINT, CLEARED!
ROGER !
SHIFT FORMAT TO PHASE TWO!
BEGIN LINKING PILOT TO UNIT-00.
PULSE AND HARMONICS NORMAL.
SYNCH IS GREEN.

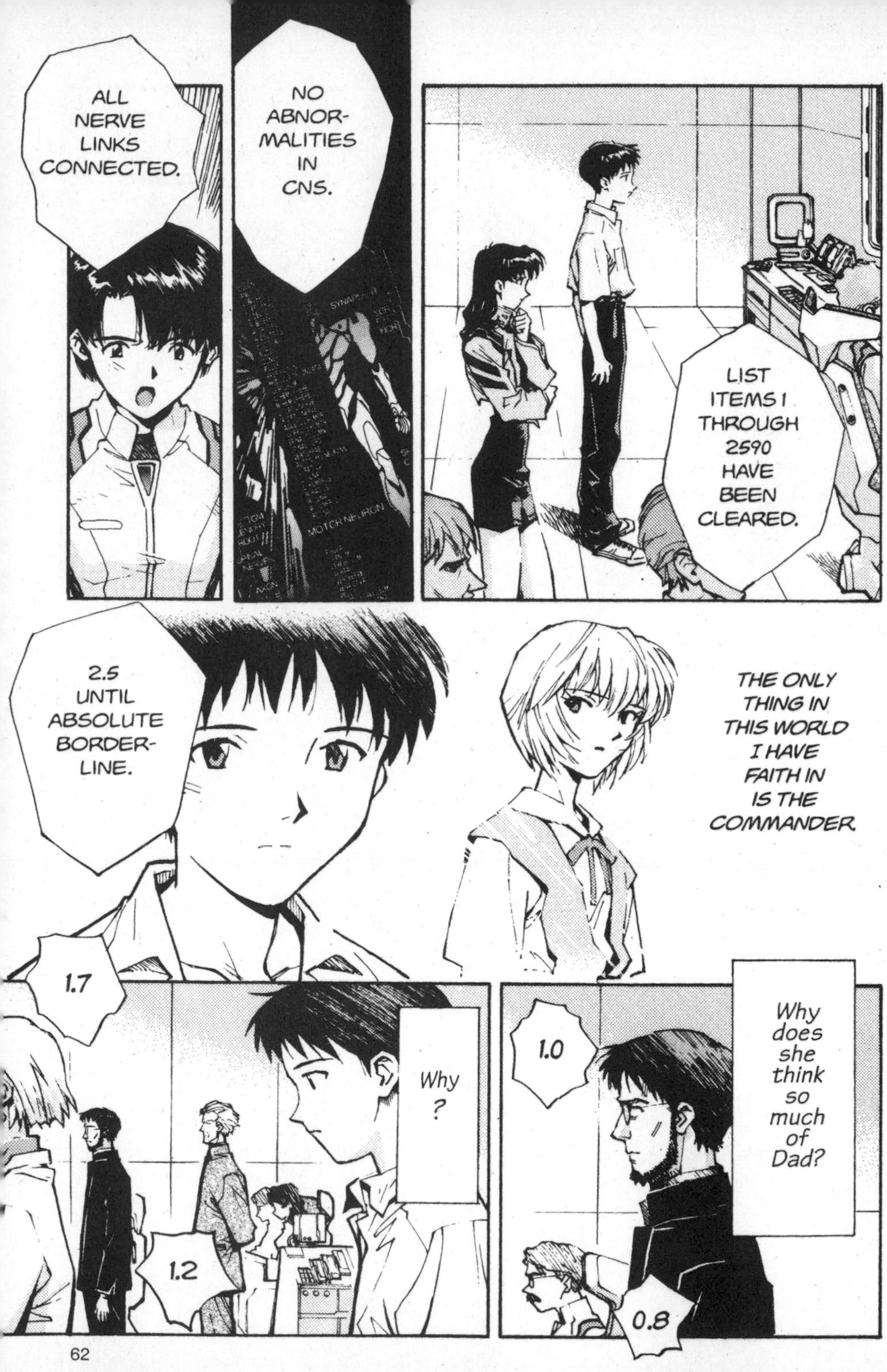
ALL NERVE LINKS CONNECTED.
NO ABNOR-MALITIES IN CNS.
LIST ITEMS 1 THROUGH 2590 HAVE BEEN CLEARED.
2.5 UNTIL ABSOLUTE BORDER-LINE.
THE ONLY THING IN THIS WORLD I HAVE FAITH IN IS THE COMMANDER.
1.7
Why?
1.2
1.0
Why does she think so much of Dad?
0.8

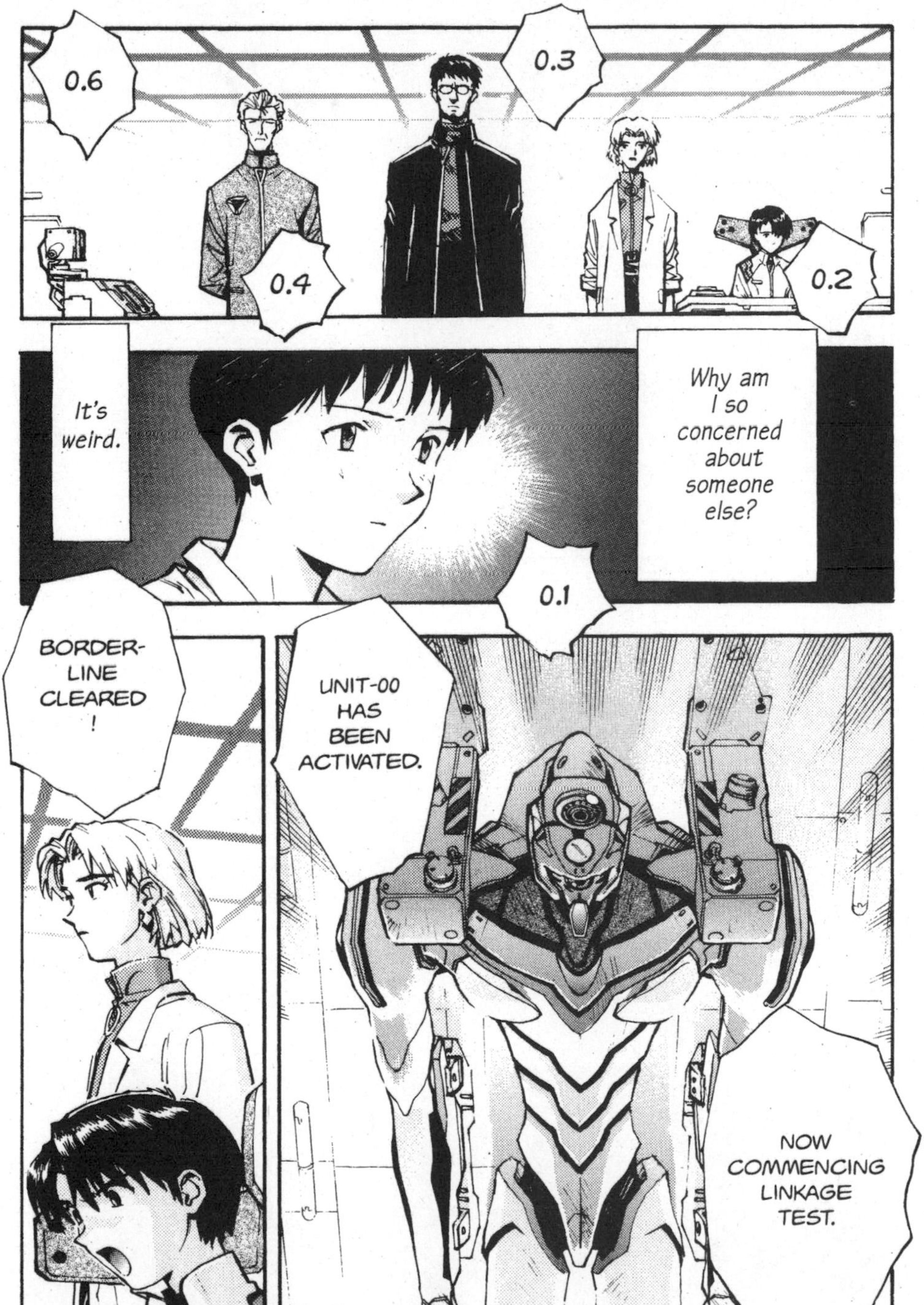
0.6
0.4
0.3
0.2
It's weird.
Why am I so concerned about someone else?
0.1
BORDER-LINE CLEARED!
UNIT-00 HAS BEEN ACTIVATED.
NOW COMMENCING LINKAGE TEST.

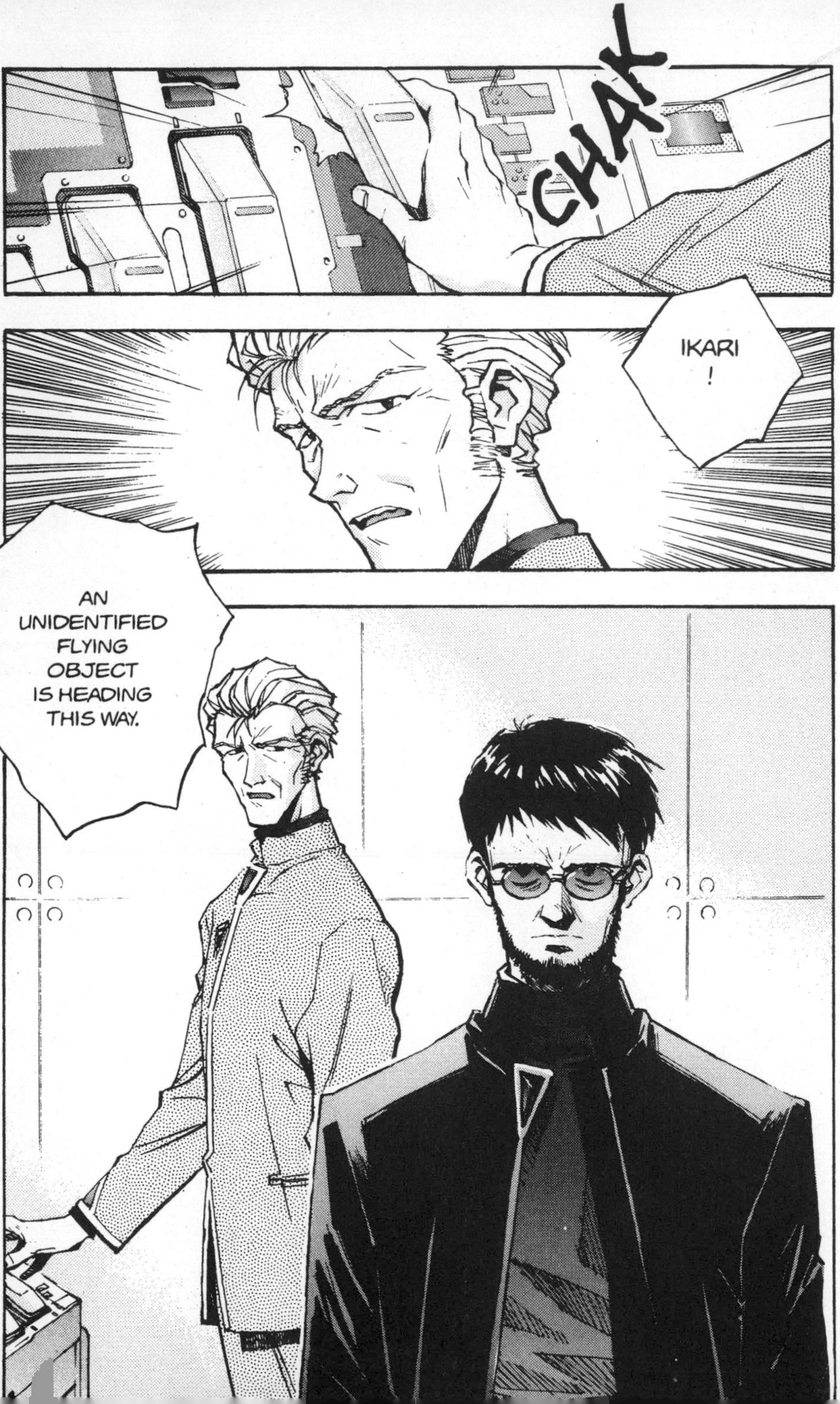
CHAK
IKARI !
AN UNIDENTIFIED FLYING OBJECT IS HEADING THIS WAY.

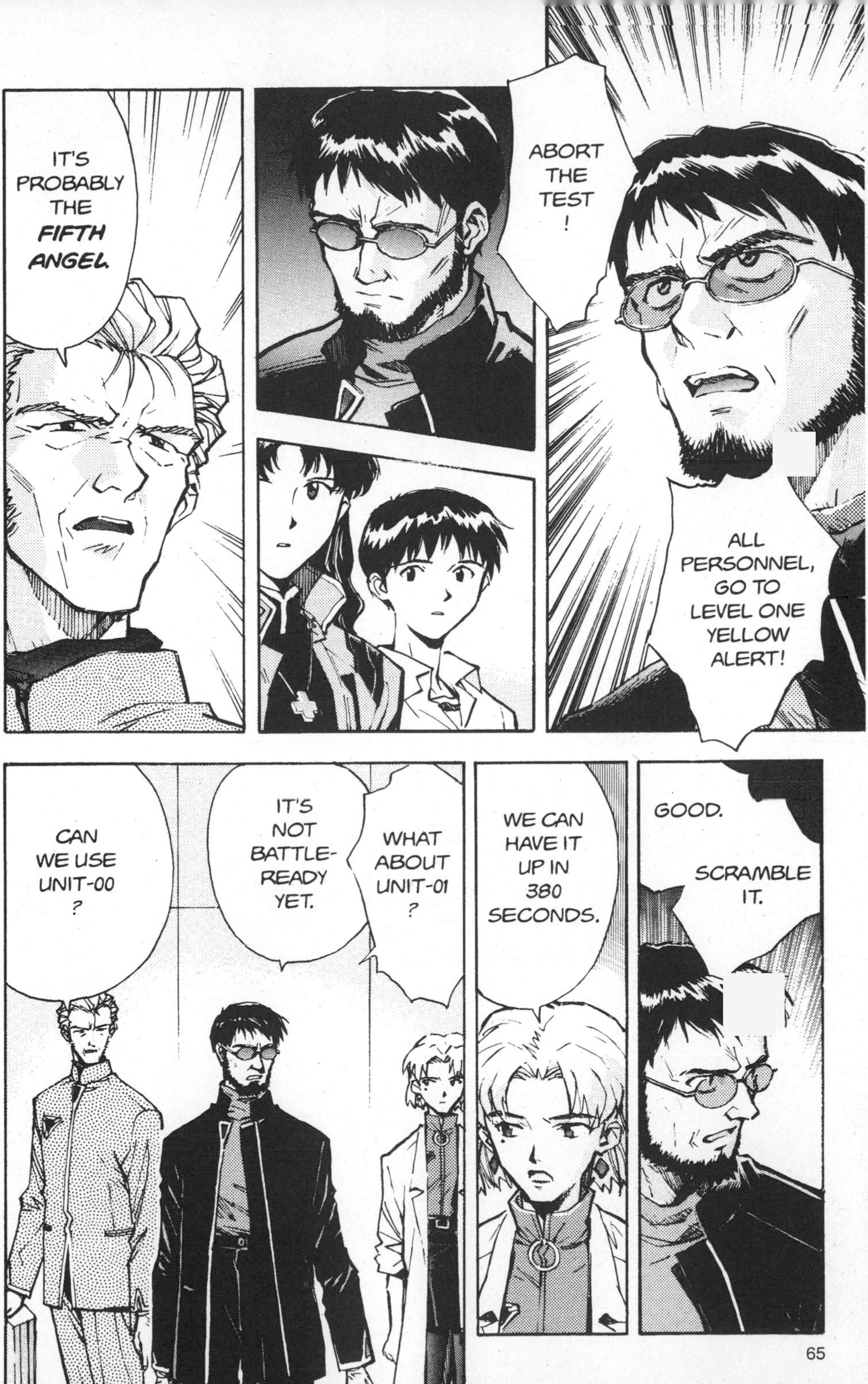
IT'S PROBABLY THE ***FIFTH ANGEL.***
ABORT THE TEST!
ALL PERSONNEL, GO TO LEVEL ONE YELLOW ALERT!
CAN WE USE UNIT-00?
IT'S NOT BATTLE-READY YET.
WHAT ABOUT UNIT-01?
WE CAN HAVE IT UP IN 380 SECONDS.
GOOD.
SCRAMBLE IT.

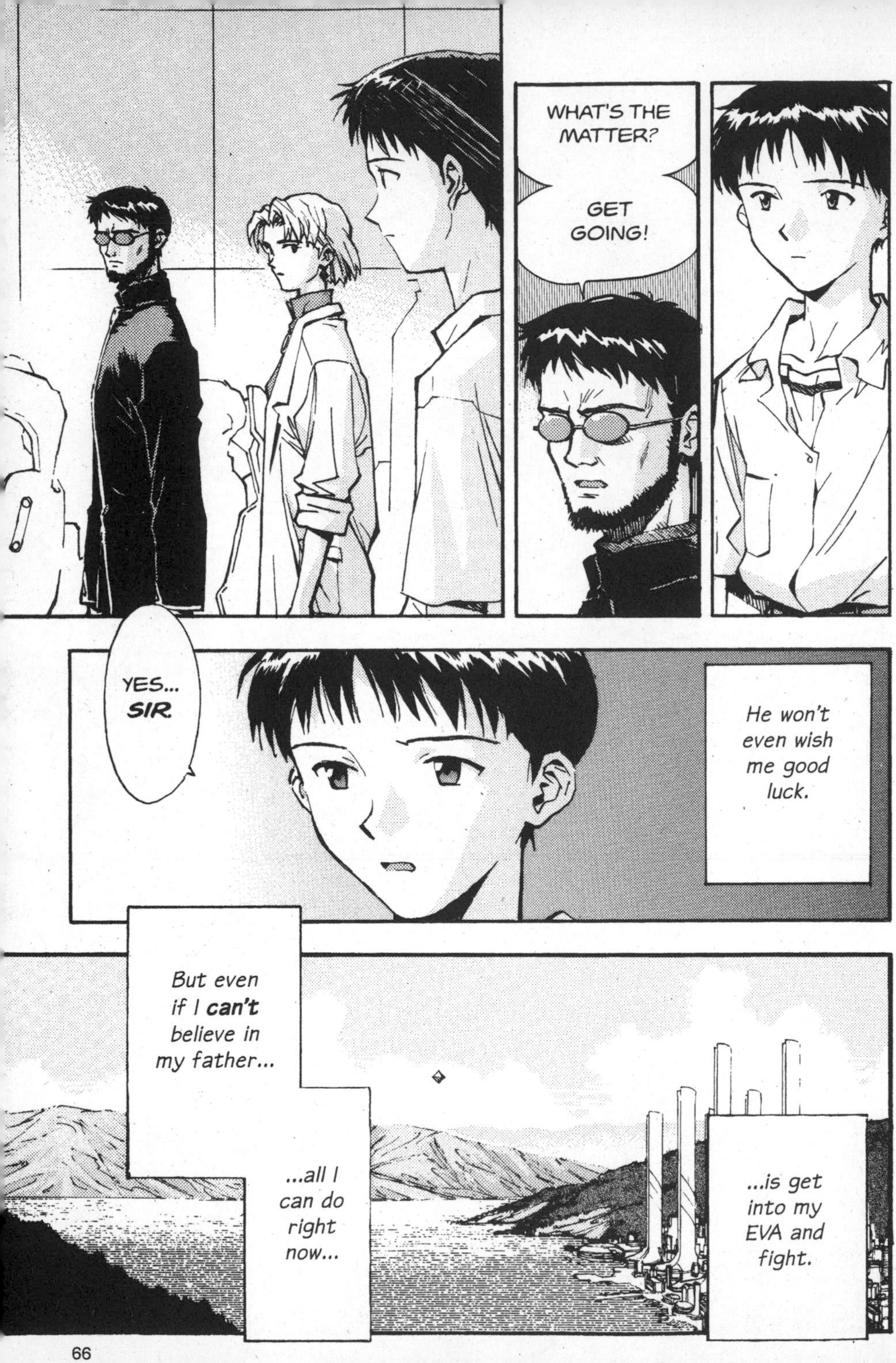
WHAT'S THE MATTER?
GET GOING!
YES... SIR.
He won't even wish me good luck.
But even if I **can't** believe in my father...
...all I can do right now...
...is get into my EVA and fight.

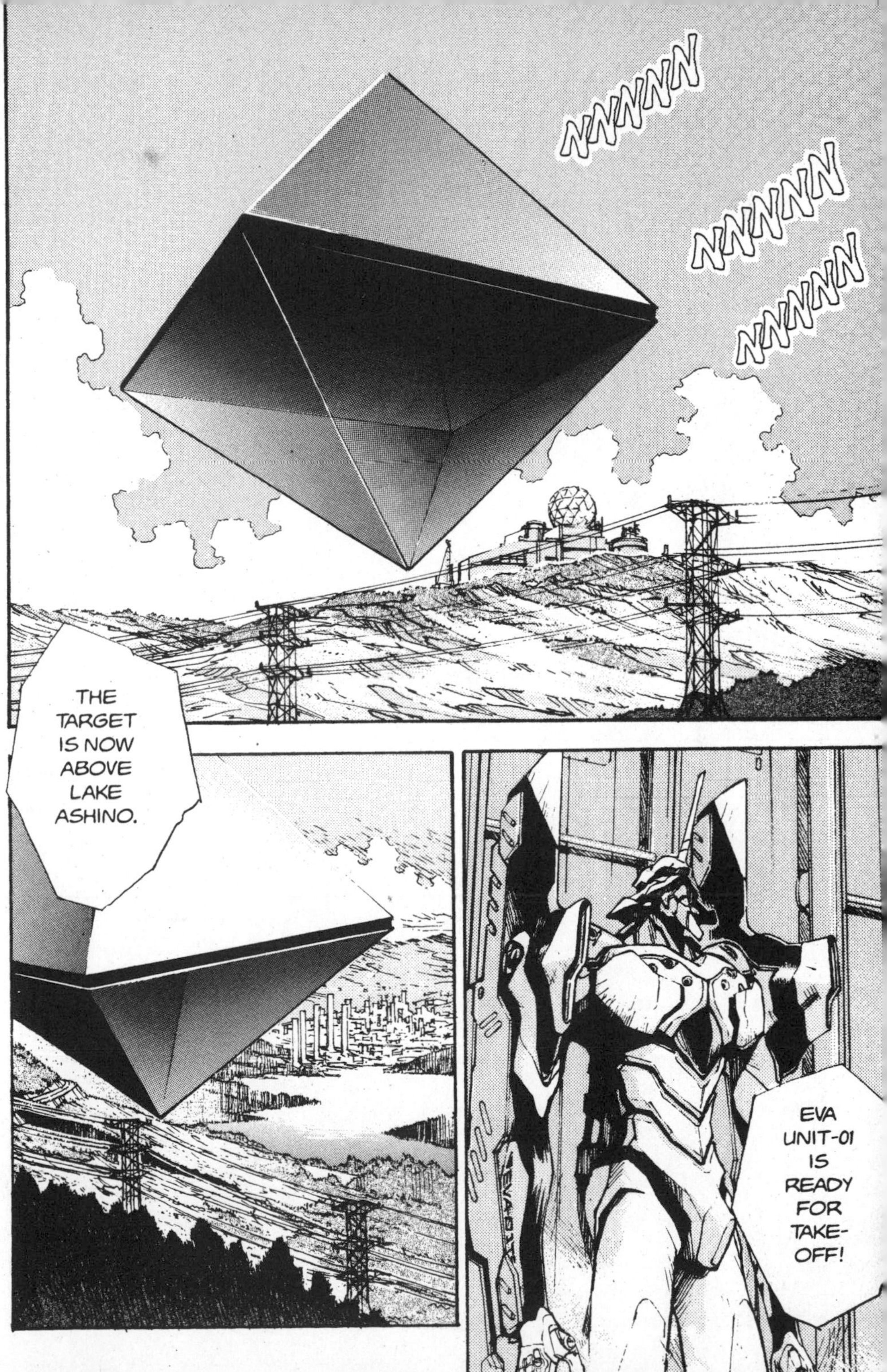
NNNNNN
NNNNNN
NNNNNN
THE TARGET IS NOW ABOVE LAKE ASHINO.
EVA UNIT-01 IS READY FOR TAKE-OFF!

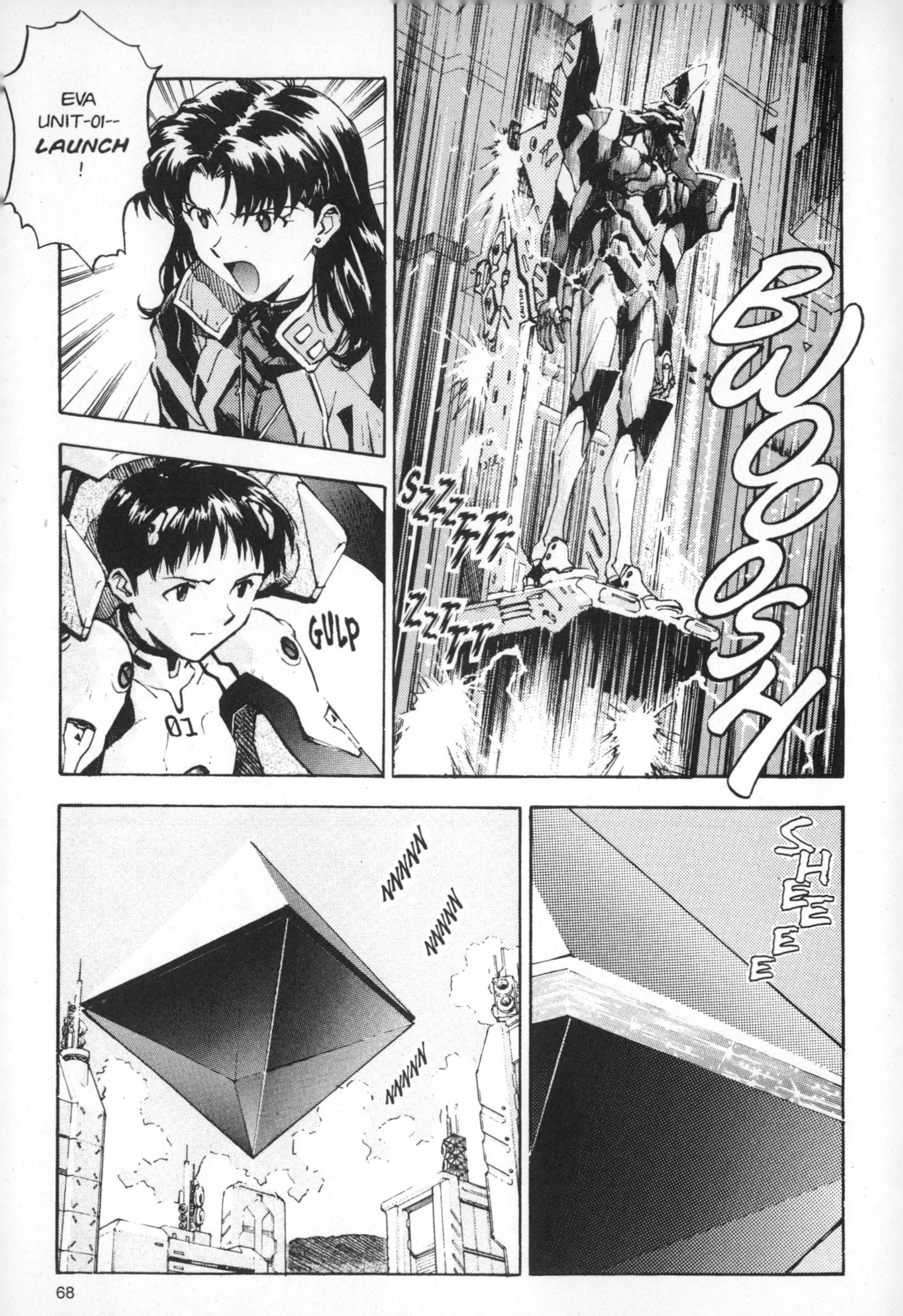
EVA UNIT-01-- **LAUNCH** !
GULP
SZZZTTT
ZZTTT
BWOOOOSH
NNNNN
NNNNN
NNNNN
SHEEEE

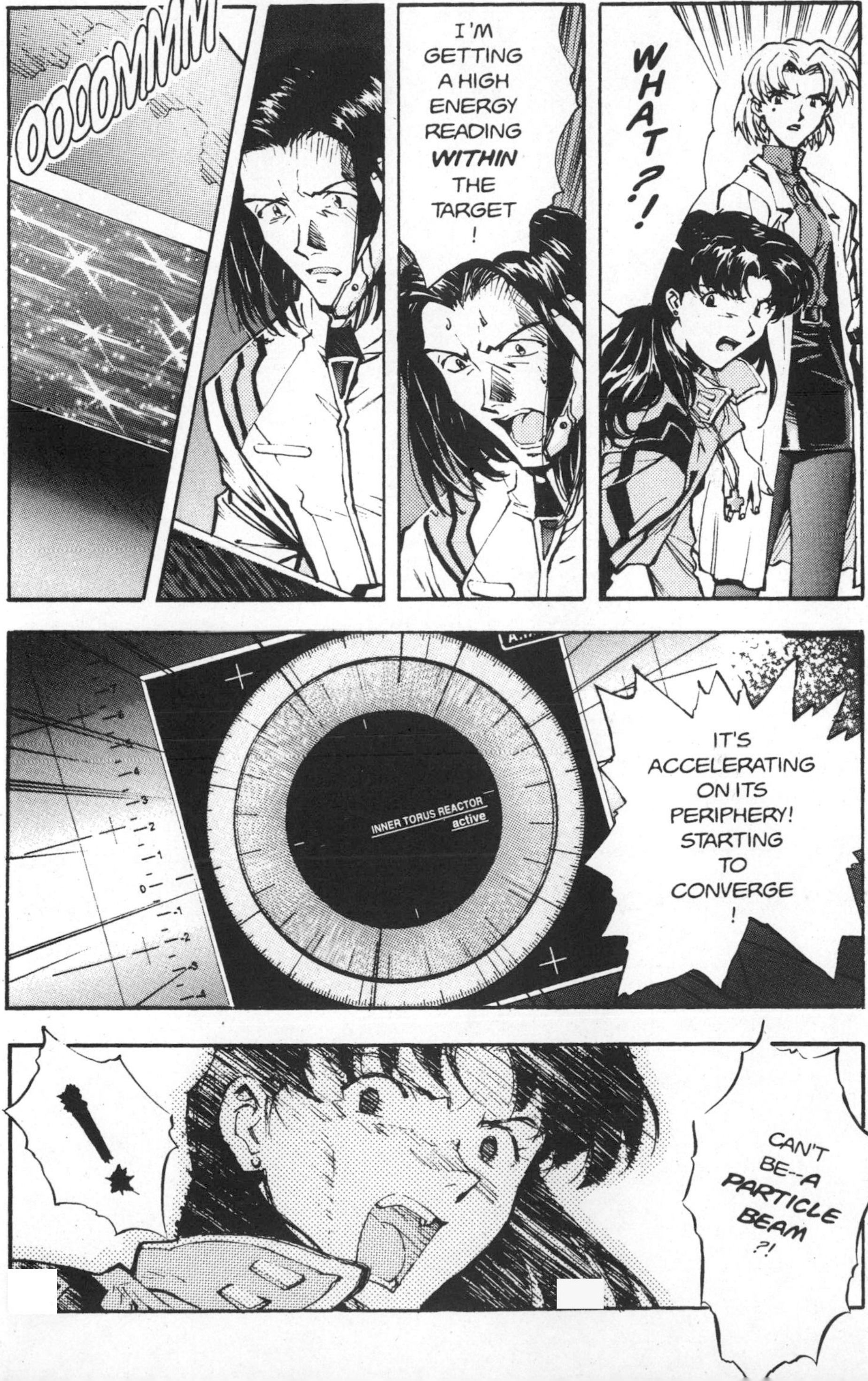
OOOOMMM
I'M GETTING A HIGH ENERGY READING WITHIN THE TARGET!
WHAT?!
INNER TORUS REACTOR active
IT'S ACCELERATING ON ITS PERIPHERY! STARTING TO CONVERGE!
!
CAN'T BE--A PARTICLE BEAM?!

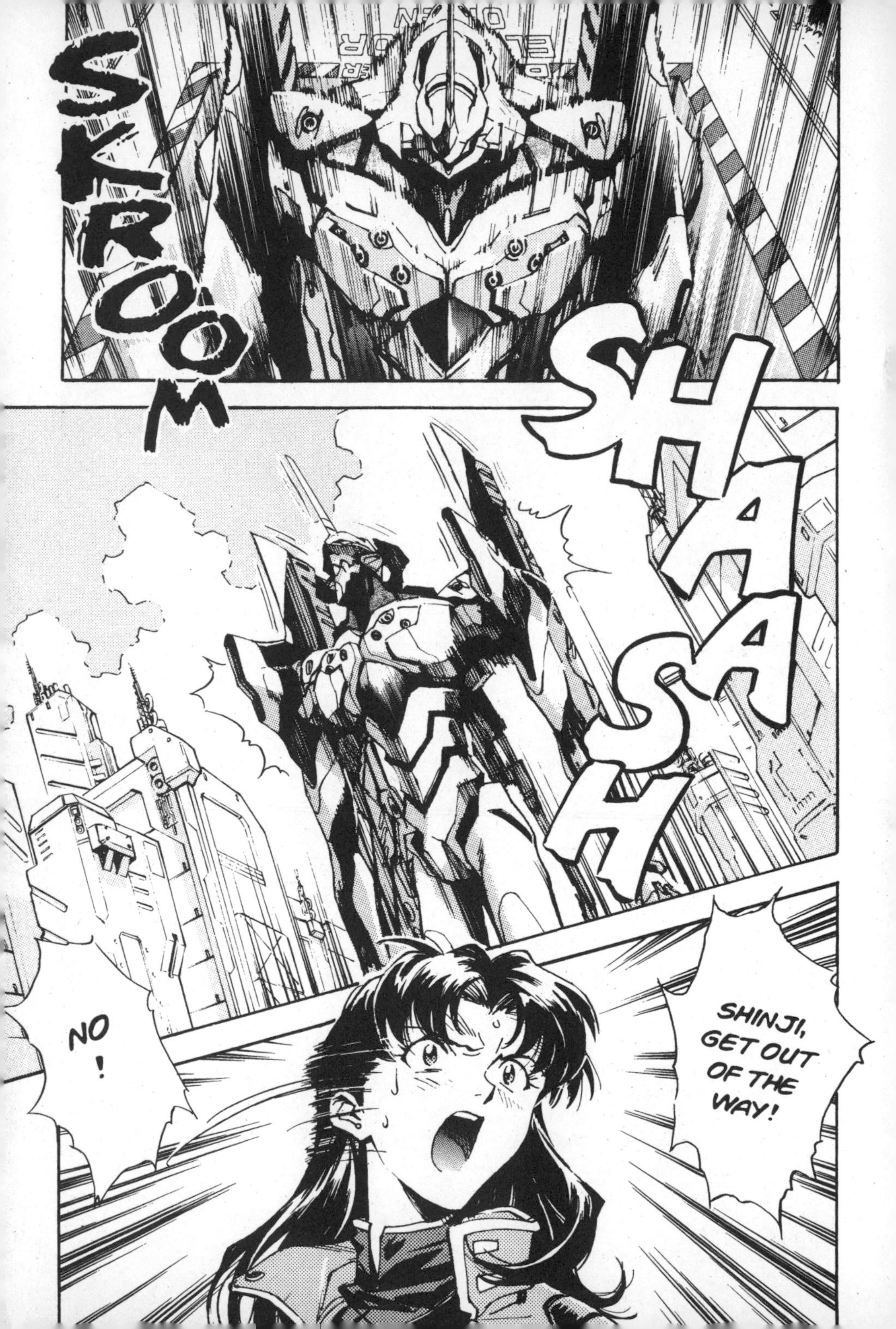
SKROOM
SHASHASH
NO!
SHINJI, GET OUT OF THE WAY!

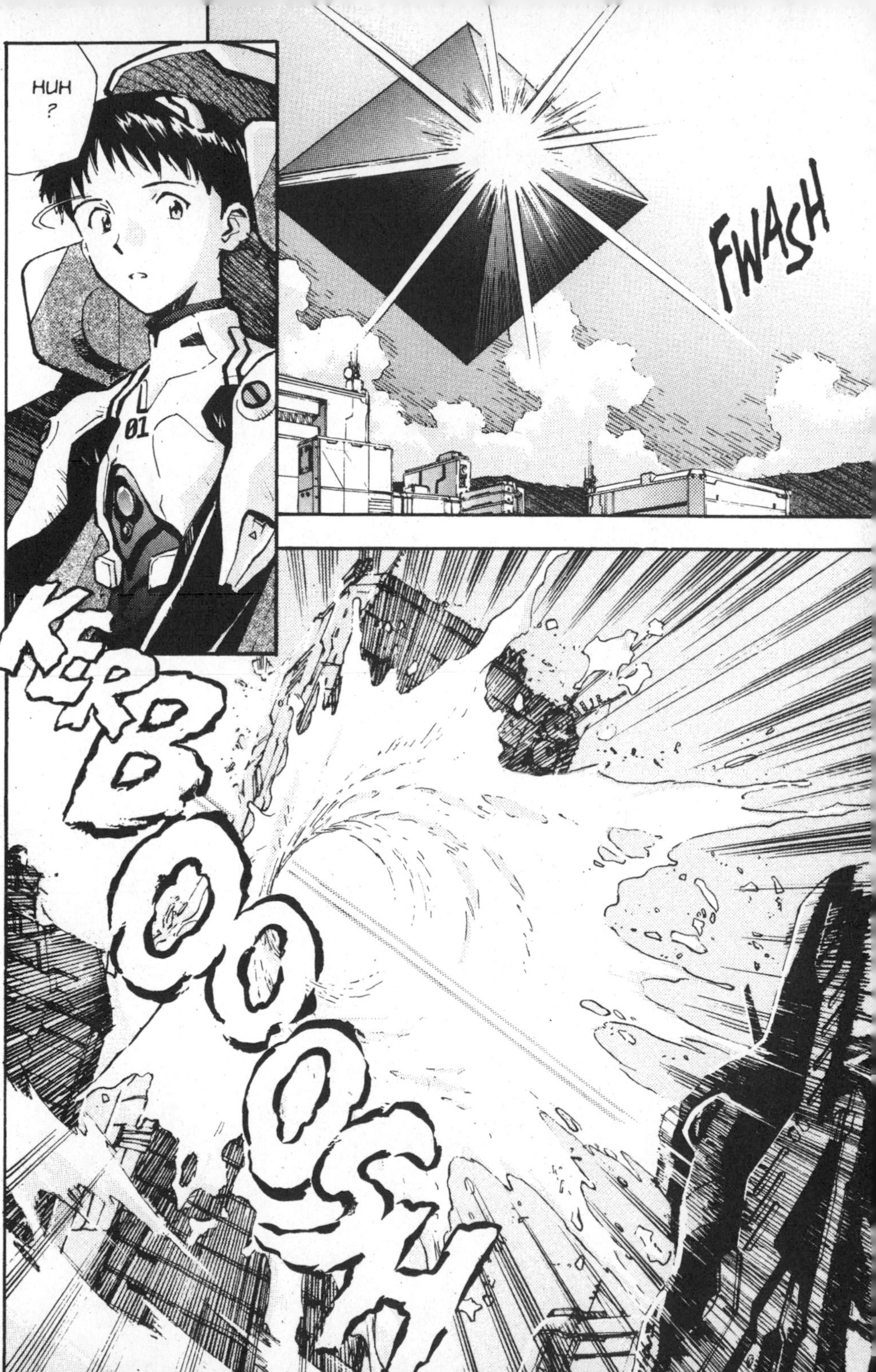
HUH
?
FWASH
KERBOOOOSH

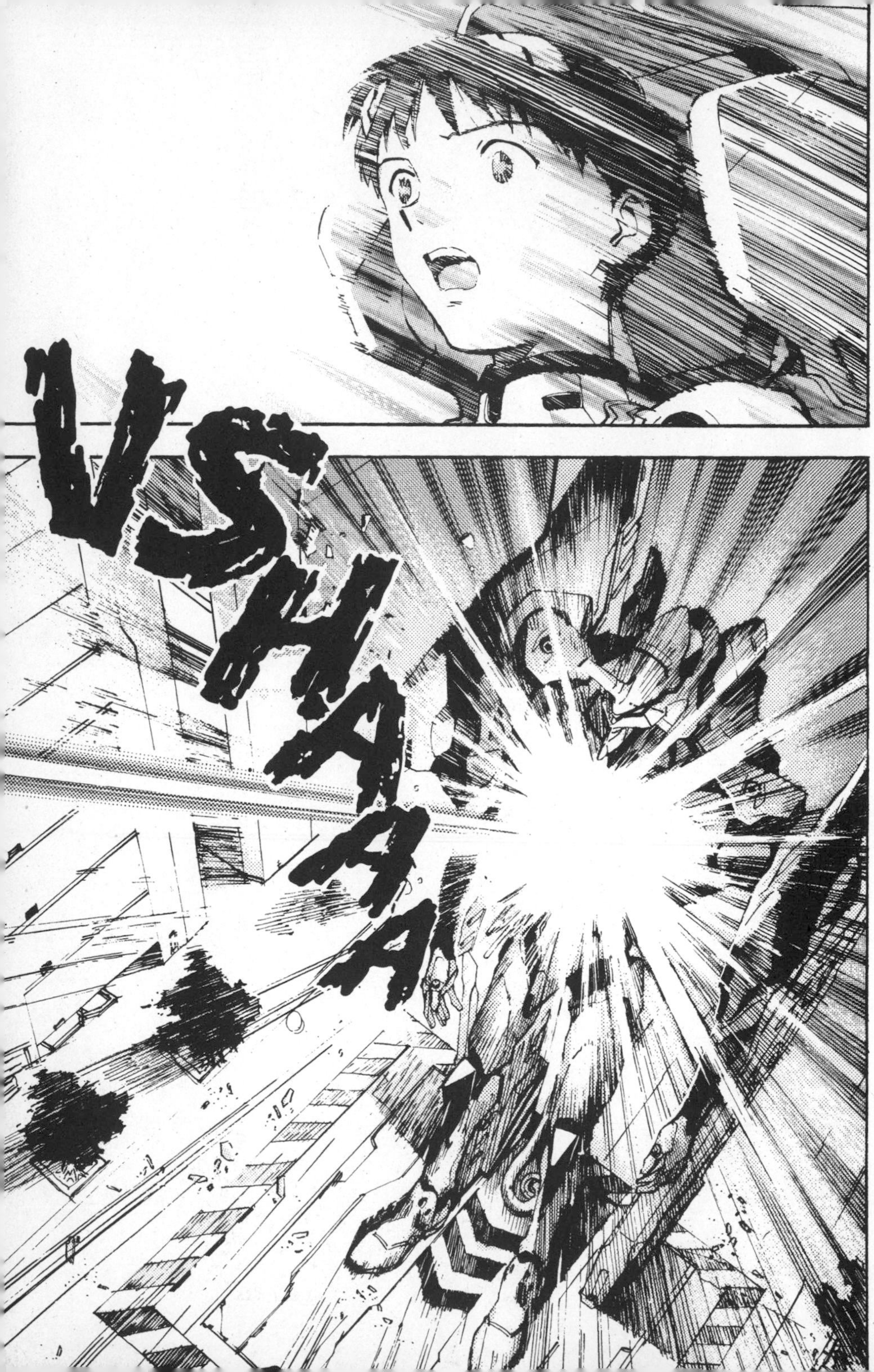
VSHAAA

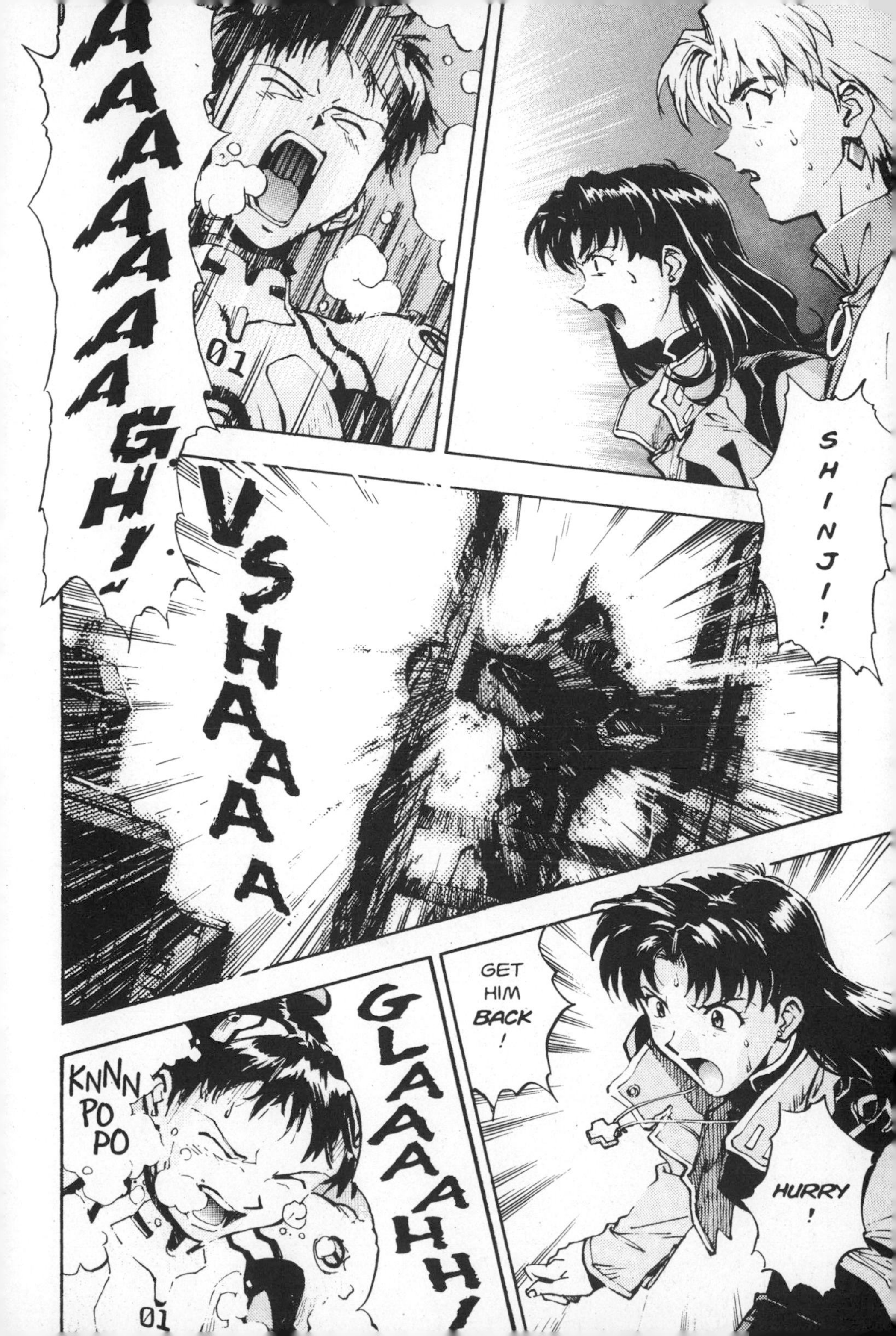
AAAAAAAAGH!
SHINJI!
VSHAAAA
KNNN
PO
PO
GLAAAAAH!
GET HIM BACK!
HURRY!

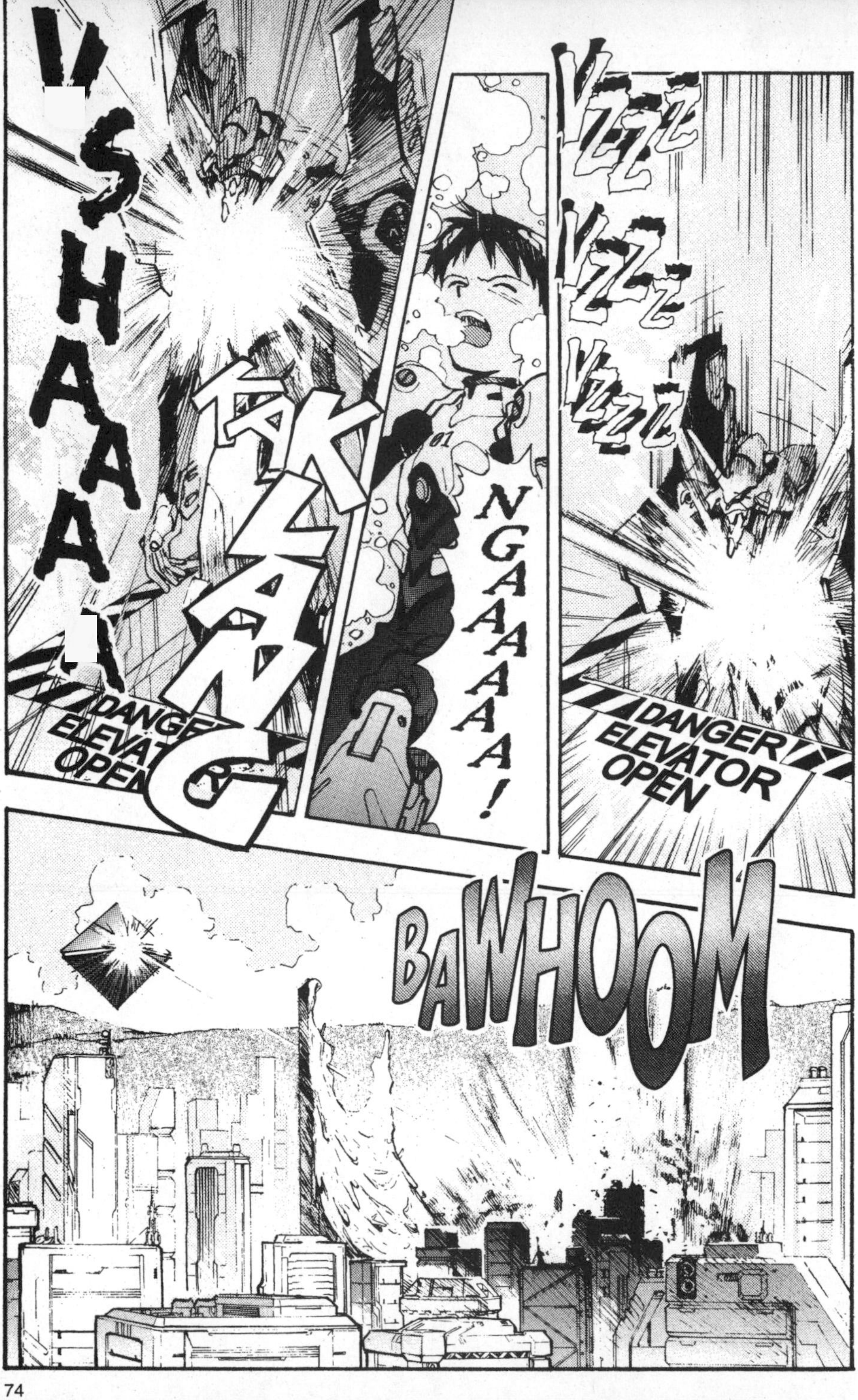
VSHAAA!
KAKLANG
DANGER
ELEVATOR
OPEN
NGAAAAAA!
VZZZ
VZZZ
VZZZ
DANGER
ELEVATOR
OPEN
BAWHOOM

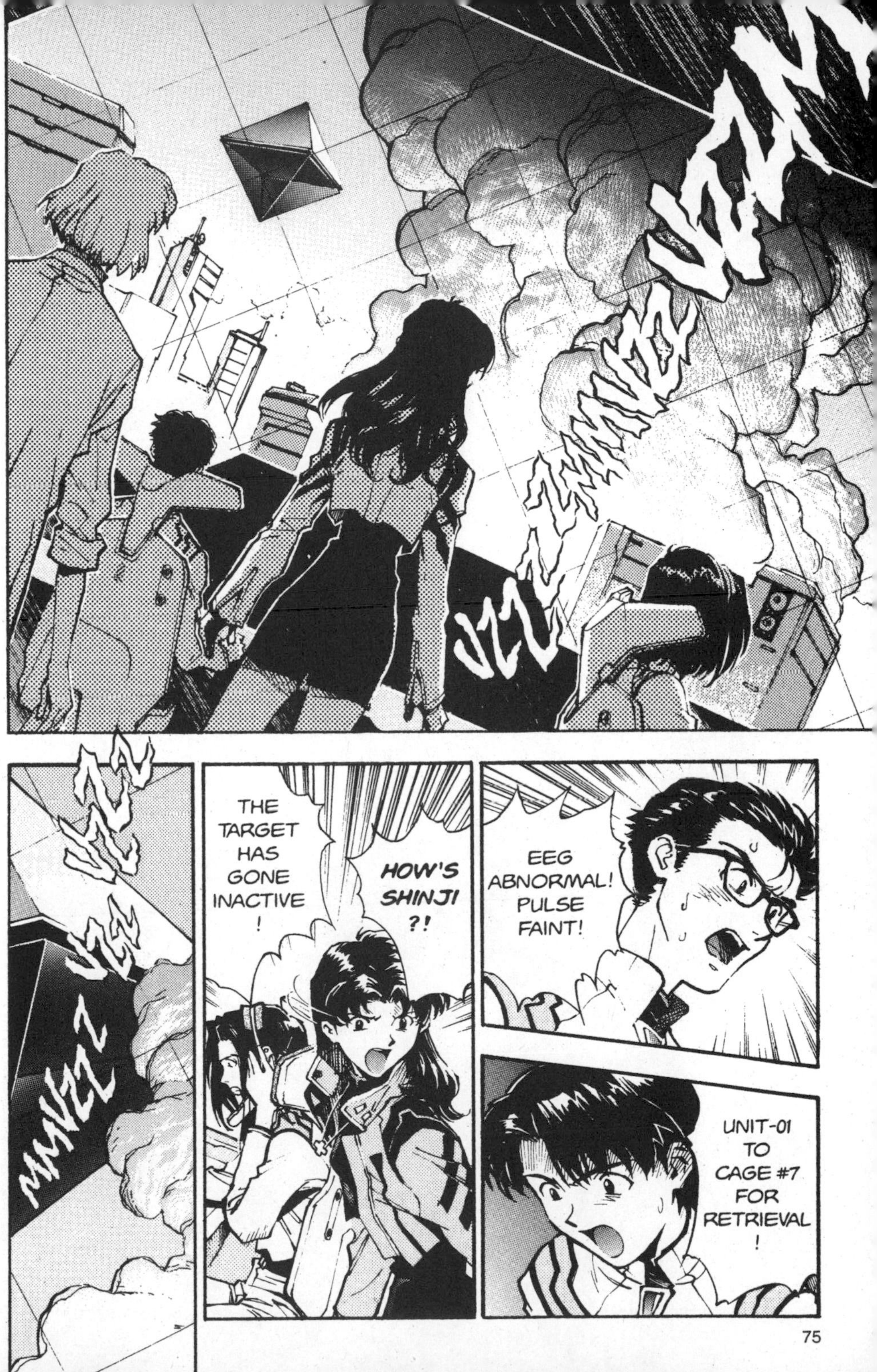
THE TARGET HAS GONE INACTIVE!
HOW'S SHINJI?!
EEG ABNORMAL! PULSE FAINT!
UNIT-01 TO CAGE #7 FOR RETRIEVAL!

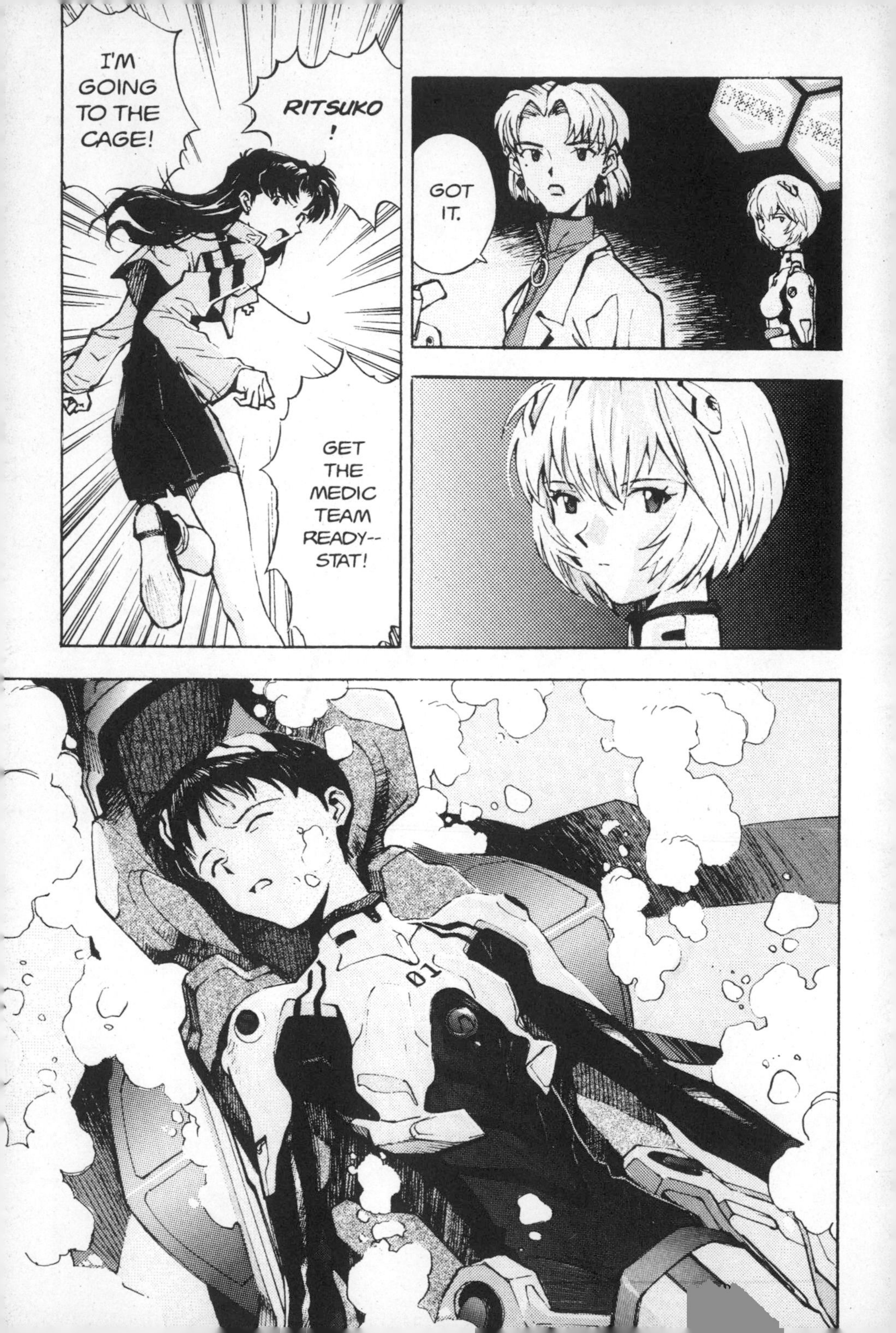
I'M GOING TO THE CAGE!
RITSUKO!
GET THE MEDIC TEAM READY-- STAT!
GOT IT.

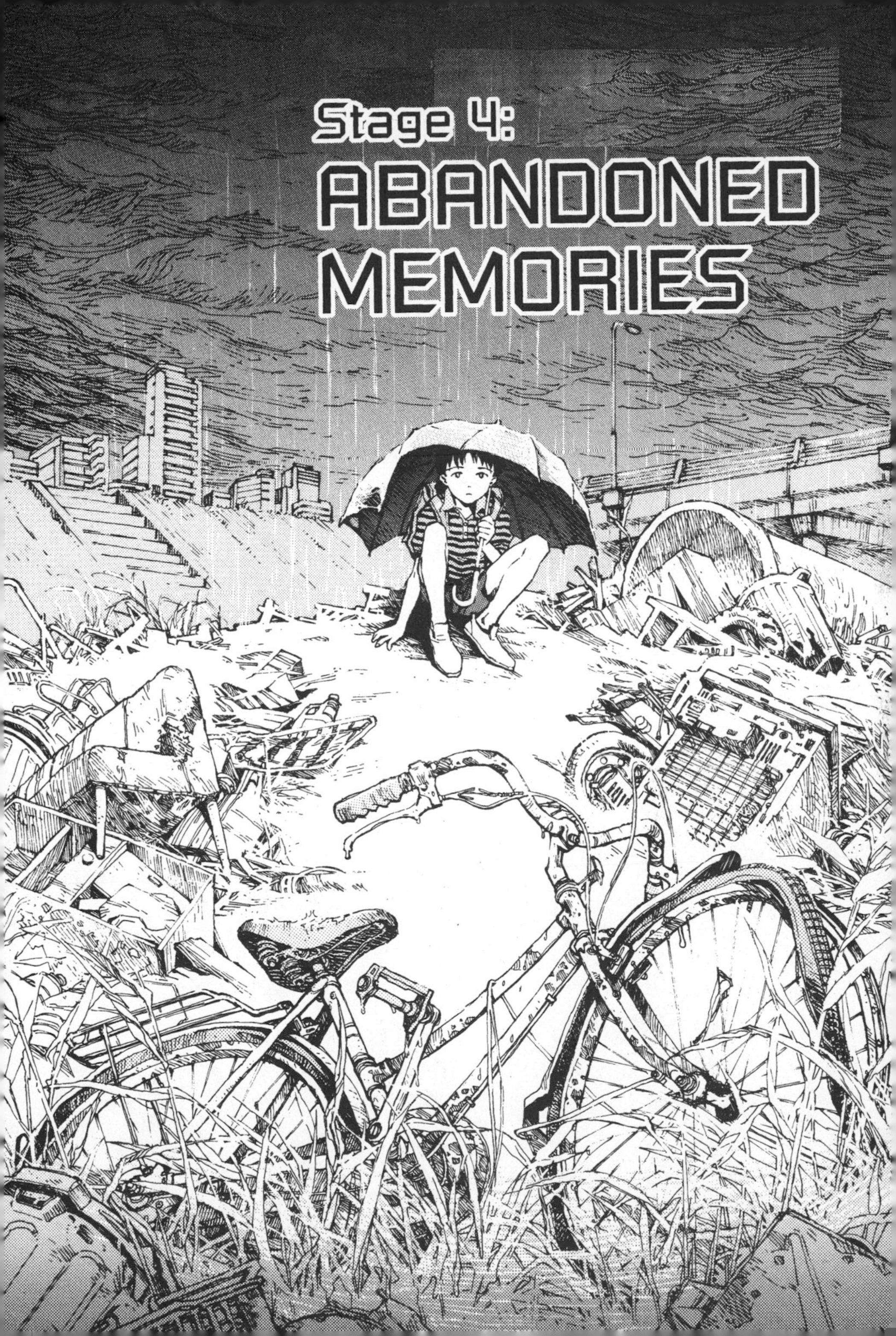
Stage 4:
ABANDONED MEMORIES

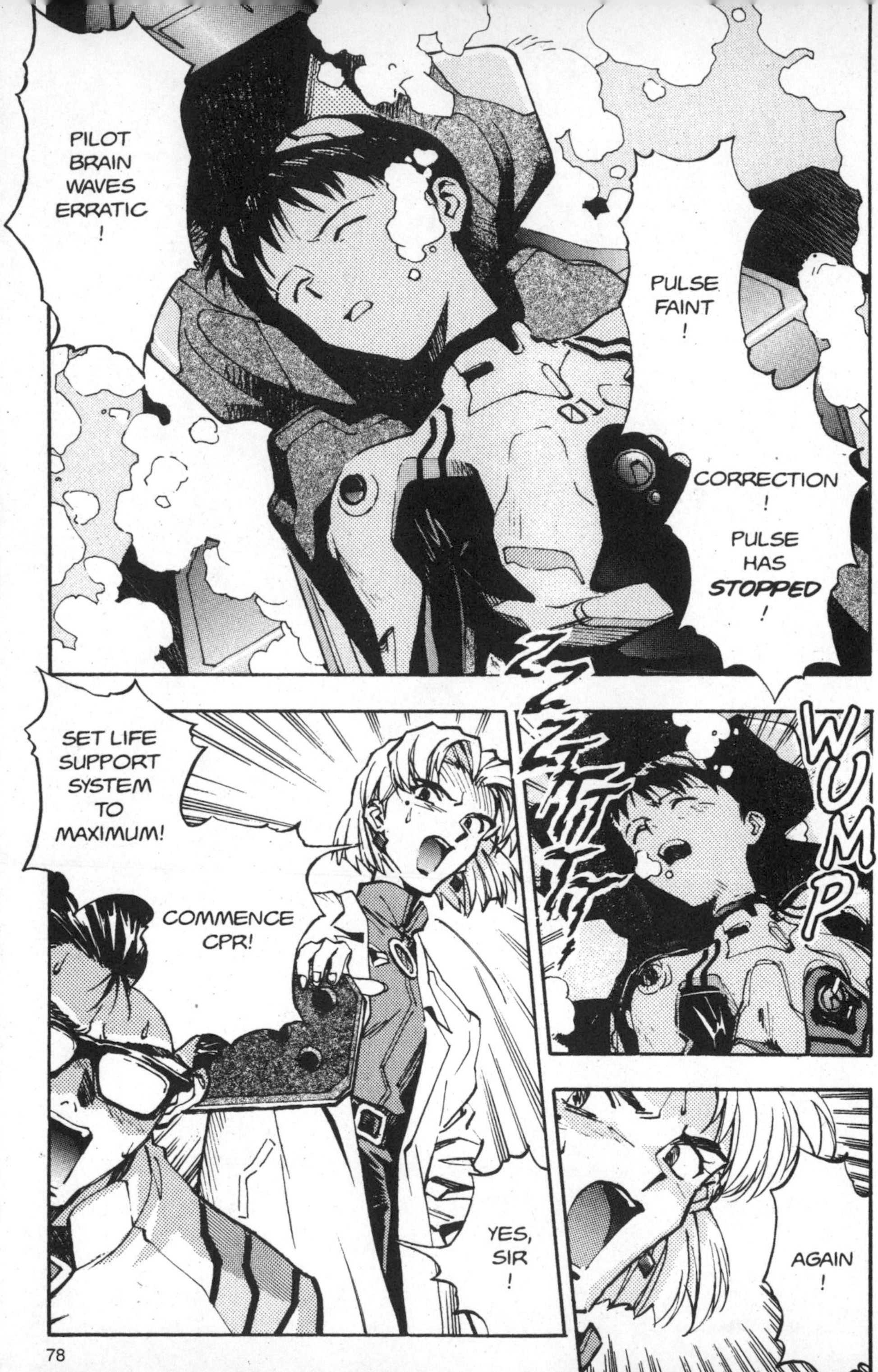
PILOT BRAIN WAVES ERRATIC!
PULSE FAINT!
CORRECTION!
PULSE HAS STOPPED!
SET LIFE SUPPORT SYSTEM TO MAXIMUM!
COMMENCE CPR!
YES, SIR!
WUMP
AGAIN!

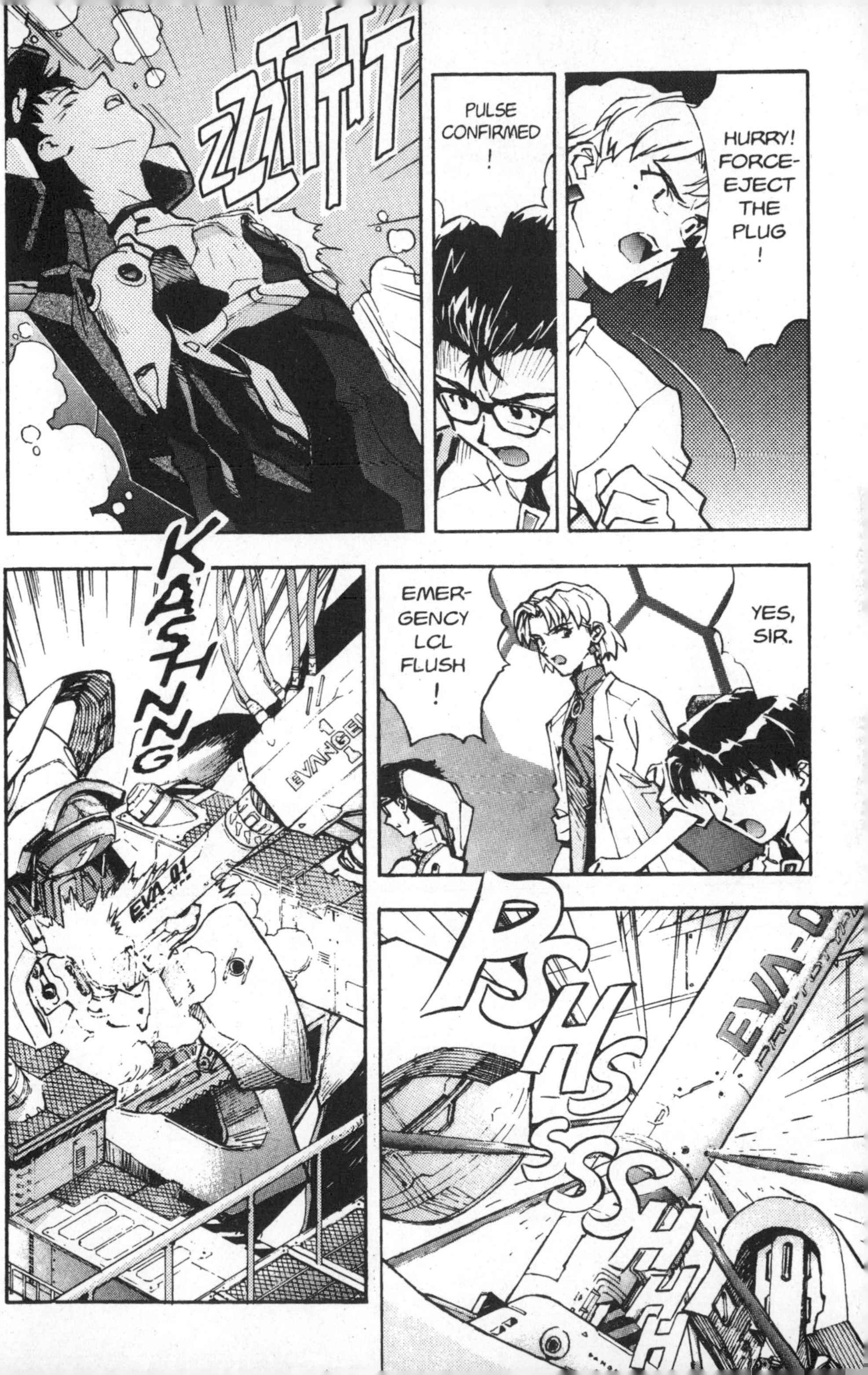
ZZZTTTT
PULSE CONFIRMED!
HURRY! FORCE-EJECT THE PLUG!
KASHNNG
EVA 01
EMERGENCY LCL FLUSH!
YES, SIR.
PSHSSSHHH

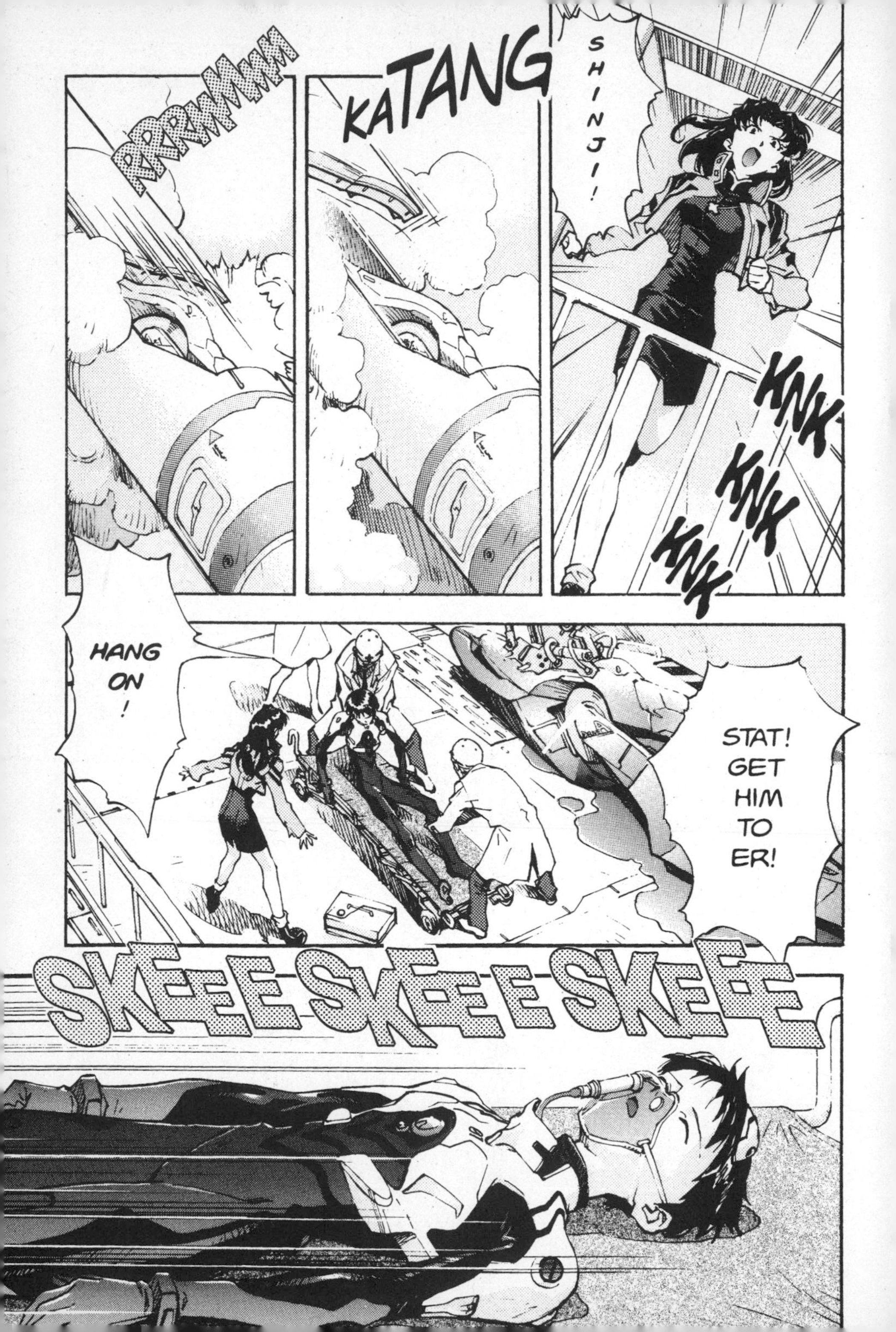
RRRRWMMM
KATANG
SHINJI!
KNK KNK KNK
HANG ON !
STAT! GET HIM TO ER!
SKEEE SKEEE SKEEE

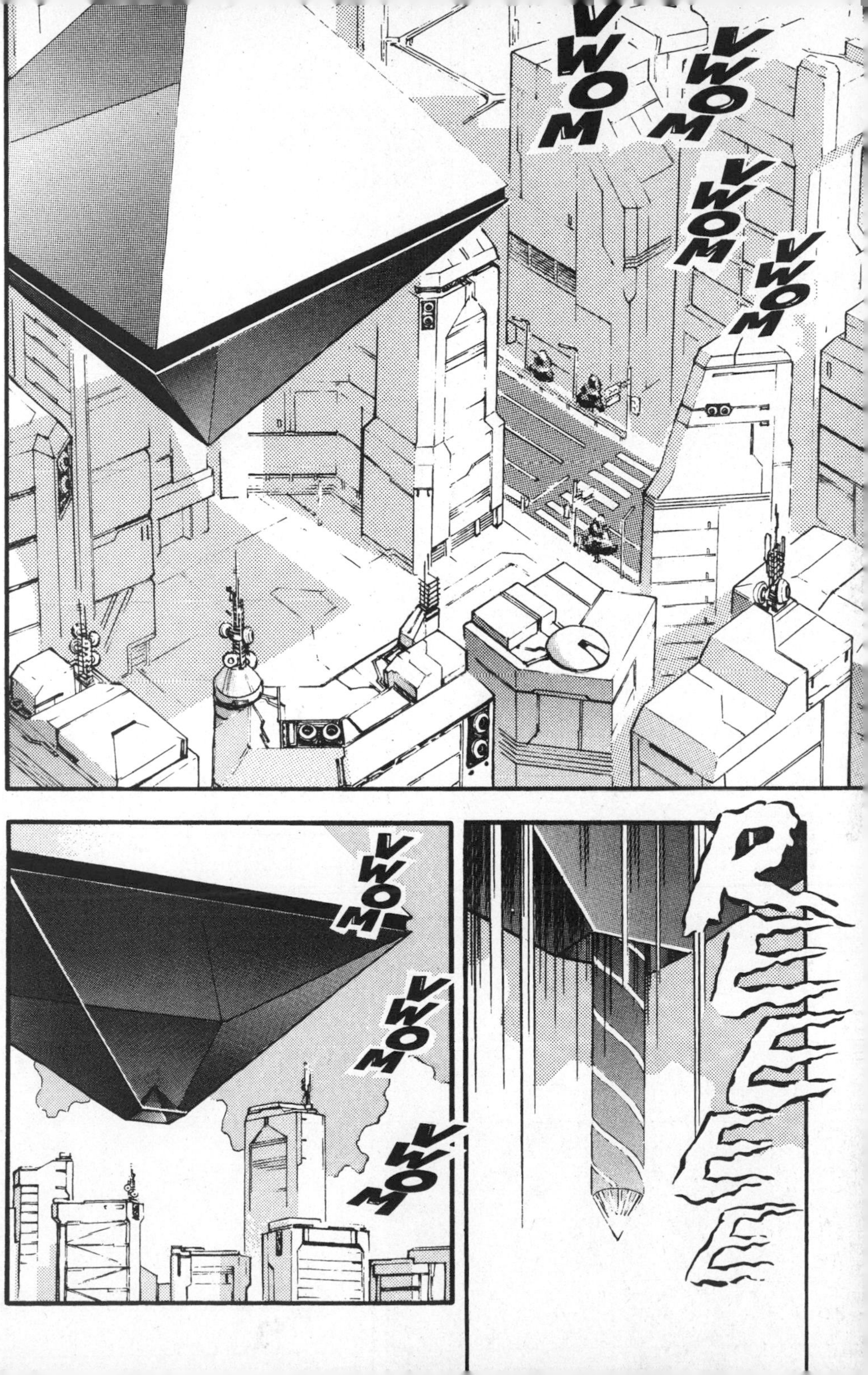
VWOM
VWOM
VWOM
VWOM
VWOM
VWOM
VWOM
REEEEE

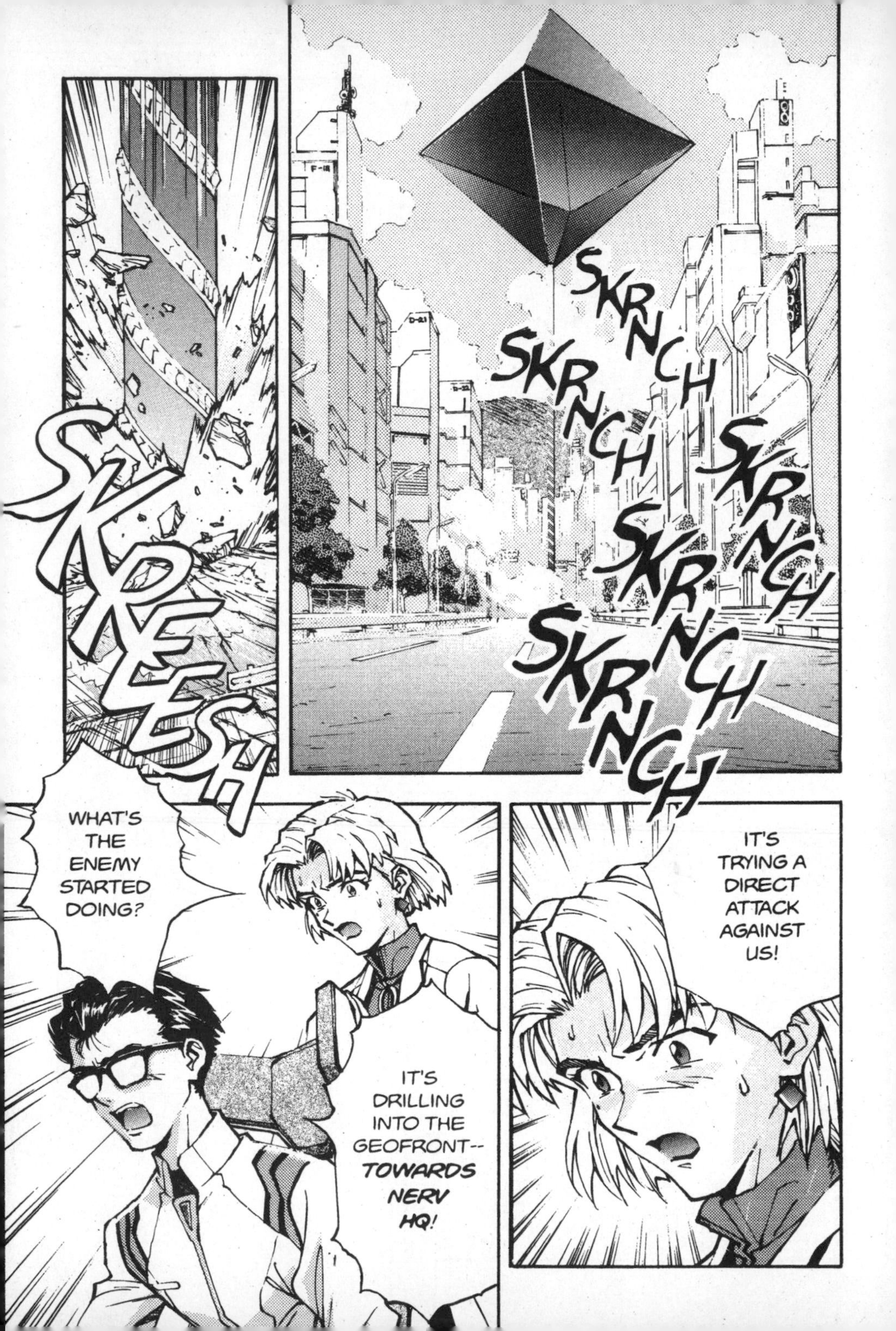
SKREESH
SKRNCH
SKRNCH
SKRNCH
SKRNCH
SKRNCH
WHAT'S THE ENEMY STARTED DOING?
IT'S DRILLING INTO THE GEOFRONT-- *TOWARDS NERV HQ!*
IT'S TRYING A DIRECT ATTACK AGAINST US!

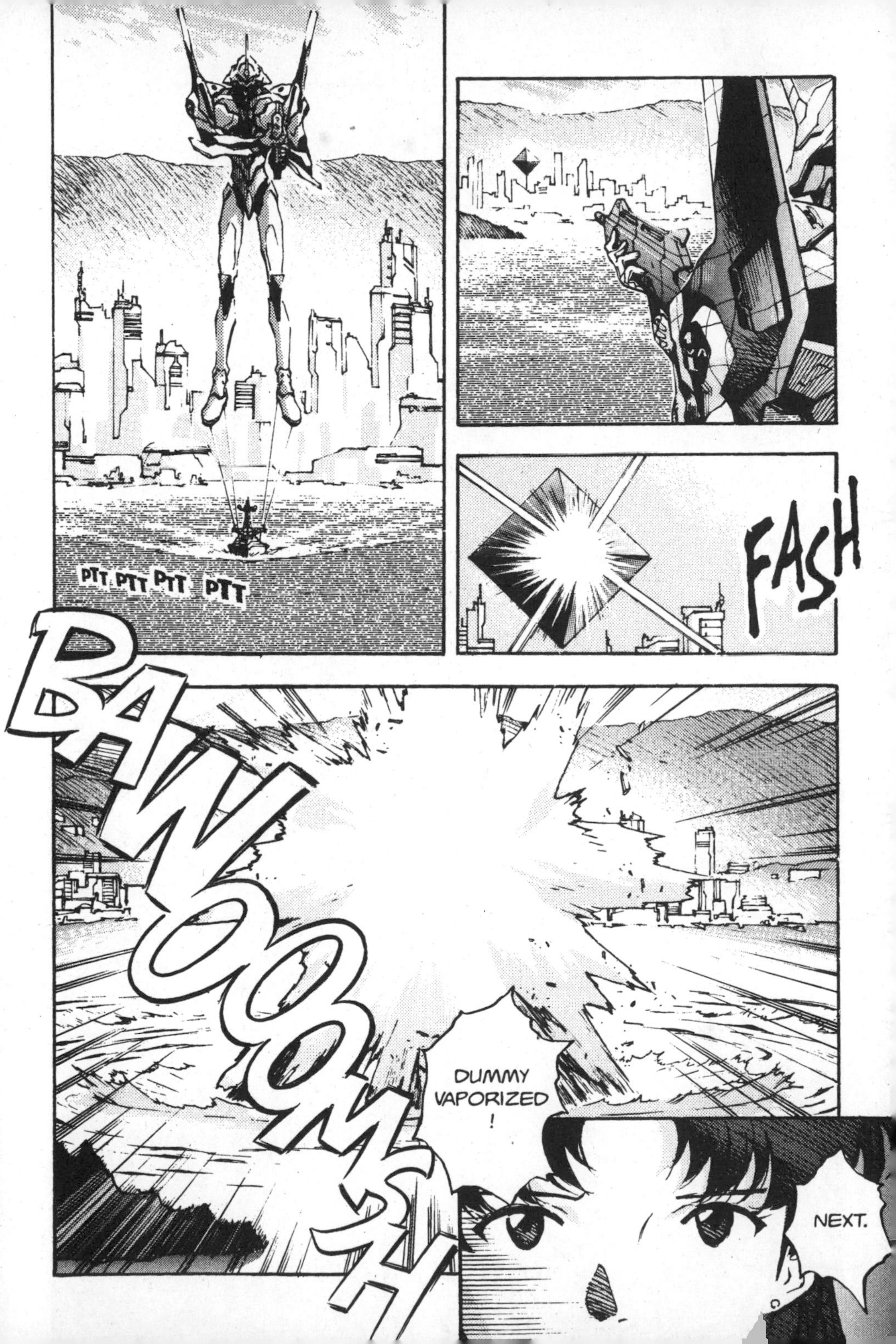
PTT PTT PTT PTT
FASH
BAWOOOMSH
DUMMY VAPORIZED !
NEXT.

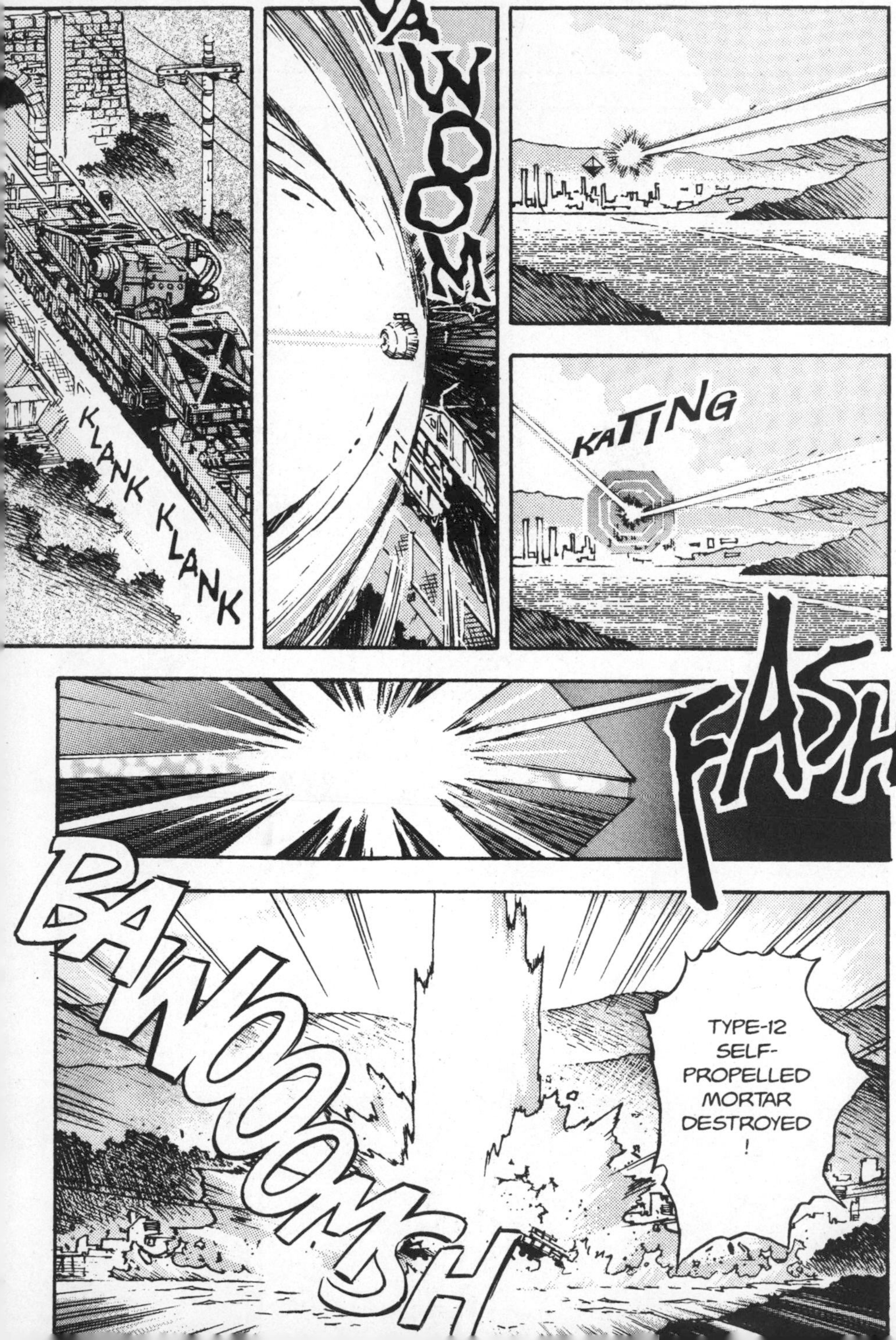
KLANK KLANK KLANK
VAWOOM
KATING
FASH
BANOOOMSH
TYPE-12 SELF-PROPELLED MORTAR DESTROYED !

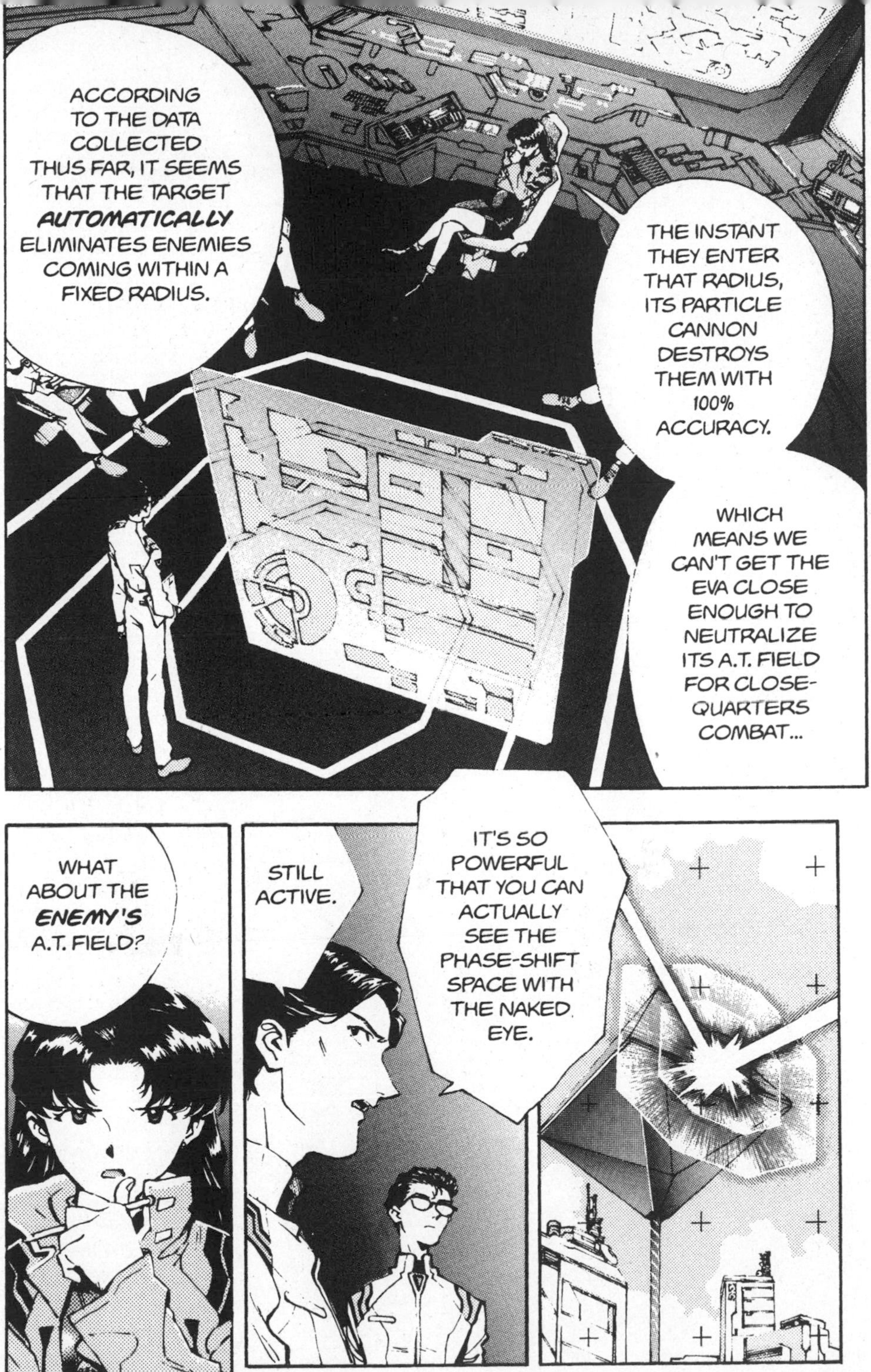
ACCORDING TO THE DATA COLLECTED THUS FAR, IT SEEMS THAT THE TARGET **AUTOMATICALLY** ELIMINATES ENEMIES COMING WITHIN A FIXED RADIUS.
THE INSTANT THEY ENTER THAT RADIUS, ITS PARTICLE CANNON DESTROYS THEM WITH 100% ACCURACY.
WHICH MEANS WE CAN'T GET THE EVA CLOSE ENOUGH TO NEUTRALIZE ITS A.T. FIELD FOR CLOSE-QUARTERS COMBAT...
WHAT ABOUT THE **ENEMY'S** A.T. FIELD?
STILL ACTIVE.
IT'S SO POWERFUL THAT YOU CAN ACTUALLY SEE THE PHASE-SHIFT SPACE WITH THE NAKED EYE.

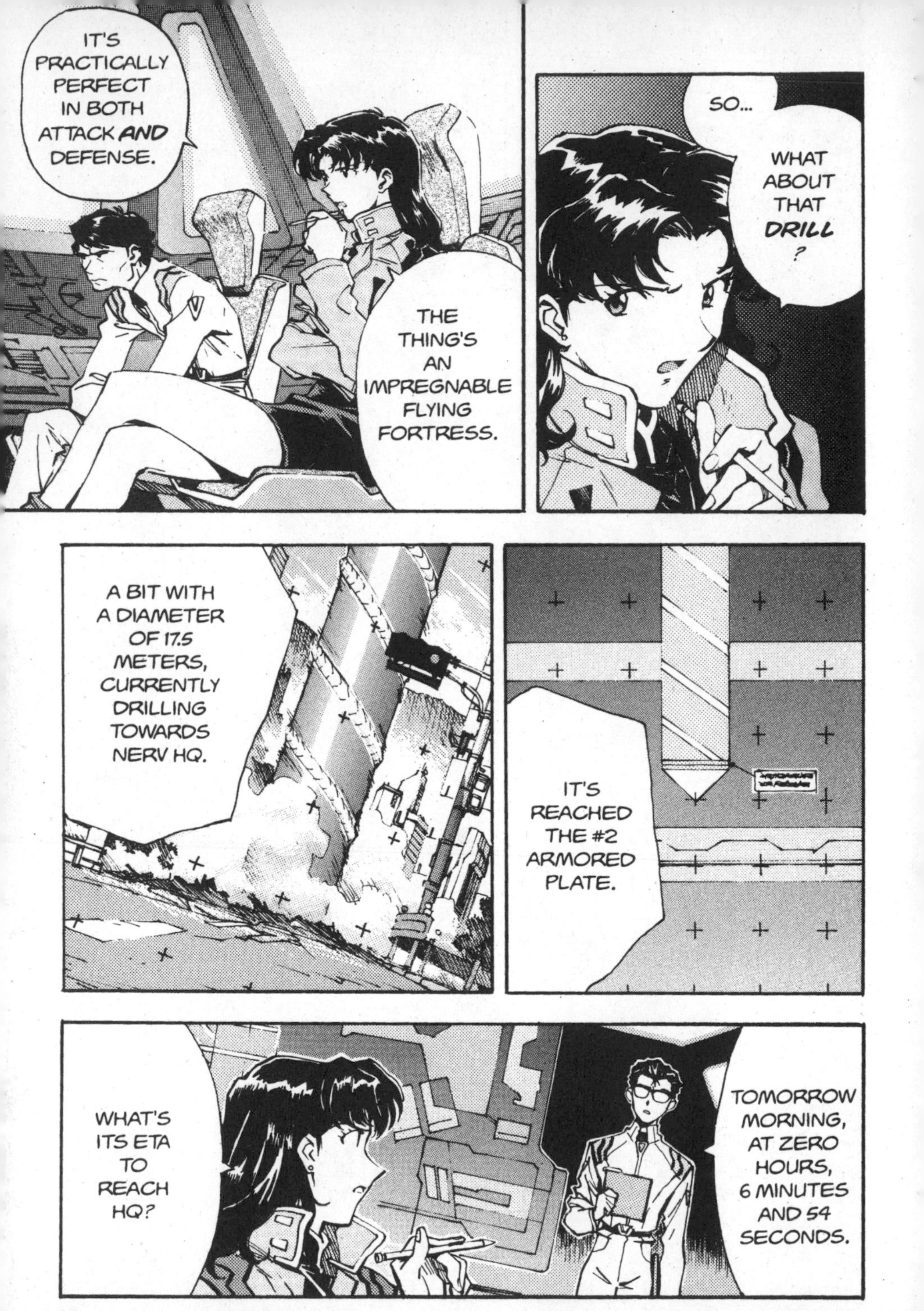
IT'S PRACTICALLY PERFECT IN BOTH ATTACK AND DEFENSE.
THE THING'S AN IMPREGNABLE FLYING FORTRESS.
SO...
WHAT ABOUT THAT DRILL?
A BIT WITH A DIAMETER OF 17.5 METERS, CURRENTLY DRILLING TOWARDS NERV HQ.
IT'S REACHED THE #2 ARMORED PLATE.
WHAT'S ITS ETA TO REACH HQ?
TOMORROW MORNING, AT ZERO HOURS, 6 MINUTES AND 54 SECONDS.

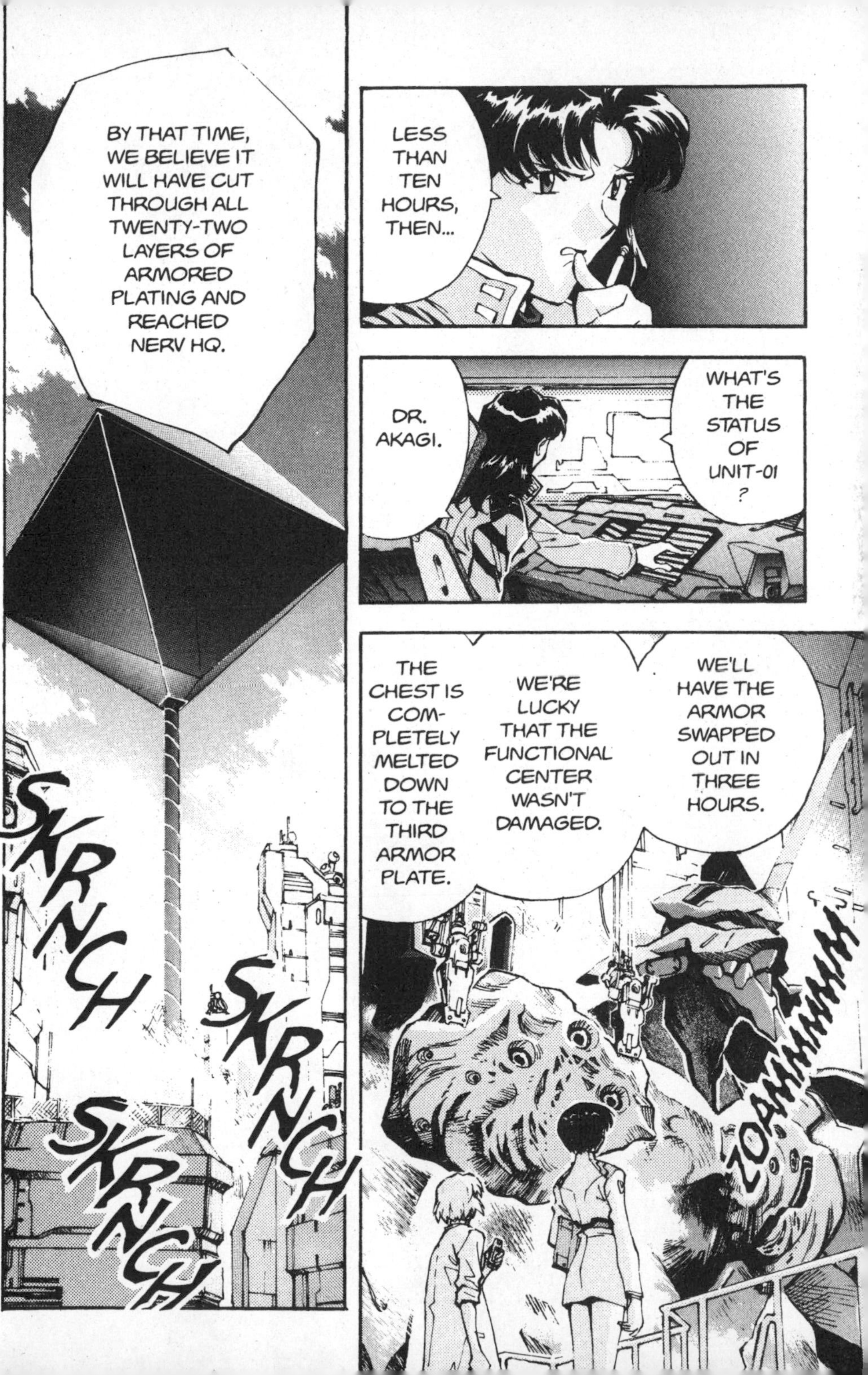
BY THAT TIME, WE BELIEVE IT WILL HAVE CUT THROUGH ALL TWENTY-TWO LAYERS OF ARMORED PLATING AND REACHED NERV HQ.
SKRNCH
SKRNCH
SKRNCH
LESS THAN TEN HOURS, THEN...
DR. AKAGI.
WHAT'S THE STATUS OF UNIT-01?
THE CHEST IS COM-PLETELY MELTED DOWN TO THE THIRD ARMOR PLATE.
WE'RE LUCKY THAT THE FUNCTIONAL CENTER WASN'T DAMAGED.
WE'LL HAVE THE ARMOR SWAPPED OUT IN THREE HOURS.
ZOAMMMMM

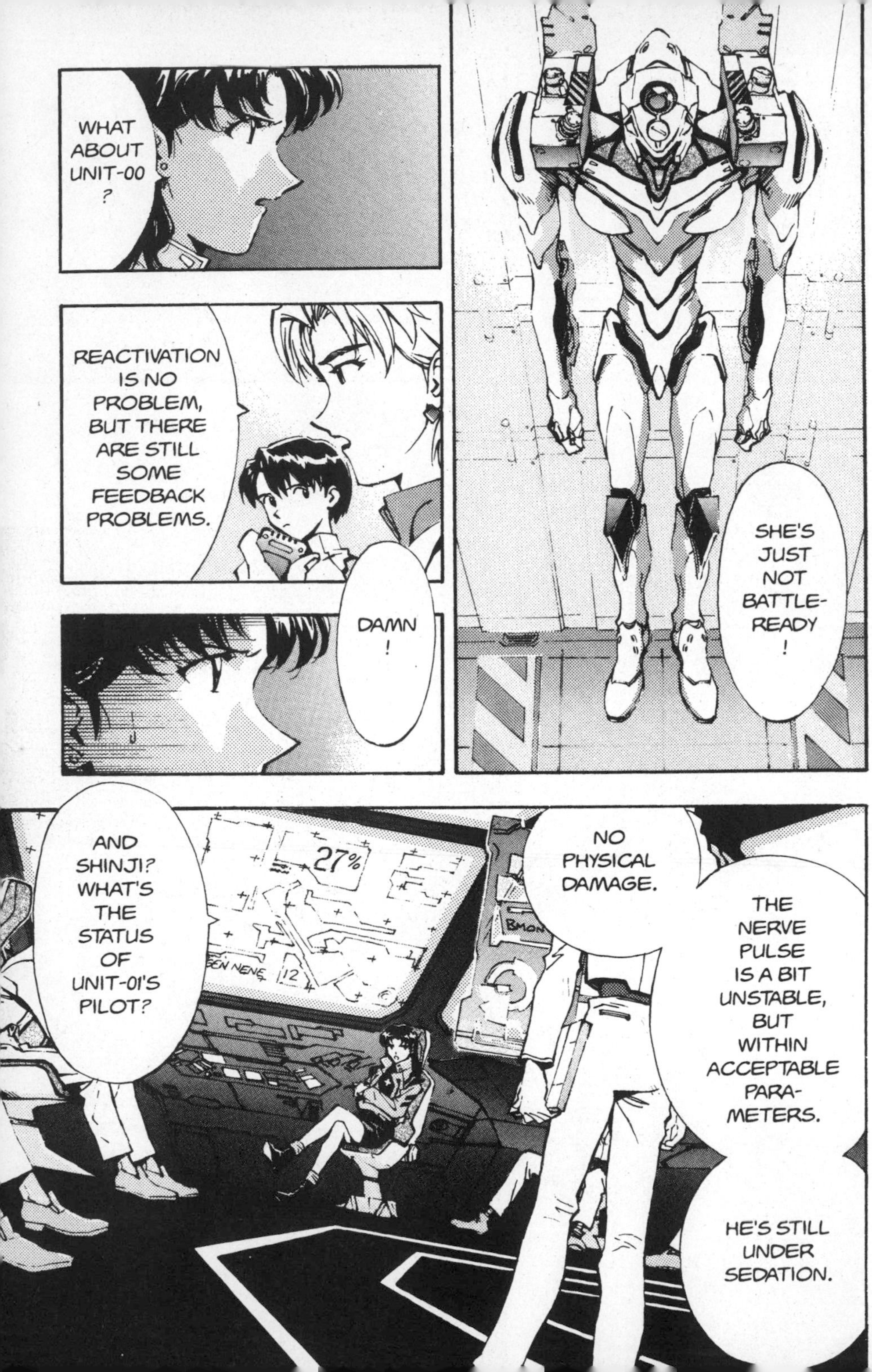
WHAT ABOUT UNIT-00 ?
REACTIVATION IS NO PROBLEM, BUT THERE ARE STILL SOME FEEDBACK PROBLEMS.
DAMN !
SHE'S JUST NOT BATTLE-READY !
AND SHINJI? WHAT'S THE STATUS OF UNIT-01'S PILOT?
27%
NO PHYSICAL DAMAGE.
THE NERVE PULSE IS A BIT UNSTABLE, BUT WITHIN ACCEPTABLE PARA-METERS.
HE'S STILL UNDER SEDATION.

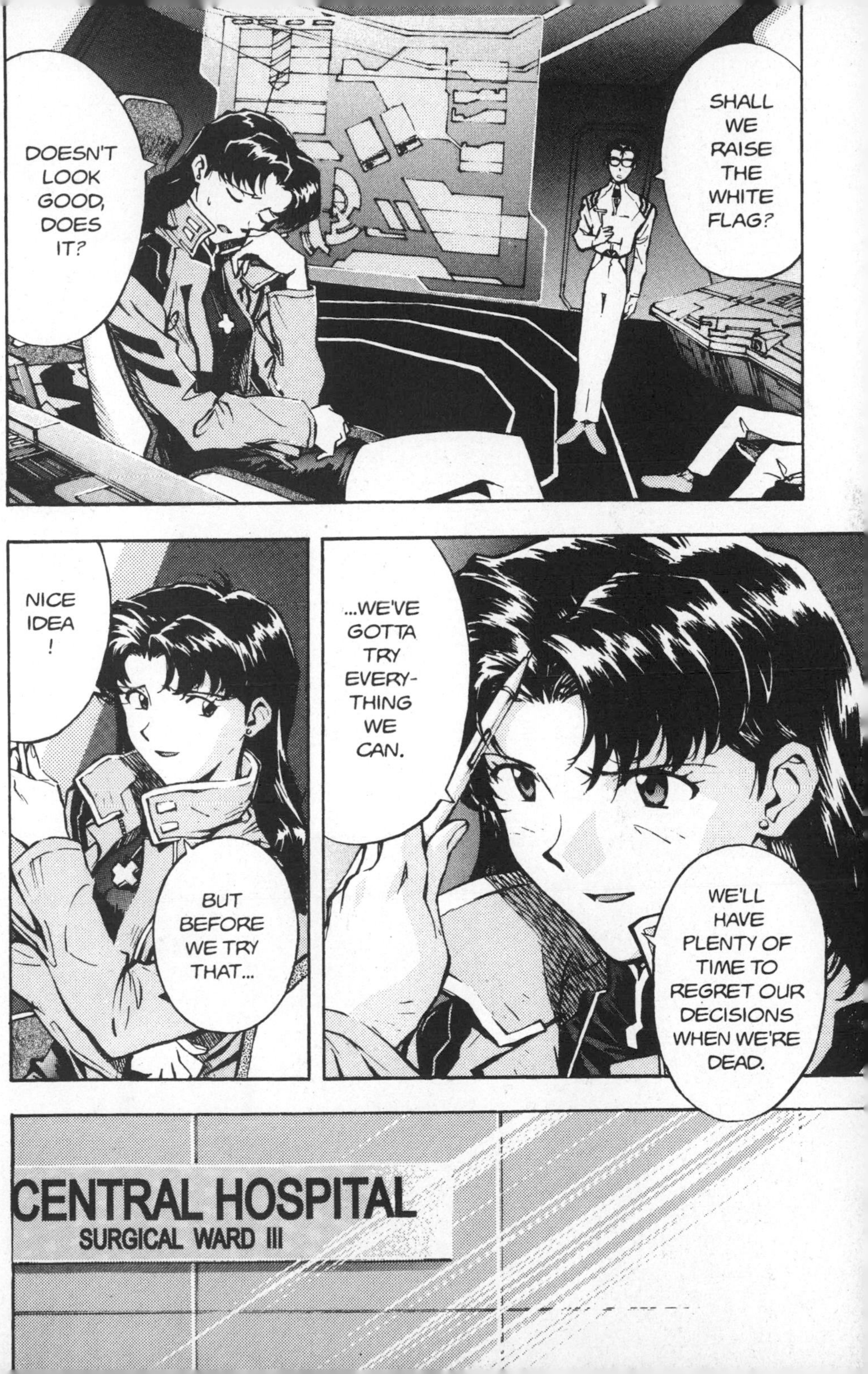
DOESN'T LOOK GOOD, DOES IT?
SHALL WE RAISE THE WHITE FLAG?
NICE IDEA!
BUT BEFORE WE TRY THAT...
...WE'VE GOTTA TRY EVERY-THING WE CAN.
WE'LL HAVE PLENTY OF TIME TO REGRET OUR DECISIONS WHEN WE'RE DEAD.
CENTRAL HOSPITAL
SURGICAL WARD III

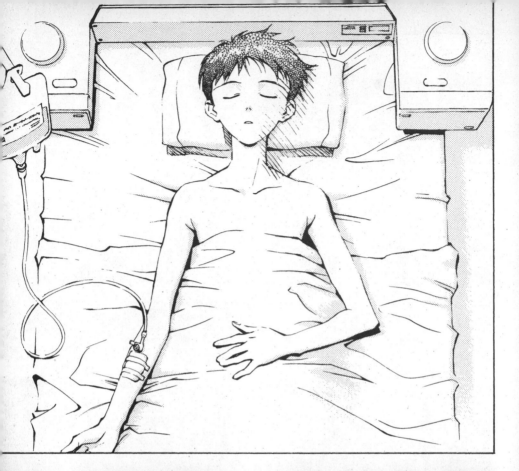

Where...

...where am I?

I wonder where I am?

It's so dark, I can't see anything.

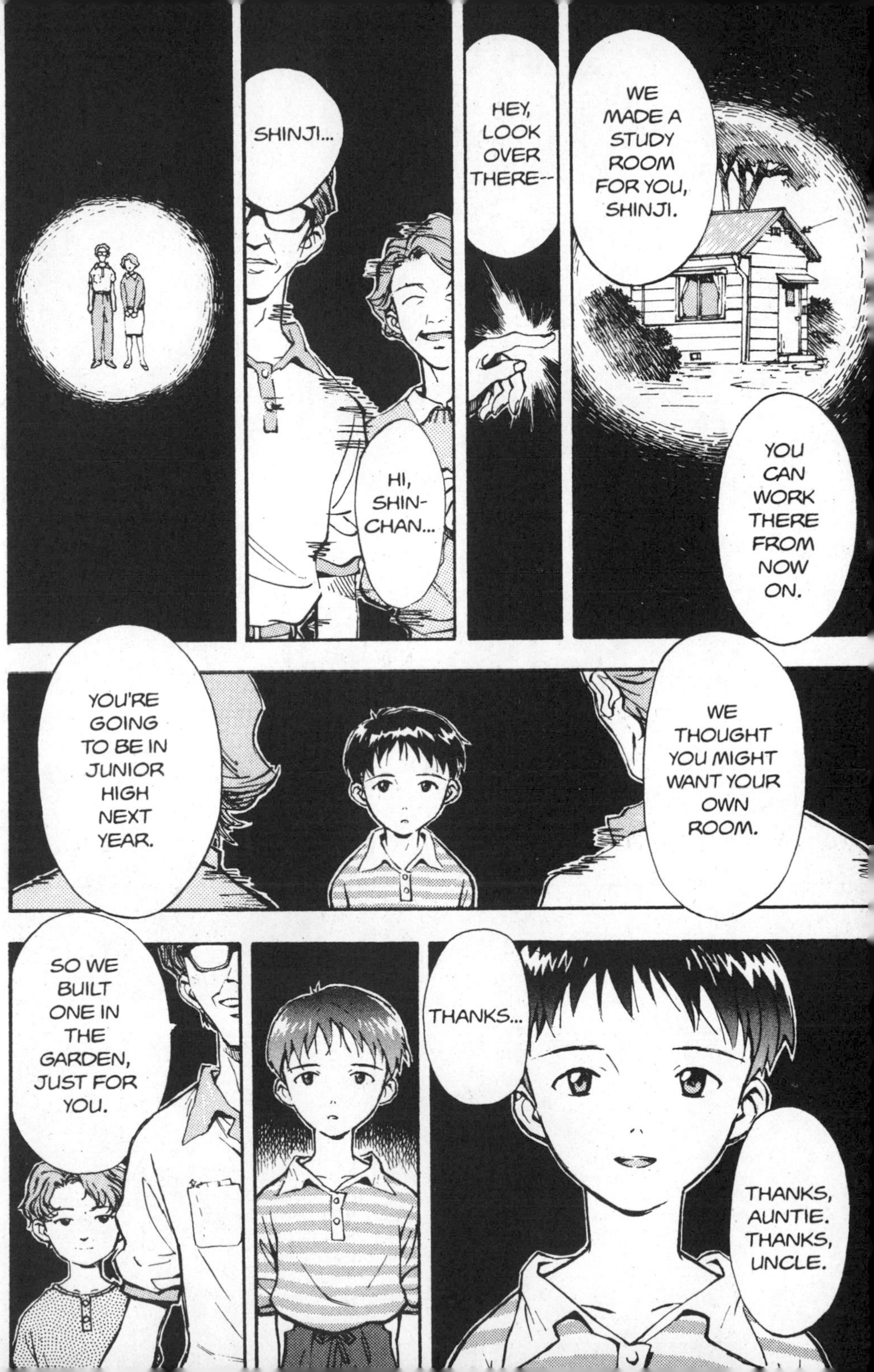
SHINJI...
HI, SHIN-CHAN...
HEY, LOOK OVER THERE--
WE MADE A STUDY ROOM FOR YOU, SHINJI.
YOU CAN WORK THERE FROM NOW ON.
YOU'RE GOING TO BE IN JUNIOR HIGH NEXT YEAR.
WE THOUGHT YOU MIGHT WANT YOUR OWN ROOM.
SO WE BUILT ONE IN THE GARDEN, JUST FOR YOU.
THANKS...
THANKS, AUNTIE. THANKS, UNCLE.

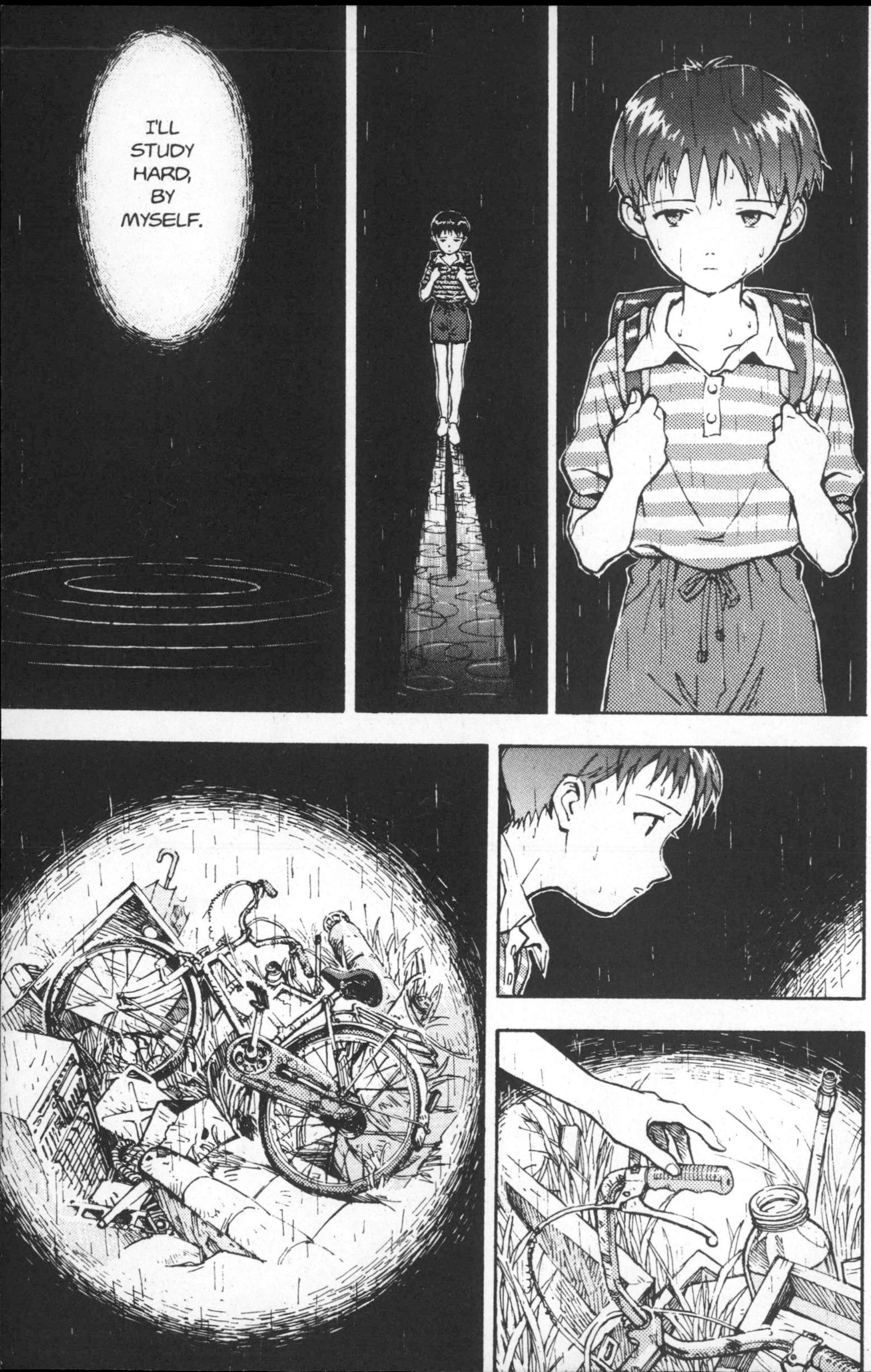
I'LL STUDY HARD, BY MYSELF.

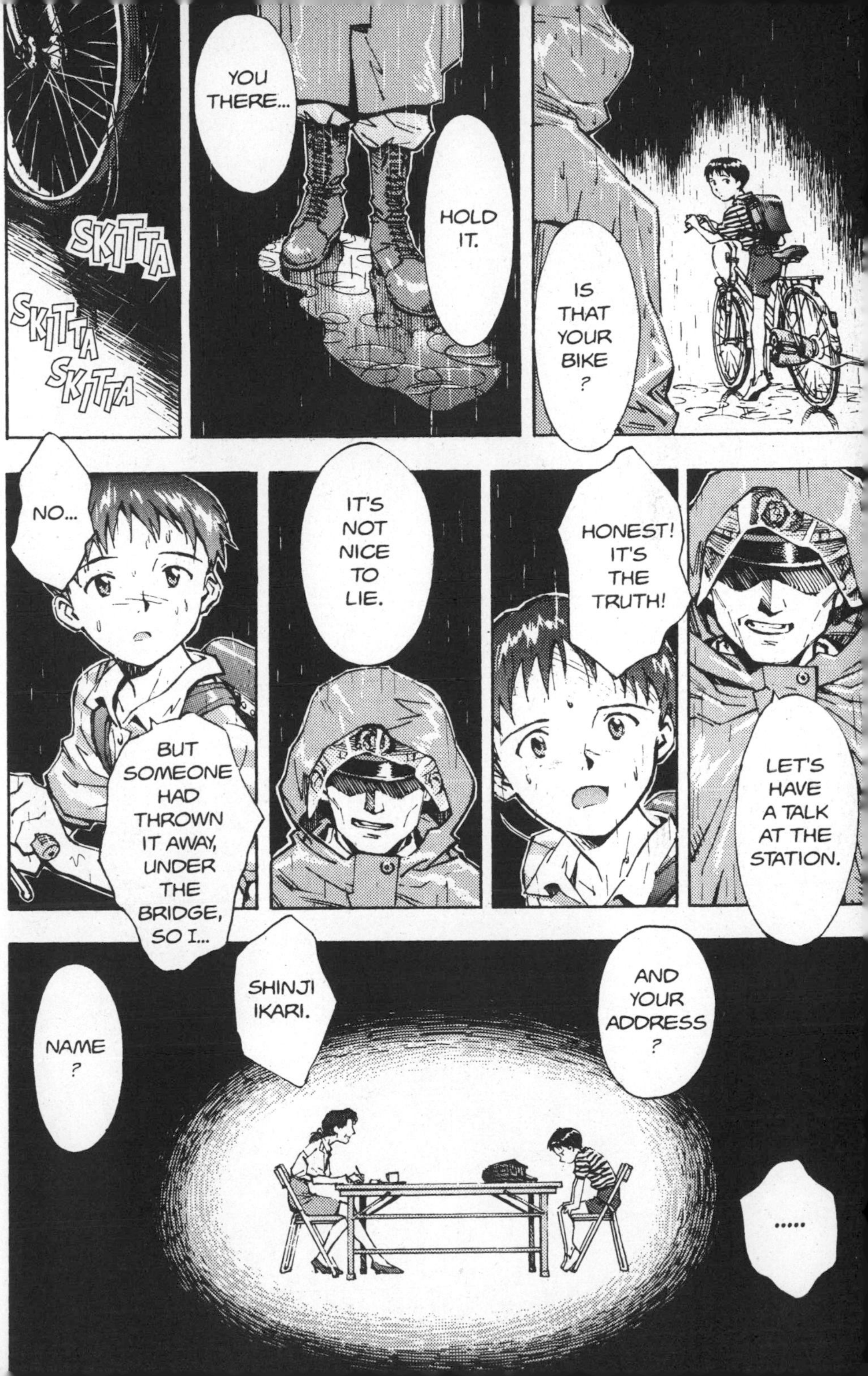
SKITTA
SKITTA
SKITTA
YOU THERE...
HOLD IT.
IS THAT YOUR BIKE ?
NO...
BUT SOMEONE HAD THROWN IT AWAY, UNDER THE BRIDGE, SO I...
IT'S NOT NICE TO LIE.
HONEST! IT'S THE TRUTH!
LET'S HAVE A TALK AT THE STATION.
NAME ?
SHINJI IKARI.
AND YOUR ADDRESS ?
.....

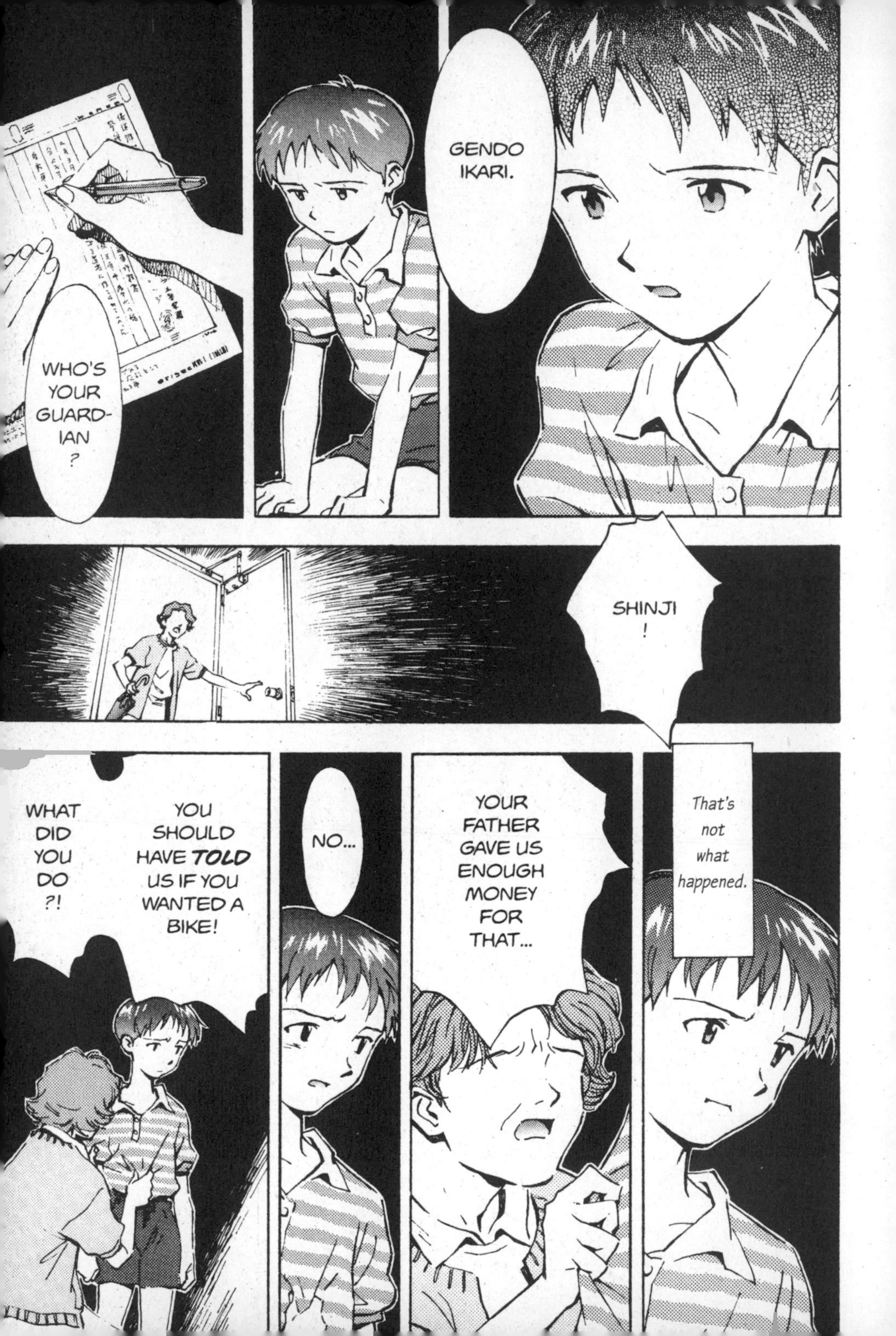
WHO'S YOUR GUARDIAN?
GENDO IKARI.
SHINJI!
WHAT DID YOU DO?!
YOU SHOULD HAVE **TOLD** US IF YOU WANTED A BIKE!
NO...
YOUR FATHER GAVE US ENOUGH MONEY FOR THAT...
That's not what happened.

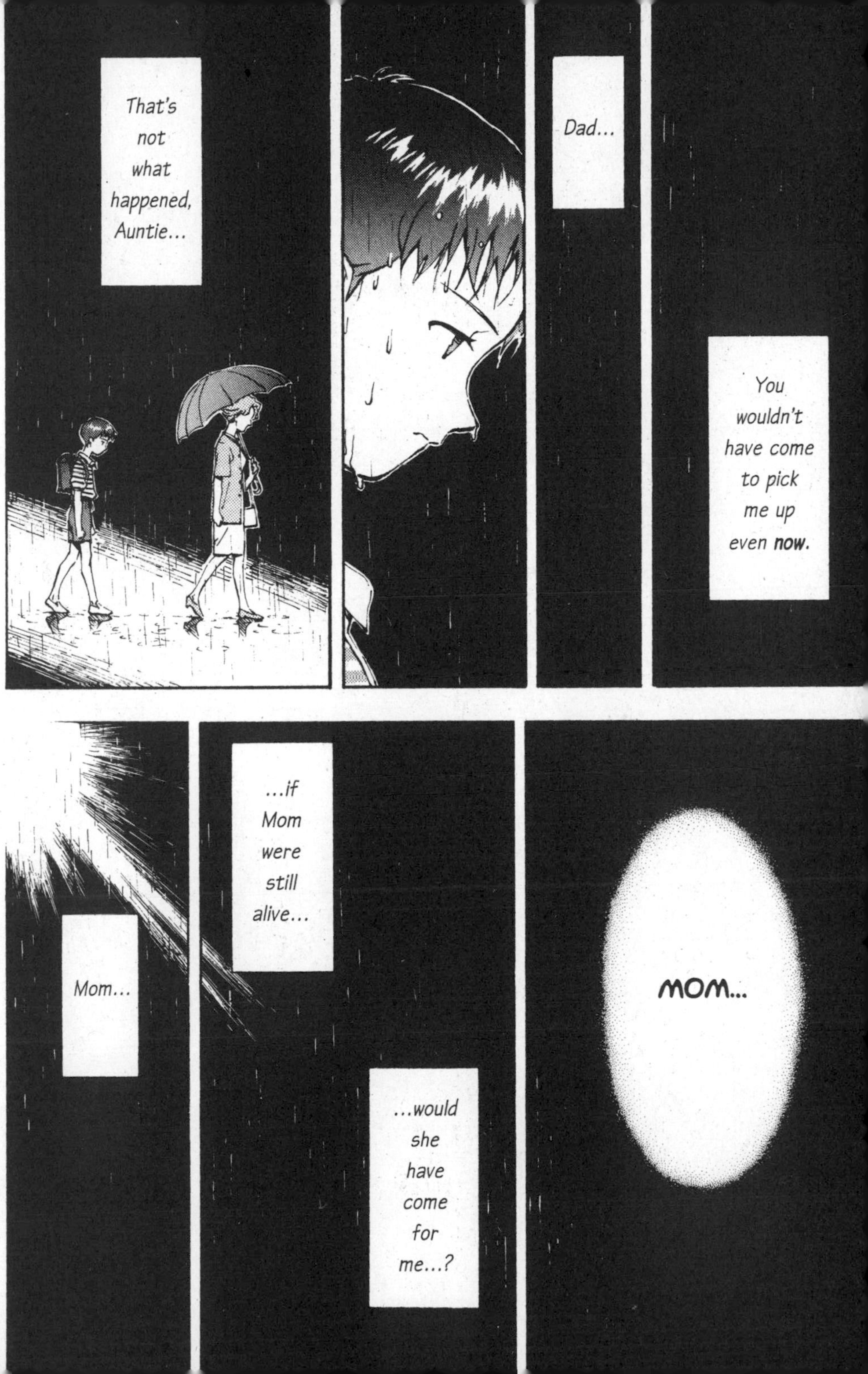
That's not what happened, Auntie...
Dad...
You wouldn't have come to pick me up even **now**.
Mom...
...if Mom were still alive...
...would she have come for me...?
MOM...

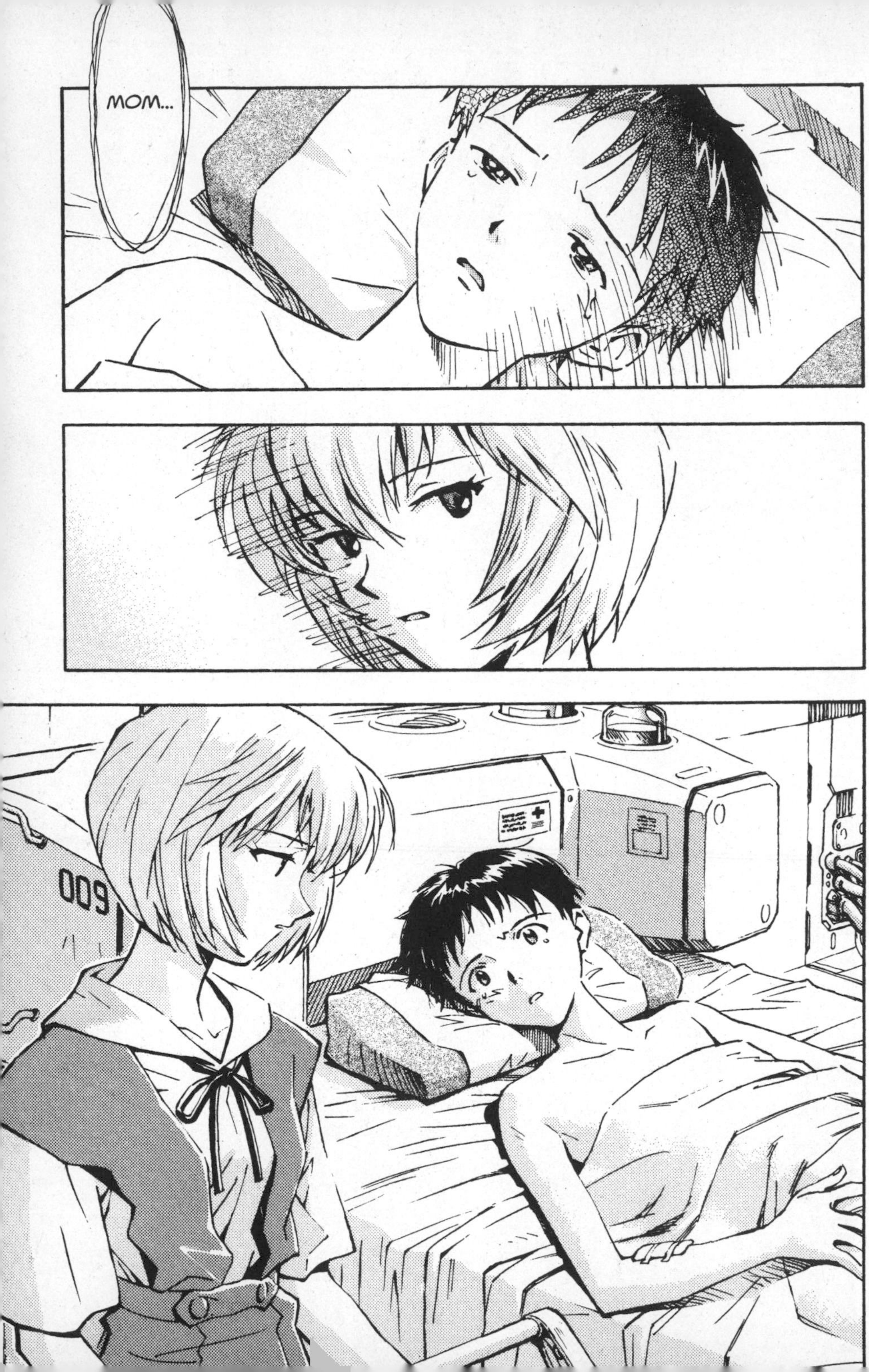
MOM...
009

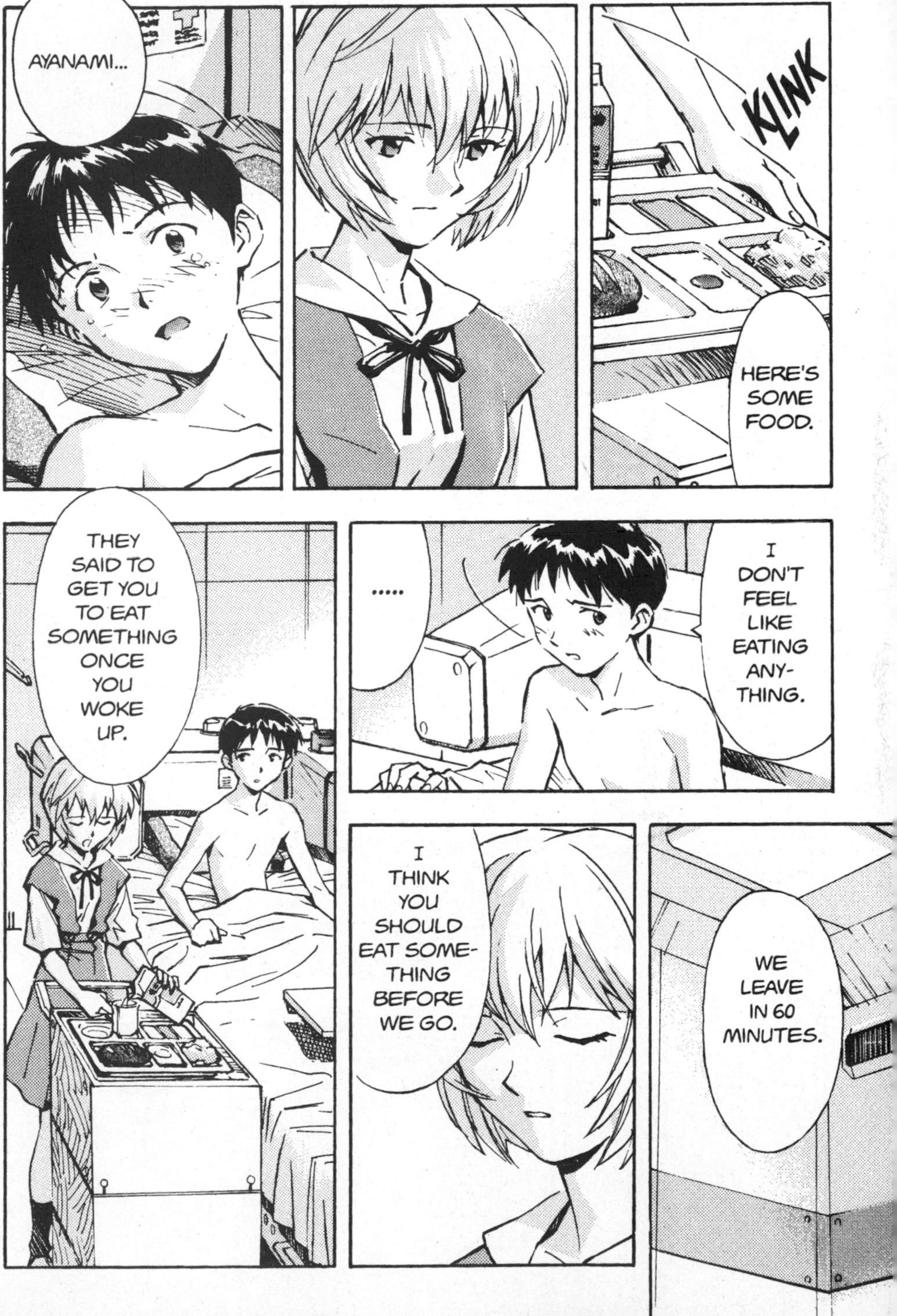
AYANAMI...
KLINK
HERE'S SOME FOOD.
THEY SAID TO GET YOU TO EAT SOMETHING ONCE YOU WOKE UP.
.....
I DON'T FEEL LIKE EATING ANY-THING.
I THINK YOU SHOULD EAT SOME-THING BEFORE WE GO.
WE LEAVE IN 60 MINUTES.

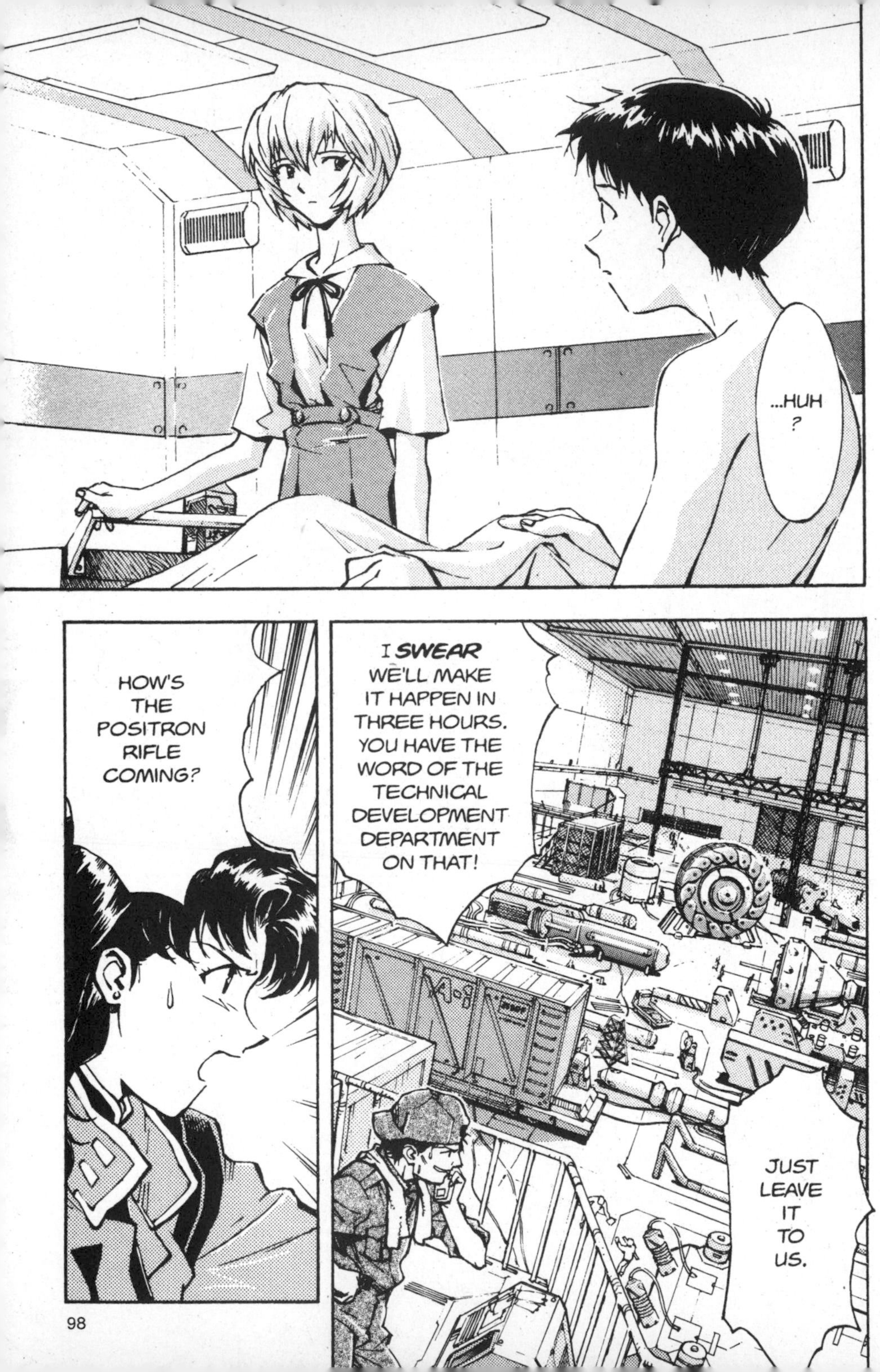
...HUH ?
HOW'S THE POSITRON RIFLE COMING?
I SWEAR WE'LL MAKE IT HAPPEN IN THREE HOURS. YOU HAVE THE WORD OF THE TECHNICAL DEVELOPMENT DEPARTMENT ON THAT!
JUST LEAVE IT TO US.

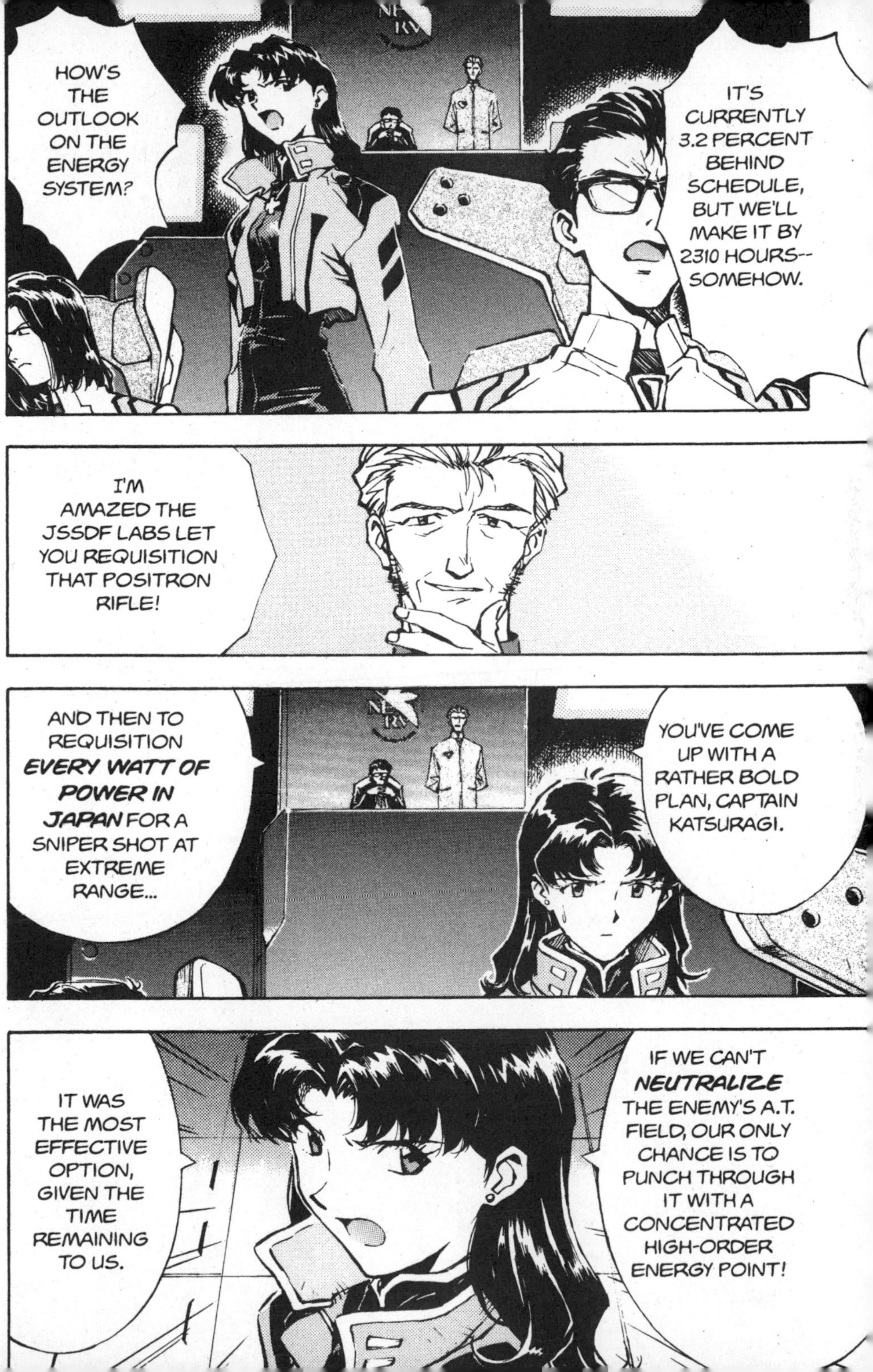
HOW'S THE OUTLOOK ON THE ENERGY SYSTEM?
IT'S CURRENTLY 3.2 PERCENT BEHIND SCHEDULE, BUT WE'LL MAKE IT BY 2310 HOURS--SOMEHOW.
I'M AMAZED THE JSSDF LABS LET YOU REQUISITION THAT POSITRON RIFLE!
AND THEN TO REQUISITION ***EVERY WATT OF POWER IN JAPAN*** FOR A SNIPER SHOT AT EXTREME RANGE...
YOU'VE COME UP WITH A RATHER BOLD PLAN, CAPTAIN KATSURAGI.
IT WAS THE MOST EFFECTIVE OPTION, GIVEN THE TIME REMAINING TO US.
IF WE CAN'T ***NEUTRALIZE*** THE ENEMY'S A.T. FIELD, OUR ONLY CHANCE IS TO PUNCH THROUGH IT WITH A CONCENTRATED HIGH-ORDER ENERGY POINT!

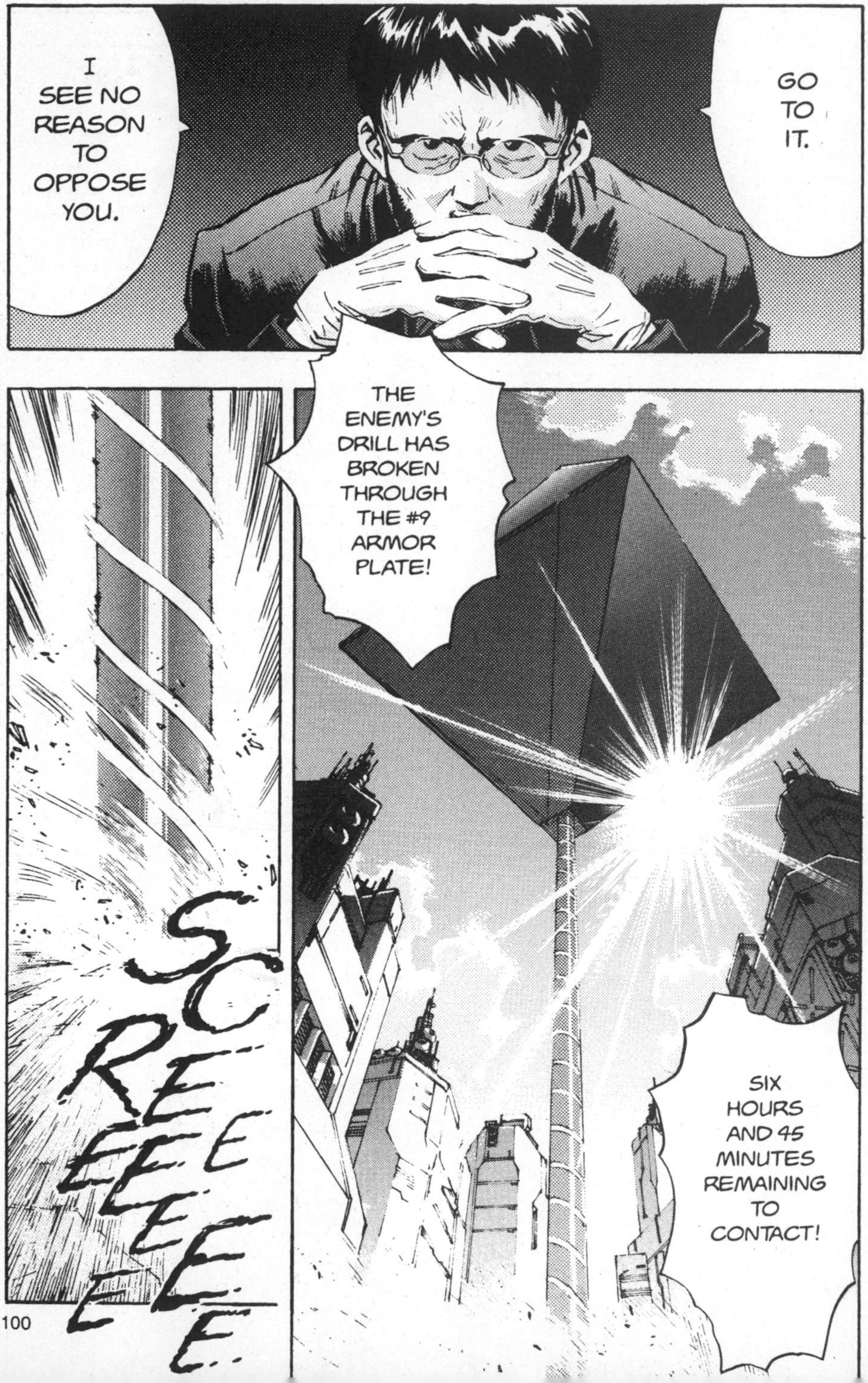
I SEE NO REASON TO OPPOSE YOU.
GO TO IT.
SCREEEEEEEEE.
THE ENEMY'S DRILL HAS BROKEN THROUGH THE #9 ARMOR PLATE!
SIX HOURS AND 45 MINUTES REMAINING TO CONTACT!

Stage 5:
THE NIGHT BEFORE BATTLE

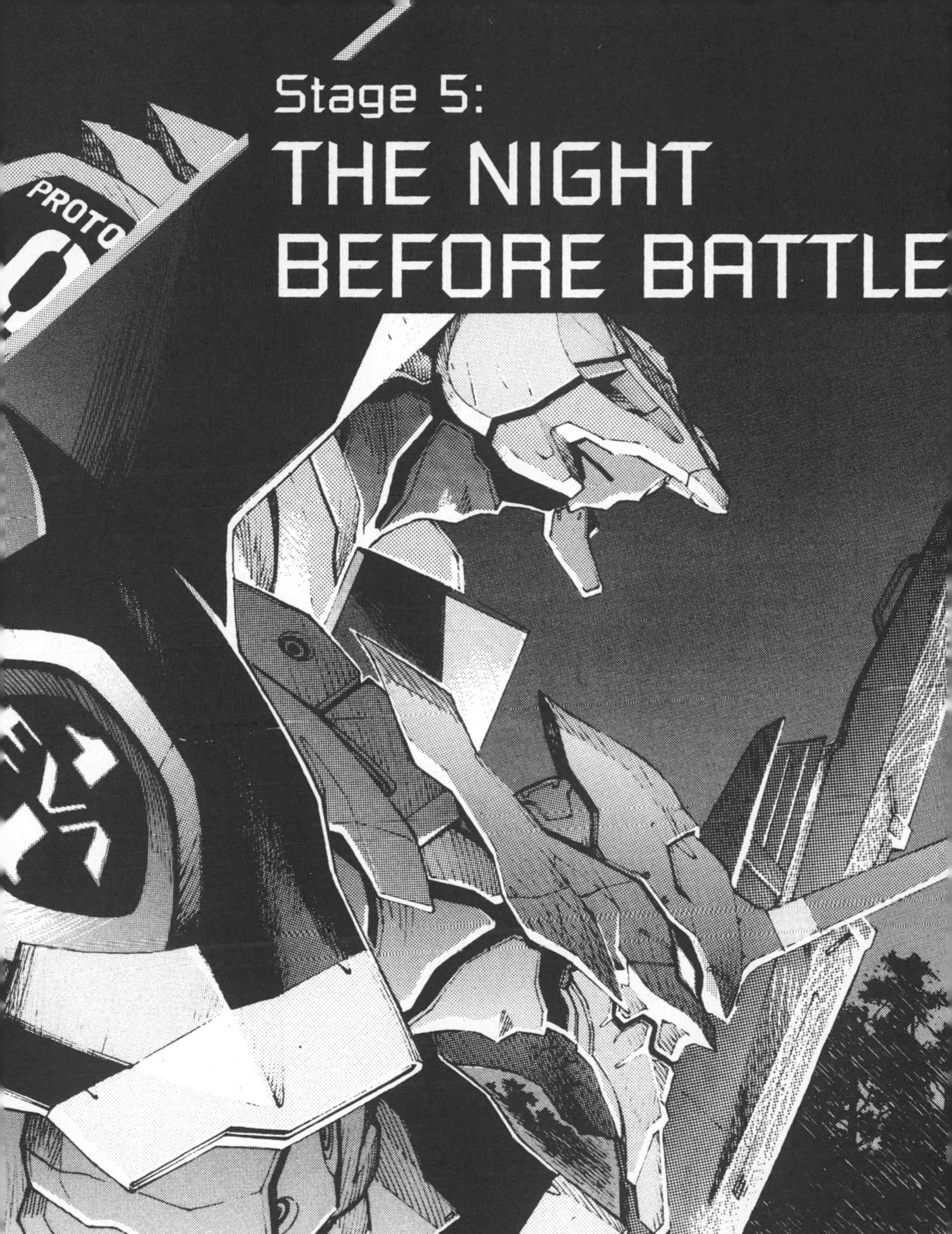
PROTO

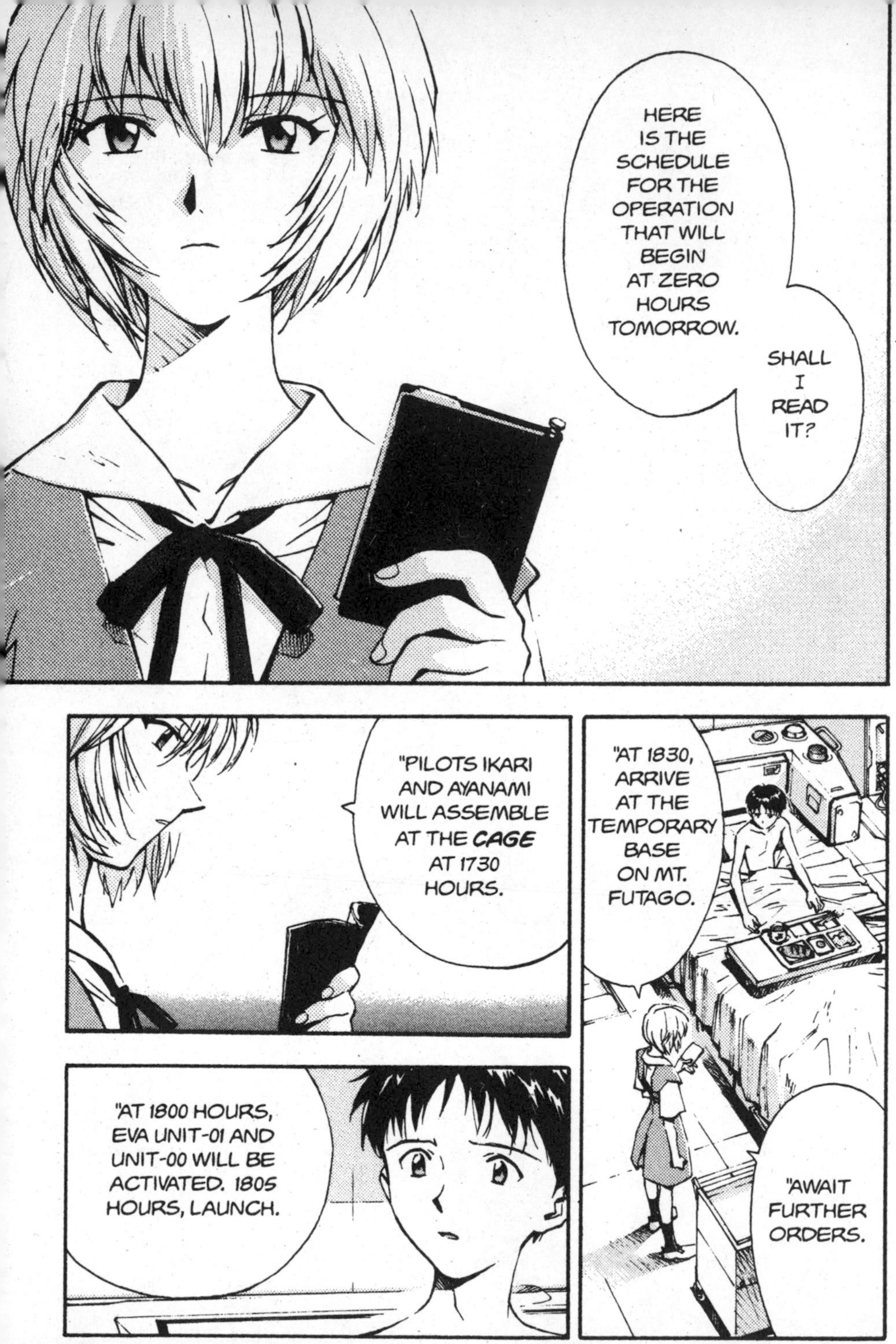
HERE IS THE SCHEDULE FOR THE OPERATION THAT WILL BEGIN AT ZERO HOURS TOMORROW.
SHALL I READ IT?
"PILOTS IKARI AND AYANAMI WILL ASSEMBLE AT THE *CAGE* AT 1730 HOURS.
"AT 1830, ARRIVE AT THE TEMPORARY BASE ON MT. FUTAGO.
"AT 1800 HOURS, EVA UNIT-01 AND UNIT-00 WILL BE ACTIVATED. 1805 HOURS, LAUNCH.
"AWAIT FURTHER ORDERS.

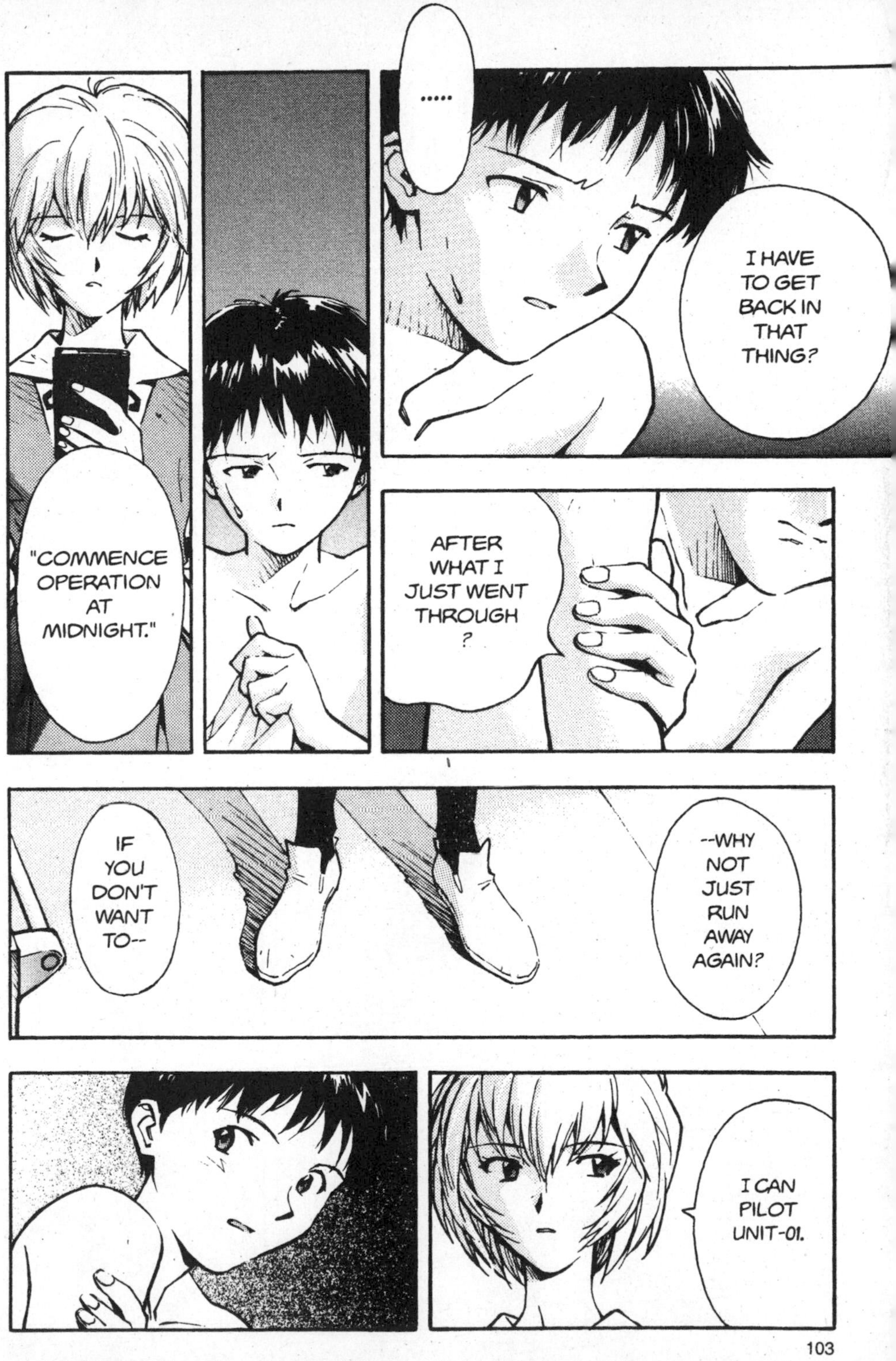
"COMMENCE OPERATION AT MIDNIGHT."
......
I HAVE TO GET BACK IN THAT THING?
AFTER WHAT I JUST WENT THROUGH?
IF YOU DON'T WANT TO--
--WHY NOT JUST RUN AWAY AGAIN?
I CAN PILOT UNIT-01.

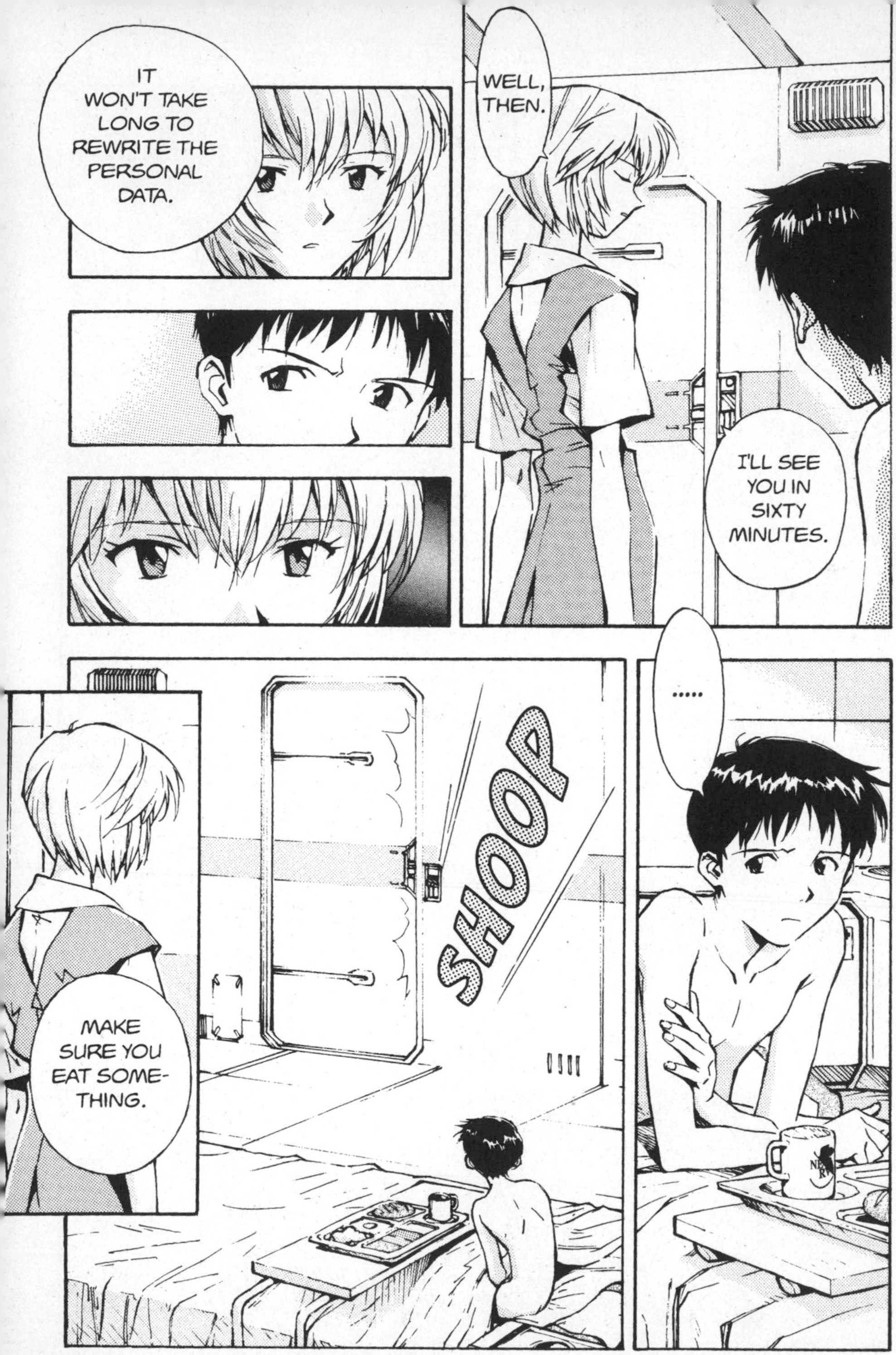
IT WON'T TAKE LONG TO REWRITE THE PERSONAL DATA.
WELL, THEN.
I'LL SEE YOU IN SIXTY MINUTES.
MAKE SURE YOU EAT SOME-THING.
SHOOP
......

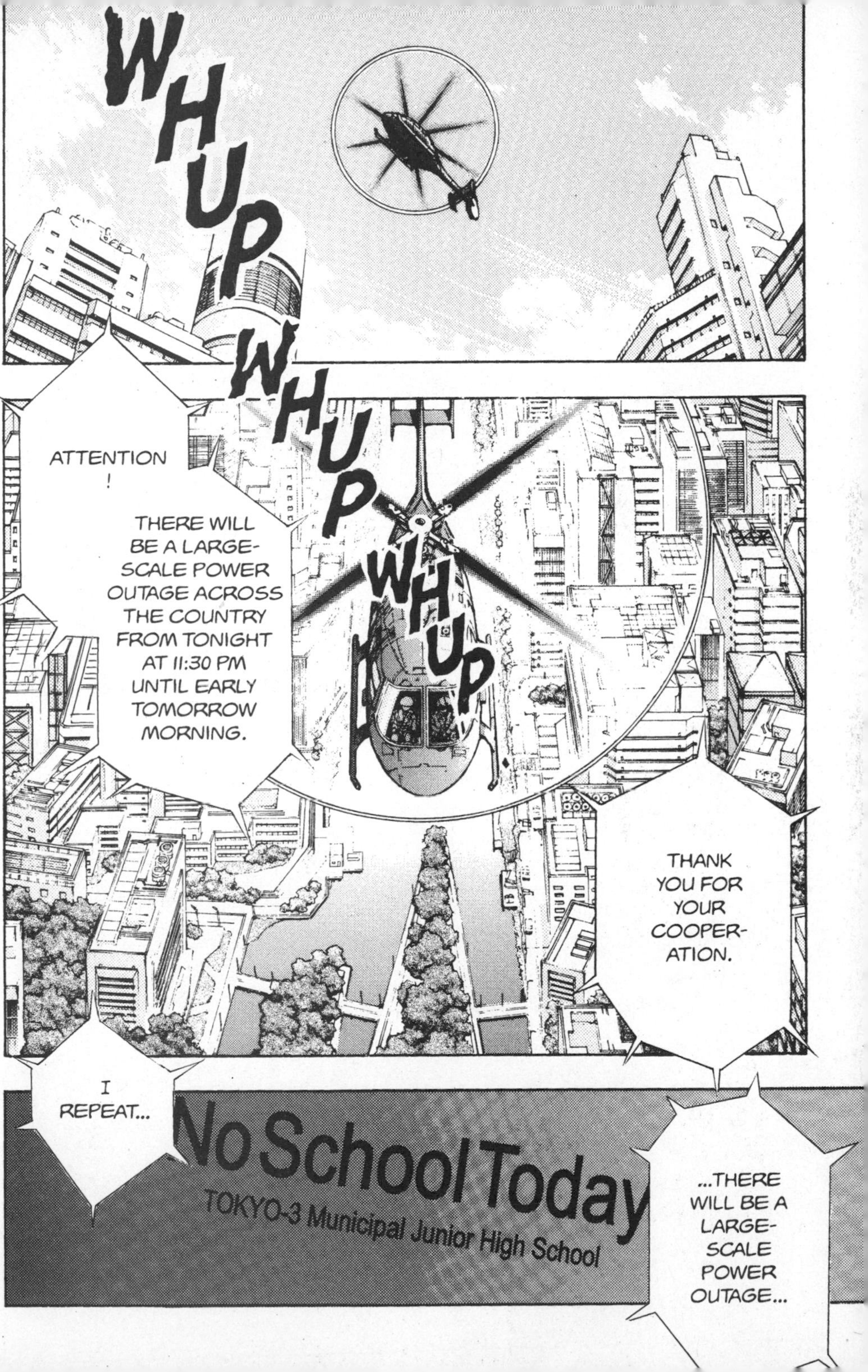
WHUP
WHUP
ATTENTION!
THERE WILL BE A LARGE-SCALE POWER OUTAGE ACROSS THE COUNTRY FROM TONIGHT AT 11:30 PM UNTIL EARLY TOMORROW MORNING.
WHUP
THANK YOU FOR YOUR COOPERATION.
I REPEAT...
No School Today
TOKYO-3 Municipal Junior High School
...THERE WILL BE A LARGE-SCALE POWER OUTAGE...

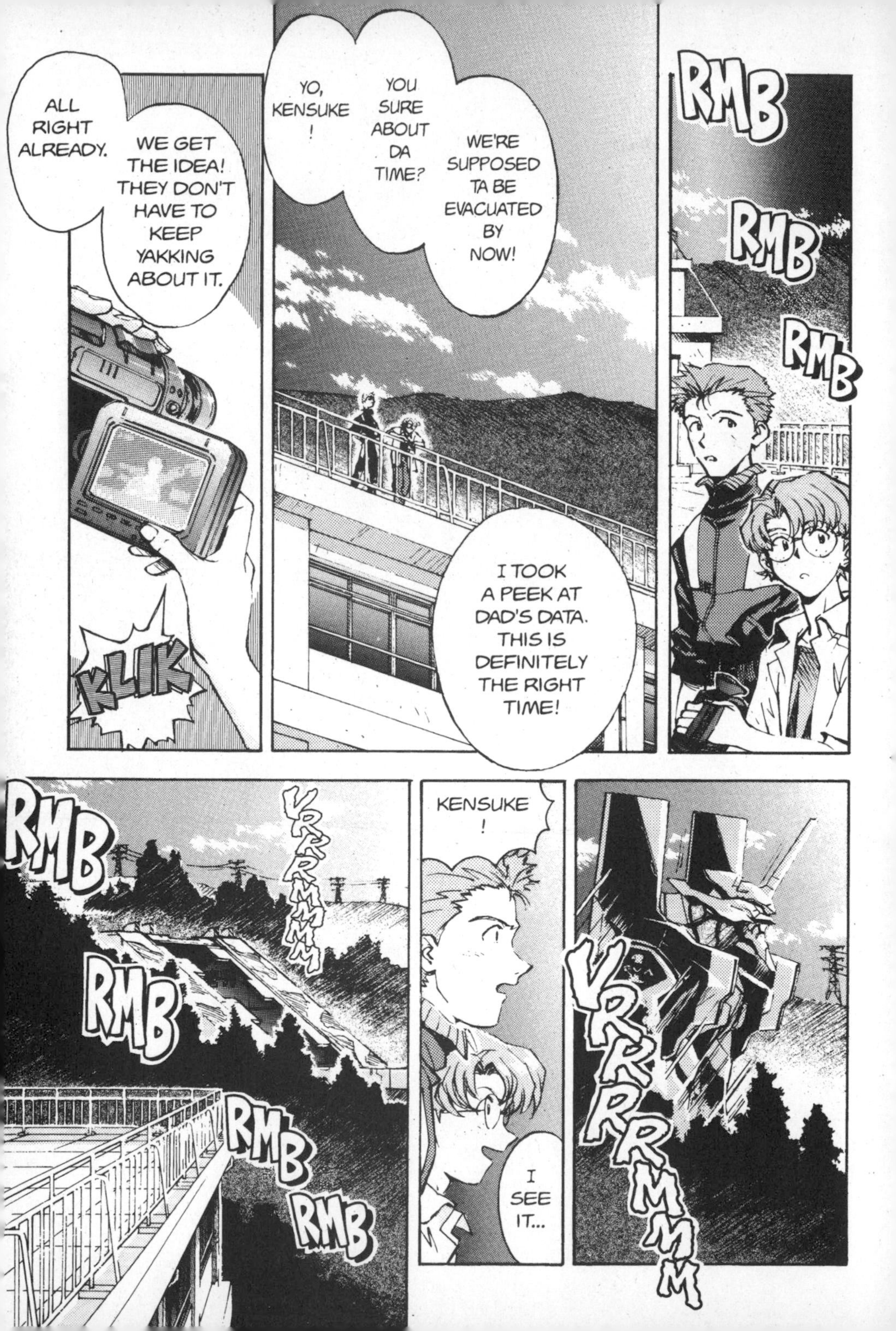
ALL RIGHT ALREADY.
WE GET THE IDEA! THEY DON'T HAVE TO KEEP YAKKING ABOUT IT.
KLIK
YO, KENSUKE!
YOU SURE ABOUT DA TIME?
WE'RE SUPPOSED TA BE EVACUATED BY NOW!
I TOOK A PEEK AT DAD'S DATA. THIS IS DEFINITELY THE RIGHT TIME!
RMB
RMB
RMB
RMB
VRRRMMMM
RMB
RMB
RMB
KENSUKE!
I SEE IT...
VRRRRMMMM

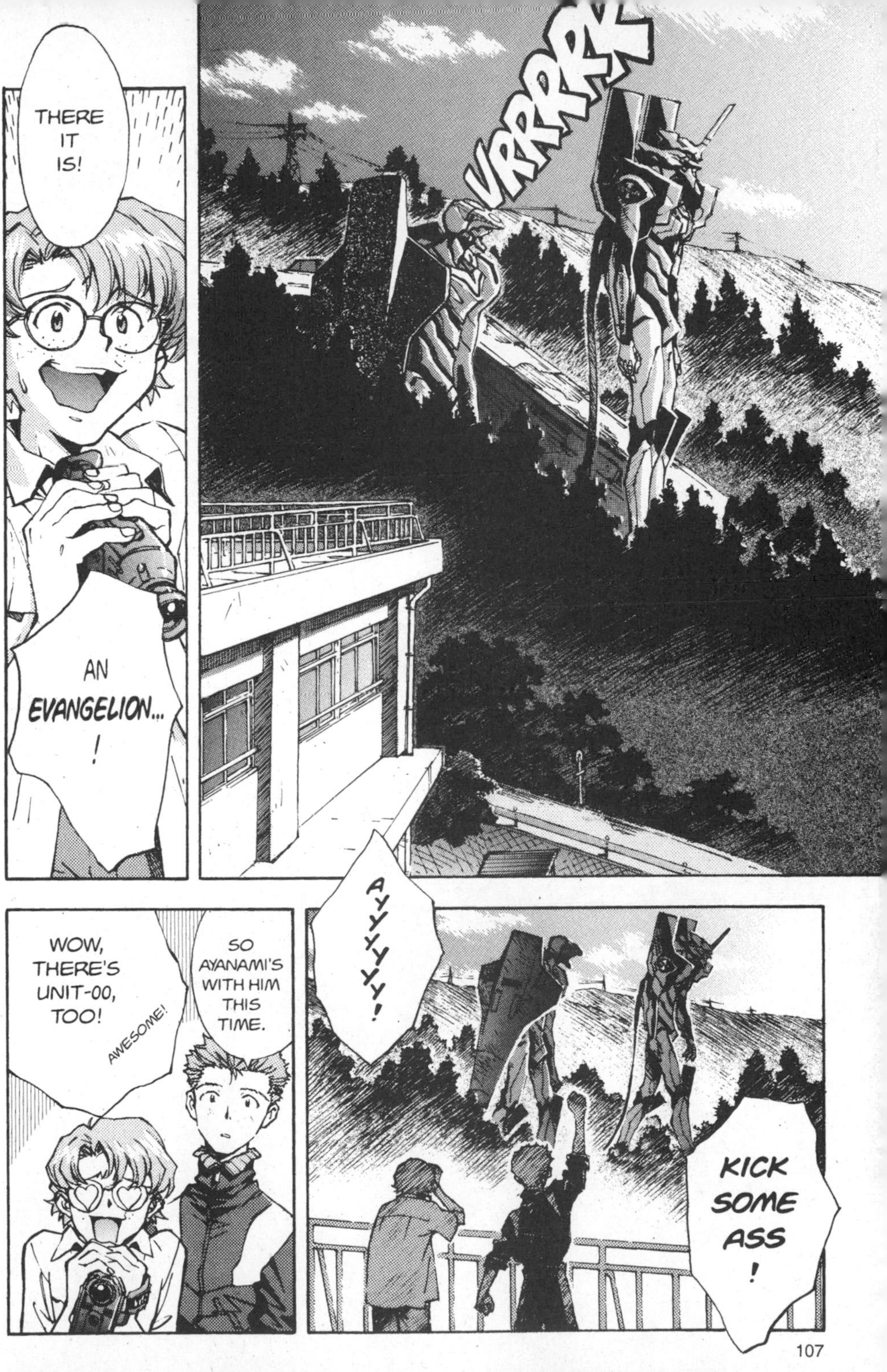

THERE IT IS!
AN EVANGELION...!
VRRRRK
WOW, THERE'S UNIT-00, TOO!
AWESOME!
SO AYANAMI'S WITH HIM THIS TIME.
AYYYYYY!
KICK SOME ASS!

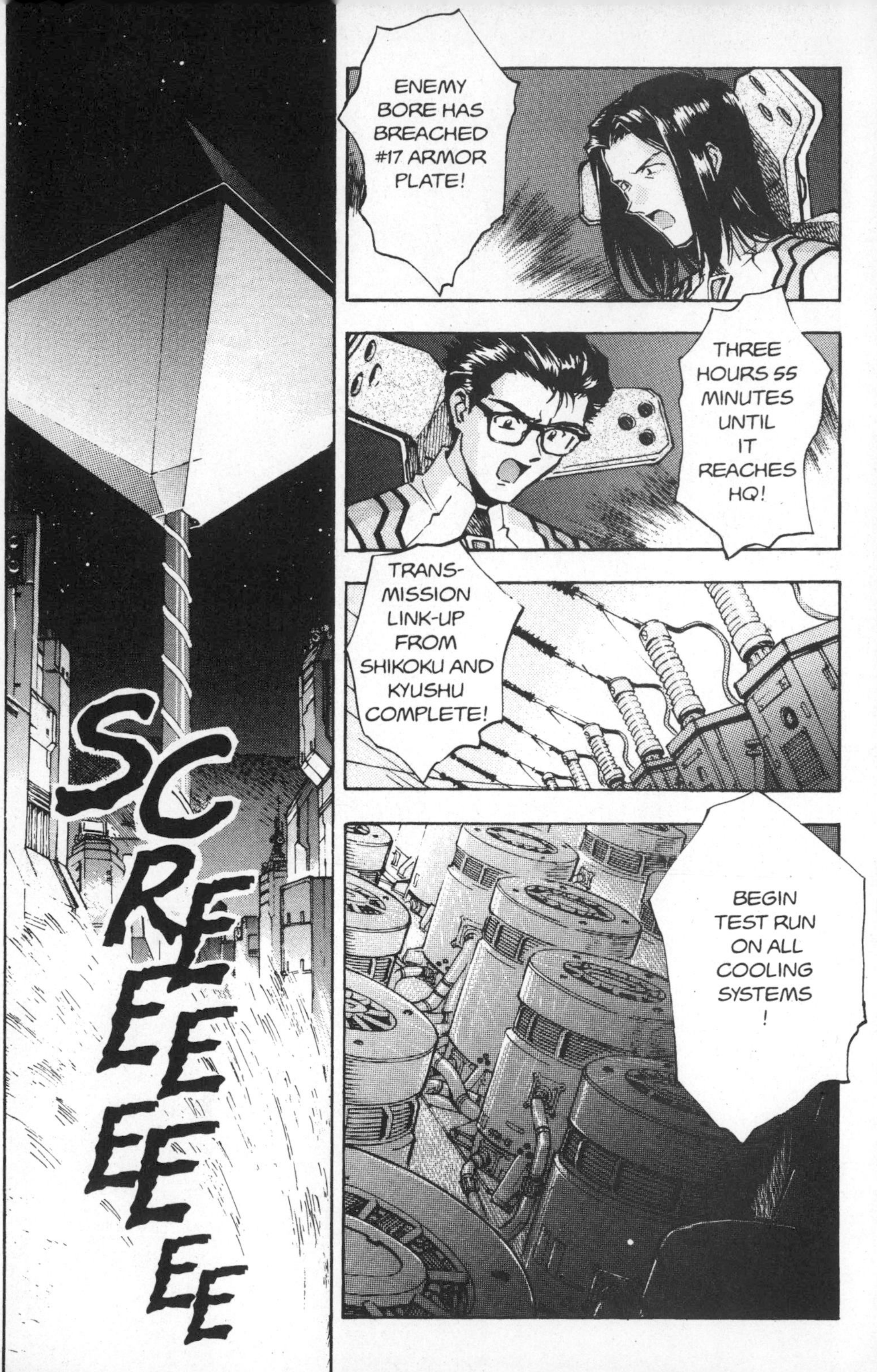
SCREEEEEEEE
ENEMY BORE HAS BREACHED #17 ARMOR PLATE!
THREE HOURS 55 MINUTES UNTIL IT REACHES HQ!
TRANS-MISSION LINK-UP FROM SHIKOKU AND KYUSHU COMPLETE!
BEGIN TEST RUN ON ALL COOLING SYSTEMS!

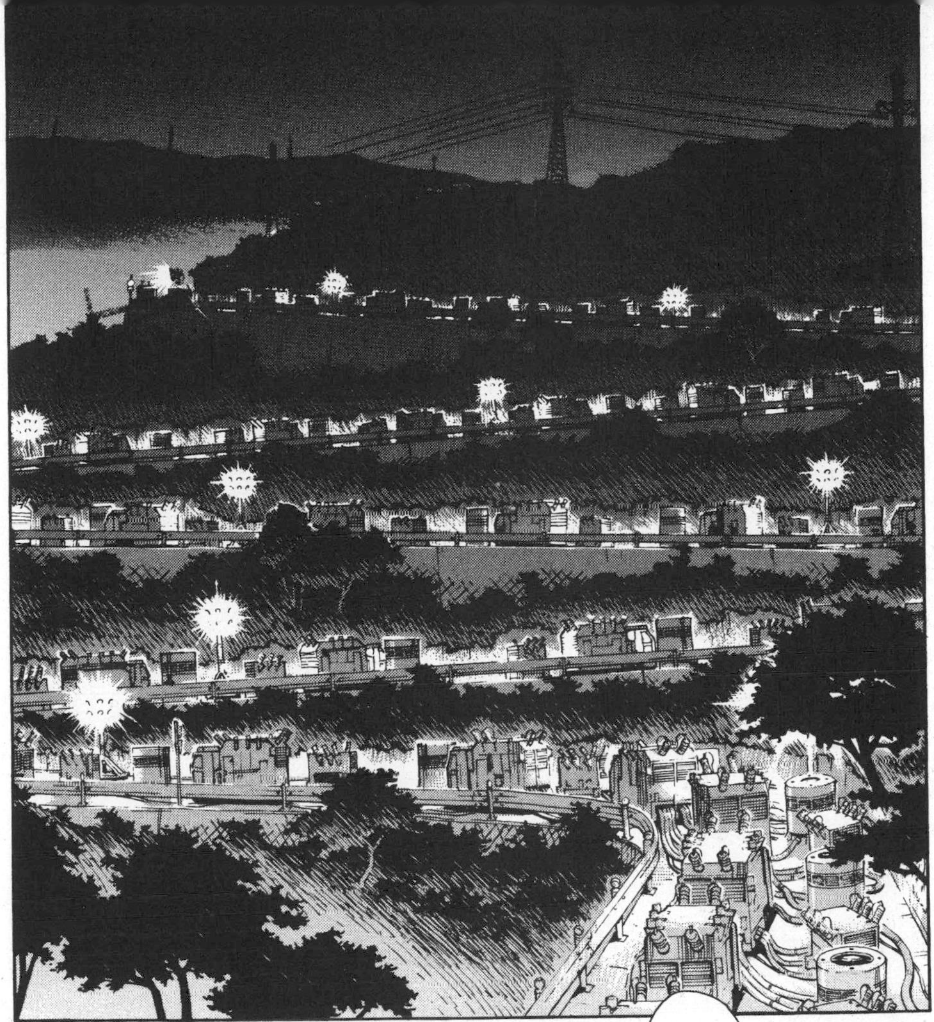

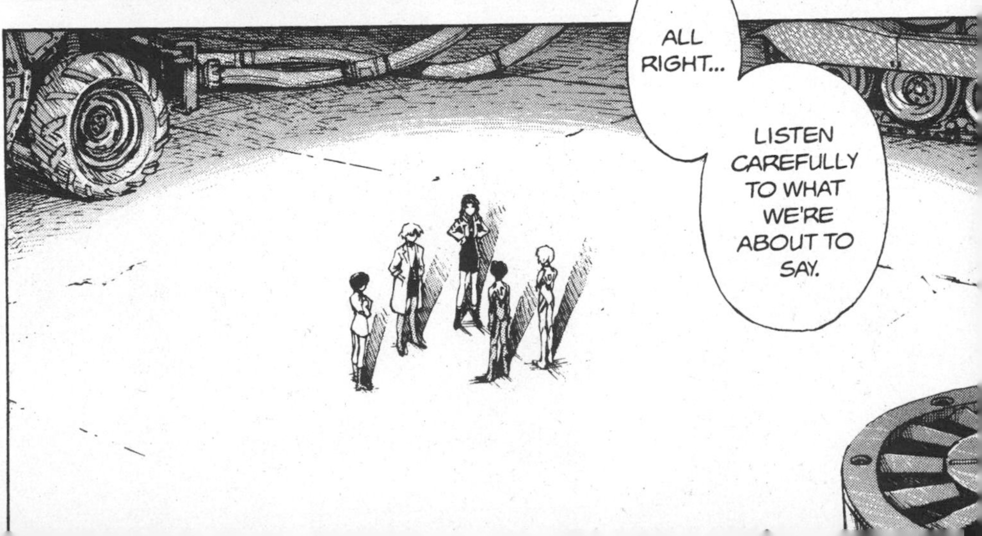
ALL RIGHT...
LISTEN CAREFULLY TO WHAT WE'RE ABOUT TO SAY.

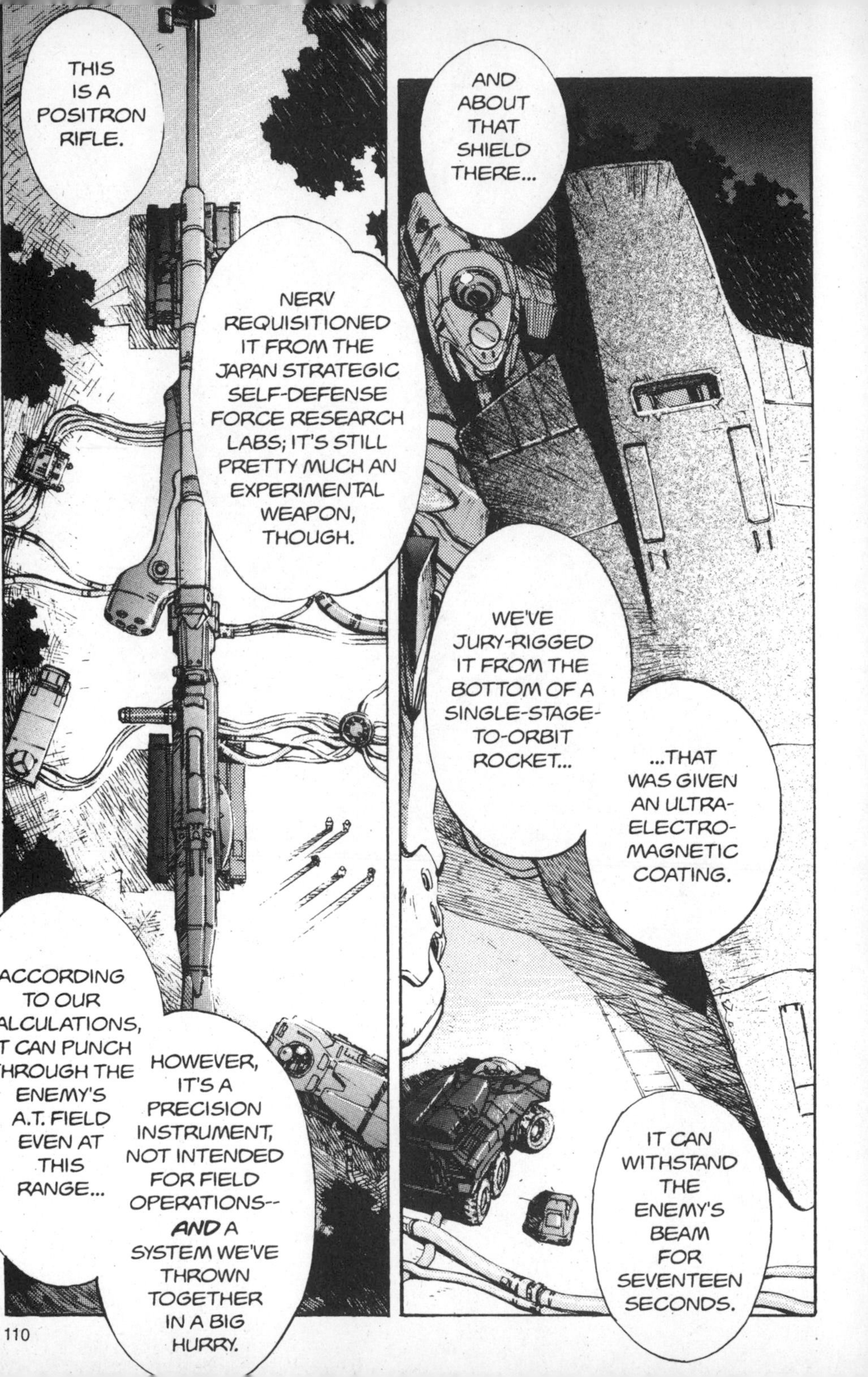
THIS IS A POSITRON RIFLE.
NERV REQUISITIONED IT FROM THE JAPAN STRATEGIC SELF-DEFENSE FORCE RESEARCH LABS; IT'S STILL PRETTY MUCH AN EXPERIMENTAL WEAPON, THOUGH.
ACCORDING TO OUR CALCULATIONS, IT CAN PUNCH THROUGH THE ENEMY'S A.T. FIELD EVEN AT THIS RANGE...
HOWEVER, IT'S A PRECISION INSTRUMENT, NOT INTENDED FOR FIELD OPERATIONS-- ***AND*** A SYSTEM WE'VE THROWN TOGETHER IN A BIG HURRY.
AND ABOUT THAT SHIELD THERE...
WE'VE JURY-RIGGED IT FROM THE BOTTOM OF A SINGLE-STAGE-TO-ORBIT ROCKET...
...THAT WAS GIVEN AN ULTRA-ELECTRO-MAGNETIC COATING.
IT CAN WITHSTAND THE ENEMY'S BEAM FOR SEVENTEEN SECONDS.

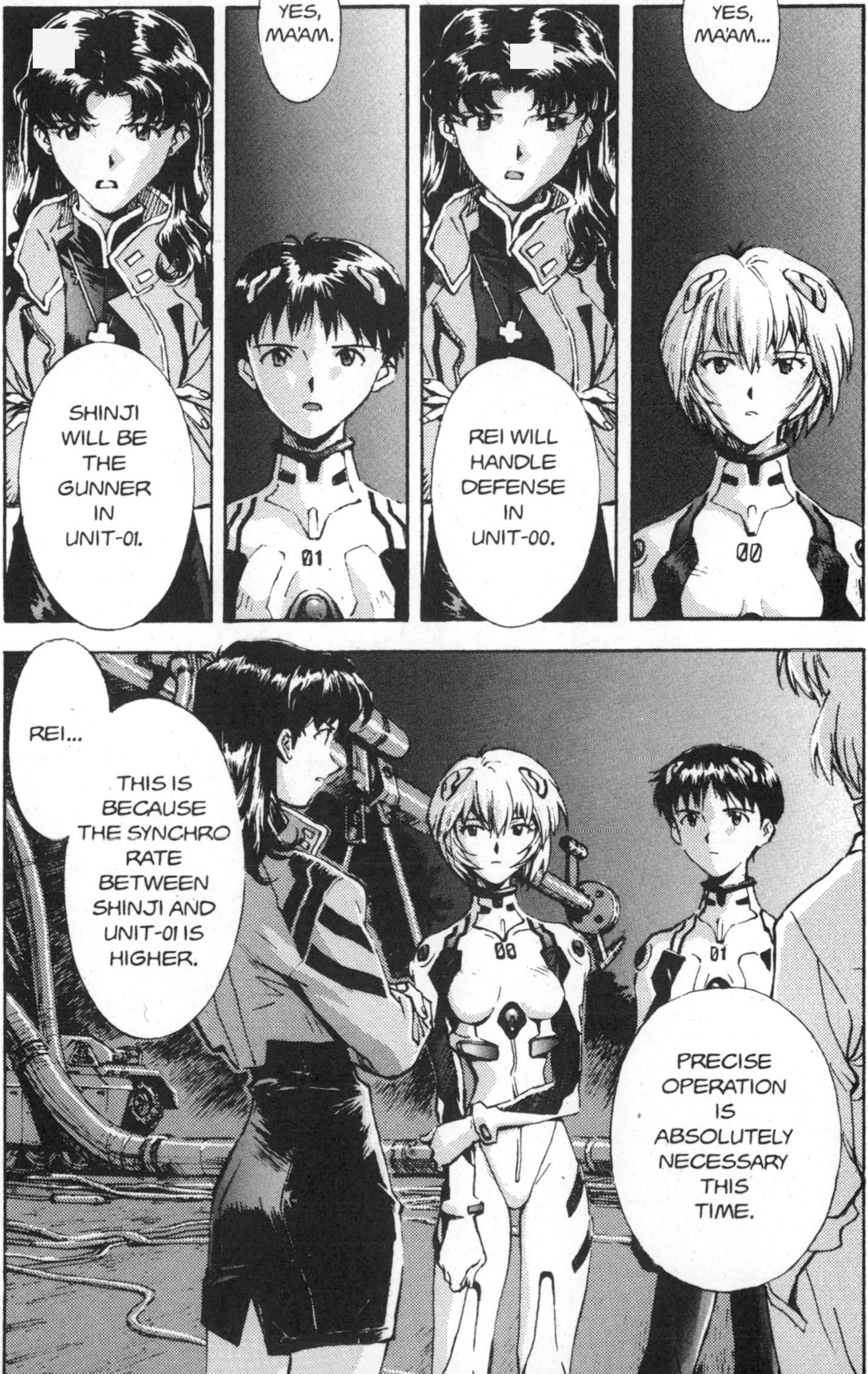
SHINJI WILL BE THE GUNNER IN UNIT-01.
YES, MA'AM.
REI WILL HANDLE DEFENSE IN UNIT-00.
YES, MA'AM...
REI... THIS IS BECAUSE THE SYNCHRO RATE BETWEEN SHINJI AND UNIT-01 IS HIGHER.
PRECISE OPERATION IS ABSOLUTELY NECESSARY THIS TIME.

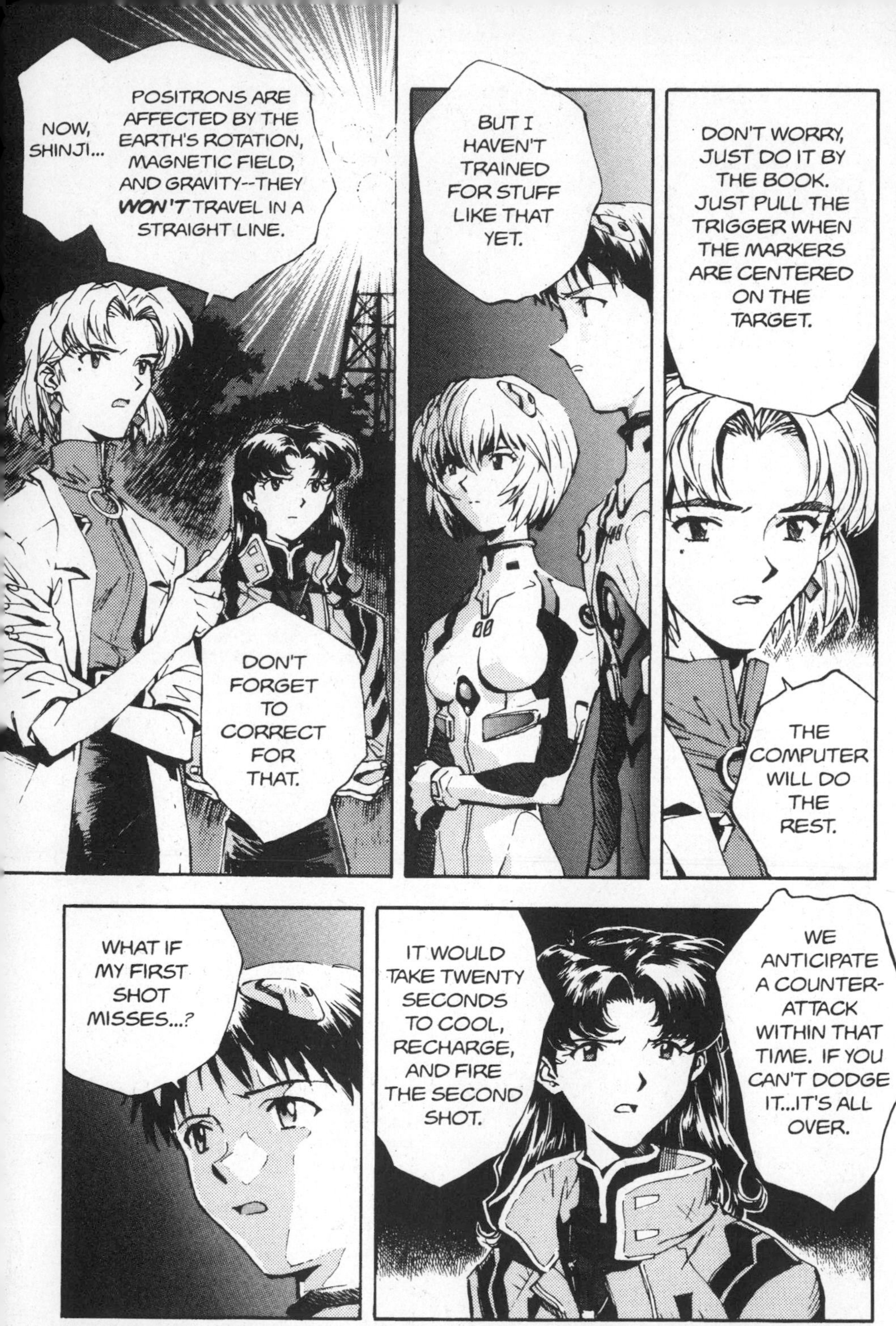
NOW, SHINJI...
POSITRONS ARE AFFECTED BY THE EARTH'S ROTATION, MAGNETIC FIELD, AND GRAVITY--THEY ***WON'T*** TRAVEL IN A STRAIGHT LINE.
DON'T FORGET TO CORRECT FOR THAT.
BUT I HAVEN'T TRAINED FOR STUFF LIKE THAT YET.
DON'T WORRY, JUST DO IT BY THE BOOK. JUST PULL THE TRIGGER WHEN THE MARKERS ARE CENTERED ON THE TARGET.
THE COMPUTER WILL DO THE REST.
WHAT IF MY FIRST SHOT MISSES...?
IT WOULD TAKE TWENTY SECONDS TO COOL, RECHARGE, AND FIRE THE SECOND SHOT.
WE ANTICIPATE A COUNTER-ATTACK WITHIN THAT TIME. IF YOU CAN'T DODGE IT...IT'S ALL OVER.

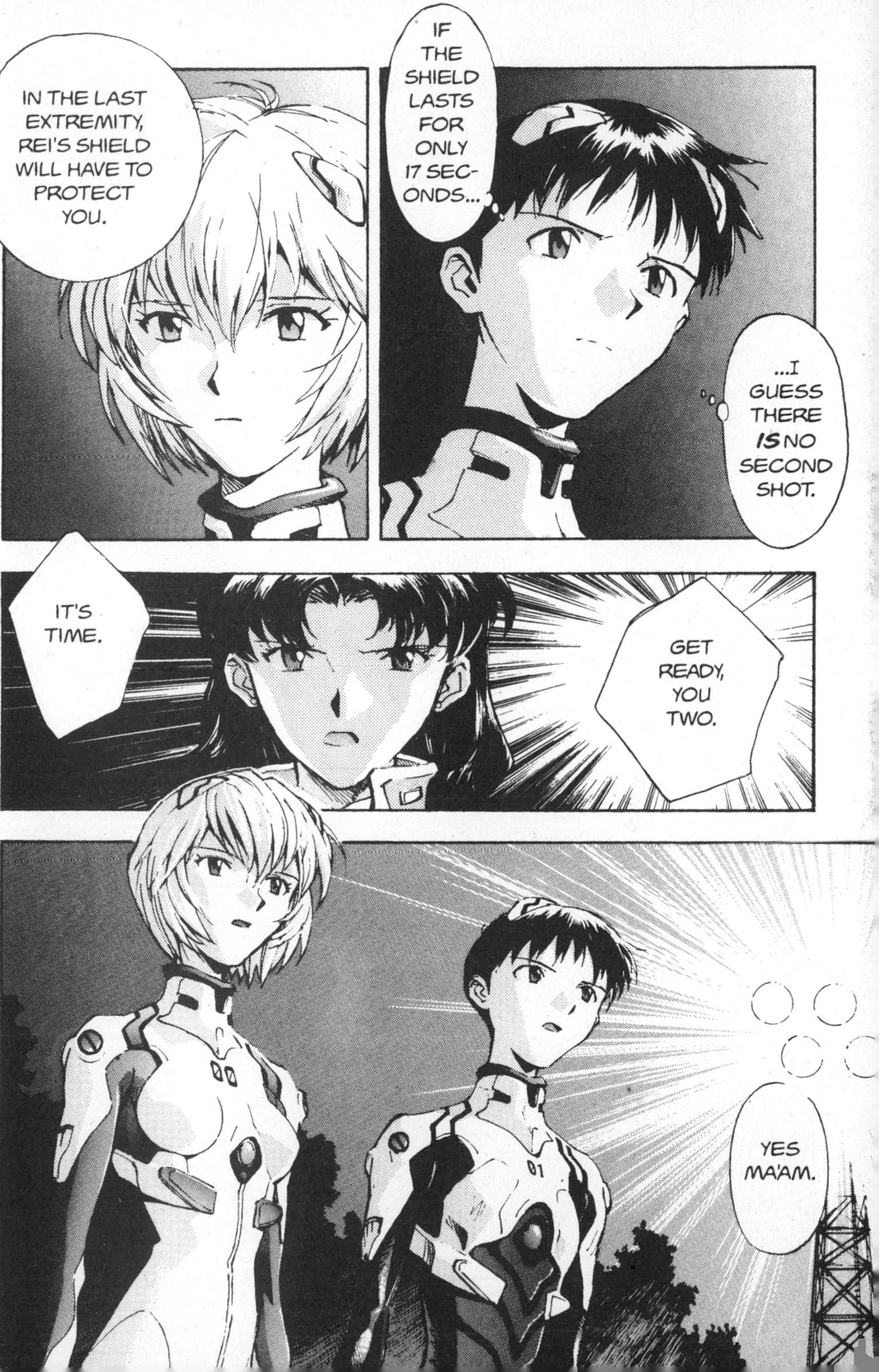
IN THE LAST EXTREMITY, REI'S SHIELD WILL HAVE TO PROTECT YOU.
IF THE SHIELD LASTS FOR ONLY 17 SECONDS...
...I GUESS THERE IS NO SECOND SHOT.
IT'S TIME.
GET READY, YOU TWO.
YES MA'AM.

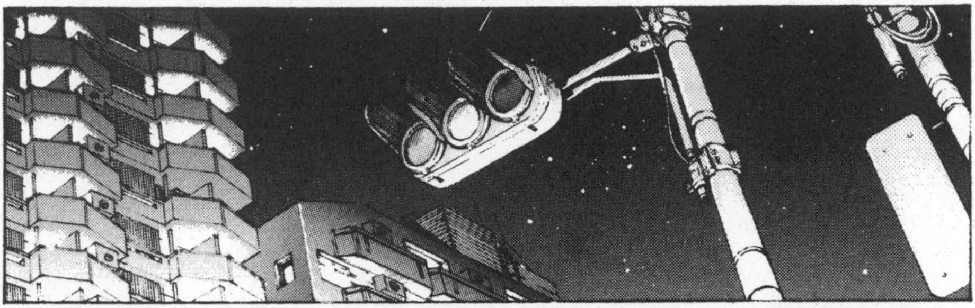

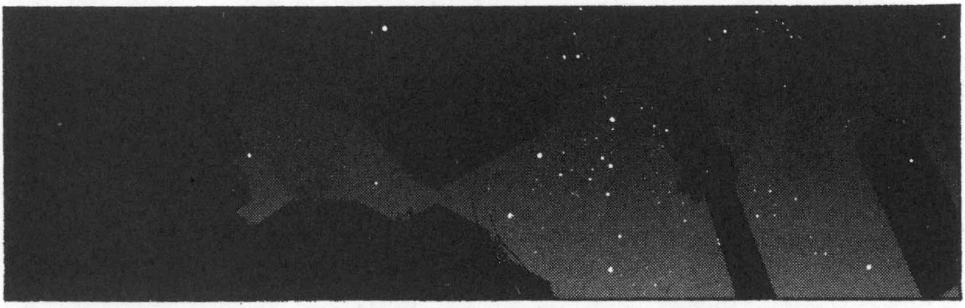

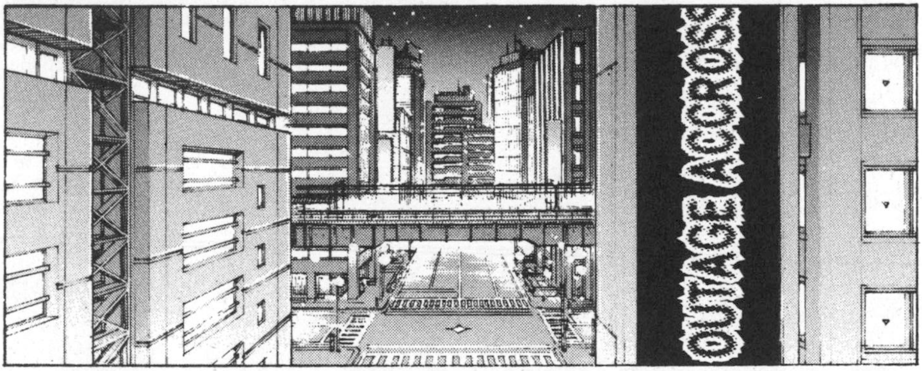
OUTAGE ACCOROSS

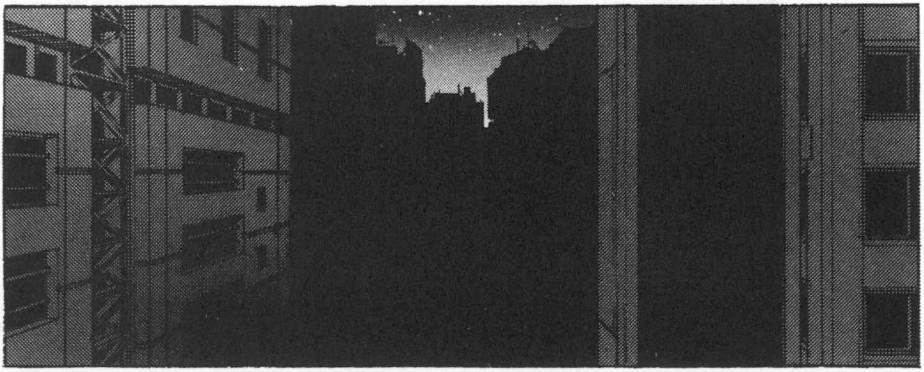

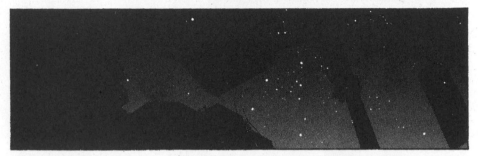

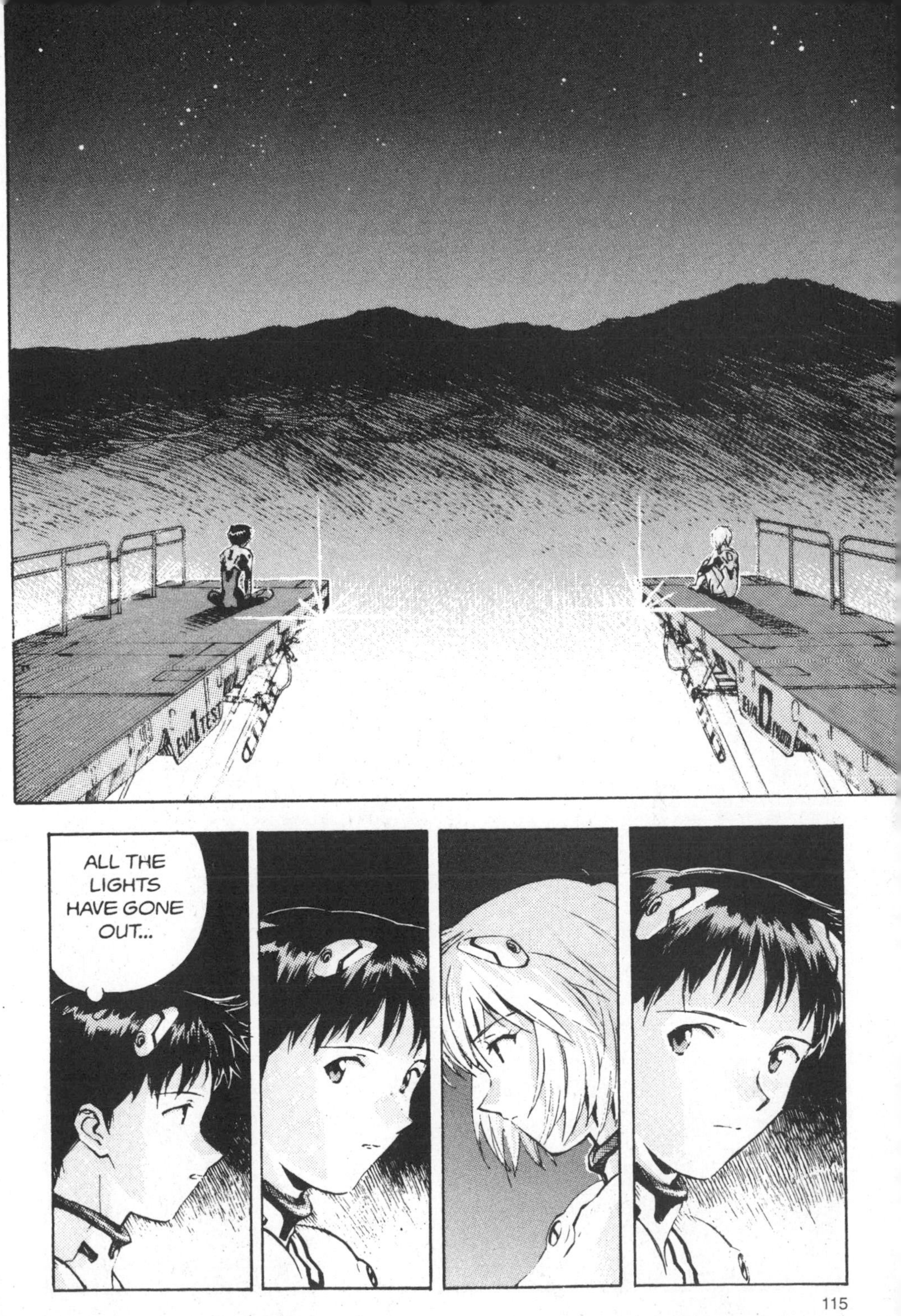
ALL THE LIGHTS HAVE GONE OUT...

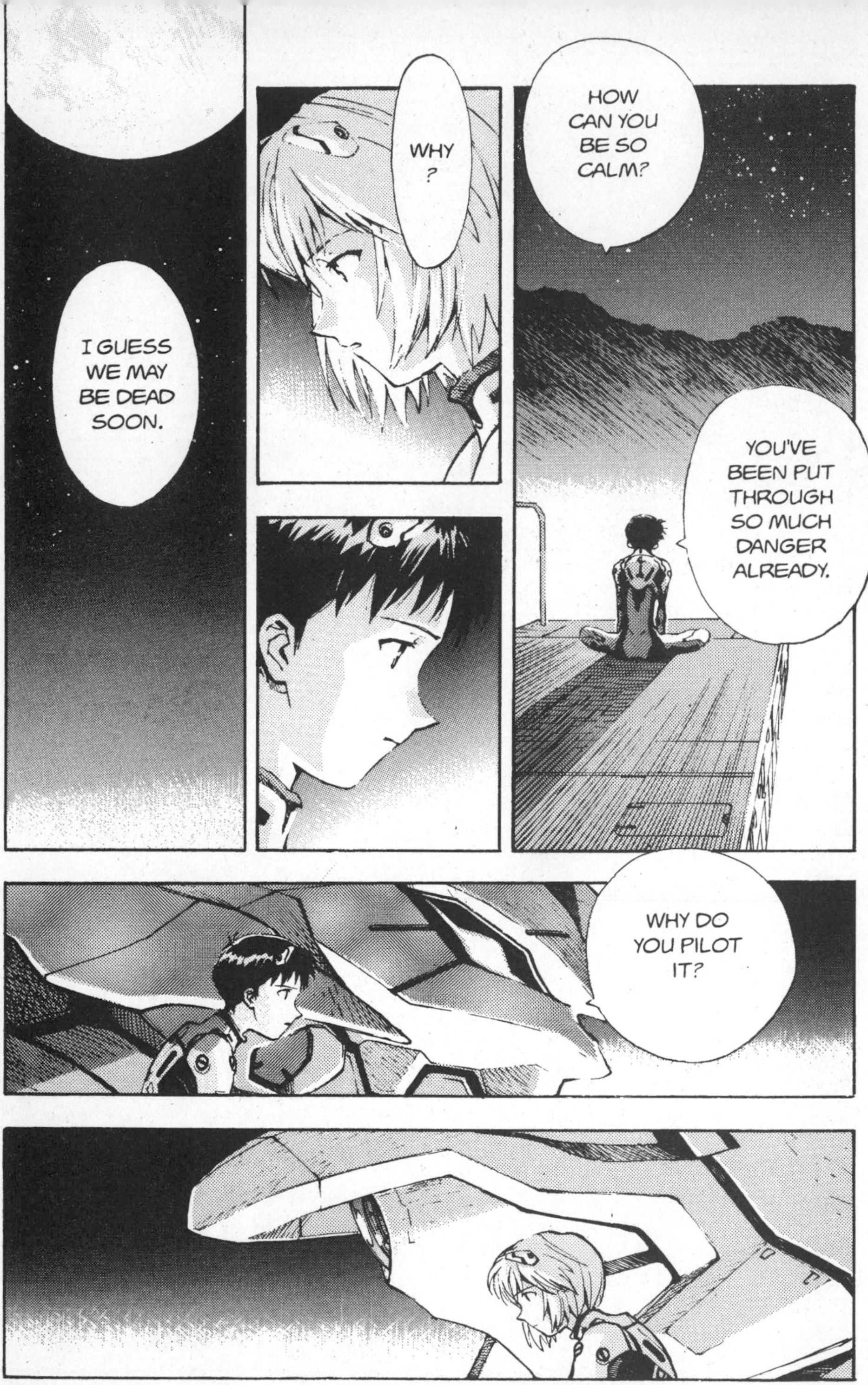
I GUESS WE MAY BE DEAD SOON.
WHY ?
HOW CAN YOU BE SO CALM?
YOU'VE BEEN PUT THROUGH SO MUCH DANGER ALREADY.
WHY DO YOU PILOT IT?

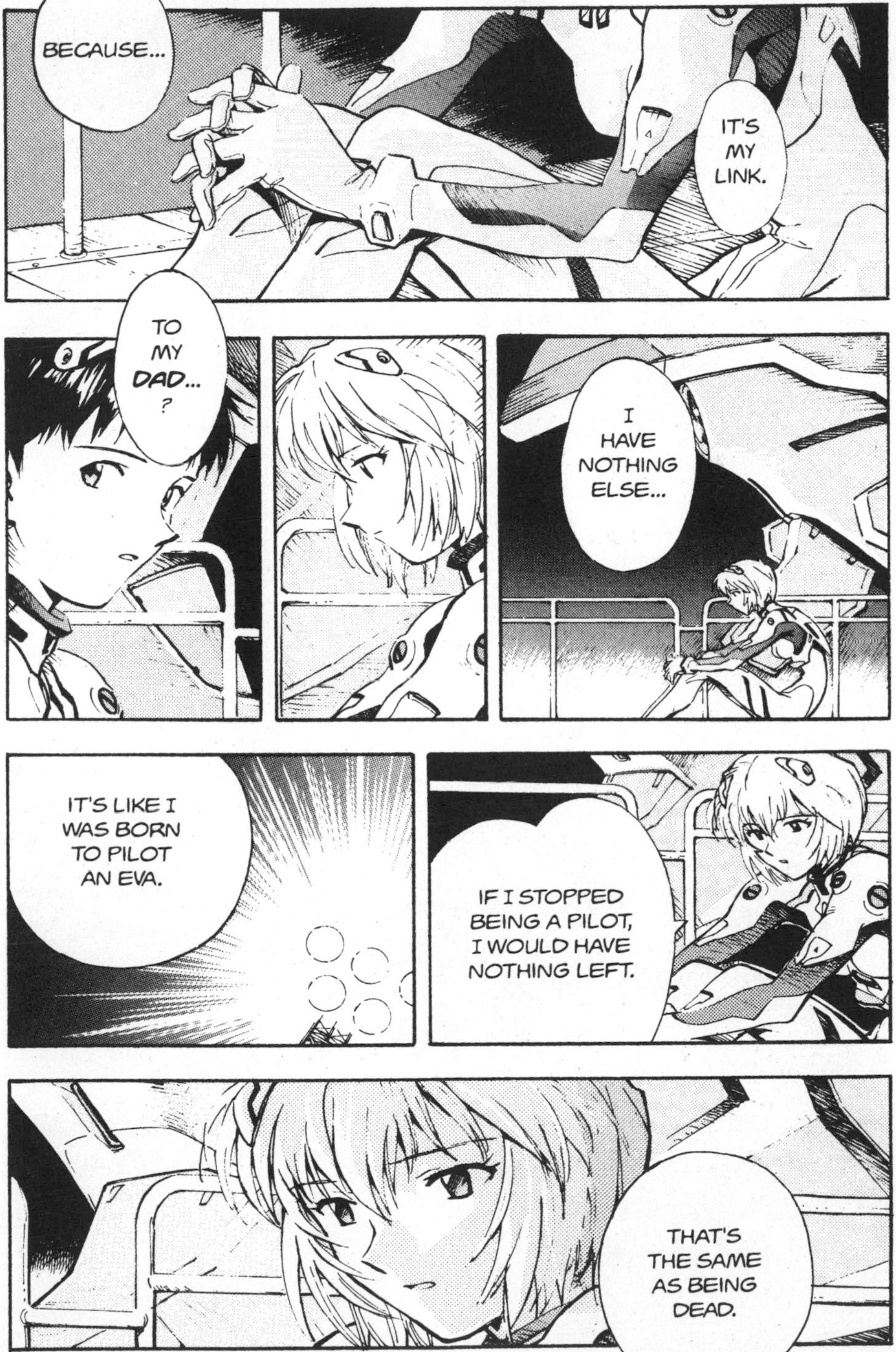
BECAUSE...
IT'S MY LINK.
TO MY DAD... ?
I HAVE NOTHING ELSE...
IT'S LIKE I WAS BORN TO PILOT AN EVA.
IF I STOPPED BEING A PILOT, I WOULD HAVE NOTHING LEFT.
THAT'S THE SAME AS BEING DEAD.

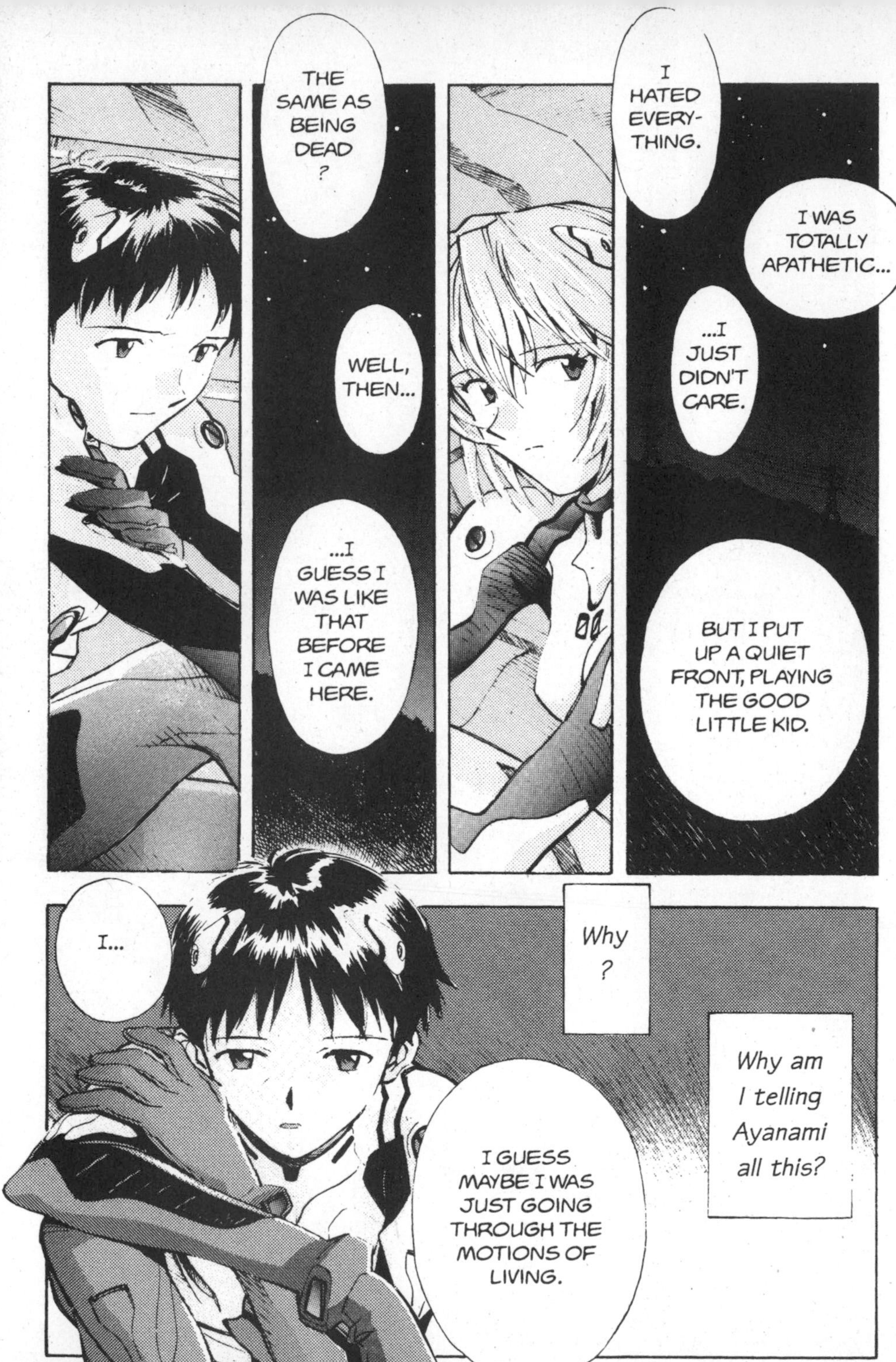
THE SAME AS BEING DEAD ?
WELL, THEN...
...I GUESS I WAS LIKE THAT BEFORE I CAME HERE.
I HATED EVERY-THING.
I WAS TOTALLY APATHETIC...
...I JUST DIDN'T CARE.
BUT I PUT UP A QUIET FRONT, PLAYING THE GOOD LITTLE KID.
I...
Why ?
Why am I telling Ayanami all this?
I GUESS MAYBE I WAS JUST GOING THROUGH THE MOTIONS OF LIVING.

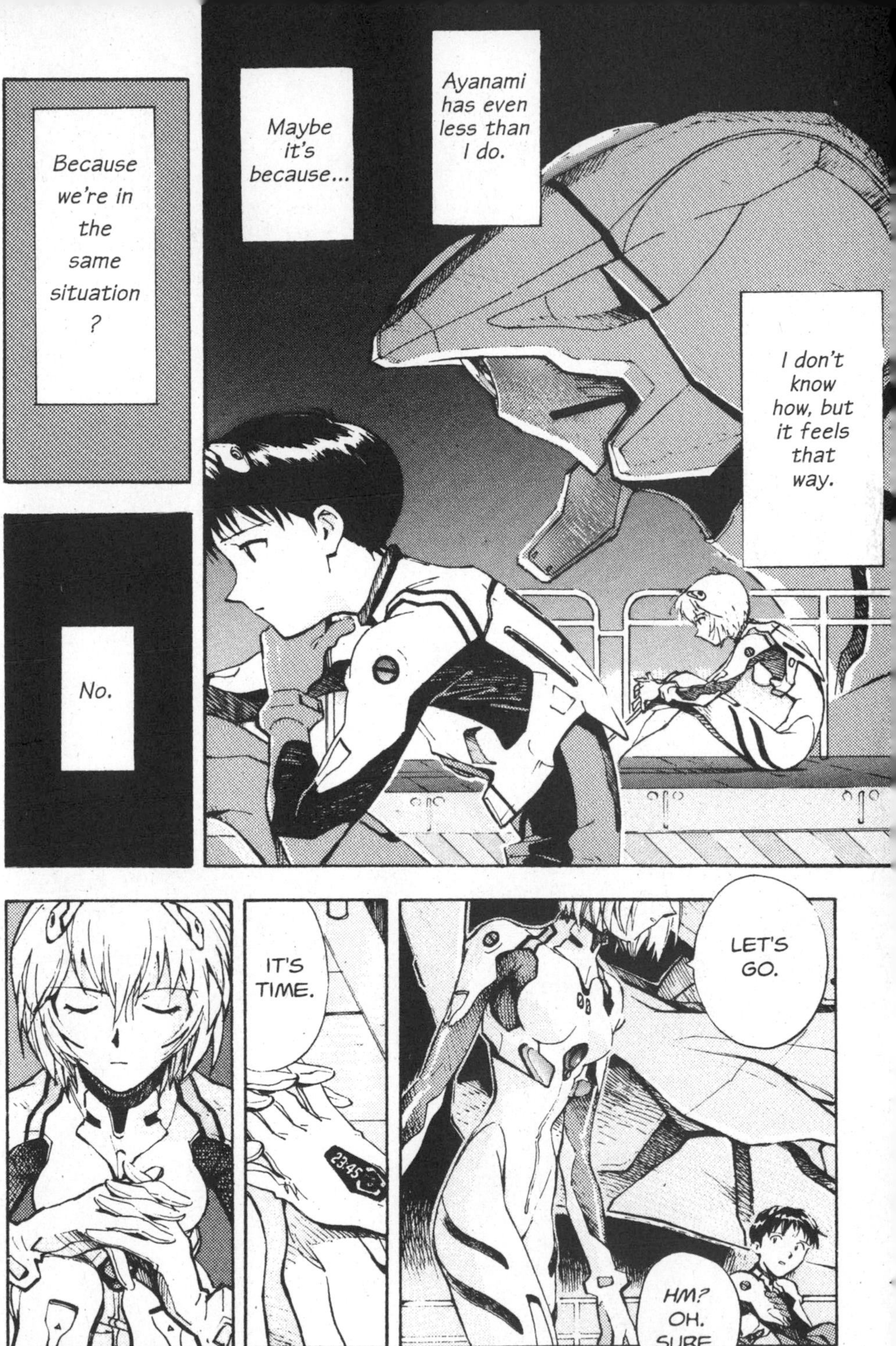
Because we're in the same situation ?
No.
Maybe it's because...
Ayanami has even less than I do.
I don't know how, but it feels that way.
IT'S TIME.
LET'S GO.
HM? OH. SURE.

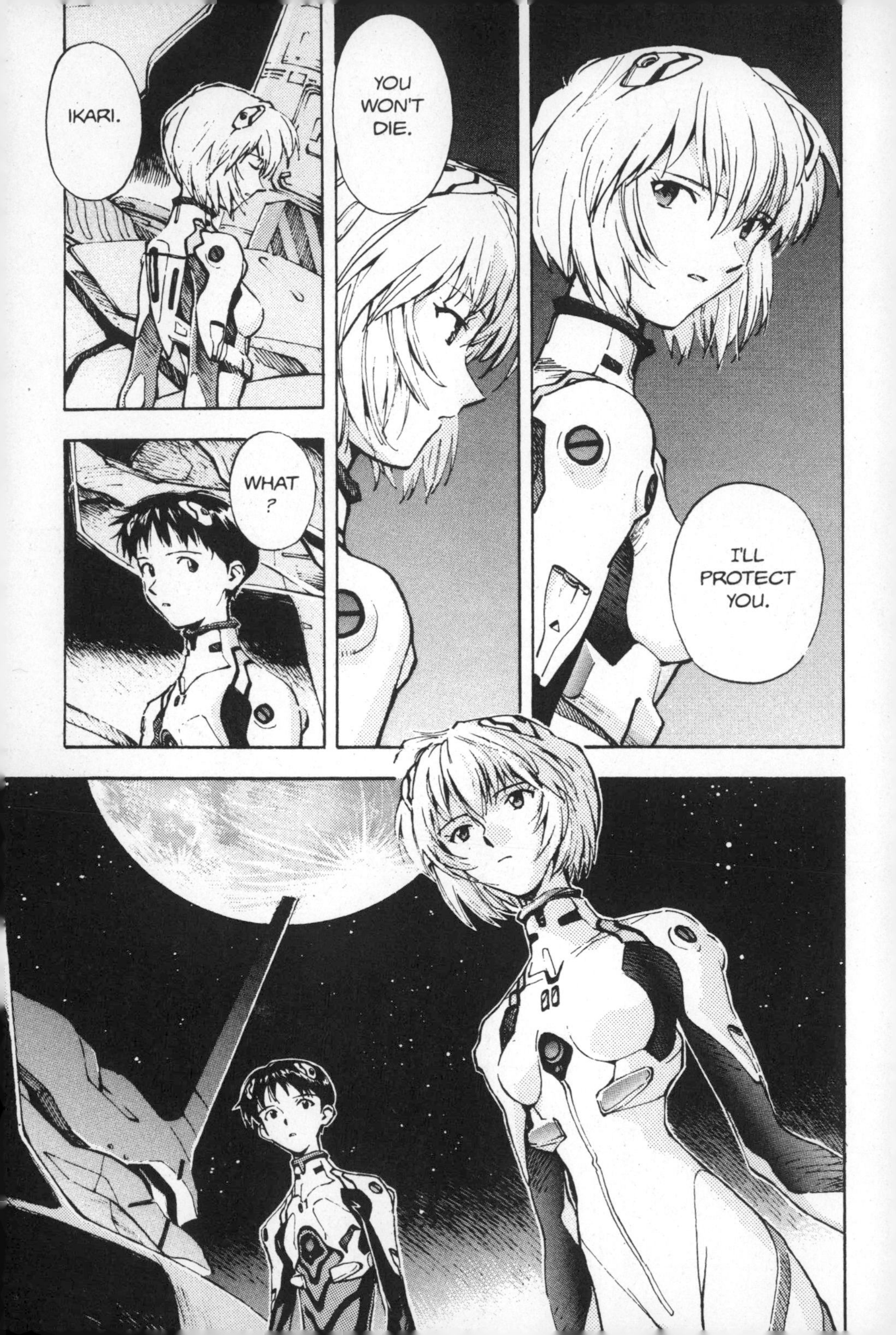
IKARI.
YOU WON'T DIE.
WHAT ?
I'LL PROTECT YOU.

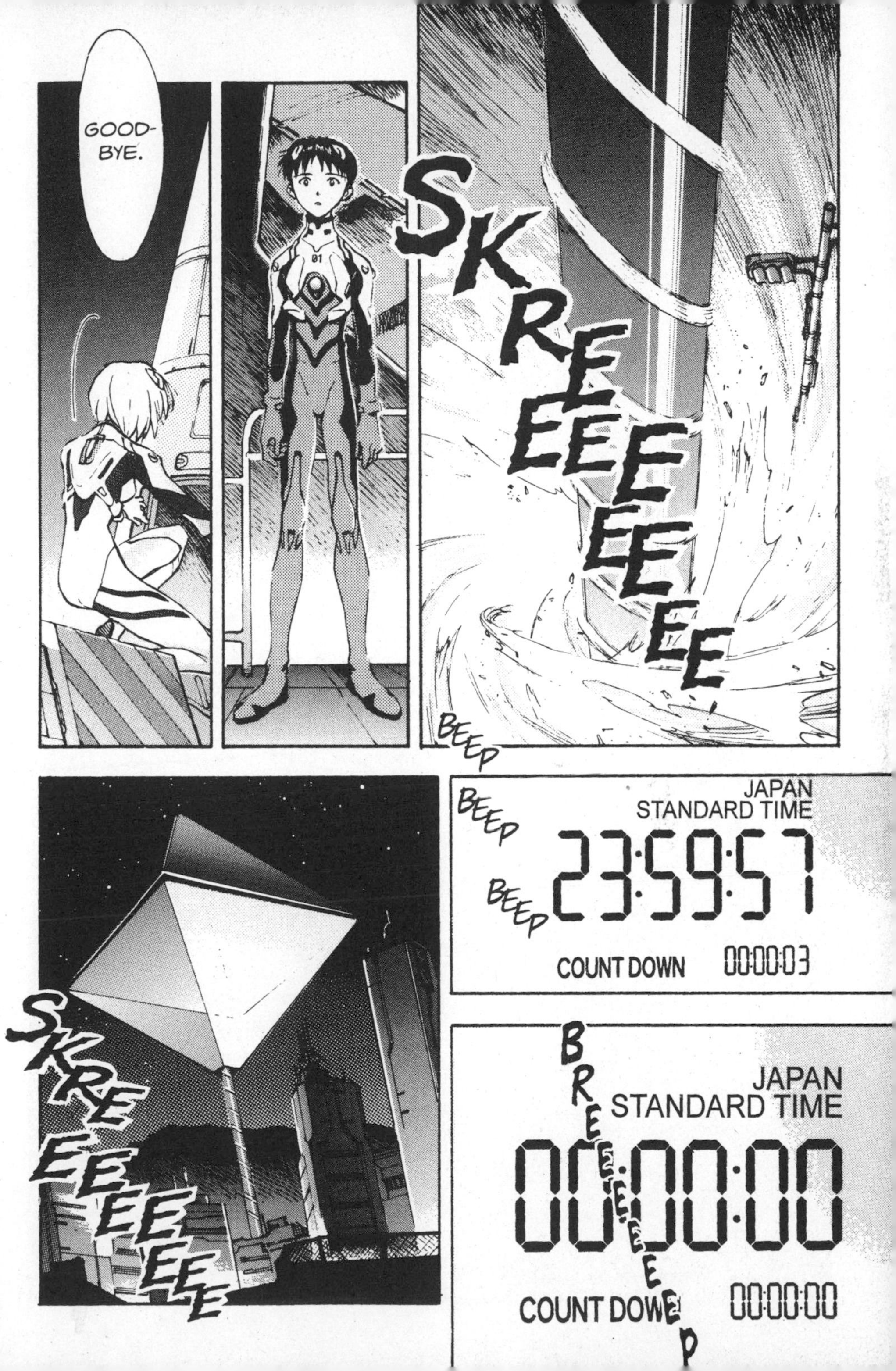
GOOD-BYE.
SKREEEEEEEEEE
BEEP
BEEP
BEEP
SKREEEEEEEEE
JAPAN STANDARD TIME
23:59:57
COUNT DOWN
00:00:03
BREEEEEEEP
JAPAN STANDARD TIME
00:00:00
COUNT DOWN
00:00:00

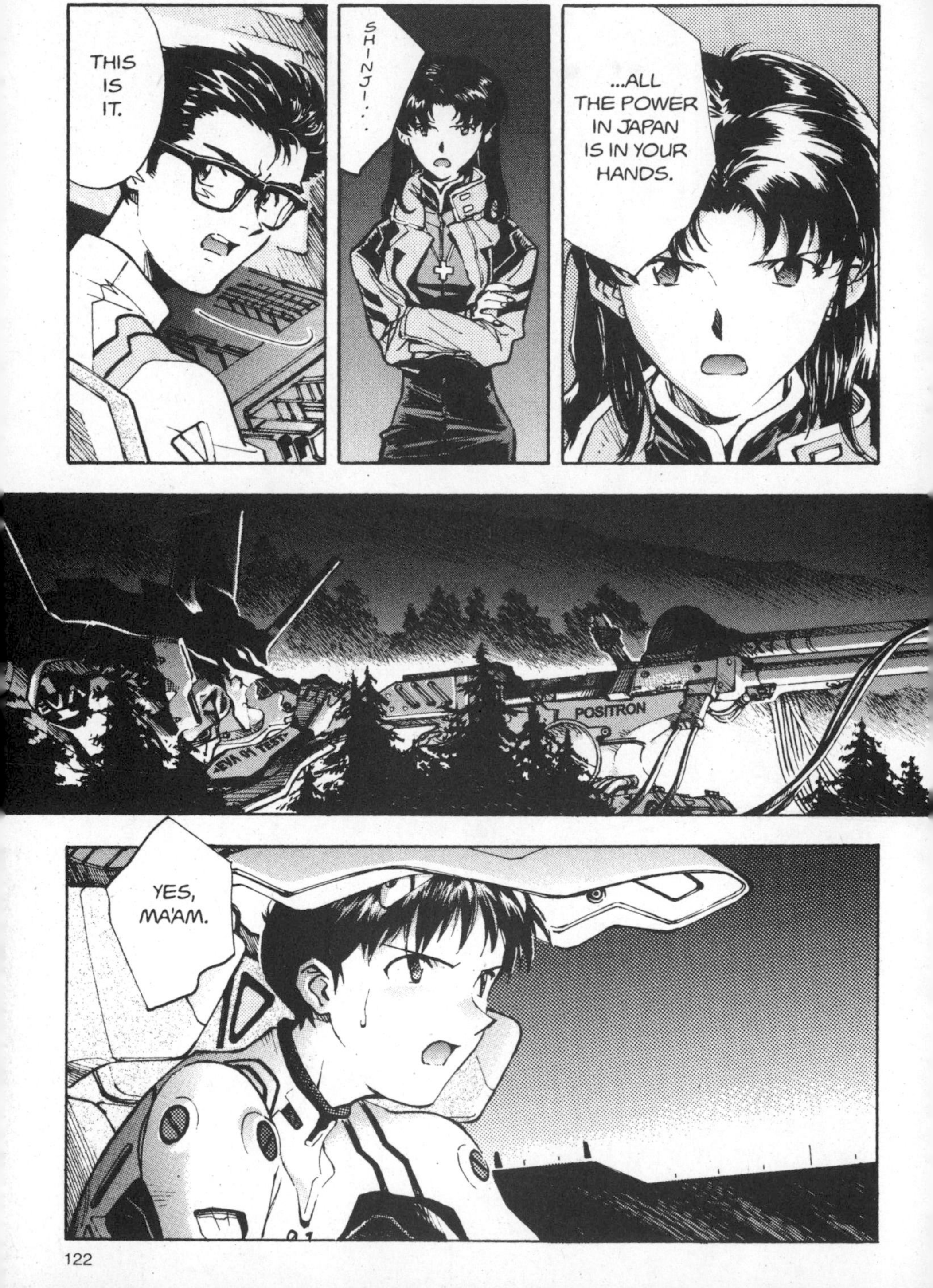
THIS IS IT.
SHINJI...
...ALL THE POWER IN JAPAN IS IN YOUR HANDS.
POSITRON
EVA 01 TEST
YES, MA'AM.

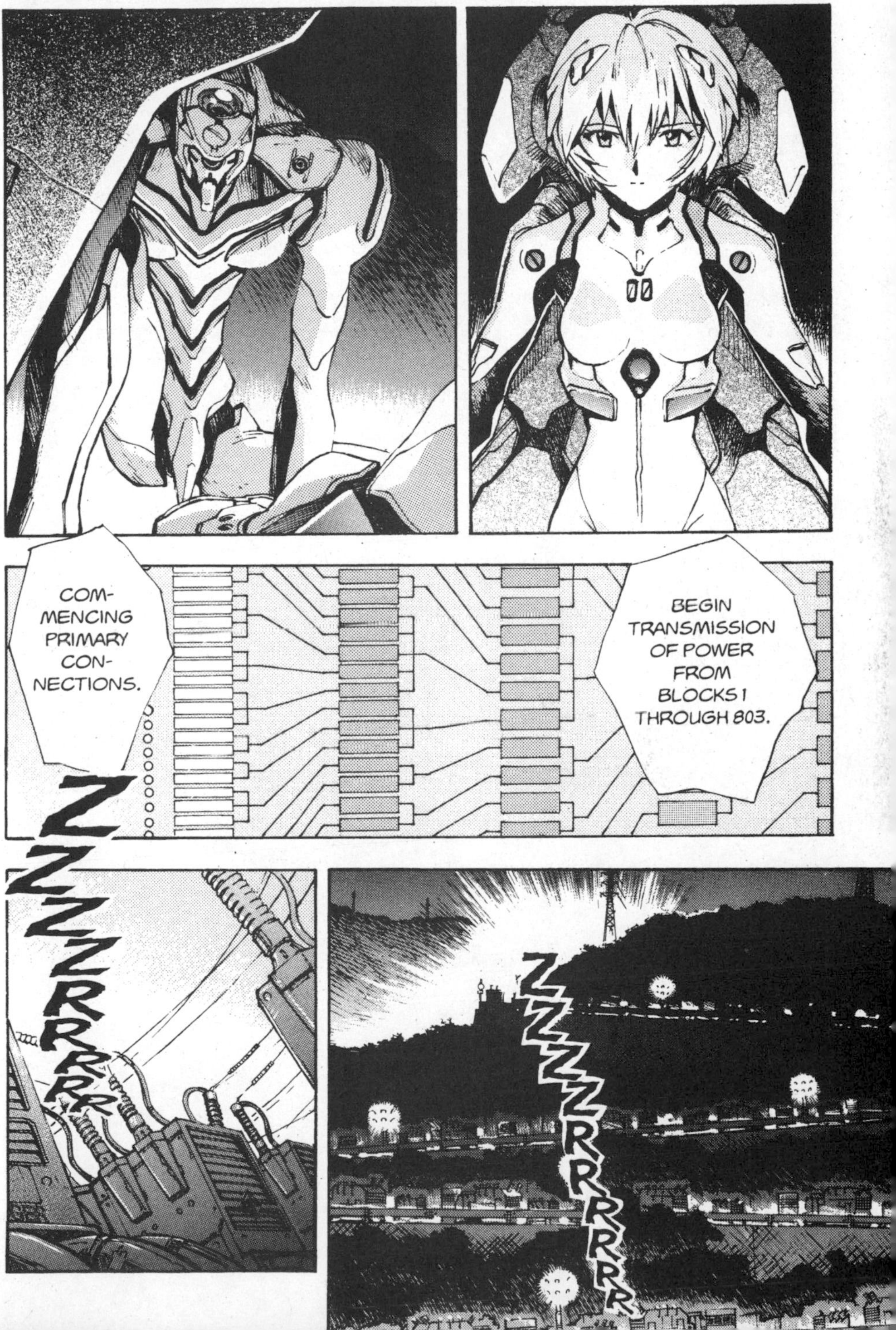
COM-
MENCING
PRIMARY
CON-
NECTIONS.
BEGIN
TRANSMISSION
OF POWER
FROM
BLOCKS 1
THROUGH 803.
ZZZZRRRRR
ZZZZZRRRRR

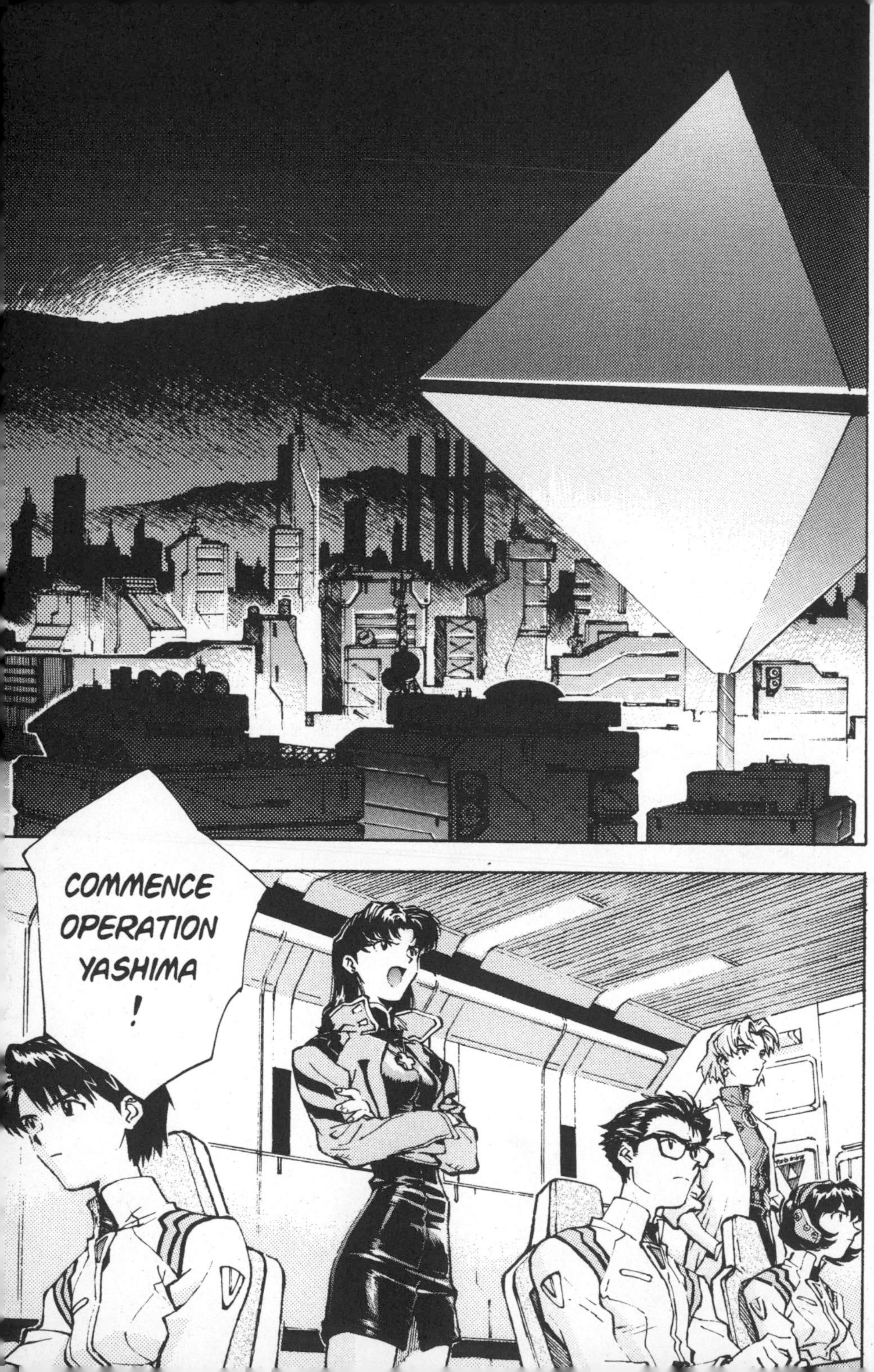
COMMENCE OPERATION YASHIMA !

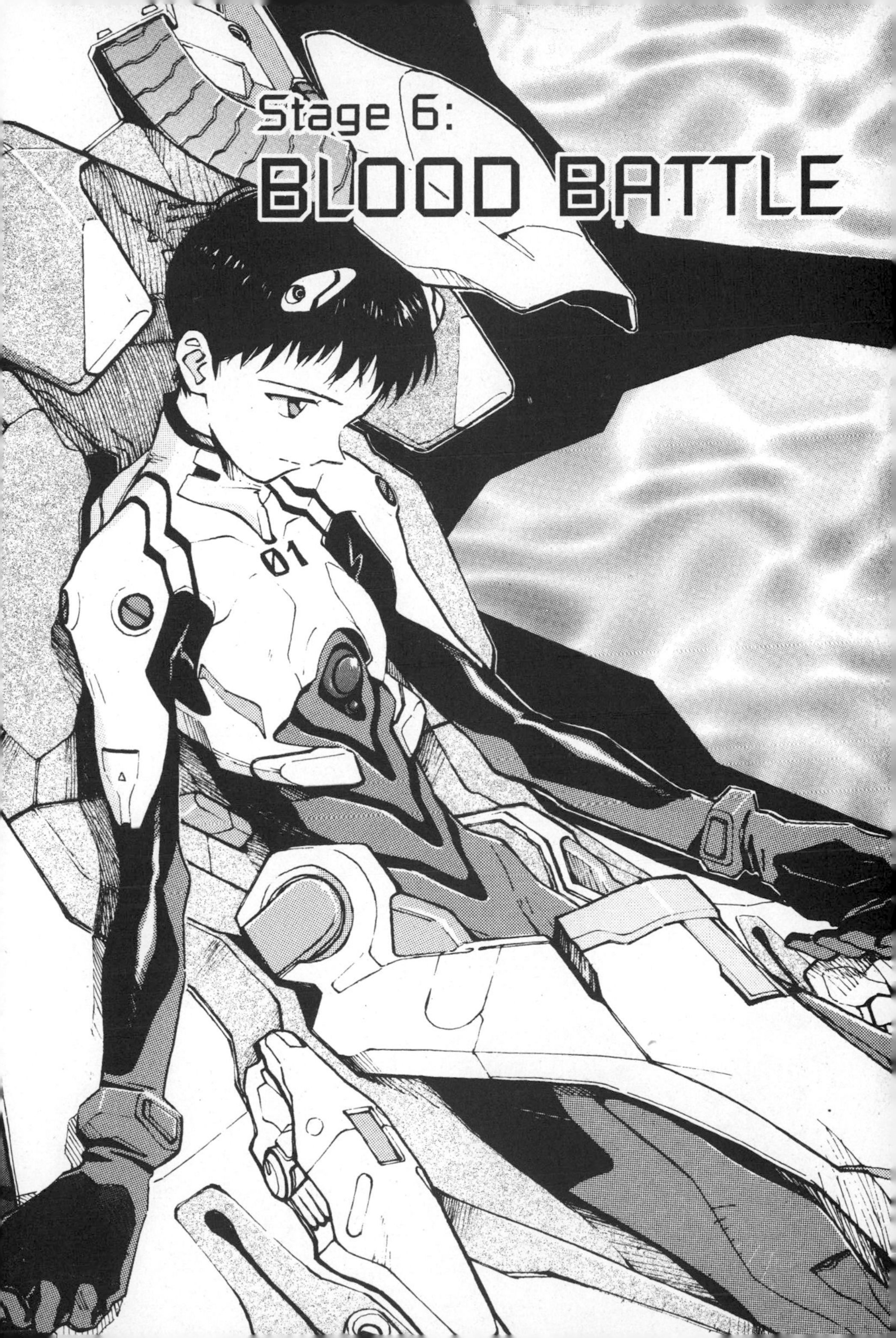
Stage 6:
BLOOD BATTLE
01

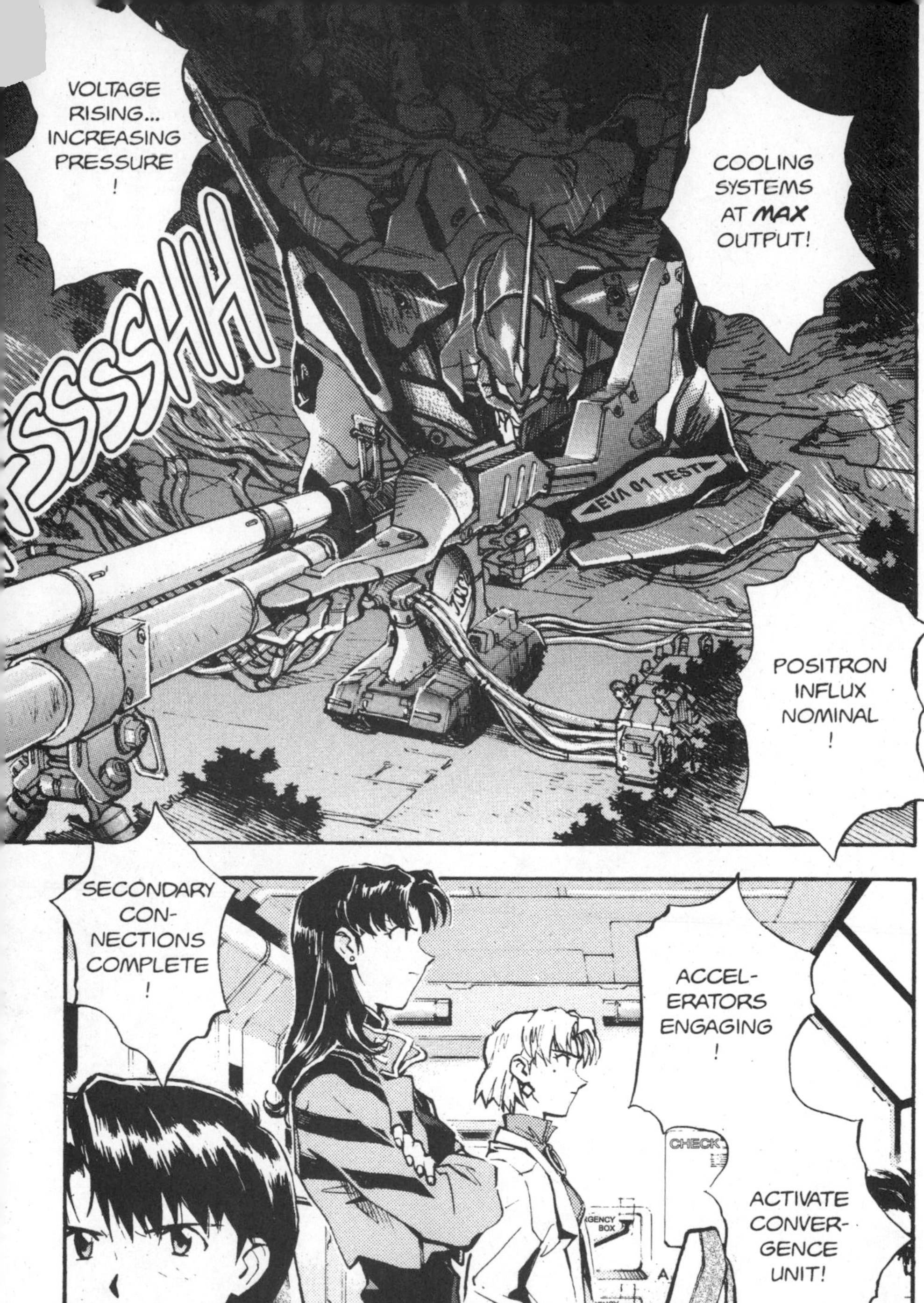
VOLTAGE RISING... INCREASING PRESSURE!
COOLING SYSTEMS AT MAX OUTPUT!
SSSSHH
EVA 01 TEST
POSITRON INFLUX NOMINAL!
SECONDARY CON-NECTIONS COMPLETE!
ACCEL-ERATORS ENGAGING!
CHECK
ACTIVATE CONVER-GENCE UNIT!

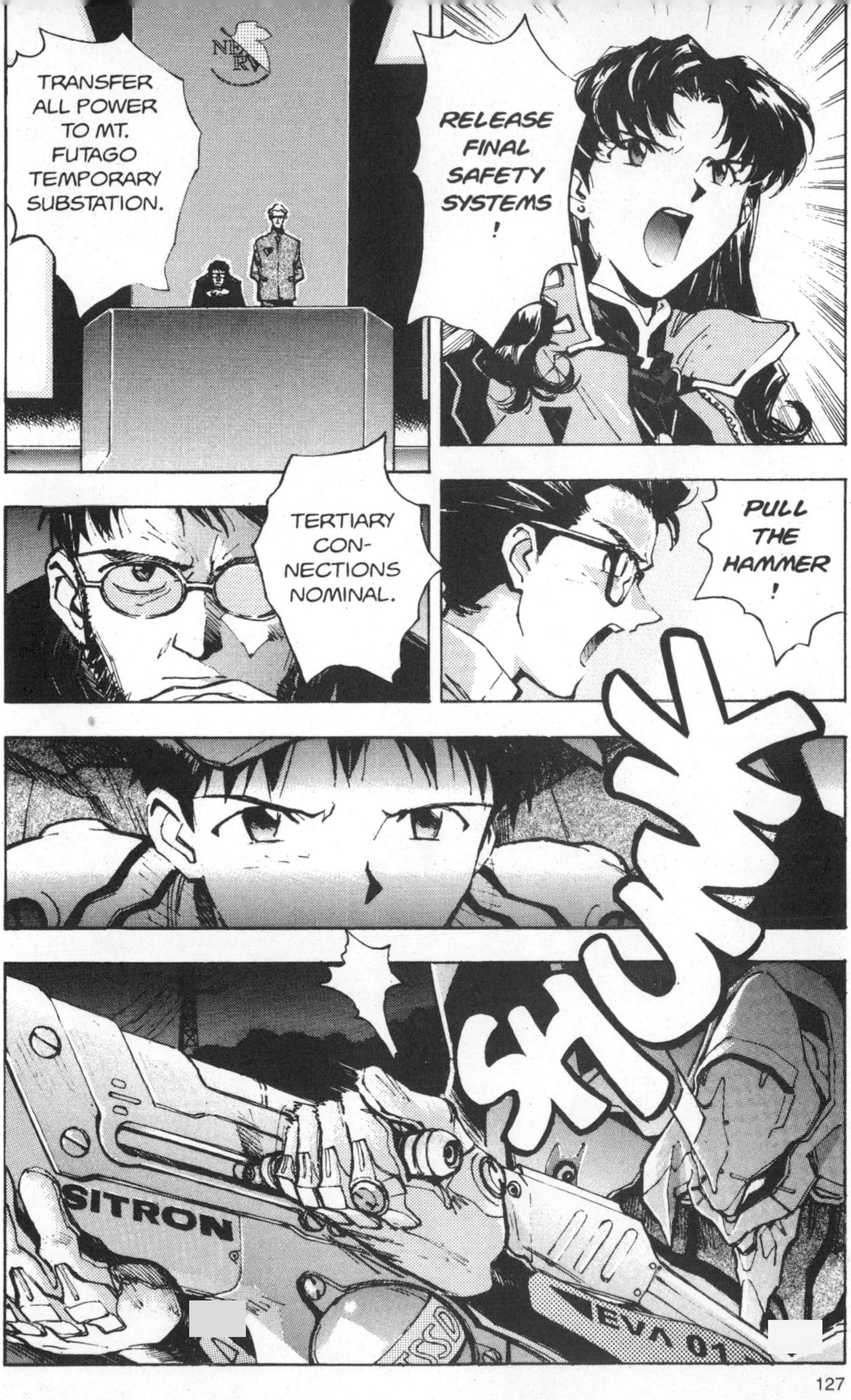
TRANSFER ALL POWER TO MT. FUTAGO TEMPORARY SUBSTATION.
RELEASE FINAL SAFETY SYSTEMS!
TERTIARY CON-NECTIONS NOMINAL.
PULL THE HAMMER!
SHUCK
SITRON
EVA 01

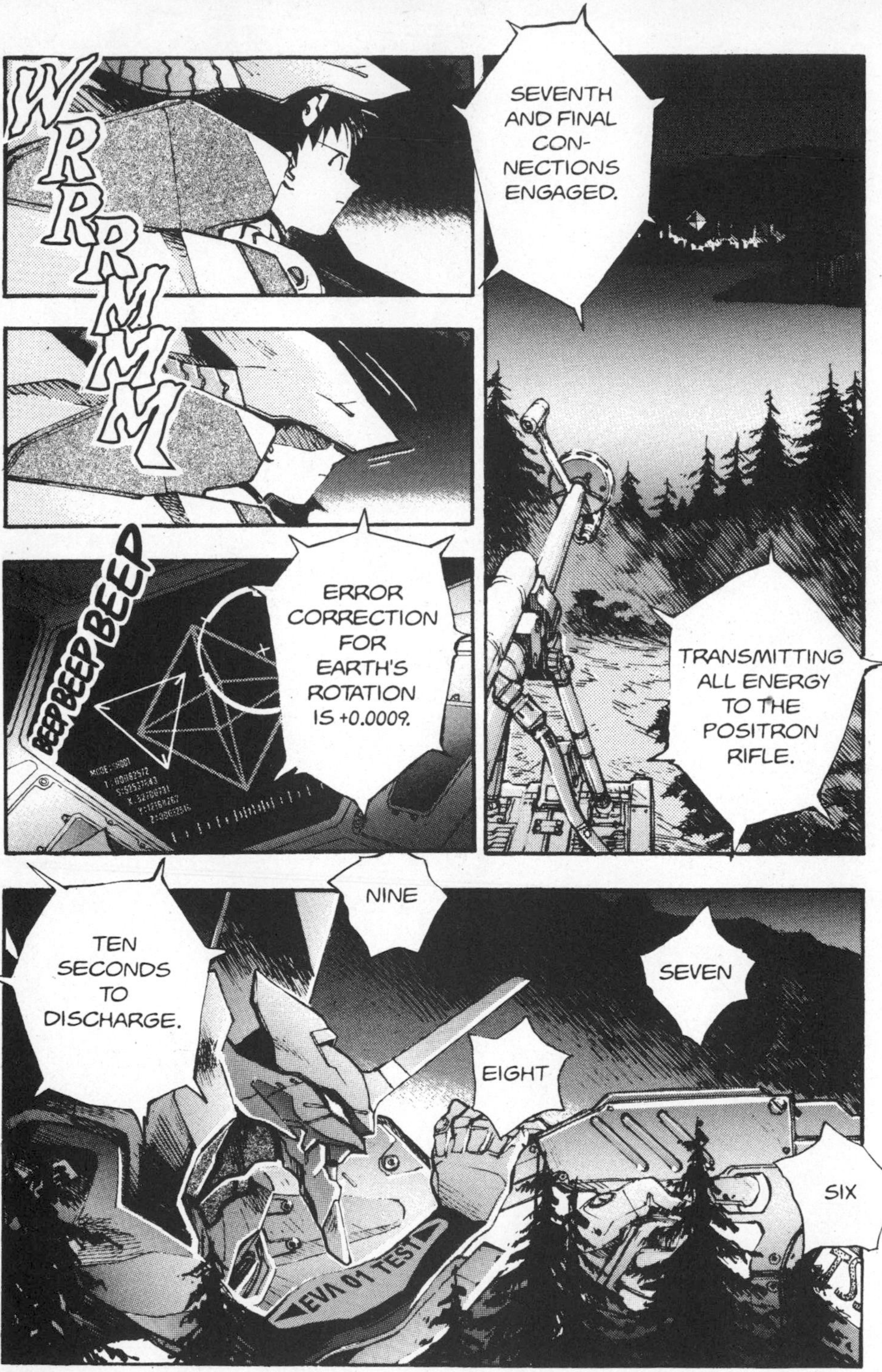

WRRRMMM
BEEPBEEPBEEP
ERROR CORRECTION FOR EARTH'S ROTATION IS +0.0009.
SEVENTH AND FINAL CON-NECTIONS ENGAGED.
TRANSMITTING ALL ENERGY TO THE POSITRON RIFLE.
TEN SECONDS TO DISCHARGE.
NINE
EIGHT
SEVEN
SIX
EVA 01 TEST

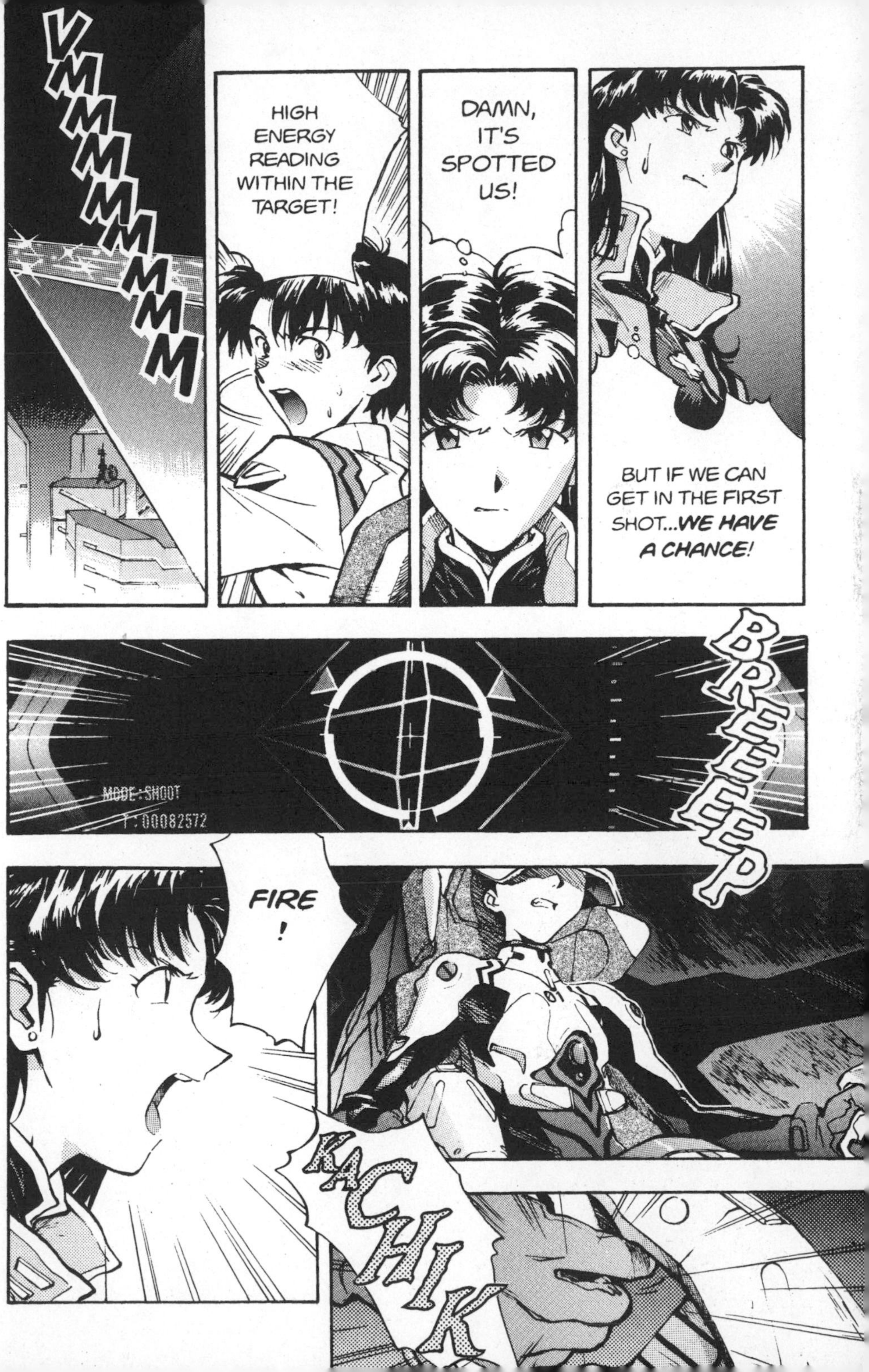
VMMMMMMMMM
HIGH ENERGY READING WITHIN THE TARGET!
DAMN, IT'S SPOTTED US!
BUT IF WE CAN GET IN THE FIRST SHOT...**WE HAVE A CHANCE!**
MODE:SHOOT
T:00082572
BREEEEP
FIRE!
KACHIK

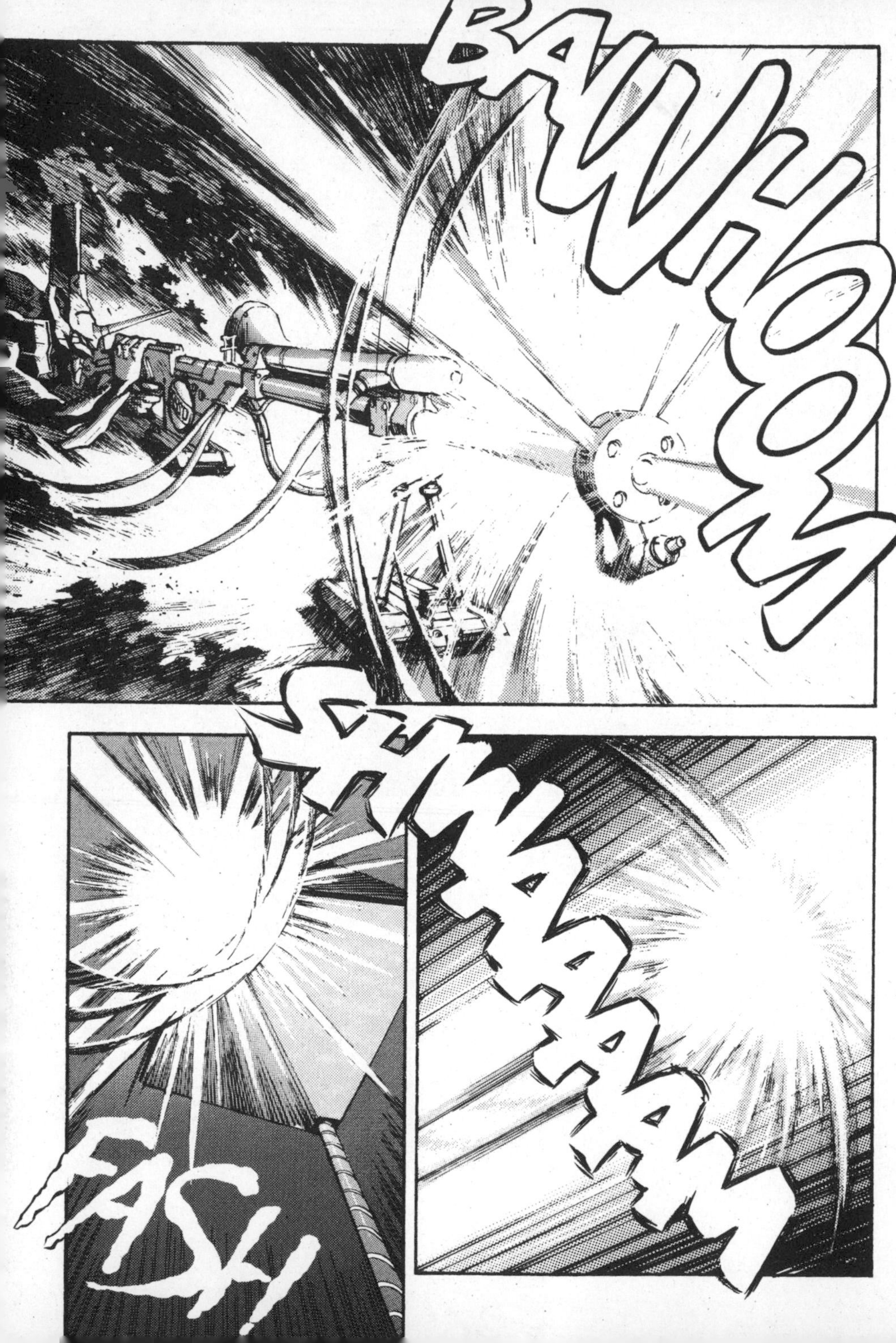
BAUHOOM
SHWAAAAM
FASH!

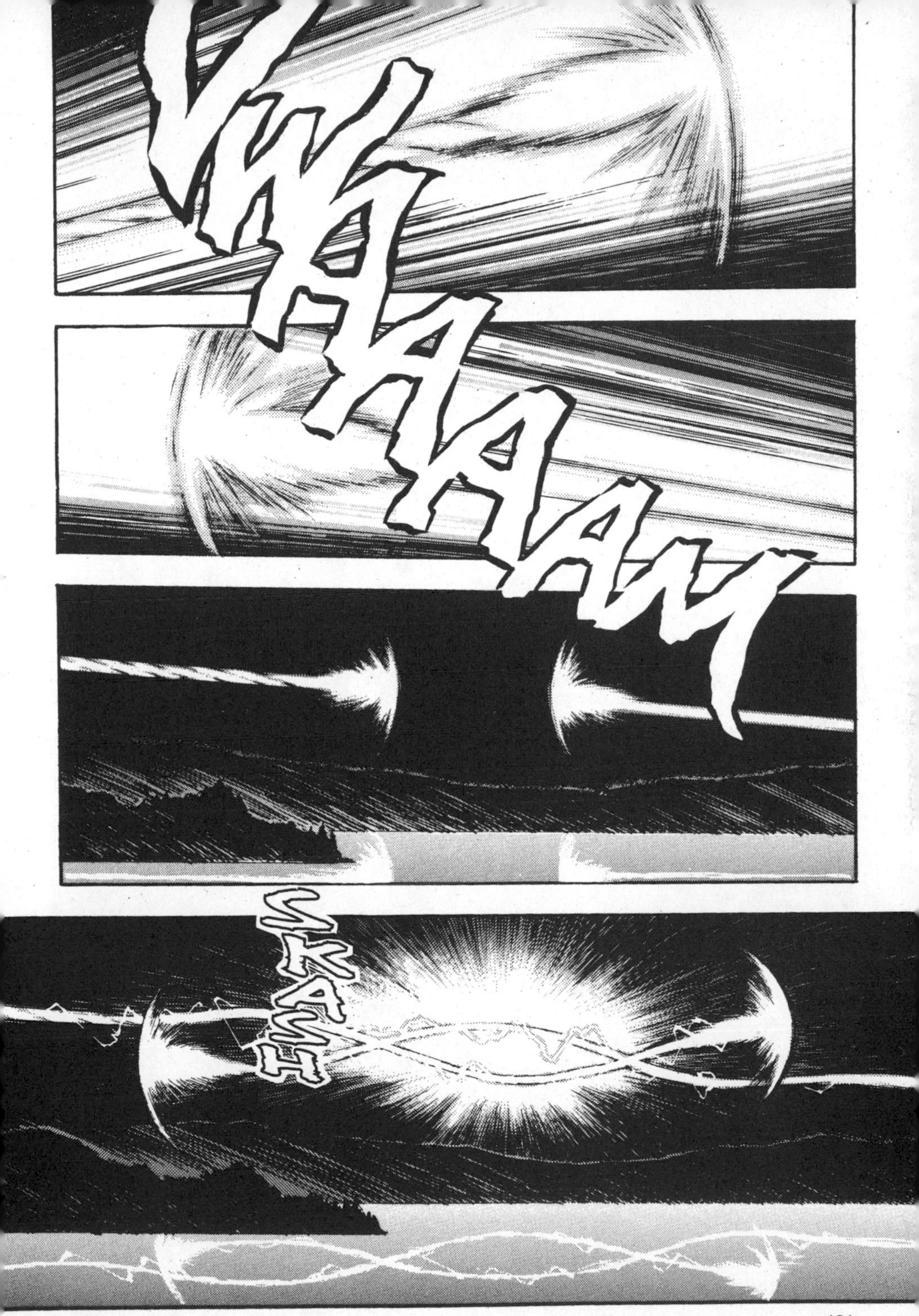
VWAAAAM
SKASH

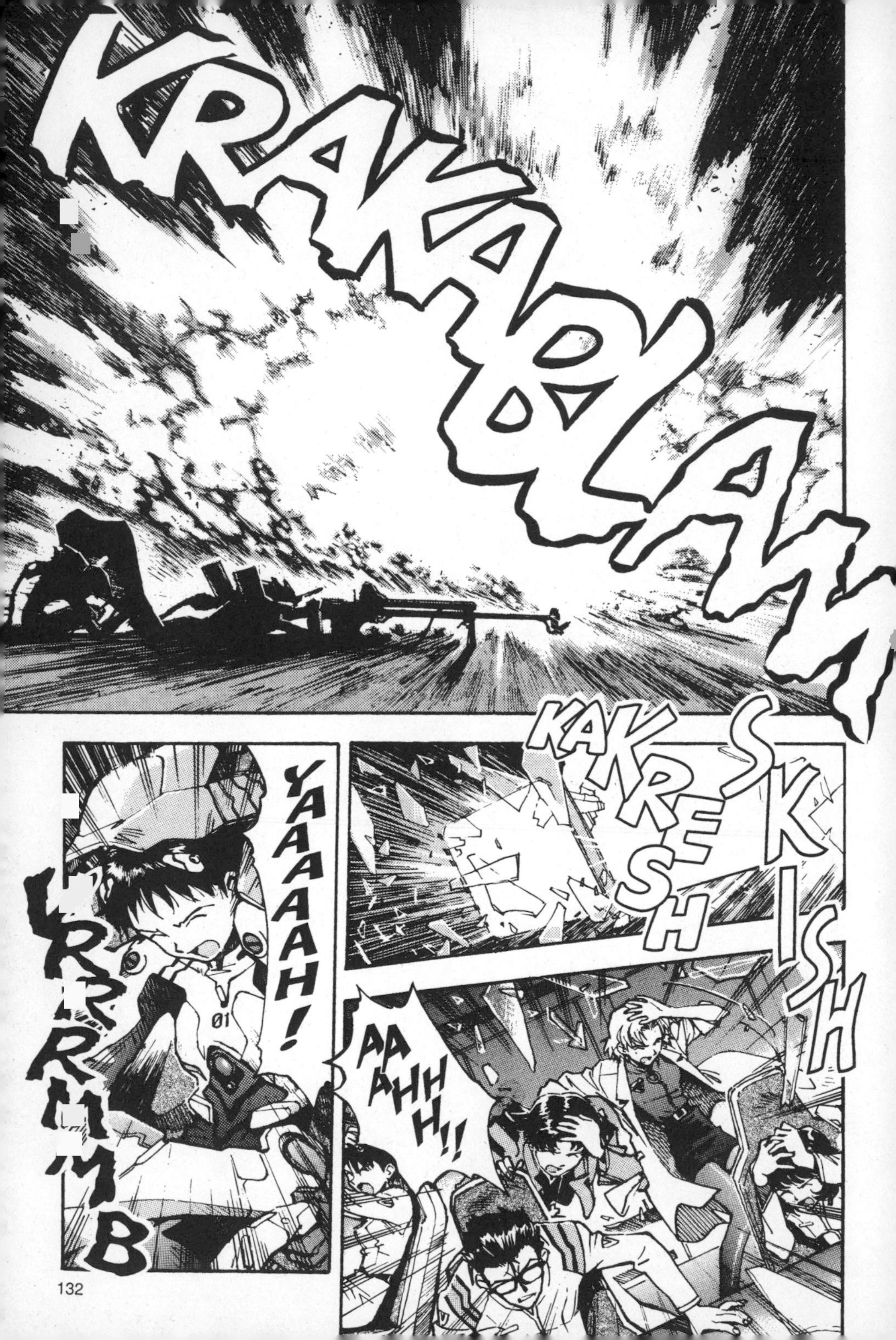
KRAKABLAM
YAAAAAAH!
RRRMMB
KAKKRESH
SKKISH
AAAHHH!!

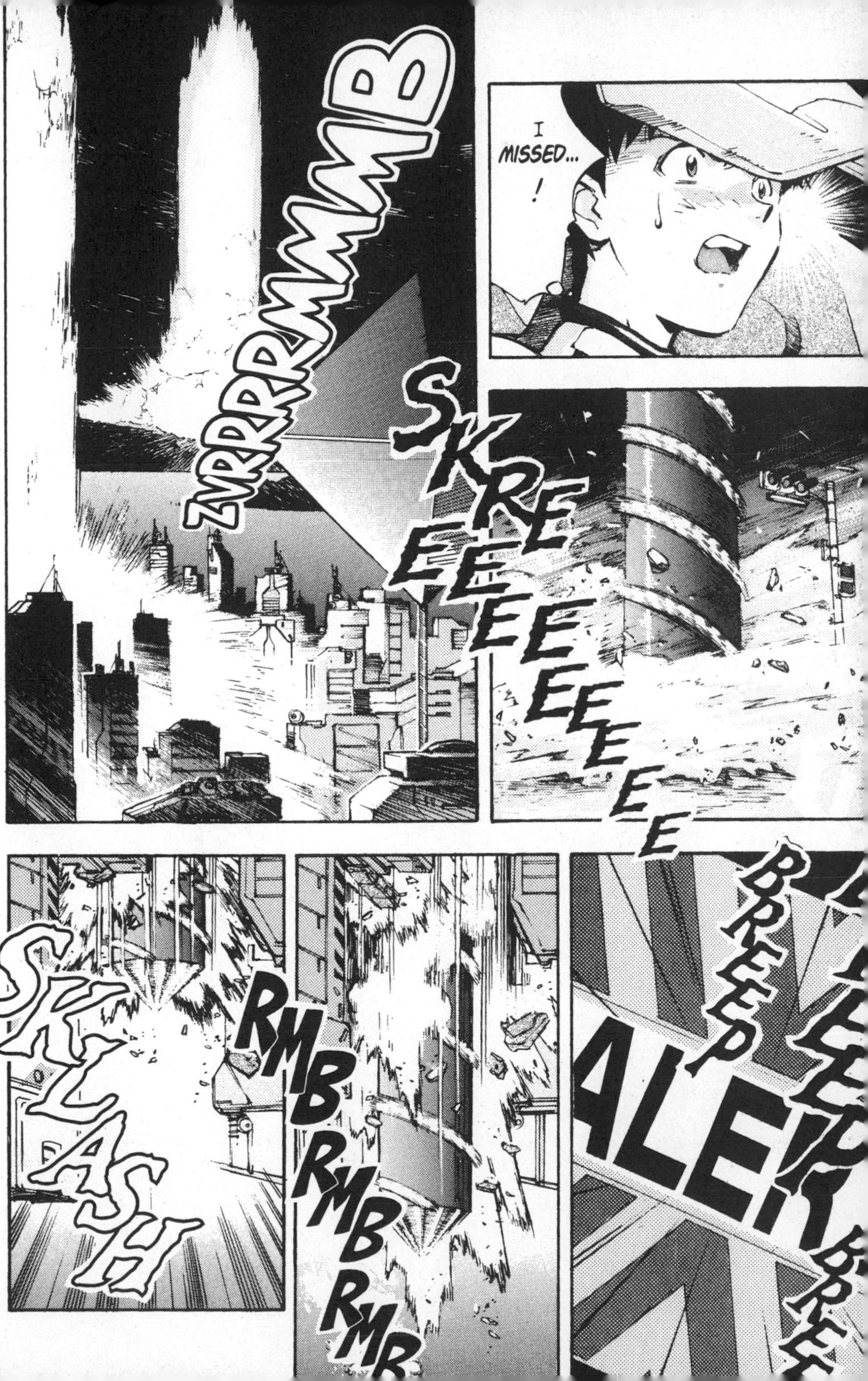

ZVRRRRMMMB
I MISSED... !
SKREEEEEEEEE
SKLASH
RMB RMB RMB RMR
BREEP
ALER

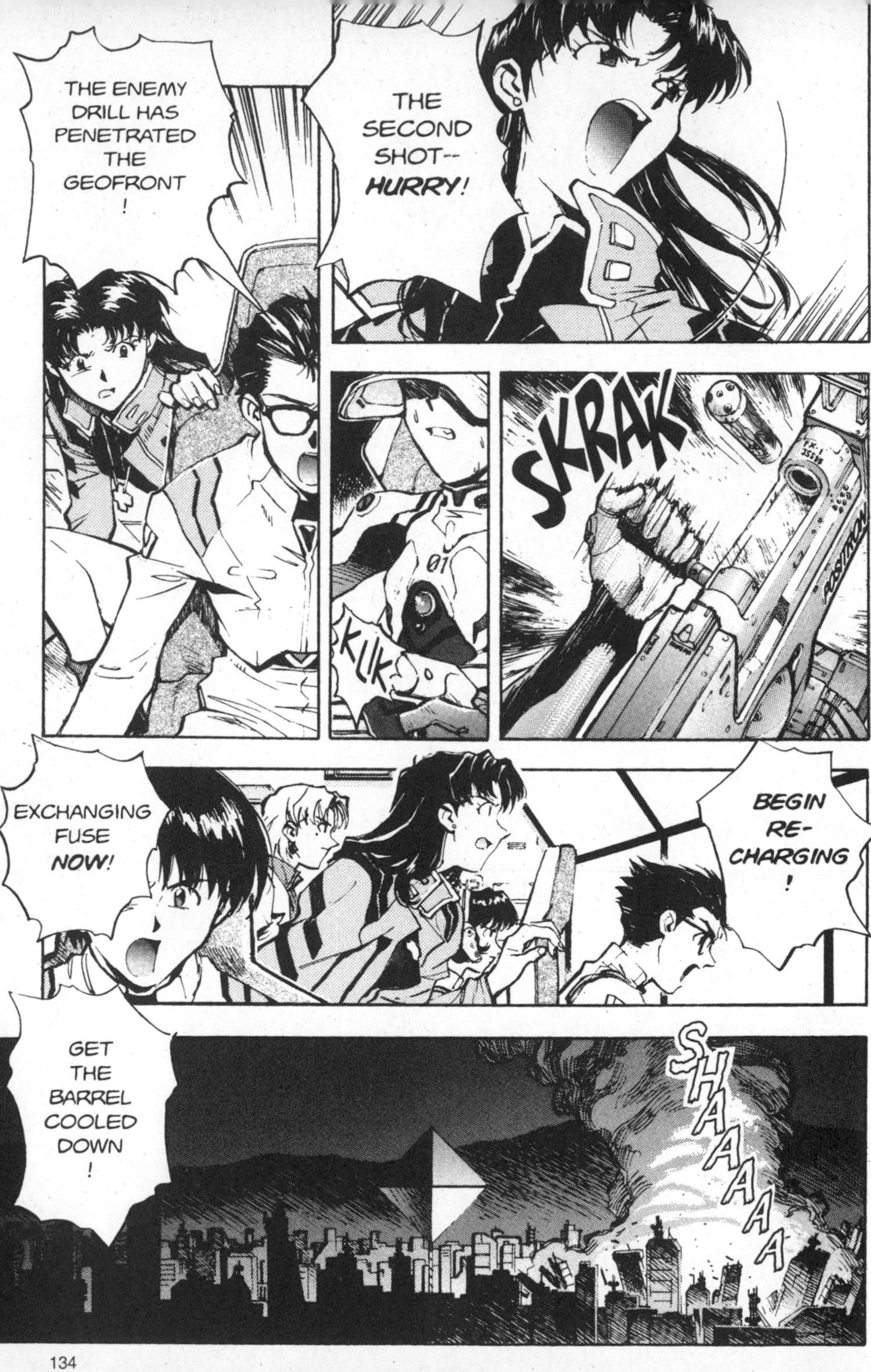
THE ENEMY DRILL HAS PENETRATED THE GEOFRONT!
THE SECOND SHOT-- HURRY!
KLIK
SKRAK
EXCHANGING FUSE NOW!
BEGIN RE-CHARGING!
GET THE BARREL COOLED DOWN!
SHAAAAA

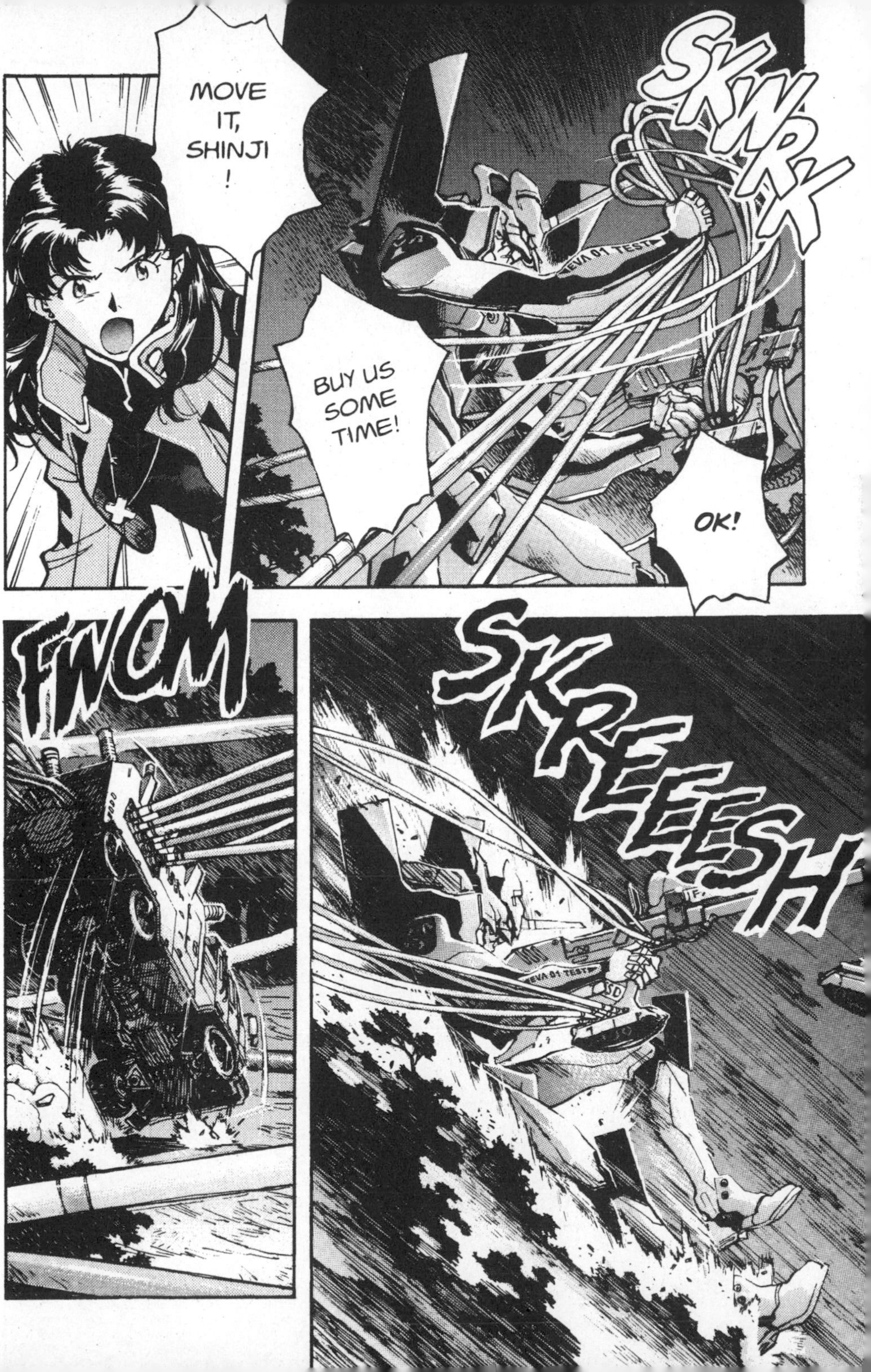
MOVE IT, SHINJI !
SKWRK
BUY US SOME TIME!
EVA 01 TEST
OK!
FWOM
SKREEESH
EVA 01 TEST

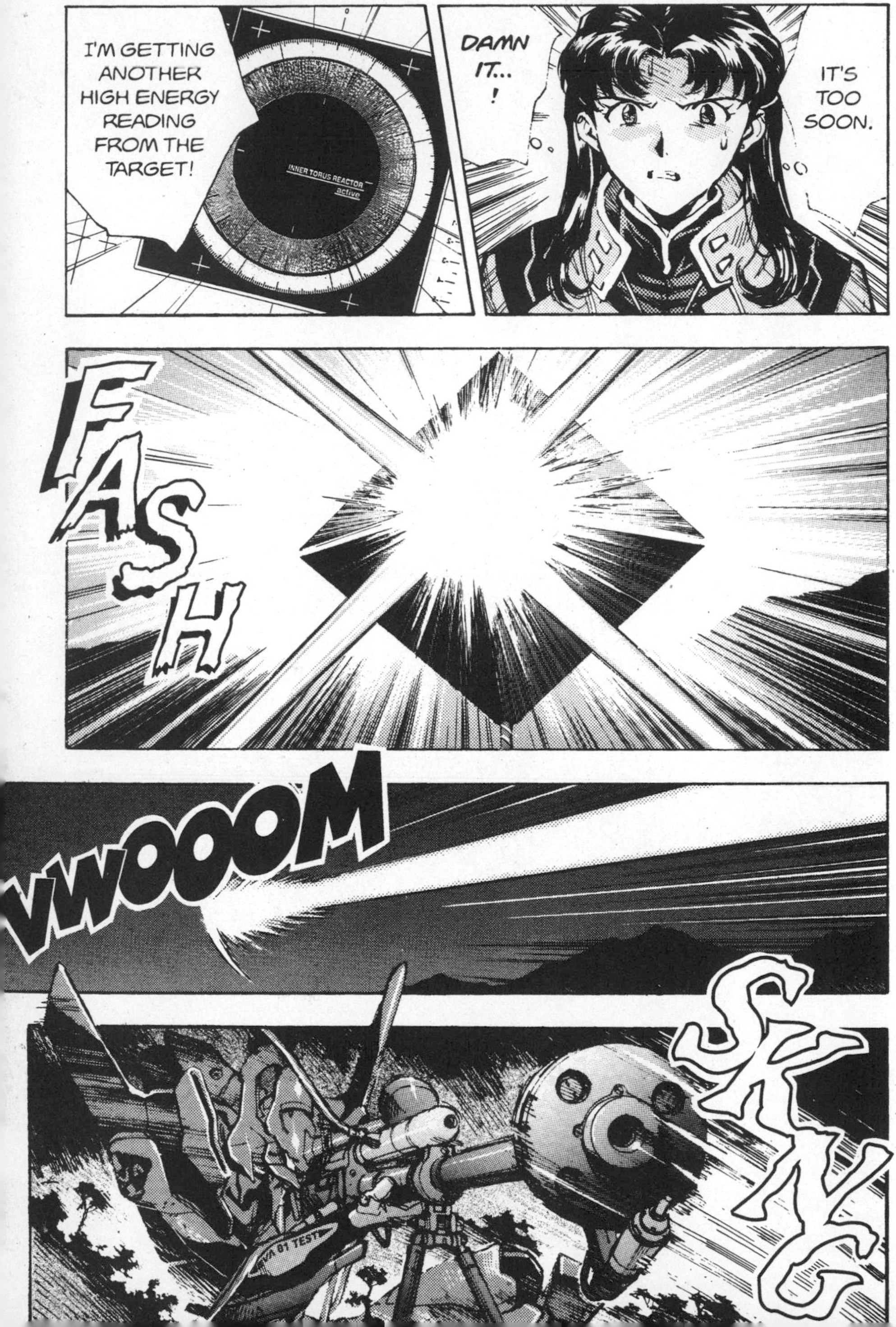
I'M GETTING ANOTHER HIGH ENERGY READING FROM THE TARGET!
INNER TORUS REACTOR
active
DAMN IT... !
IT'S TOO SOON.
FASH
VWOOOM
SKYG
EVA 01 TEST

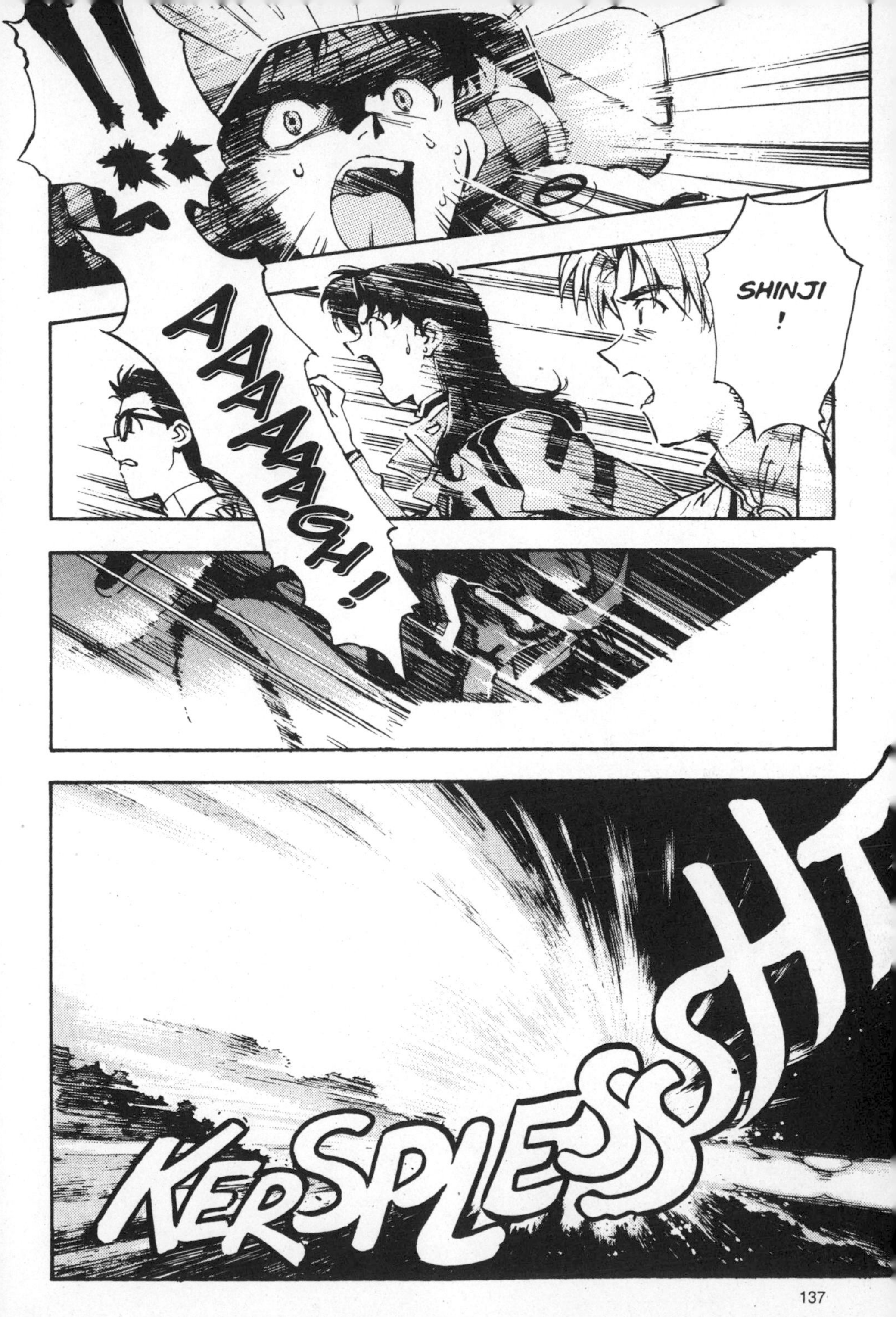
!!
SHINJI!
AAAAAAGH!!
KERSPLESSSHT

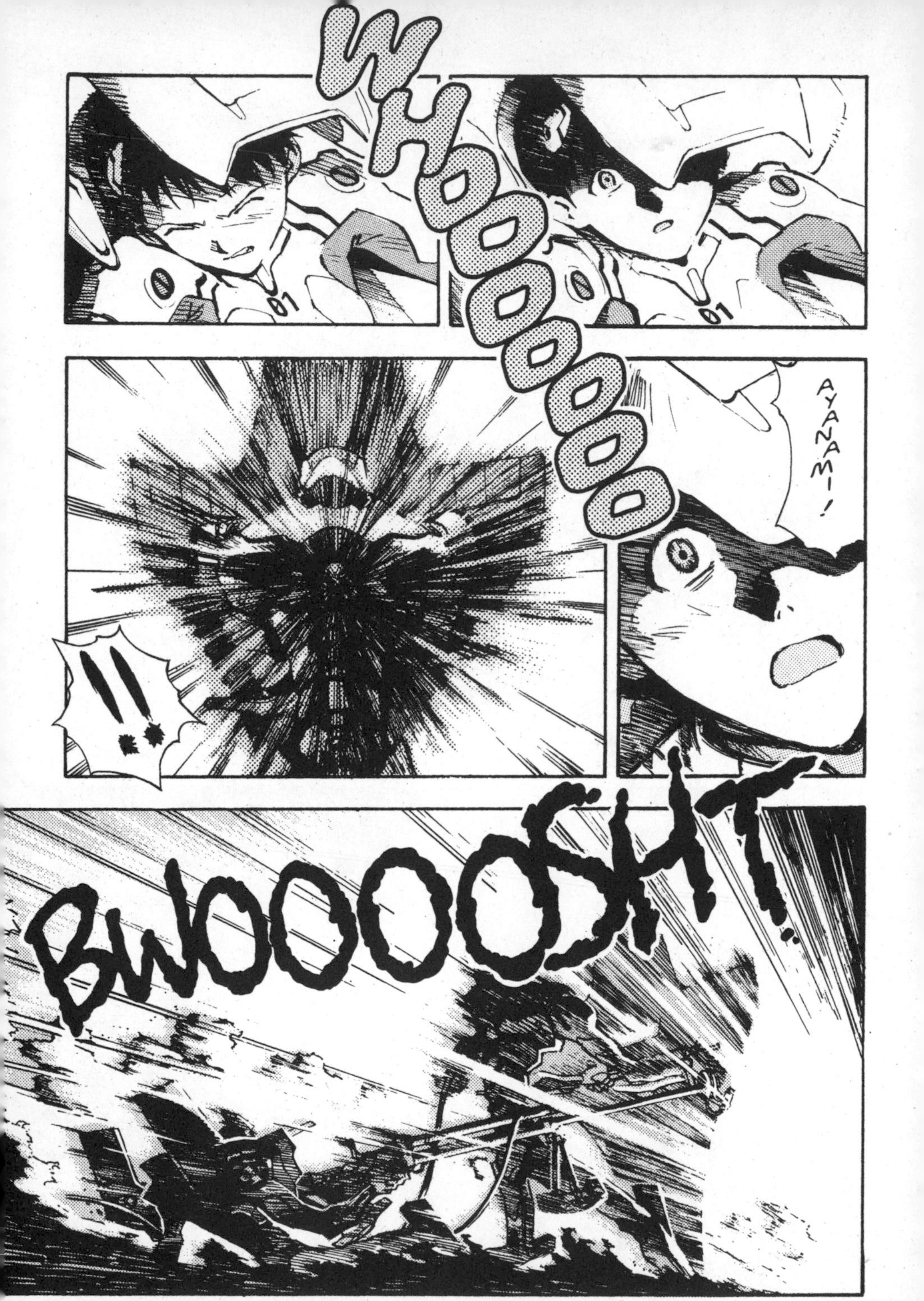
WHOOOOOOOO
AYANAMI!
!!
BWOOOOSHT..

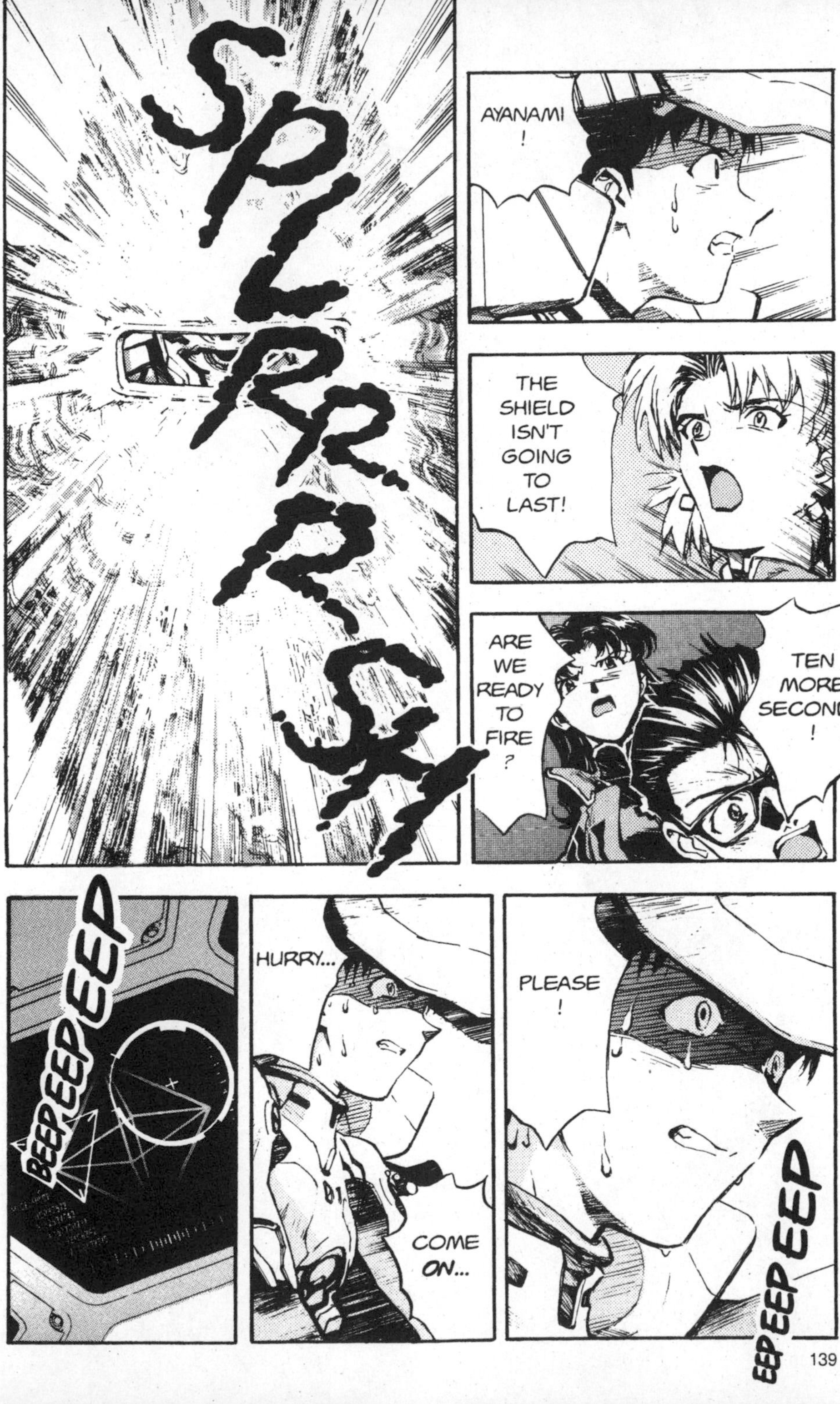

SPLRRRSH
AYANAMI!
THE SHIELD ISN'T GOING TO LAST!
ARE WE READY TO FIRE?
TEN MORE SECONDS!
BEEP EEP EEP
HURRY...
COME ON...
PLEASE!
EEP EEP EEP

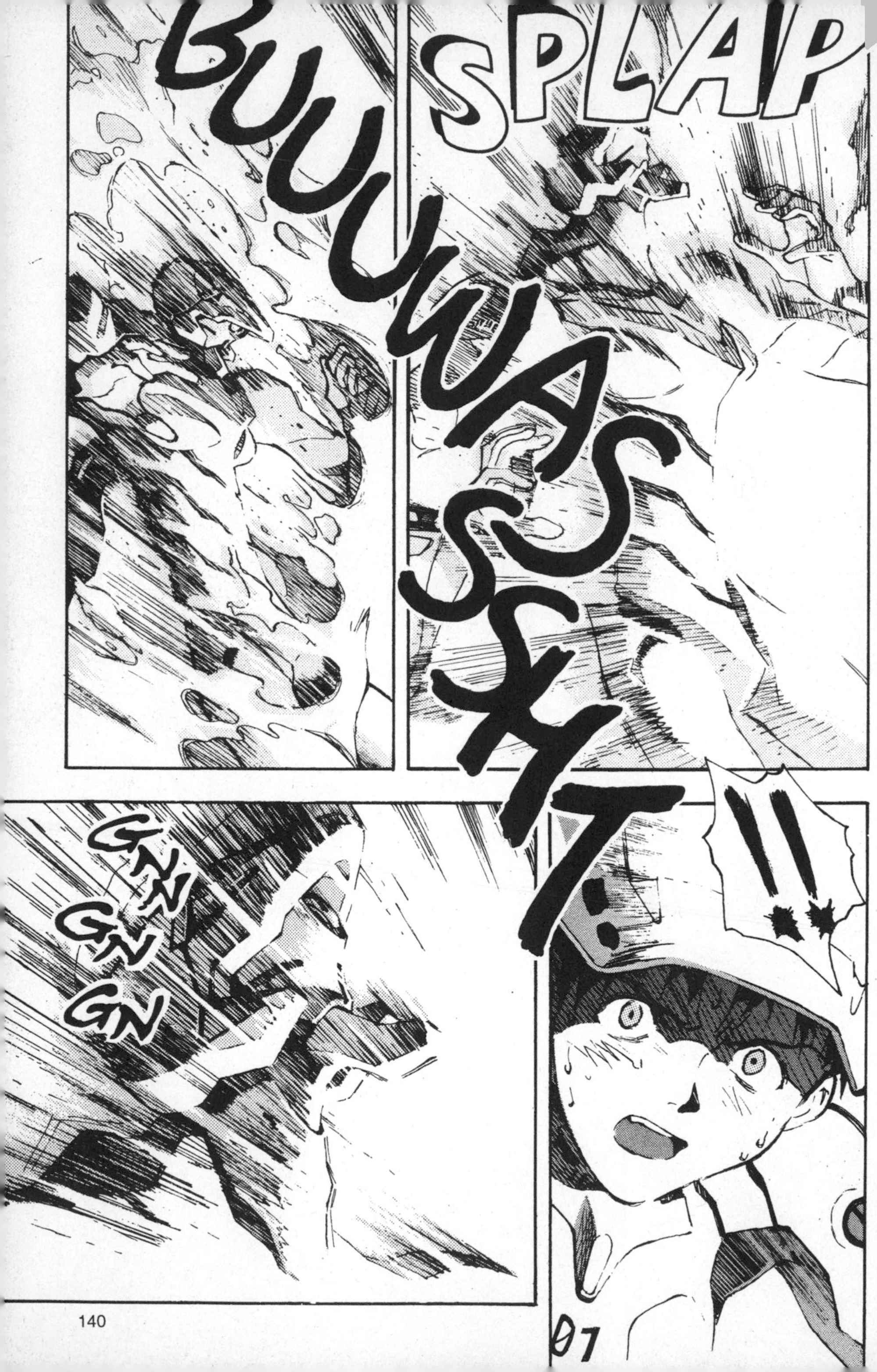
BUUUWASSHT
SPLAP
GNN
GN
GN
!!

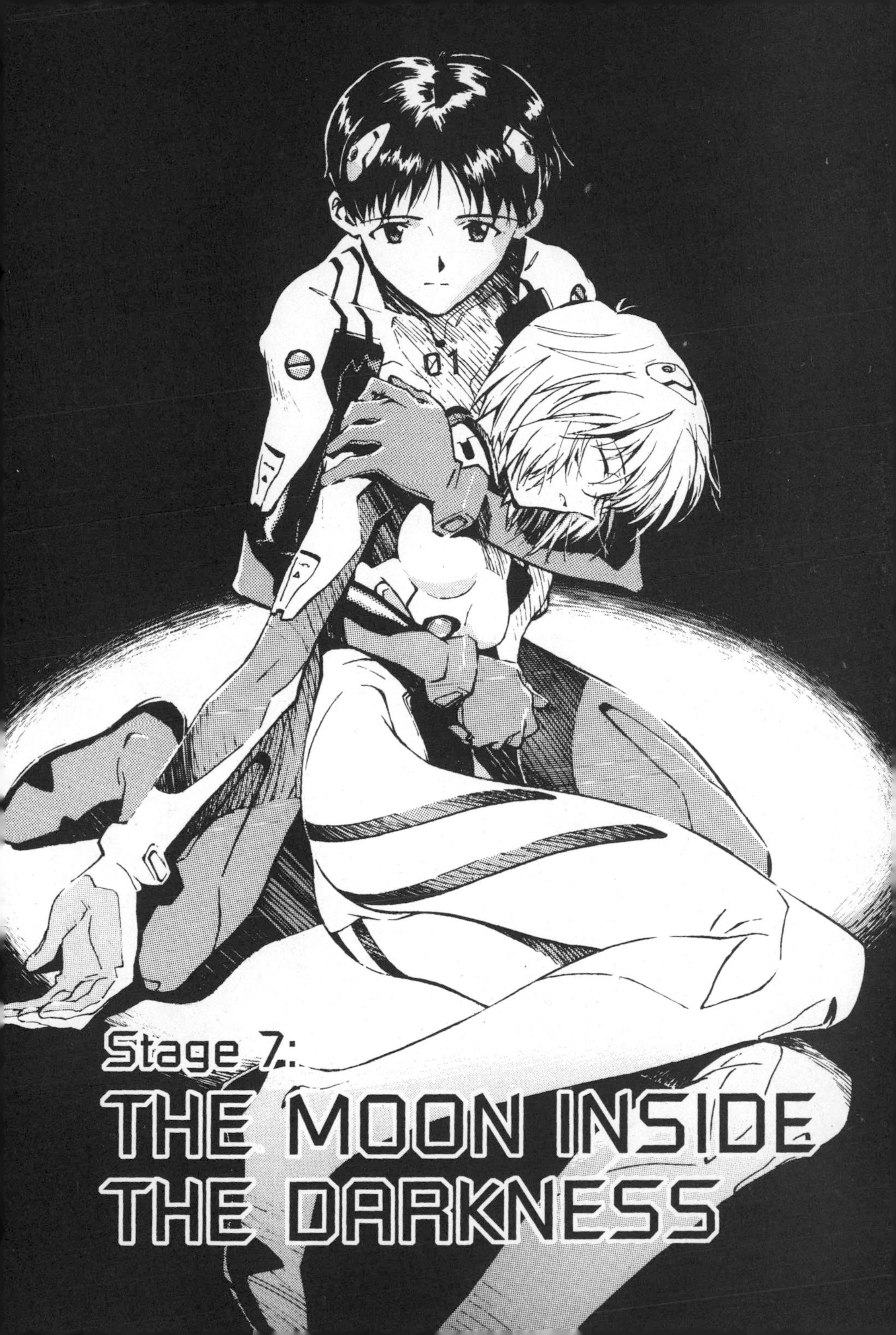
01

Stage 7: THE MOON INSIDE THE DARKNESS

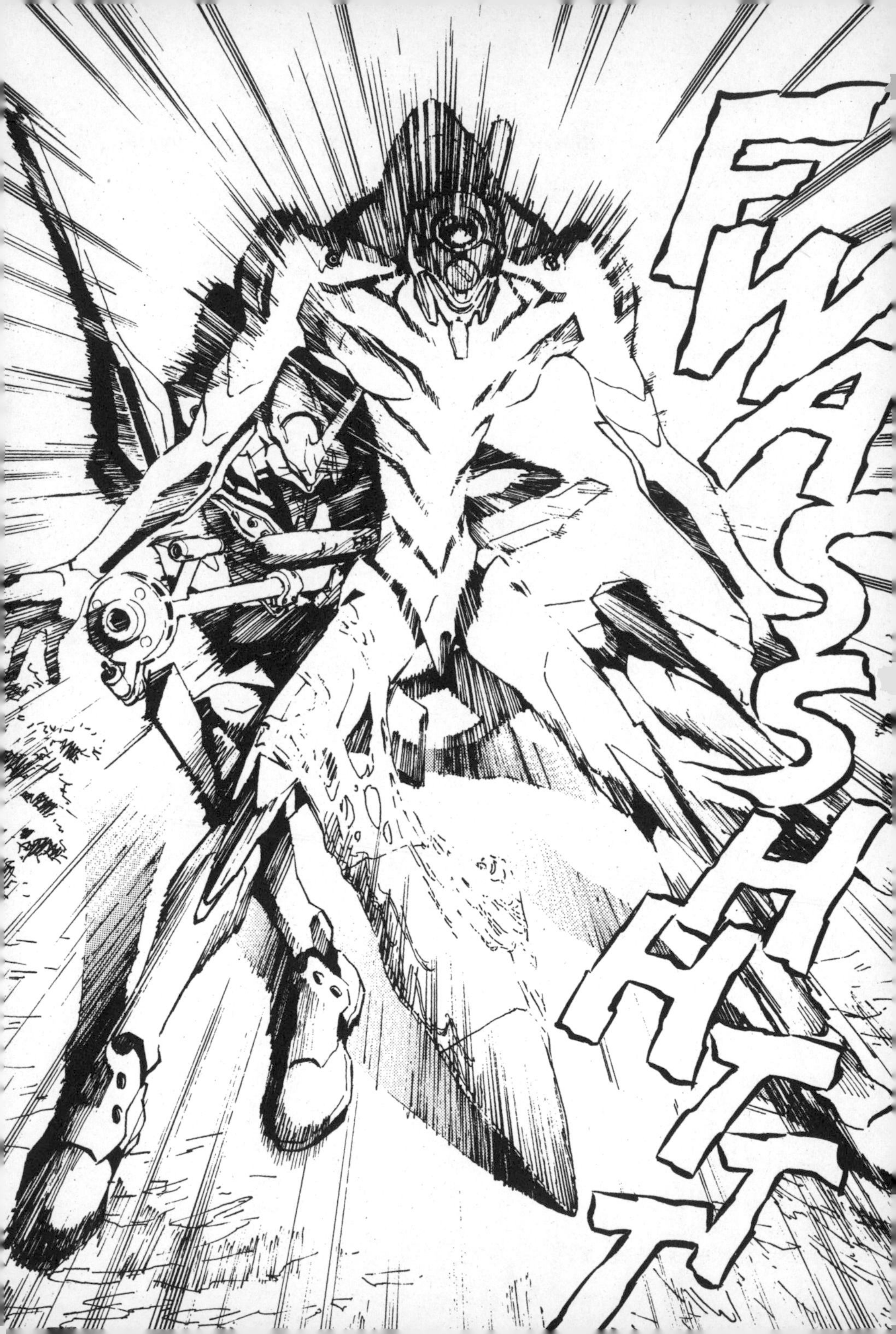
FWASHTT

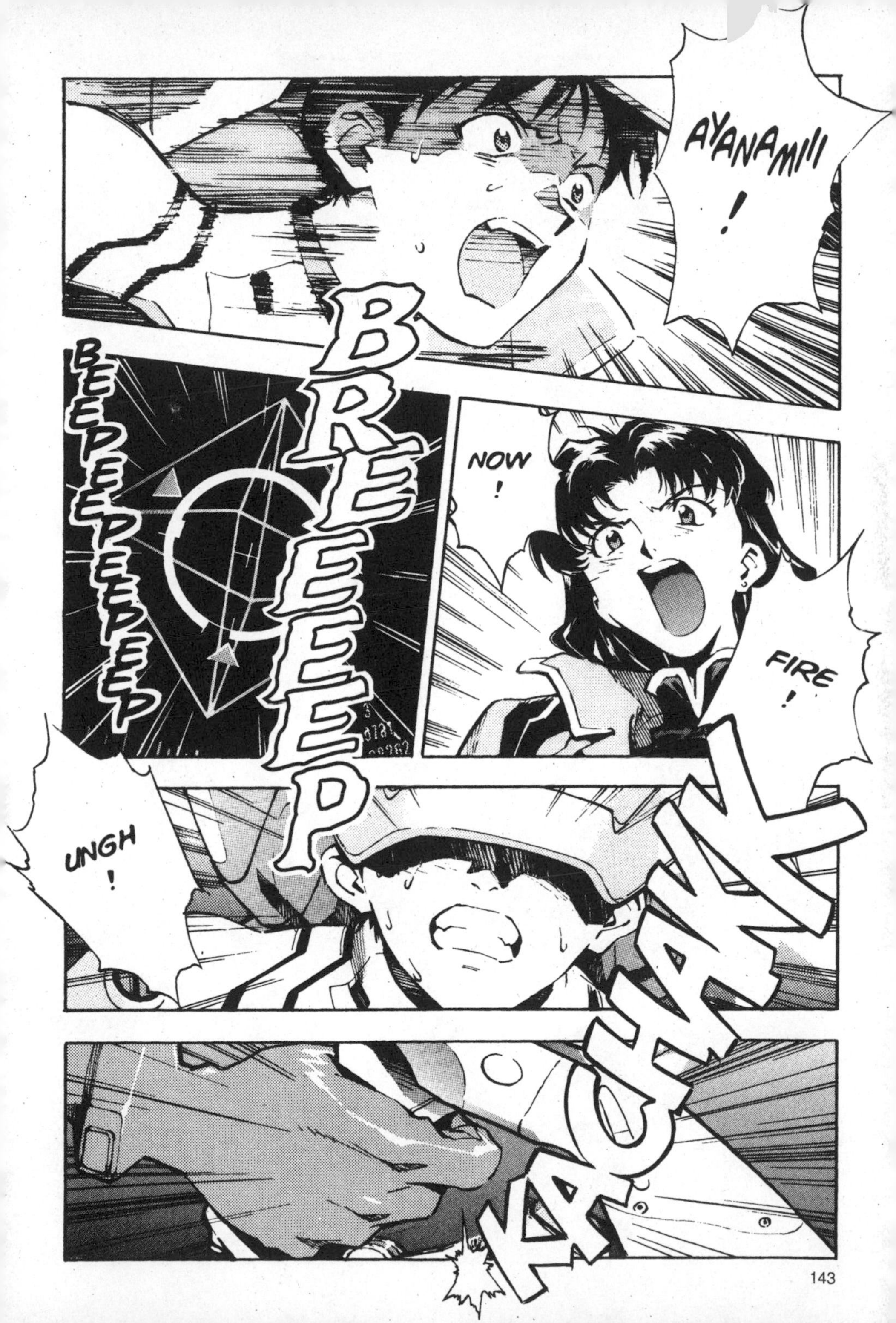
AYANAMI!!!
BREEEEEP
BEEPEEPEEPEEP
NOW!
FIRE!
UNGH!
KACHAK

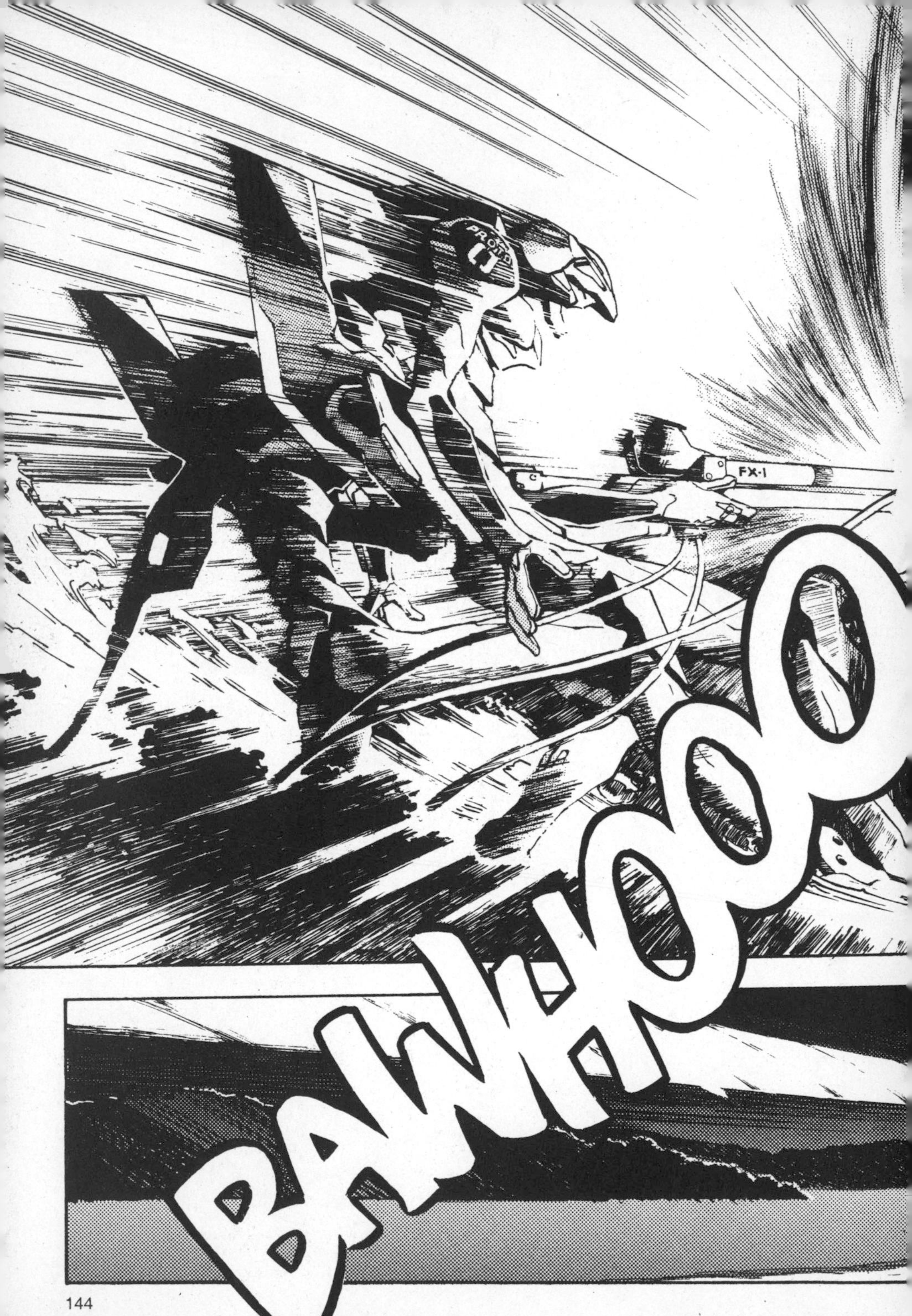
FX-1
BAWHOOO

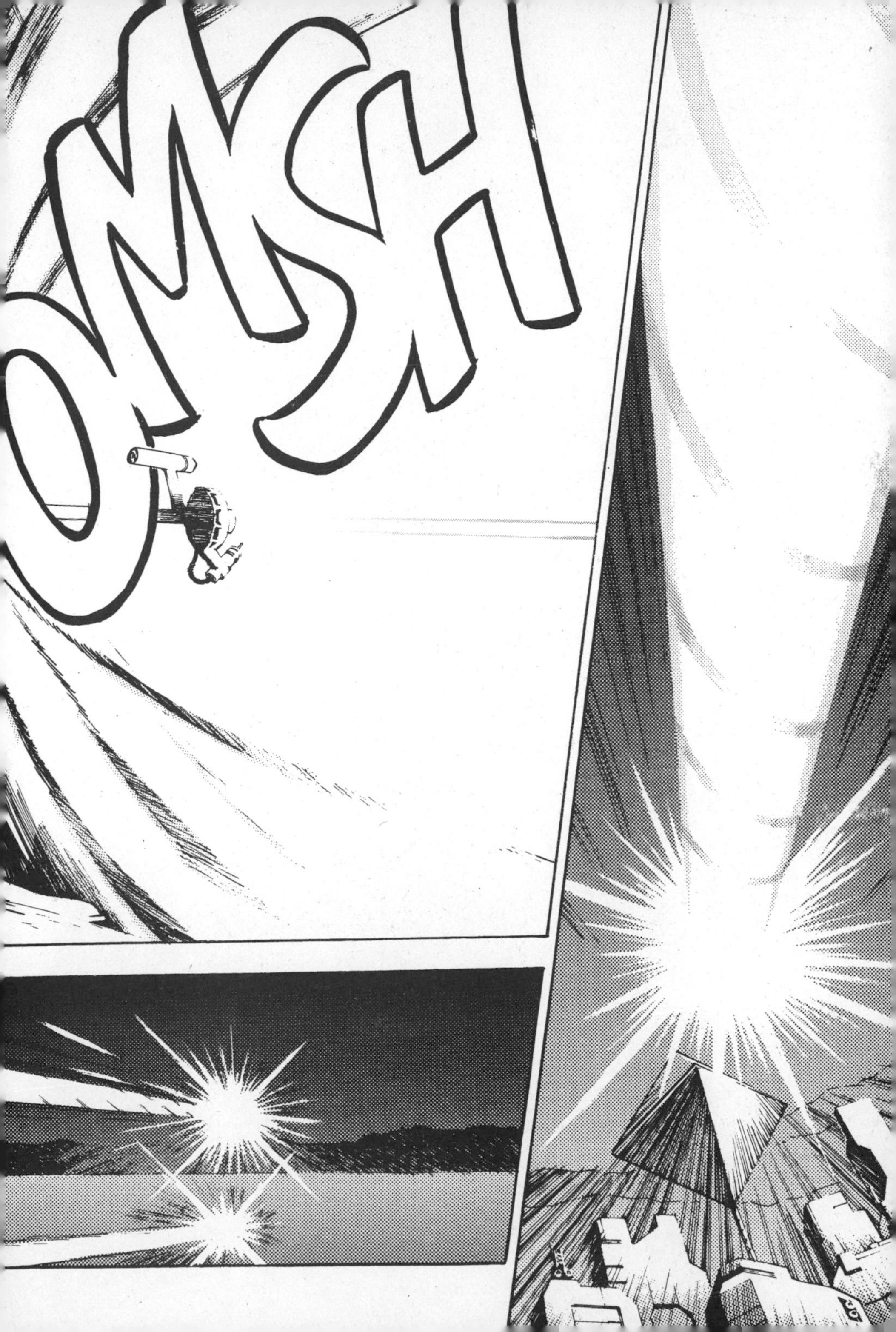
OMSH

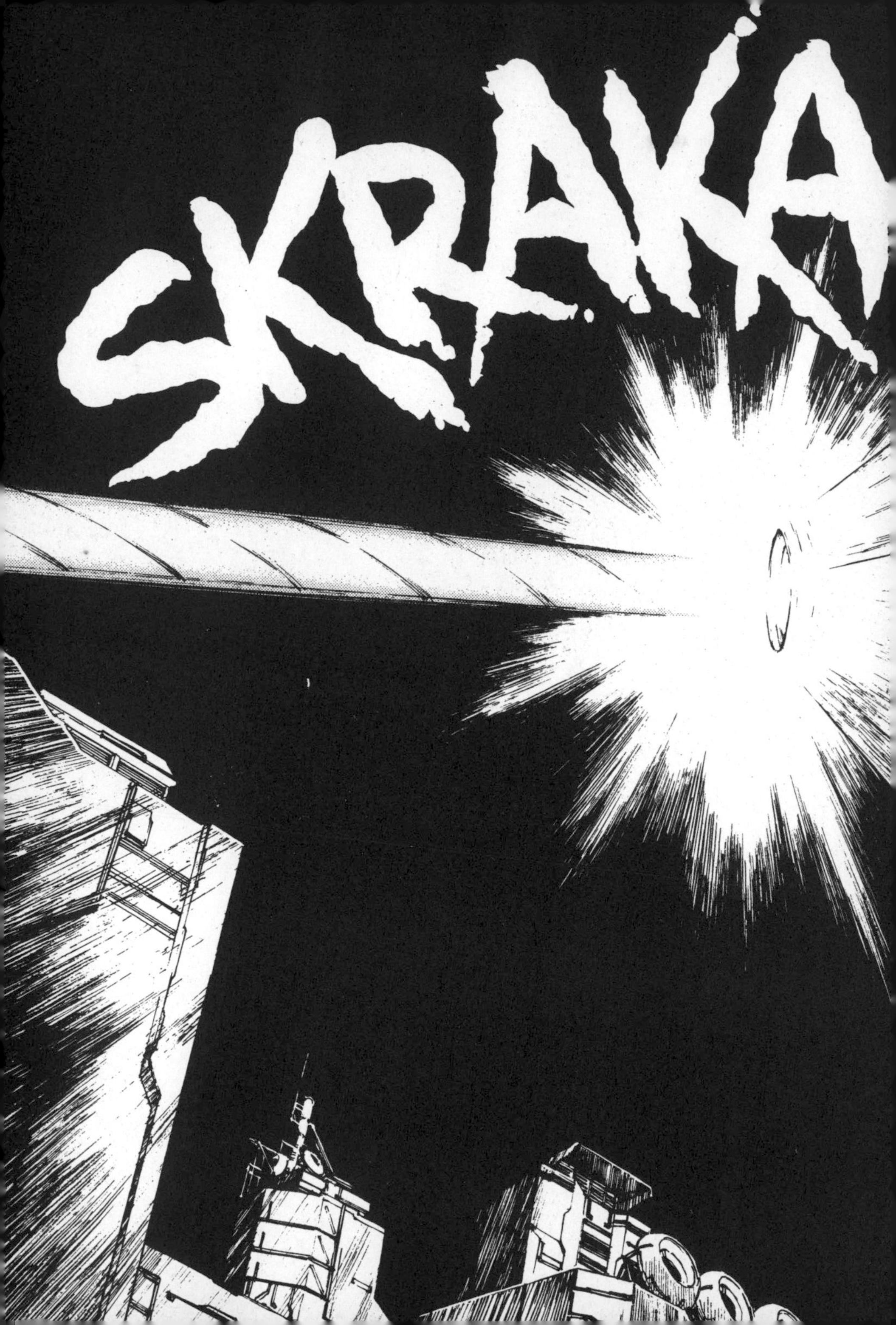
SKRAKA

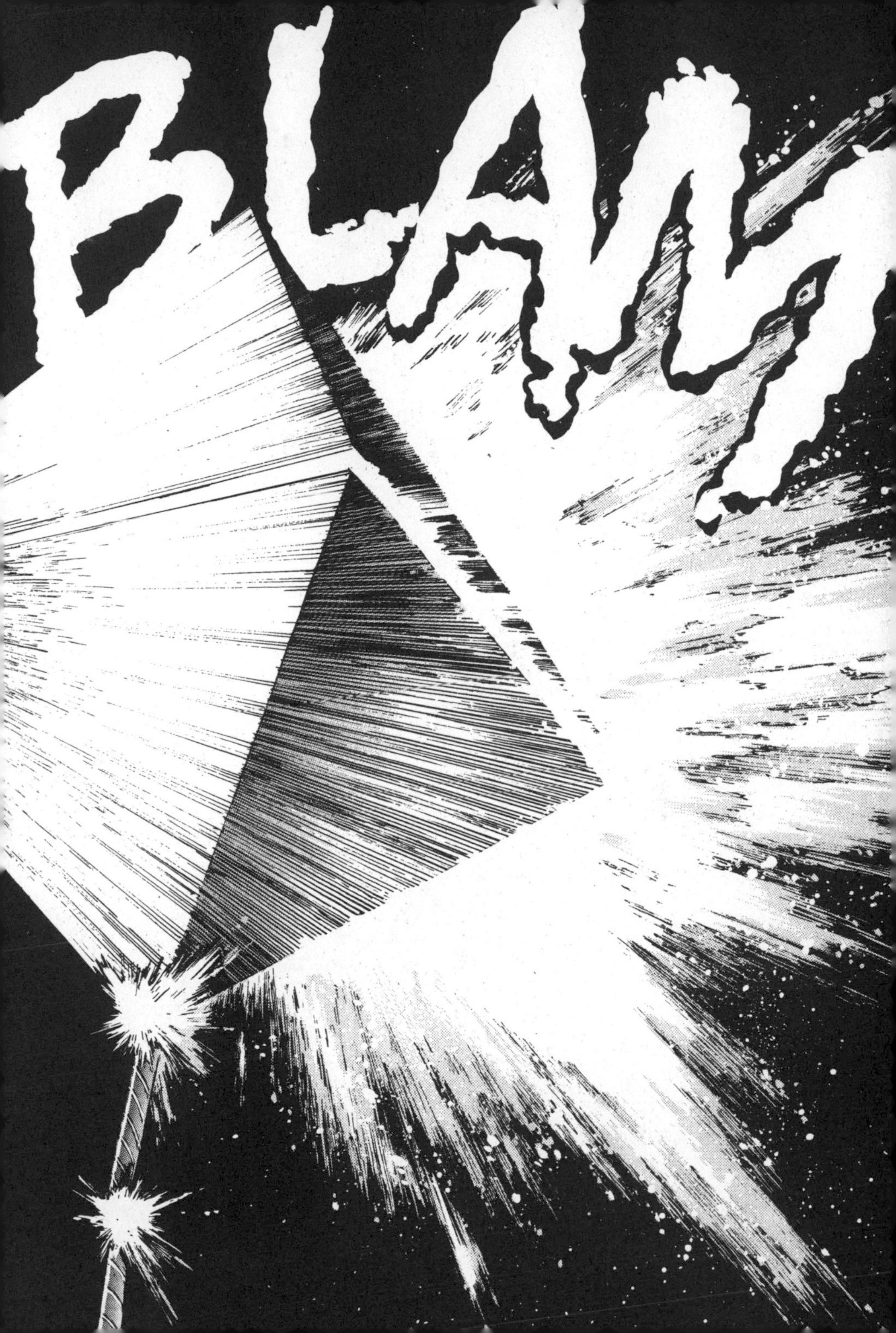
BLAM!

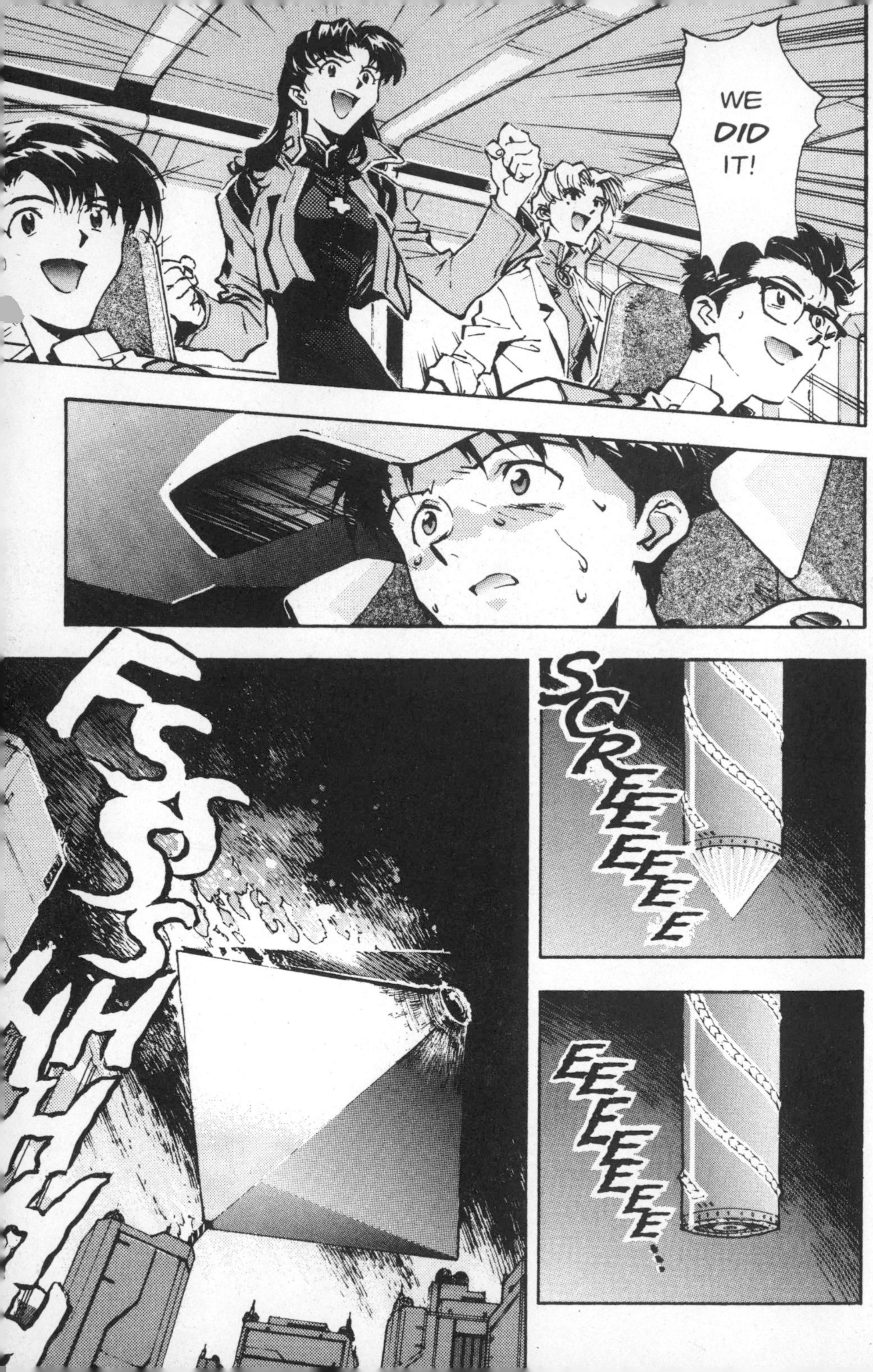
WE DID IT!
SCREEEEEEE
EEEEEEE...

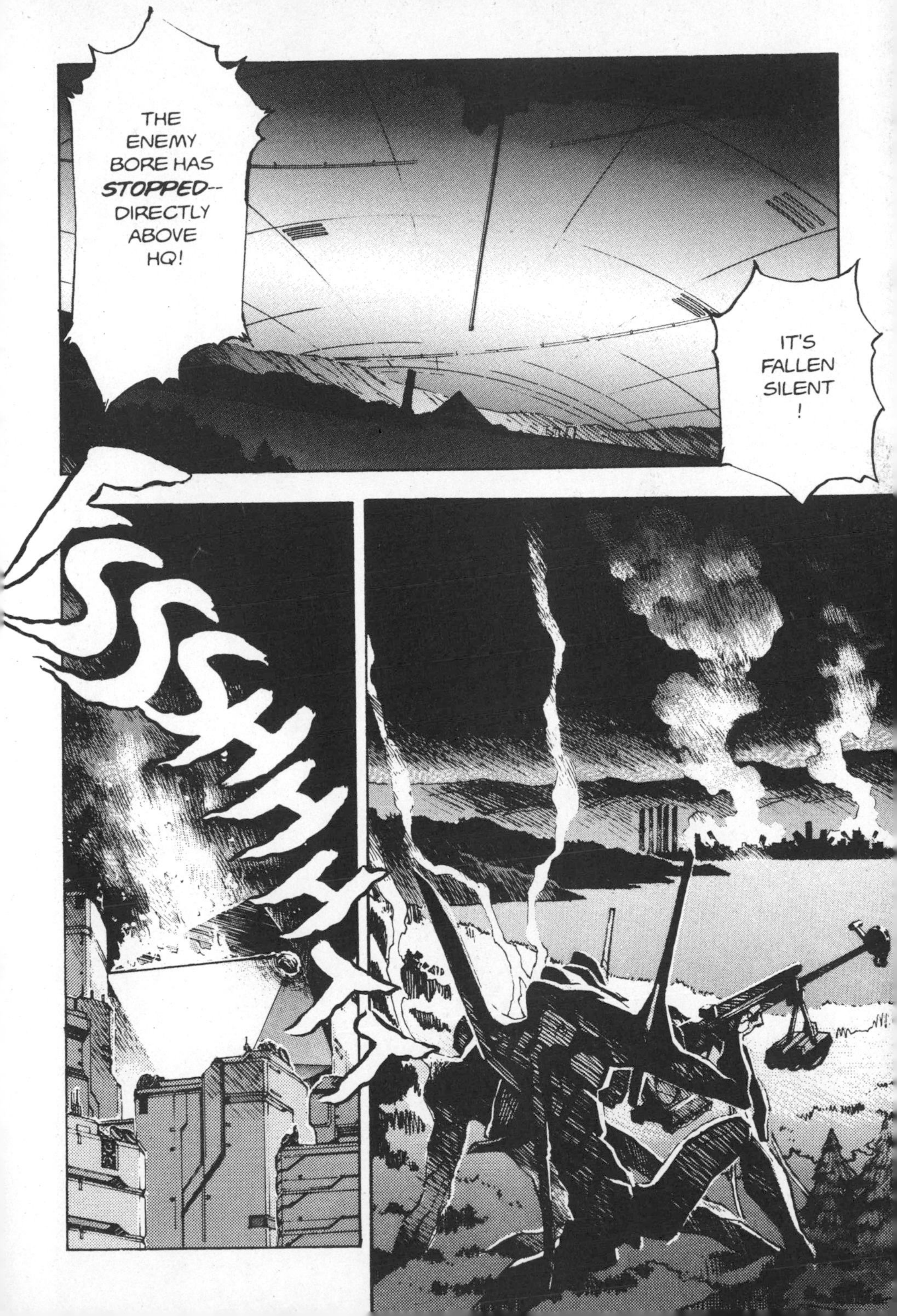
THE ENEMY BORE HAS **STOPPED**-- DIRECTLY ABOVE HQ!
IT'S FALLEN SILENT !

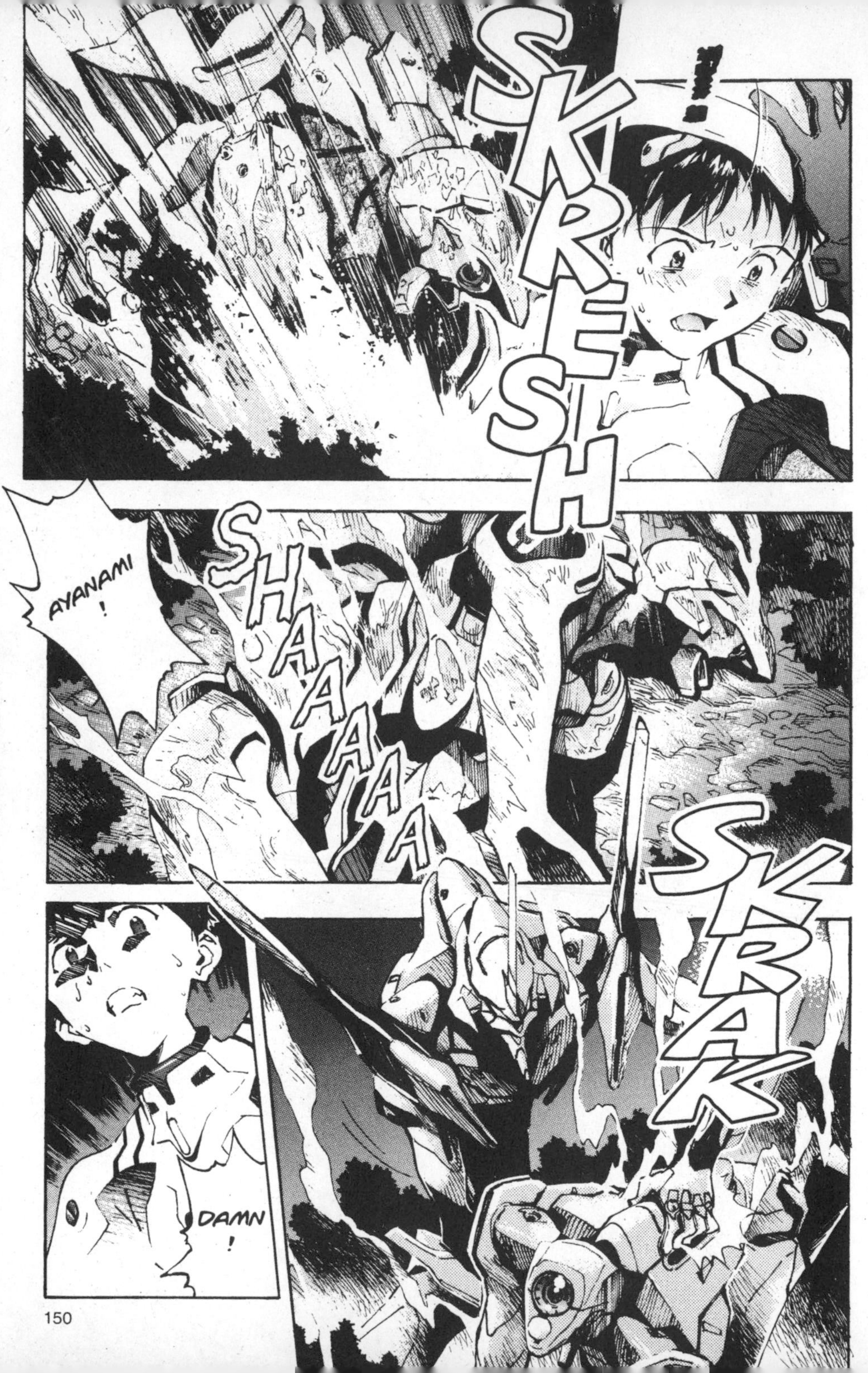
SKRESH
!!
AYANAMI!
SHAAAAAA
DAMN!
SKRAK

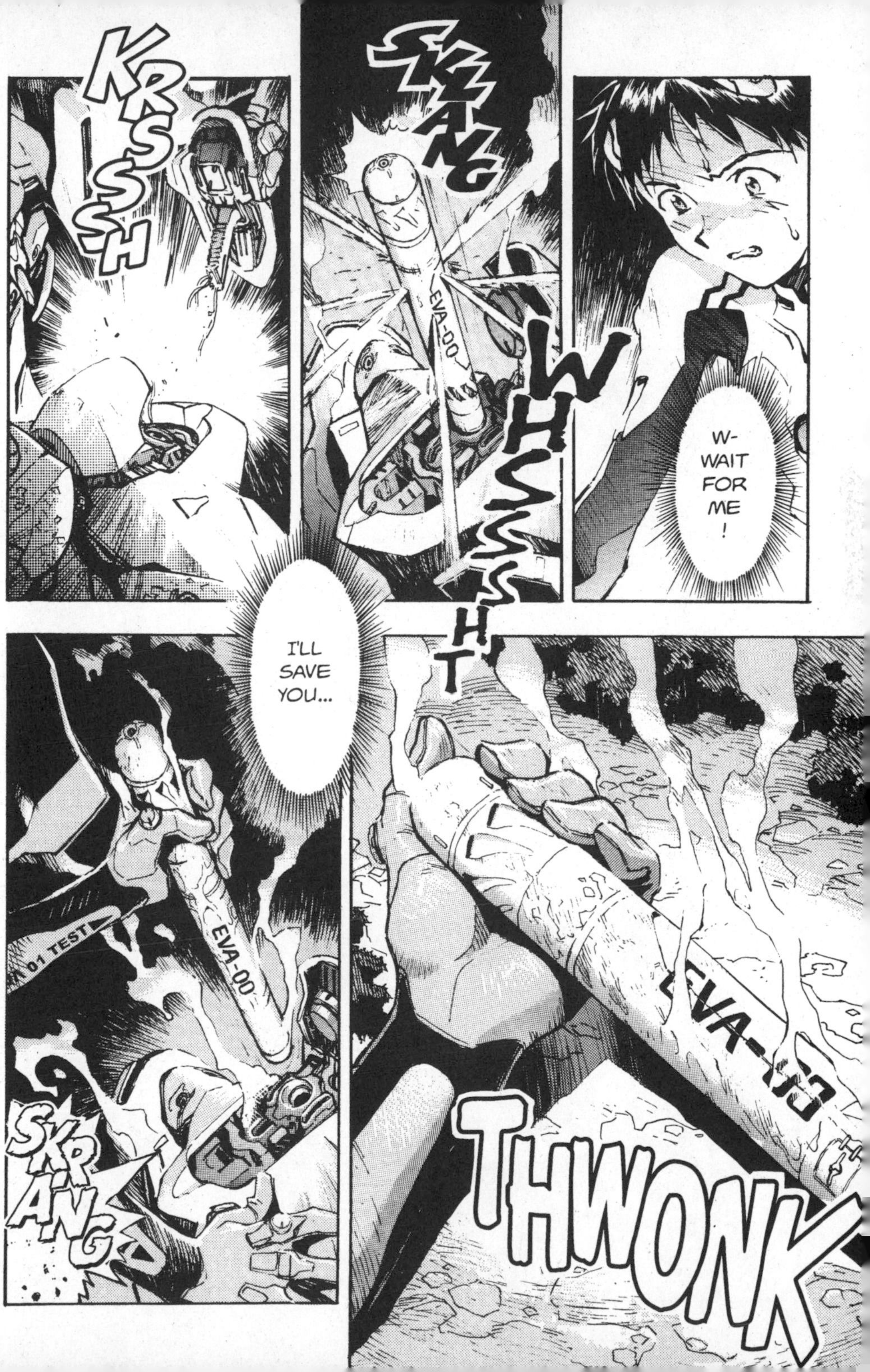
KRSSSH
SKZANG
EVA-00
WHSSSSHT
W-WAIT FOR ME!
I'LL SAVE YOU...
01 TEST
EVA-00
SKPANG
EVA-00
THWONK

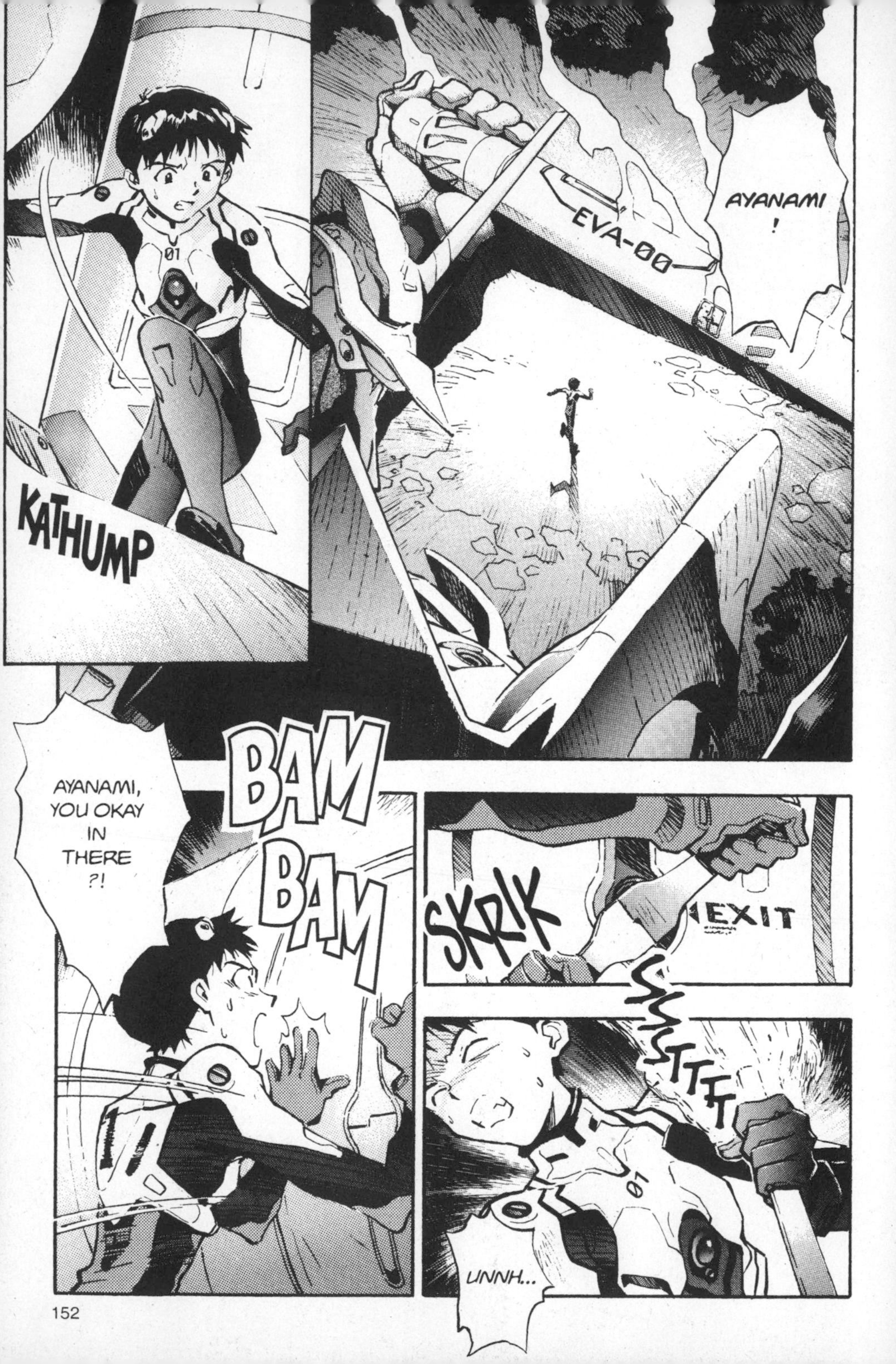
KATHUMP
EVA-00
AYANAMI !
BAM
BAM
AYANAMI, YOU OKAY IN THERE ?!
SKRIK
EXIT
UNNH...

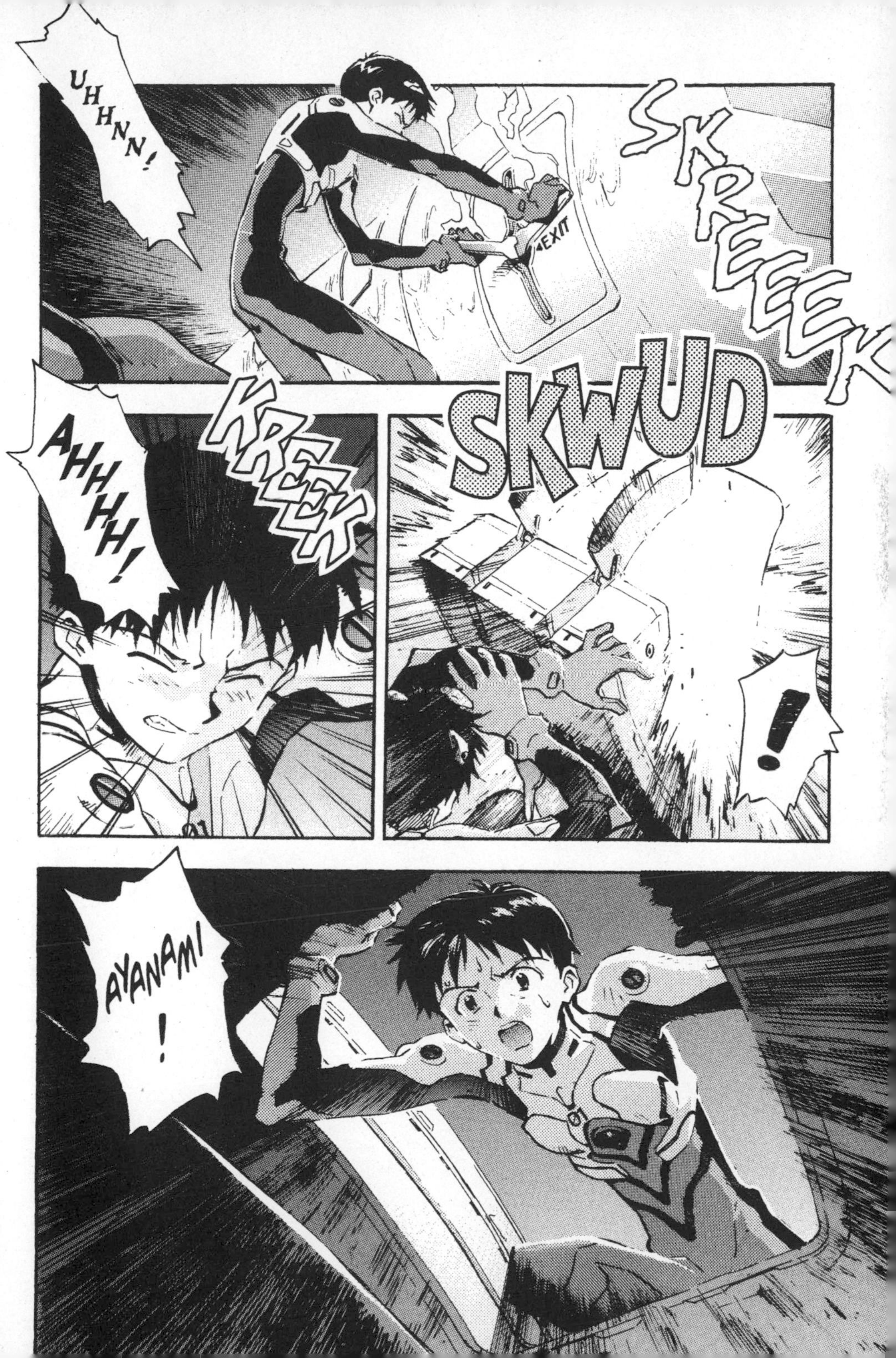
UHHNN!
SKREEEEK
AHHHH!
KREEK
SKWUD
!
AYANAMI!

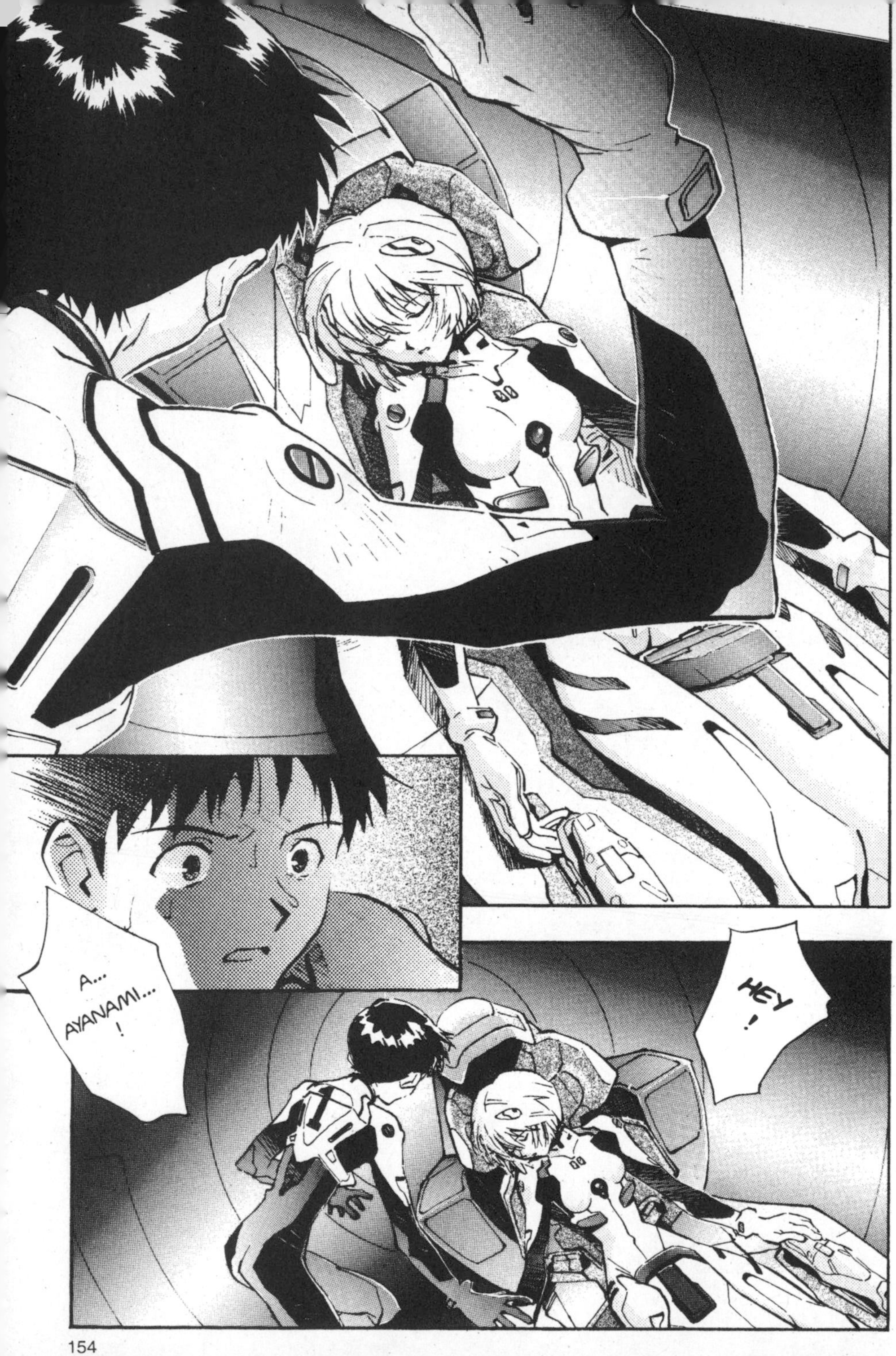
A... AYANAMI...!
HEY!

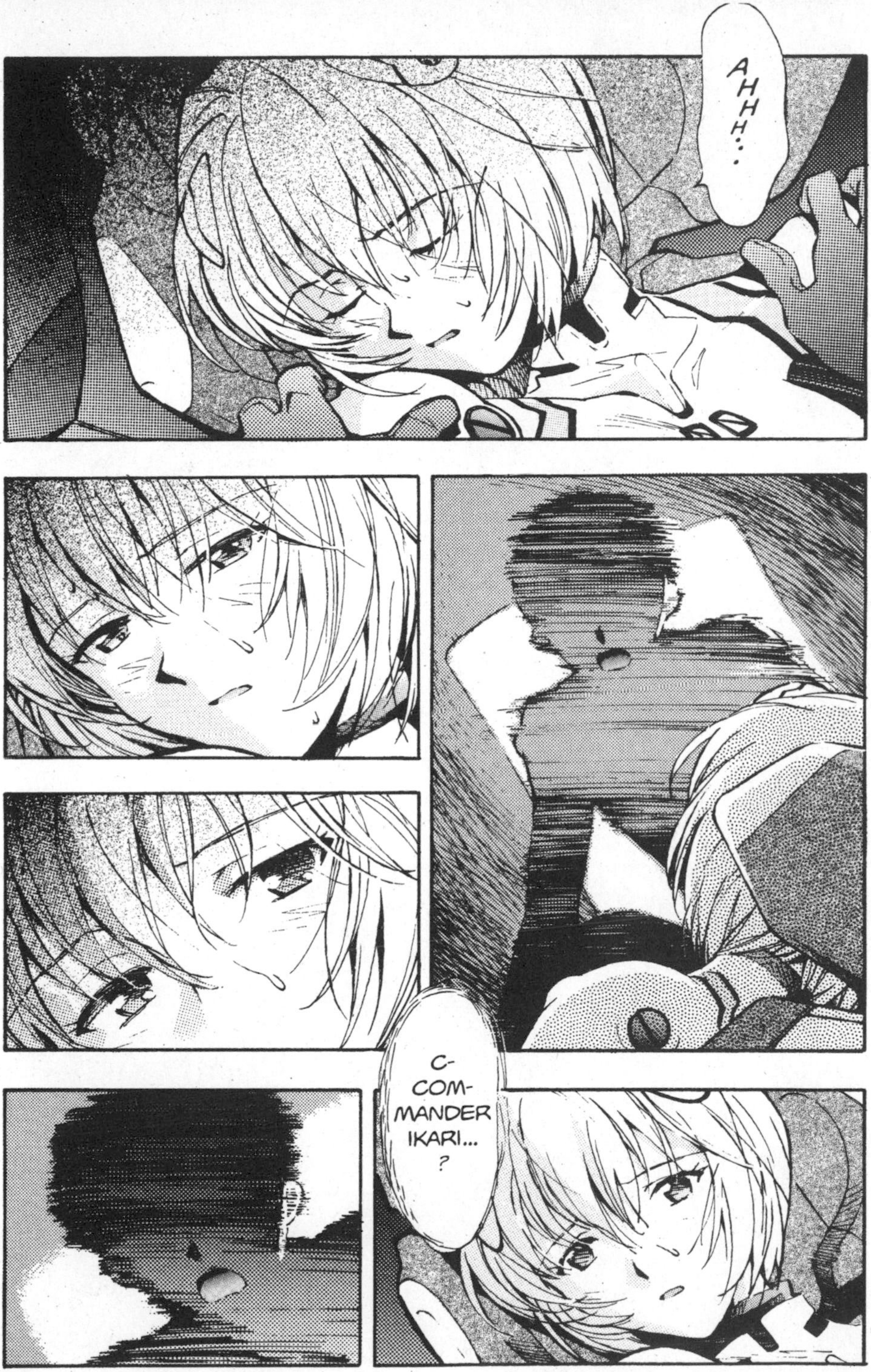
AHHH...
C-COM-MANDER IKARI...?

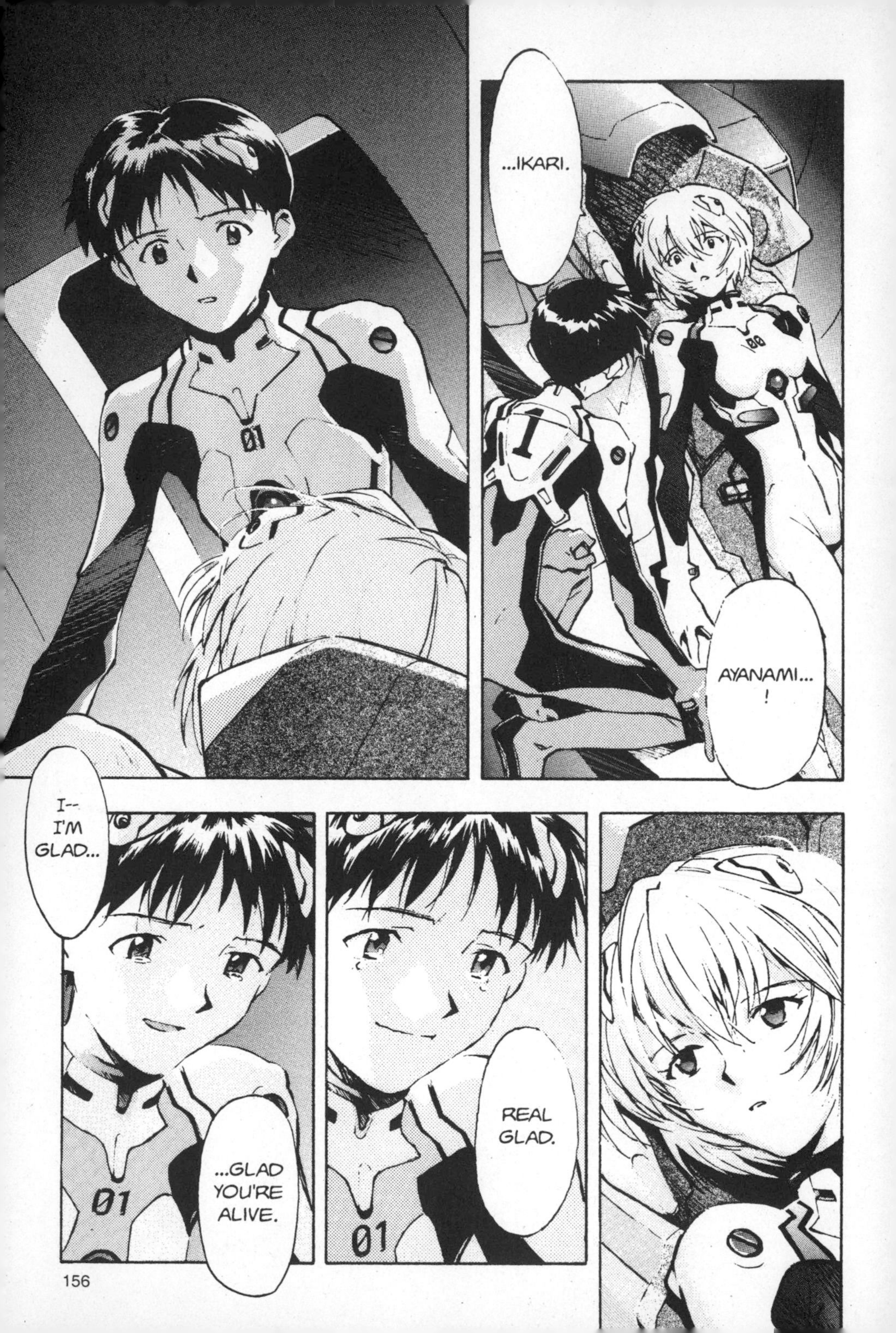
...IKARI.
AYANAMI... !
I-- I'M GLAD...
...GLAD YOU'RE ALIVE.
REAL GLAD.

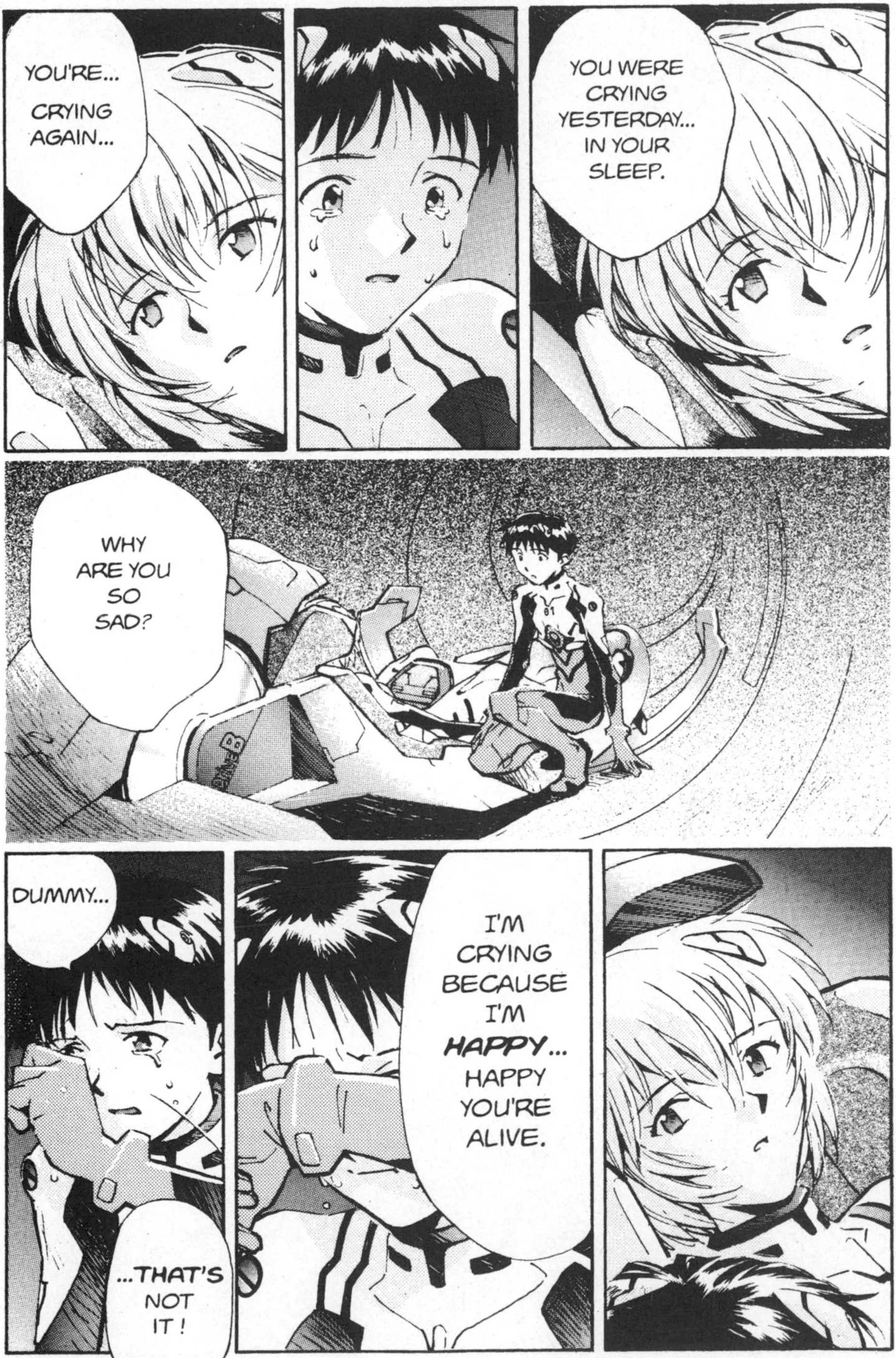
YOU'RE... CRYING AGAIN...
YOU WERE CRYING YESTERDAY... IN YOUR SLEEP.
WHY ARE YOU SO SAD?
DUMMY...
...THAT'S NOT IT!
I'M CRYING BECAUSE I'M ***HAPPY***... HAPPY YOU'RE ALIVE.

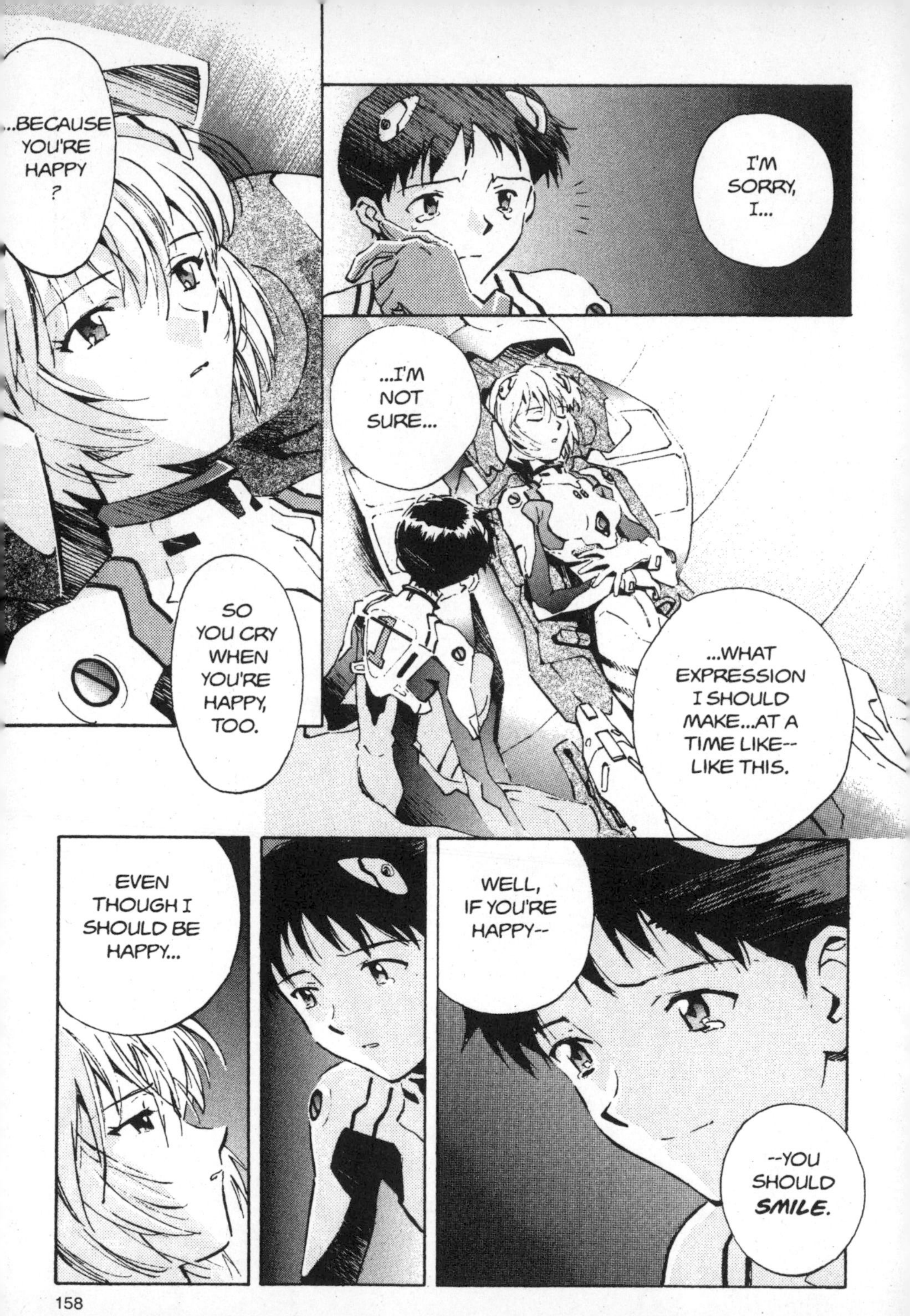
...BECAUSE YOU'RE HAPPY?
SO YOU CRY WHEN YOU'RE HAPPY, TOO.
I'M SORRY, I...
...I'M NOT SURE...
...WHAT EXPRESSION I SHOULD MAKE...AT A TIME LIKE--LIKE THIS.
EVEN THOUGH I SHOULD BE HAPPY...
WELL, IF YOU'RE HAPPY--
--YOU SHOULD SMILE.

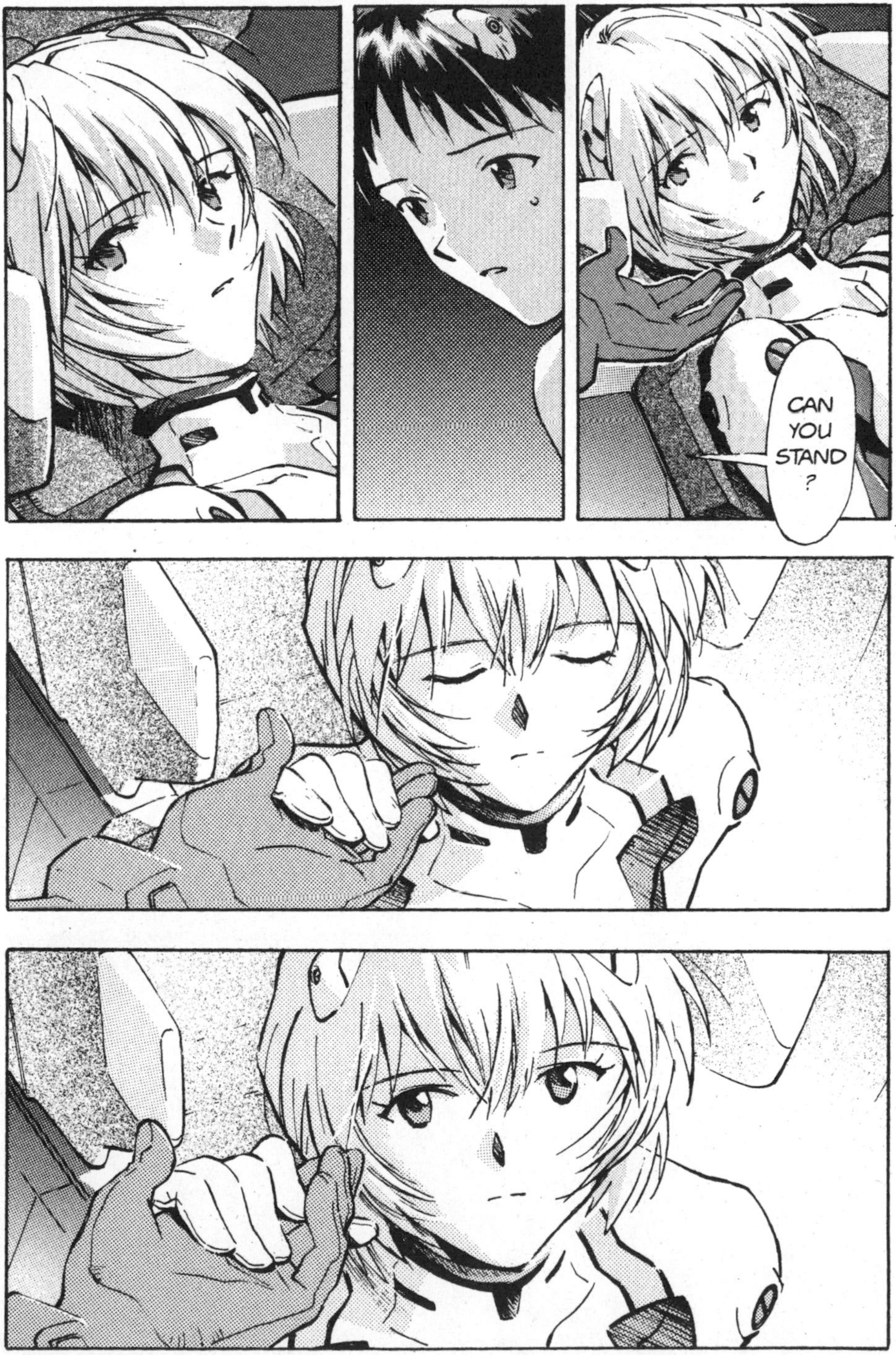
CAN YOU STAND ?

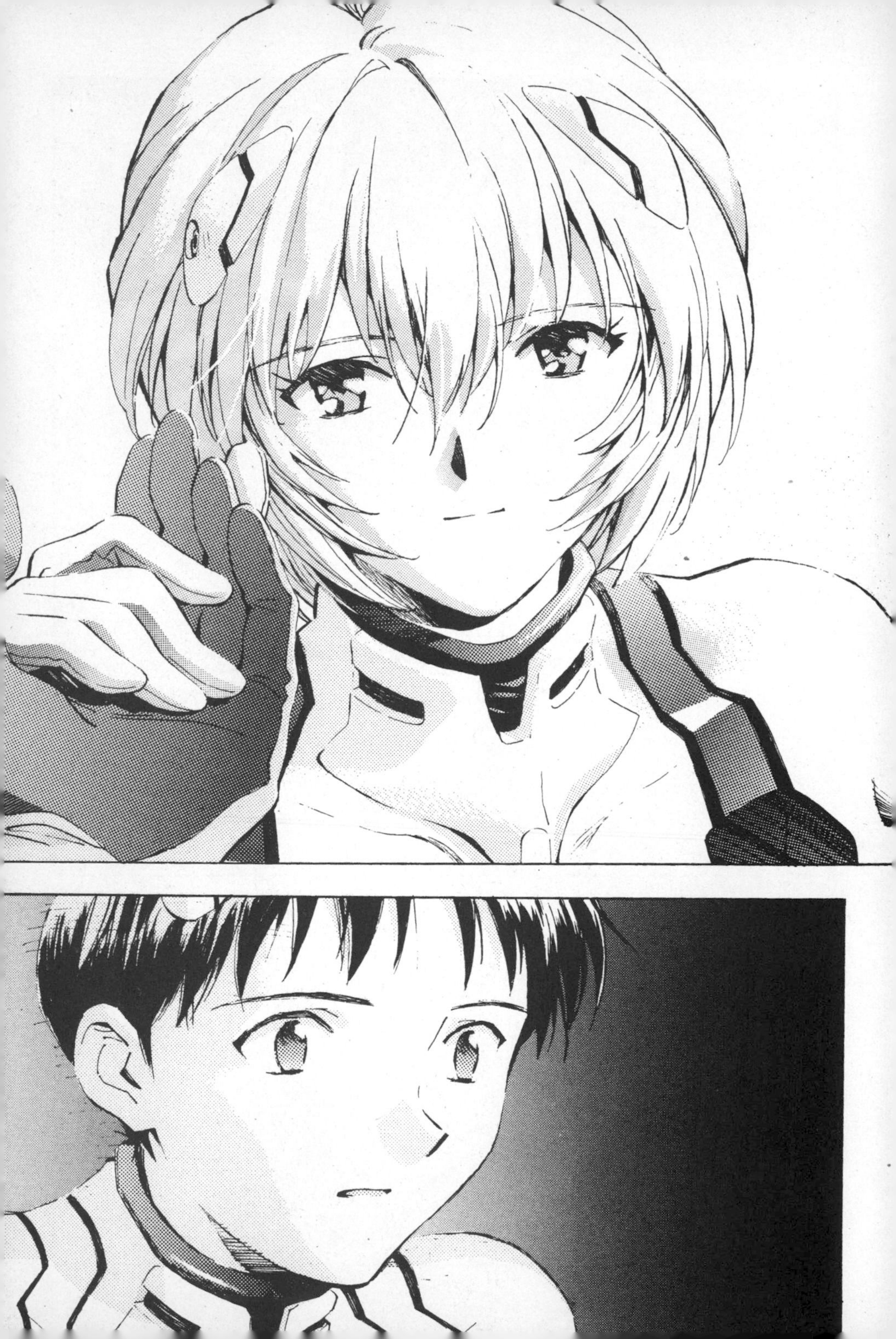

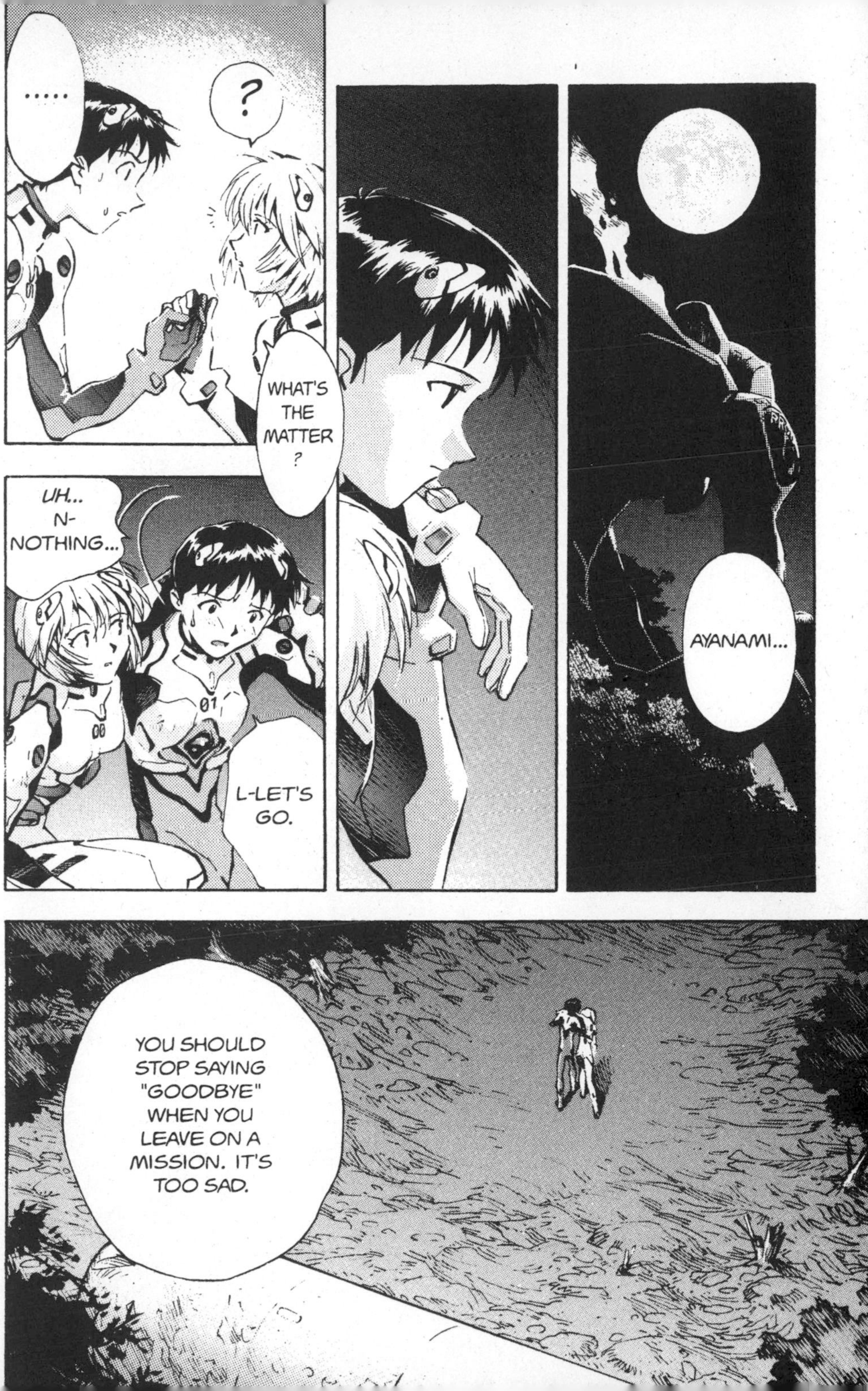
......
?
WHAT'S THE MATTER ?
UH... N-NOTHING...
L-LET'S GO.
AYANAMI...
YOU SHOULD STOP SAYING "GOODBYE" WHEN YOU LEAVE ON A MISSION. IT'S TOO SAD.

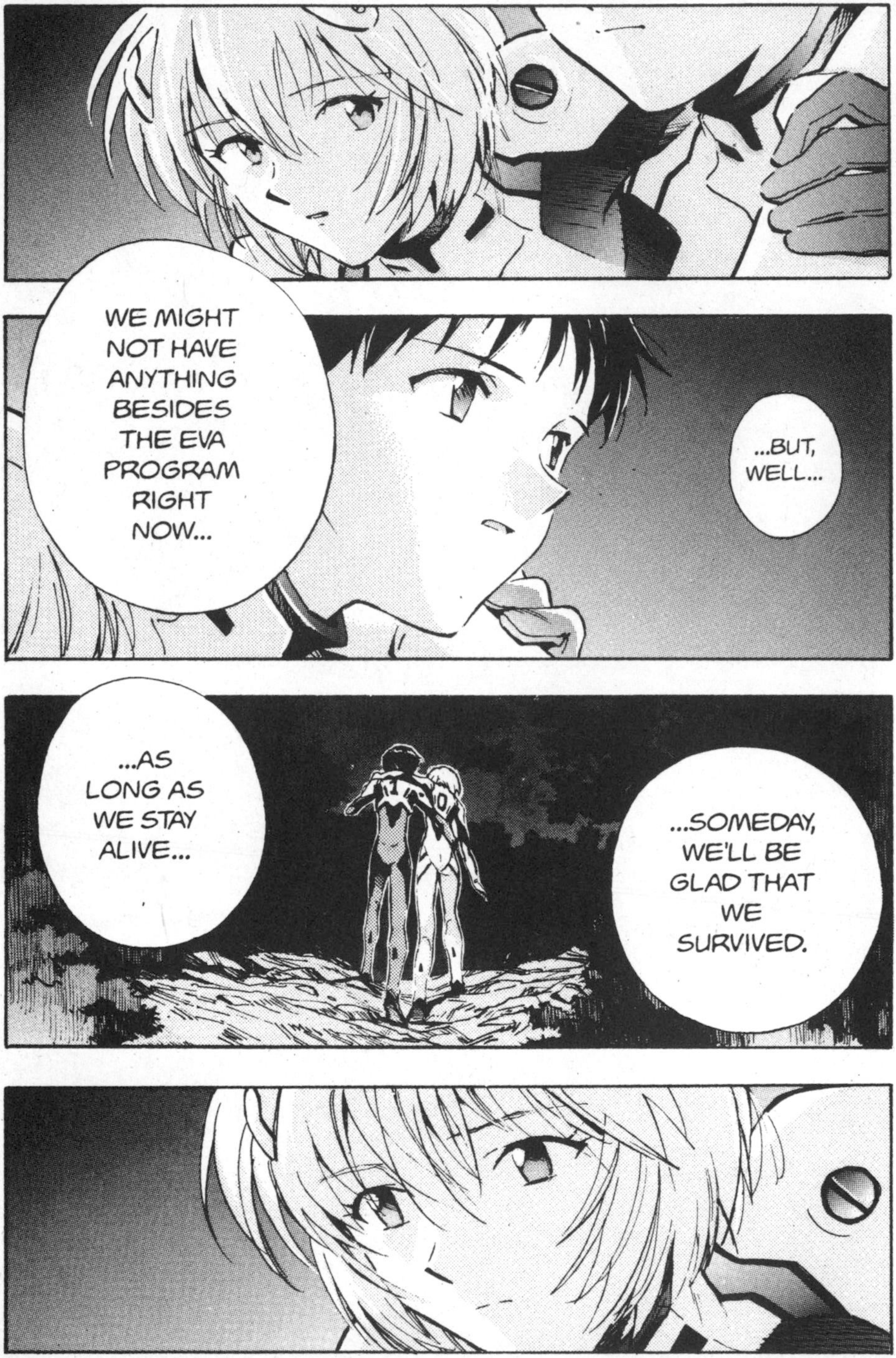
WE MIGHT NOT HAVE ANYTHING BESIDES THE EVA PROGRAM RIGHT NOW...
...BUT, WELL...
...AS LONG AS WE STAY ALIVE...
...SOMEDAY, WE'LL BE GLAD THAT WE SURVIVED.

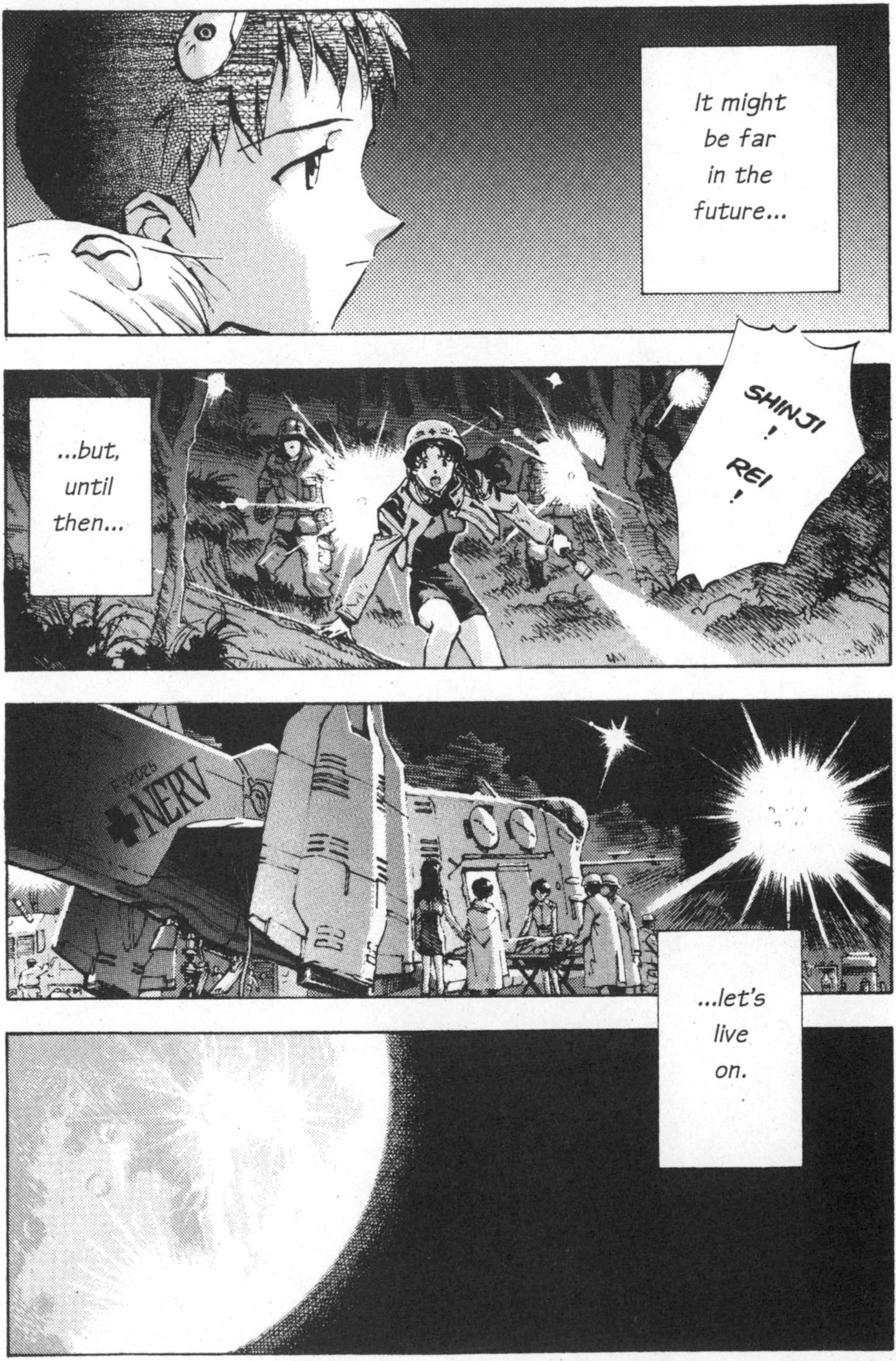
It might be far in the future...
...but, until then...
SHINJI! REI!
...let's live on.

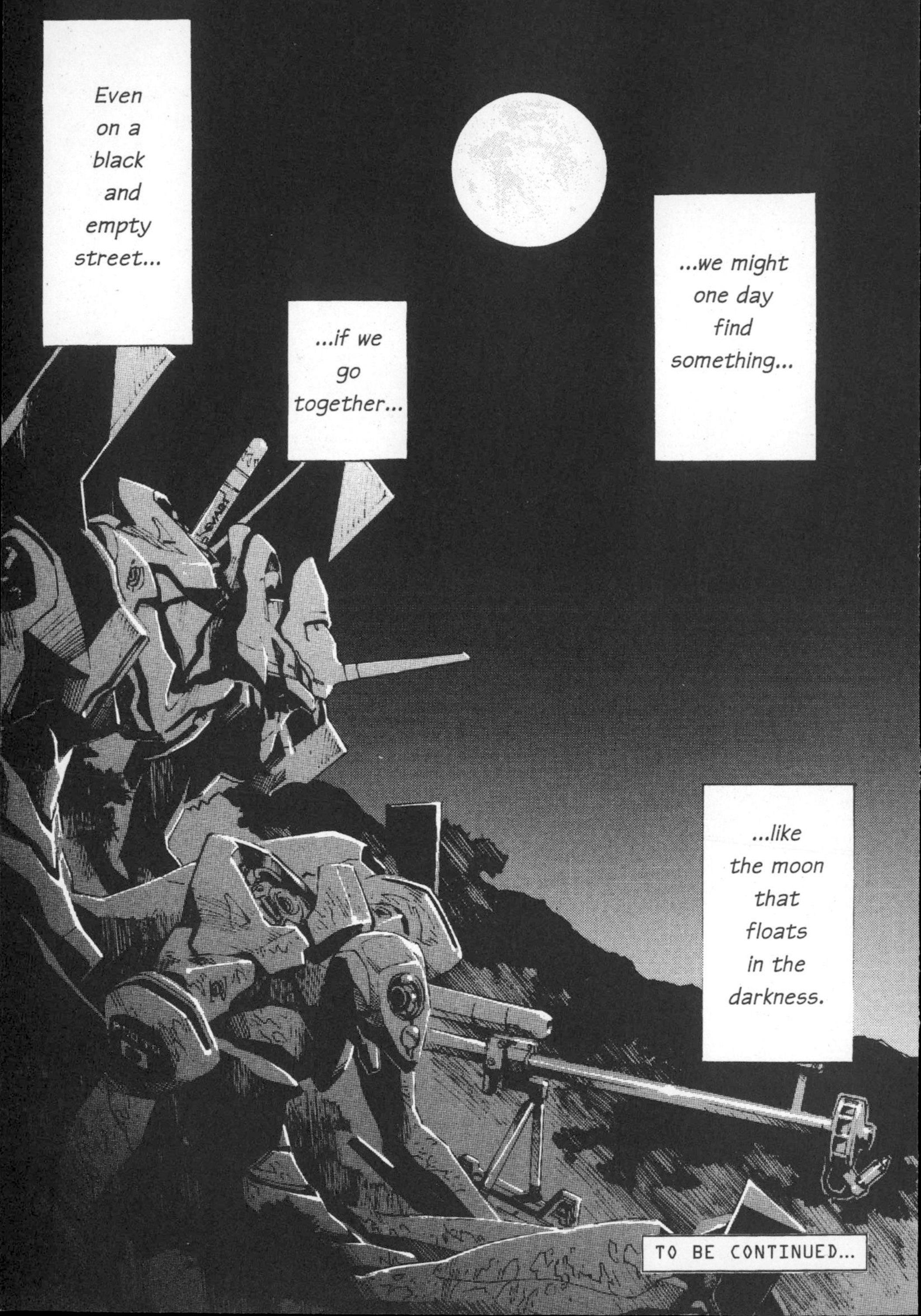
Even on a black and empty street...
...if we go together...
...we might one day find something...
...like the moon that floats in the darkness.
TO BE CONTINUED...

YUKO MIYAMURA

Voice of Asuka Langley Soryu

A Place For Asuka In The Heart

(Translated By William Flanagan)

Asuka was a young girl—a "part" that taught me a lot. She wasn't so much a part of my personality, as a separate entity inside of me—something close to a friend. It's like she and I are studying the human condition together.

Now get this clear, I'm not talking about *Sybil*, or anything like that. It's not a split personality inside of me alone. I think it is in all of us. You know, how everybody has different sides to their personality. Something like that.

I think it's just because I'm an actress that I had the chance to approach the character called Asuka. I'm sure that you're thinking that an inexperienced actress like me is out of her league writing these words, and if you do, I apologize. What I really wanted to write about was what an actress does when she tries to act. What approach she takes to the work. There are all types of actors out there, so I suppose there are as many approaches. And this is how my relationship with Asuka began.

Just to let you know, Asuka wasn't the most open-hearted character I've met. When I act out Asuka's part, I try to synchronize myself with her 400%. But every time I tried to draw myself in closer synchronization, Asuka would never allow herself to synch with *me*. Even in the end, she would never step across the line and draw closer to me. One day, I figured out that there was a wall in Asuka's heart. But there's a problem with that. If I did all the work and allowed myself to be submerged in Asuka's feelings (her self-absorption, her fears, her loneliness, all those things I would feel once I came over the wall in her heart and feel as she felt them), I would suffer the same spiritual damage she's suffered. I couldn't. I just couldn't do it.

Even as I tried to pull down the wall, it would grow taller and taller. I guess that's only natural. The more you push, the greater the power to resist becomes, until it started to look as if I would be the one to break. It seemed much like a fight between a married couple. Then I decided to accept Asuka and the wall in her heart as she is. I decided to reserve a small part of my heart for Asuka to live in and do my best to protect it. So even now, there's a line drawn in my heart that separates Asuka from myself, and it is there that Asuka still lives.

I can analyze it with calm detachment now, but when I was playing Asuka, it was a battle. Maybe it was something like the relationship between Helen Keller and Anne Sullivan. Asuka would cry out, "Don't you dare come inside my mind!" Her plea

came out so amazingly strong, it was painful to portray her. I'd ask myself why it was so painful, and I wouldn't know the answer, so the pain grew more intense. If the reward for pain is greater experience, then Asuka gave me quite enough experience to last me for a long while.

The thing I would like to say to the friend in my heart is, "Asuka, you're just a 14-year-old kid, aren't you?" 14 is a time of life when you are thrown against the wall of life. You are forced to learn. It's puberty, where you decide what kind of life you're going to live, right? *Evangelion* came to its climax just as you hit that point, but after that, what would your choices be, Asuka? What good would you try to do? What kind of adult would you grow into? Asuka, I want you to stay in that place in my heart and grow into an adult at your own pace. And I'll keep up, and grow up right alongside you. You're thrown against that wall, but the thicker that wall gets, the more weapons come to hand that will allow you to break through it. You're in training for life every day. So let's not share our pain—let's share our happiness and do our best to become good friends. There's no need to over think it. If you come to a mountain, learn to eat mountains. If you come to an ocean, learn to drink oceans. Each is delicious in its own way, so taste it! Life is fun, Asuka!

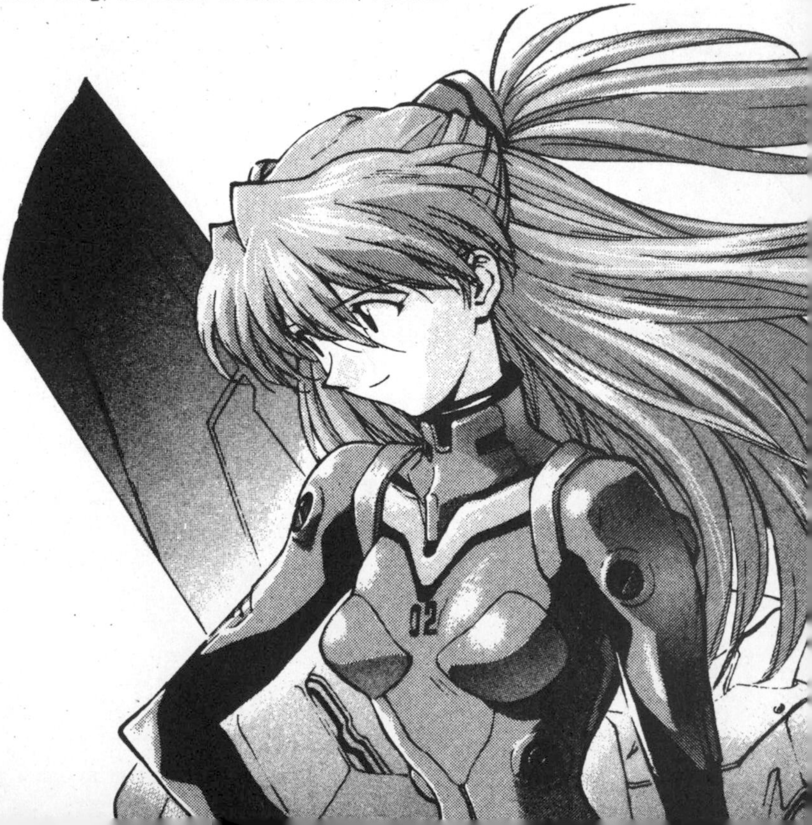